SHOWMANSHIP:
THE CINEMA OF WILLIAM CASTLE

JOE JORDAN

SHOWMANSHIP: THE CINEMA OF WILLIAM CASTLE
©2014 JOE JORDAN
ALL RIGHTS RESERVED.
All rights reserved. No part of this book may be reproduced or distributed, in print, recorded, live or digital form, without express written permission of the copyright holder. However, excerpts of up to 500 words may be reproduced online if they include the following information, "This is an excerpt from *Showmanship: The Cinema of William Castle* by Joe Jordan."

Published in the USA by:
BearManor Media
P O Box 71426
Albany, Georgia 31708
www.bearmanormedia.com

ISBN: 9781593935849
Printed in the United States of America
Book design by Robbie Adkins

TABLE OF CONTENTS

FOREWORD BY BELA G. LUGOSI VII
INTRODUCTION BY THOMAS PAGE IX
ACKNOWLEDGEMENTS.. XIII

PART I, THE THIRTY-NINE STEPS 1
CHAPTER ONE THE CHANCE OF A LIFETIME (1943) 3
CHAPTER TWO KLONDIKE KATE (1943) 9
CHAPTER THREE THE WHISTLER (1944) 13
CHAPTER FOUR SHE'S A SOLDIER TOO (1944) 21
CHAPTER FIVE WHEN STRANGERS MARRY (1944) 25
CHAPTER SIX THE MARK OF THE WHISTLER (1944) 33
CHAPTER SEVEN THE CRIME DOCTOR'S WARNING (1945) 37
CHAPTER EIGHT VOICE OF THE WHISTLER (1945) 41
CHAPTER NINE JUST BEFORE DAWN (1946) 47
CHAPTER TEN MYSTERIOUS INTRUDER (1946) 51
CHAPTER ELEVEN THE RETURN OF RUSTY (1946) 55
CHAPTER TWELVE CRIME DOCTOR'S MAN HUNT (1946) 59
CHAPTER THIRTEEN THE CRIME DOCTOR'S GAMBLE (1947) 65
CHAPTER FOURTEEN TEXAS, BROOKLYN, AND HEAVEN (1948) 71
CHAPTER FIFTEEN THE GENTLEMAN FROM NOWHERE (1948) 75
CHAPTER SIXTEEN JOHNNY STOOL PIGEON (1949) 79
CHAPTER SEVENTEEN UNDERTOW (1949) 85
CHAPTER EIGHTEEN IT'S A SMALL WORLD (1950) 89
CHAPTER NINETEEN THE FAT MAN (1951) 95
CHAPTER TWENTY HOLLYWOOD STORY (1951) 101
CHAPTER TWENTY-ONE CAVE OF OUTLAWS (1951) 107
CHAPTER TWENTY-TWO SERPENT OF THE NILE (1953) 111
CHAPTER TWENTY-THREE FORT TI (1953) 117
CHAPTER TWENTY-FOUR CONQUEST OF COCHISE (1953) 123
CHAPTER TWENTY-FIVE SLAVES OF BABYLON (1953) 129
CHAPTER TWENTY-SIX DRUMS OF TAHITI (1954) 133
CHAPTER TWENTY-SEVEN CHARGE OF THE LANCERS (1954) 137
CHAPTER TWENTY-EIGHT BATTLE OF ROGUE RIVER (1954) 143
CHAPTER TWENTY-NINE JESSE JAMES VS. THE DALTONS (1954).... 149
CHAPTER THIRTY THE IRON GLOVE (1954) 153
CHAPTER THIRTY-ONE THE SARACEN BLADE (1954) 159
CHAPTER THIRTY-TWO THE LAW VS. BILLY THE KID (1954) 163

CHAPTER THIRTY-THREE MASTERSON OF KANSAS (1955) 167
CHAPTER THIRTY-FOUR THE AMERICANO (1955) 173
CHAPTER THIRTY-FIVE NEW ORLEANS UNCENSORED (1955) 179
CHAPTER THIRTY-SIX THE GUN THAT WON THE WEST (1955) 185
CHAPTER THIRTY-SEVEN DUEL ON THE MISSISSIPPI (1955) 191
CHAPTER THIRTY-EIGHT THE HOUSTON STORY (1956) 195
CHAPTER THIRTY-NINE URANIUM BOOM (1956) 201

PART II, SHOWTIME! 207
CHAPTER FORTY MACABRE (1958) 209
CHAPTER FORTY-ONE HOUSE ON HAUNTED HILL (1958) 221
CHAPTER FORTY-TWO THE TINGLER (1959) 233
CHAPTER FORTY-THREE 13 GHOSTS (1960) 245
CHAPTER FORTY-FOUR HOMICIDAL (1961) 257
CHAPTER FORTY-FIVE MR. SARDONICUS (1961) 269
CHAPTER FORTY-SIX ZOTZ! (1962) 283
CHAPTER FORTY-SEVEN 13 FRIGHTENED GIRLS! (1963) 291
CHAPTER FORTY-EIGHT THE OLD DARK HOUSE (1963) 297
CHAPTER FORTY-NINE STRAIT-JACKET (1964) 307
CHAPTER FIFTY THE NIGHT WALKER (1964) 323
CHAPTER FIFTY-ONE I SAW WHAT YOU DID (1965) 329
CHAPTER FIFTY-TWO LET'S KILL UNCLE (1966) 337
CHAPTER FIFTY-THREE THE BUSY BODY (1967) 353
CHAPTER FIFTY-FOUR THE SPIRIT IS WILLING (1967) 363
CHAPTER FIFTY-FIVE PROJECT X (1968) 369
CHAPTER FIFTY-SIX SHANKS (1974) 377
AUTHOR'S NOTE 383
BIBLIOGRAPHY 385

for Jennifer

FOREWORD
BY BELA G. LUGOSI

Joe Jordan, author of *Showmanship: The Cinema of William Castle*, has spent a significant amount of time researching the life and career of a man who is considered to be one of Hollywood's most underappreciated filmmakers. It is clear to me that Mr. Jordan is passionate about the subject of which he writes. His thorough analysis, in addition to the exclusive interviews he conducted with several notables of the era, reveals that there is more to Hollywood's great showman than people realize. The feature of Joe's book I find most interesting is that it covers every film William Castle directed.

In his autobiography, William Castle related that his career was given its start when Bela Lugosi thoughtfully suggested him for a stage job with a road company tour of *Dracula*. There, William Castle, a high school dropout, introduced to the film industry the idea of promotional gimmicks and showmanship for which he has become famous.

William Castle's encounters with Dad were a familiar story – a generous, humble, gentle man – but also one whose mere presence could terrify.

My own experience with Dad was the same. He was principled, kind and generous, hardworking, and full of life. He was intense in all that he did, yet he actually had a good sense of humor.

Time has proven that Bela Lugosi and his performance as Dracula are responsible for the start of the horror genre in films and for the initial success of Universal Studios. As it is important to be included as part of Dad's legacy, I am proud to acknowledge Bela Lugosi's influence on the film career of William Castle.

INTRODUCTION
BY THOMAS PAGE

Everyone who knew William Castle admired him as both a producer and a genuine artist. I completely agree with that assessment.

As a movie producer under Harry Cohn, Castle was so prolific he was never certain how many movies he had made in his lifetime. The total meandered between ninety-six and 102 during the three weeks I worked with him on turning my novel, *The Hephaestus Plague*, into his last movie, *Bug*.

One hundred movies!

Bill Castle began in the golden age of producing films. Today, a director is lucky if he or she can count a dozen features in a lifetime of work, not including television.

I can attest Bill Castle knew more about the process and business of producing movies than any other person I ever met. From the germ of an idea in his head, to costing a script, purchasing raw stock, hiring actors, wardrobe, directors, lighting equipment, Castle had the numbers in his head and time worked out to the second. He produced, directed, financed, edited, booked, and promoted his own work.

He was also undeniably an artist. Here, descriptions become complicated. What kind of artist was he?

He was a superbly skilled producer, an efficient director, a fine actor, and a world-class genius of a promoter.

Castle believed that promotion should be an integral part of the entire movie going experience. Film promotion should never be separated from film creation. Every moviegoer today sits through twenty to thirty minutes of trailers when they go to a film, and more than a few will confess these trailers are very enjoyable.

He was prescient in this respect. Movie posters, which were throwaways, now sell for thousands of dollars. Making movie promotional trailers is a big business, complete with awards and huge expenditures that match the cost of the films being promoted.

To Bill Castle, his business, his life's work and passion, was bigger than simple movies and advertising and promotion.

His artistry was being a professional entertainer like Shakespeare, Hitchcock, Howard Hawks, and John Ford. His life's passion and artistic ambition was the insanely difficult and complex process of enabling millions of people all over the world to add two or three hours of enjoyment to their lives.

Being an entertainer is a very high and noble calling, and it is a tough one. Castle had the kind of guts that only a great gambler possessed. His life was about mortgaging his house over and over to finance movies. He was a plunger, which is a gift great movie producers possess – or are possessed by.

Anyone doubting the gambling aspect of producing should read the crucial hours between the time Castle optioned *Rosemary's Baby* and nailed the deal with Charles Bluhdorn, Robert Evans, and Paramount to produce it. This is nail-biting suspense in real life and real time.

It is also crucial to understanding not just William Castle, but the artistic success of Hollywood movies in general. Castle took pride in his work, but he produced movies to please people, not to educate or improve them. He did not promote his own political beliefs or tell an audience what is right or wrong.

The past century may have been the age of social and political conscience: Stanley Kramer hectoring us with *High Noon* and *On the Beach*, Costa-Gavras with *Z*.

This was not for William Castle. His social conscience and personal beliefs were nobody's business.

Simple entertainment, devoid of preaching or passionate political purpose, is the most difficult and fragile of creations. His best work began in a famous instance in the 1950s when he saw a huge line of people waiting to see a French film entitled *Les Diaboliques*. He realized that, among other emotions, people enjoyed being scared! From roller coasters to ghost stories to movie monsters, fear is a thrilling and enjoyable and legitimate way to pass a few hours!

So he embarked on a career of delicious fear. His entertainments began days before the actual movie appeared with outlandishly imaginative promotion – insuring audiences from dying of fright, stationing nurses in movie theatres, colored goggles for seeing ghosts – and culminated with ridiculously enjoyably scary movies.

The key to his success, it was his ability to observe what other people enjoy.

Rosemary's Baby was an outlandish and brilliant idea. It also was the perfect vehicle for Bill Castle's sensibility. It was crazy, outlandish, totally unbelievable, and with almost no social significance at all – in short, a singular, original, and brilliant work of art. As a novel, it was exciting as a movie, a work of art. Castle spotted its value instantly and went through a famous, wrenching punch-out with Robert Evans and Charles Bluhdorn to get it.

When I worked with him on the script for *Bug*, I realized I was dealing with an enormously sophisticated man. One of his passions was live theatre, and he was still tapped to be an actor in varied movies. Roman Polanski wanted him to be the satanic doctor in *Rosemary's Baby*, and he would have been perfect. But producing the film was more than enough to occupy him.

I was proud to have known Castle for those three weeks and became terribly sad when he passed away. He had more great movies in his head, and also had the energy and skill to bring them off. He was a master entertainer, and that is artistry of the rarest type. I miss him and so does the rest of the world.

I am delighted that the readers of this book will have the superb expertise that the author, Joe Jordan, brings to the subject of William Castle. It has taken over thirty years for the world to appreciate Castle's films, as well as the clever totality of his work. It has taken even longer for a growing number of students to perceive the personality and artistry of William Castle as considerably more polished and complex than audiences realized when he was alive.

Joe Jordan has avoided all the traps critics and even fervent fans made in looking at Castle's work. The smiling producer with the big cigar was a skillful artist and a clever trickster whose complexity eluded even the most discerning observers. Castle was proud of his work, but he was mysterious and modest to a fault, even in his autobiography. His gifts did not elude Mr. Jordan, who shows that Castle was a craftsman whose work is far more nuanced than audiences realized.

Jordan's work and observations are by far the most insightful of any other works I have read. They are solid contributions to understanding a personality whose work seems even to have inspired Hitchcock himself.

ACKNOWLEDGEMENTS

Much can be said in regard to the life and career of William Castle. He was an individual who worked tirelessly to make a name for himself in the motion picture industry. *Showmanship: The Cinema of William Castle* is aptly titled because Castle was a showman in the truest sense of the word. The promotional gimmicks of his most popular films are a testament to his success. But Castle's knack of reaching out to the public did not begin during the latter part of his career. Inspired by P. T. Barnum, he expressed a desire to interact with his audiences at a very young age. His autobiography, *Step Right Up! I'm Gonna Scare the Pants Off America*, offers an entertaining account of his life and must be purchased by all Castle fans. Some have questioned if Castle's retelling of his story is completely accurate. Perhaps, a few details were embellished. But it is evident that Castle was a passionate writer. I can imagine him sitting in front of his typewriter, charged with an extraordinary amount of energy as he churned out chapter after chapter. I would not be surprised if his autobiography was completed in less than a week. In short, it has been an incredibly valuable resource to me. Yet, *Showmanship: The Cinema of William Castle* is more about the films Castle directed than his amazing life story. Furthermore, it does not include a chapter pertaining to *Rosemary's Baby*, as the critically acclaimed film was directed by Roman Polanski.

Castle may not be known to every film buff, but without question, he made his mark on the industry. Every Halloween, several television networks air his films as part of an annual showcase. It is a popular tradition, and it appears to have no end in sight. Vincent Price once said, "Castle's films don't date, they just become more fun as the years go by." Over time, many have laughed, albeit good naturedly, at his pictures. A selection of Castle's films have been classified as campy (referring to a production that is amusing because it was intended to scare audiences, but also appears to be ridiculing itself). It is a word I avoid within my analyses simply because I attempt to interpret Castle's films as works of art. For several years, I was fortunate to teach a William Castle appreciation course to young adults. My lectures were based off of the chapters in this book. Perhaps, some may question my interpretations. For example, in regard to *House on Haunted Hill*, I make reference to the *mise-en-scène* and how it invokes a feeling of dread. Some may not take my analyses seriously, claiming Castle was not an auteur. Nevertheless, through the years, my students have been quite appreciative of his work. Our discussions frequently spanned ninety minutes, which happened to be the entire length of the class period. Therefore, it is in my humble opinion that Castle's films, like any work of art, are worthy of discussion and appreciation. Furthermore, I frequently make reference to his motifs. A motif is defined as "a recurrent thematic element in an artistic work," and considerable attention must be granted towards Castle's motifs, as they reveal much about the director's persona.

I have stated that every Castle fan should be in possession of his autobiography. In addition, I highly recommend a viewing of *Spine Tingler! The William Castle Story*, the award-winning documentary directed by Jeffrey Schwarz. In fact, in order to better understand *Showmanship: The Cinema of William Castle*, it would be ideal to view as many Castle-directed films as possible. The chapters of this book, arranged according to the release dates of his films, will simply be more informative if the reader has a good understanding of the material. Furthermore, it is not necessary to read the chapters in chronological order, but some may contain spoilers of other films. For example, when reading the chapter pertaining to *The Night Walker*, it is best to view *House on Haunted Hill*, *Homicidal*, and, of course, *The Night Walker* prior to doing so.

As I write this introduction, the date of April 24, 2014, looms on the horizon. It is only a couple of months away and is to be a very special day, as the date marks what would have been Castle's hundredth birthday. Since his unfortunate passing in 1977 at the age of sixty-three, he has been remembered primarily for his horror films. But throughout Castle's storied career, he had the opportunity to direct pictures of several different genres (i.e., film noir, Western). Furthermore, many Hollywood notables were afforded the opportunity to receive direction from Castle prior to reaching the primes of their careers. These performers include, but are not limited to,

Shelley Winters (*She's a Soldier Too* and *Johnny Stool Pigeon*), Lloyd Bridges (*She's a Soldier Too*), Robert Mitchum (*When Strangers Marry*), Audie Murphy (*Texas, Brooklyn, and Heaven*), Tony Curtis (*Johnny Stool Pigeon*), Rock Hudson (*Undertow* and *The Fat Man*), Jayne Meadows (*The Fat Man*), Julie Adams (*Hollywood Story*), Julie Newmar (*Serpent of the Nile* and *Slaves of Babylon*), Raymond Burr (*Serpent of the Nile*), Lee Majors (*Strait-Jacket*), and Richard Pryor (*The Busy Body*).

In closing, I would like to thank the following individuals who, at one time or another, contributed either their ideas or support towards the completion of this book: Scott Andrews, David J. Skal, Marina Knapp, Carla Sapon, Skip McClintock, Tom Page, Bela G. Lugosi, Peter Leyva, Gary Davis, Beth Holt, Gint Valiulis, Jeffrey Schwarz, David Maqui, Michelle Morgan, Sandy Grabman, Dave Menefee, Tavi Benjamin, Robbie Adkins, and John Badham. I am also grateful to Mickey Kuhn, Marvin Kaplan, Rhonda Fleming, Joyce Taylor, Joyce Meadows, and Pat Cardi for granting me the opportunity to interview them. Furthermore, William Castle's legacy has continued to thrive well into the twenty-first century, and much of this is due to the vibrancy and passion of his daughter, Terry Castle. I would like to thank Terry for all of her support through the years. I will never forget the time she made a special appearance in my classroom to visit with my students. In addition to writing fiction based on her father's world of the macabre, Terry proudly produced the remakes of *House on Haunted Hill* (1999) and *13 Ghosts* (retitled *Thir13en Ghosts*, 2001). I also want to acknowledge Lucy Chase Williams, Tom Weaver, and Ben Ohmart for entrusting their faith in me. Had it not been for them, *Showmanship: The Cinema of William Castle* would not have come to full fruition. In regard to my family, I want to acknowledge the support I have received over the course of many years from my parents, Joseph C. Jordan and Rosetta P. Jordan (1933-1983), and my siblings, Paul Jordan (1962-2009), Marie Shapiro, and Thomas Jordan. I would like to express my affection and appreciation for my daughter, Jocelyn Jordan, and my son, Justin Jordan. Words cannot express how grateful I am for having the both of them in my life. Finally, I especially want to recognize Jennifer Jordan, my wife of over ten years, and the individual to whom this book is dedicated, for never giving up on me. As I conducted my research, she willingly joined me during many screenings of Castle's films and subsequently took an avid interest in his work. I owe all of my success to her.

J. J.
Los Angeles
February 17, 2014

PART I
THE THIRTY-NINE STEPS

Chester Morris and George E. Stone.

CHAPTER ONE
THE CHANCE OF A LIFETIME (1943)

After three years of learning the ropes of the film business, Columbia Pictures was ready to give William Castle his shot at the director's chair. Harry Cohn, the infamous head of the studio, handed his young apprentice a script that was originally perceived as "lousy, dull, contrived, [and] miserable." Castle wanted to make revisions, but Irving Briskin, the executive in charge of low-budget B films for Columbia, was quite adamant. The script was to be shot word for word – no exceptions. Castle almost filed a complaint with Cohn, but later decided against it. There was much that needed to be done before filming commenced, and Castle was grateful enough to have such an opportunity in the first place. He was being offered the chance of a lifetime, which, ironically, was the name of the script he almost rejected.

The Chance of a Lifetime, Castle's directorial debut, was the sixth installment in Columbia's *Boston Blackie* series. The saga was loosely based on the short stories of author Jack Boyle. His works, published in magazines during the 1910s, evolved around the daring escapades of a clever jewel thief. Several film adaptations were produced during the silent era, but it was not until the early 1940s that the popularity of Boyle's creation increased due to Columbia's revival of the material. Unlike before, the refashioned Horatio "Boston Blackie" Black (Chester Morris) would no longer behave in an immoral, criminal-like manner. Often finding himself on the wrong side of the law due to false accusations, Blackie and his sidekick, The Runt (George E. Stone), would fight to restore justice to society. Castle made every effort to familiarize himself with the characters of *The Chance of a Lifetime* despite his skepticism of the script. And on the first day of production, he reported to the studio with the confidence and determination of an A-list director preparing to direct a film as worthy as *Gone with the Wind*.

Boston Blackie conducts a sociological experiment beginning with a formal plea to the governor. If a select group of well-behaved prisoners are to be paroled, they could contribute to society by working in the steel factory of Arthur Manleder (Lloyd Corrigan), a local entrepreneur. Inspector John Farraday (Richard Lane), Blackie's somewhat friendly nemesis, vehemently opposes the plan. But the governor grants Blackie a three-month trial period. Dooley Watson (Erik Rolf), serving time for armed robbery, is one of the chosen parolees. But he forgoes his first day of work in order to recover a load of stolen money. His accomplices, "Nails" Blanton (Douglas Fowley) and "Red" Taggart (John Harmon), come out of hiding to demand their share of the loot. Watson kills Red in self-defense, but Nails escapes as Blackie arrives on the scene. Blackie collects the money from Watson and orders him back to the factory. An attempt by Blackie and the Runt to conceal Red's body is cut short when Farraday catches them in the act. Protecting the integrity of his experiment, Blackie takes the blame for Red's death, claiming to have wanted the loot all for himself. The money is turned over to Farraday. Blackie escapes with the intention of finding Nails. Watson soon learns that his wife (Jeanne Bates) and child (Larry Olsen) have been kidnapped. Nails will not release them until he gets his share of the money, but it is locked in a safe at police headquarters. In disguise, Blackie and the Runt steal the money with the hopes of bringing Nails out of hiding. Manleder and the remaining parolees set a trap at Blackie's apartment. Nails falls into it and confesses the details of Red's death, thereby exonerating Watson.

Castle completed his direction of *The Chance of a Lifetime* in twelve days. Once the final cut had been assembled, he viewed it with Briskin, who did not waste any time slamming the film as the lights came on in the screening room. Even worse, Briskin attempted to make his own modifications to the print. He began by removing a portion of one reel and splicing it into another. The carnage continued and eventually culminated with the removal of one reel in its entirety. In his less-than-valiant attempt to assume the role of film editor, Briskin destroyed Castle's original vision of what was to be. When the film was released to the public, its reception was lousy. Although *The Chance of a Lifetime* was a failure partly due to Briskin's manipulation of the final cut, the narrative's heightened suspense, offbeat humor, and introduction of a significant Castle motif made it a qualified failure.

The scene in which Nails and Red make their surprise visit to Watson's apartment is one of the better parts of the film (until the absurd scuffle) primarily because of its heightened suspense. A stuffed animal, complete with a detachable head, makes this possible. A knock on the door is heard, and the loot is quickly stashed inside the plush toy, thus making it the center of attention. Nails becomes comfortable in a nearby armchair and collects the inanimate puppy simply because it happens to be in his way. He fiddles with its head, completely unaware that the fortune he desperately seeks is within his grasp. Although Nails eventually returns the toy to the foot of the chair, the immediate future remains uncertain. Watson feeds his visitors bold-faced lies, and Castle's camera captures the entire living room so that we are very much aware of the stuffed animal's location. The unexpected then occurs when Johnny, Watson's young son, enters the scene from his bedroom:

> JOHNNY: I want my doggy, Mommy.
>
> NAILS: Get him outta here!
>
> Johnny picks up the puppy and holds it upright. He walks over to Nails and mimics a barking sound, giggling in the process.
>
> NAILS: Will you stop that?
>
> JOHNNY: The head comes off. Wanna see?
>
> He begins to turn the head, but it suddenly becomes stuck.
>
> JOHNNY: It won't come off. Will you help me?
>
> He tries handing the toy (and money) to Nails, who refuses to acknowledge Johnny altogether.

The tension is partly broken when Watson punches Nails, leading to the wacky scuffle that costs Red his life. Very little time passes from the moment the money is hidden inside the puppy to the point when the fight begins. However, it is a period of uncertainty. Through the stuffed animal, Castle builds suspense. Furthermore, he persuades his audience to root for Watson, despite Watson's deliberate disobeying of Blackie. The mood is tense, but it does not necessarily set the tone for the remainder of the film.

Through the inept character of Detective Sgt. Matthews (Walter Sande), Castle makes the best of a lackluster script with an effective display of offbeat humor. Farraday sets a trap for Blackie at Nails's apartment, but the plan is far from foolproof. Blackie and The Runt, confined to a windowless kitchen, seek refuge in a dumbwaiter. The two are able to descend a safe distance from the apartment around the time Farraday and Matthews realize what is happening. The dumbwaiter is supported by a single rope. Matthews grabs a knife:

> FARRADAY: You can't cut that rope! They'll drop five floors!
>
> MATTHEWS: Yeah, but we can scare 'em.
>
> FARRADAY: Yeah!
>
> Farraday peers down into the darkness of the shaft.
>
> FARRADAY: Alright, Blackie! You asked for it!
>
> Matthews attempts to slice the rope, but does so with the dull edge of the knife. Blackie looks up towards the light of the kitchen.
>
> BLACKIE (undeterred): You're gonna cut the rope, Matthews! Better use the sharp edge of the knife!
>
> A disgusted Farraday smacks Matthews in the arm.

Blackie always appears to be one step ahead of the police. The dumbwaiter incident is primarily comical because he does not care about the potential danger involved. Instead, a confident Blackie encourages and invites the inept Matthews to continue. Of course, after the chain of events has run its course, nobody is hurt. Aside from its humor, the scene is noteworthy because it contains the motif of dumbwaiters (later to be seen in *13 Frightened Girls!*) But a more significant motif lies elsewhere within Castle's first film.

The Chance of a Lifetime introduces the popular motif of cigars, an item many would come to associate with Castle, especially during the latter part of his career. At the factory, Manleder attempts to distract Farraday and Matthews with a pair of delectable Corona Coronas. The inspector refuses, but his partner's temptation is obvious. Coincidentally, Matthews is later seen to be delightfully puffing on a cigar that, courtesy of Blackie, was indirectly purchased by Farraday. For Castle, the unwavering passion for cigars began in 1939 when the great Orson Welles offered him a savory Churchill. Although Castle had never smoked a cigar in his life, the lone experience would hook him for the rest of his days. On many occasions, Castle was rarely seen without a cigar. Furthermore, his trademark logo, featuring his familiar silhouette, revealed a cigar protruding from his mouth. In regard to Castle's films, the motif was quite popular and appeared in future productions such as *The Crime Doctor's Gamble*, *It's a Small World*, and many more.

During the climax at Blackie's apartment, Nails yells, "You been seein' too many bad movies, Blackie!" One can only wonder if this was an indirect reference to the impending reception of *The Chance of a Lifetime*. Critics from *The Hollywood Reporter* and *Variety* slammed Castle's direction. But some aspects of the production were beyond his control, as Briskin stepped in to make "corrections" to the final cut. Although he served as the film's executive producer, Briskin's name is missing from the credits. *The Chance of a Lifetime* was to be Castle's first, and only, contribution to the *Boston Blackie* series. After fourteen films, the saga concluded in 1949. However, *The Chance of a Lifetime* was the only installment to pave the way for a special debut. Because several months following the release of Castle's film, the *Boston Blackie* radio program hit the airwaves, thereby taking the popularity of Boyle's original creation to new levels.

CHAPTER TWO
KLONDIKE KATE (1943)

In 1941, just two years prior to directing his first motion picture, William Castle crafted a story for Universal. Shortly thereafter, a film based on his idea was produced. But it was presented to audiences as *Jack London's North to the Klondike*. Some theories suggest the picture was based on a short story of London's. Others claim no such story existed, and that the late author's name was merely used to garner attention.

Nevertheless, Castle was ultimately awarded a "based on a story by" credit. The film, directed by Erle C. Kenton, was set in Alaska. In 1943, upon completing *The Chance of a Lifetime*, Castle revisited the northern territory within another narrative. *Klondike Kate*, his second motion picture, takes place in the fictional town of Totem Pole, Alaska. The film is set at the turn of the twentieth century and tells the tale of the "QUEEN OF THE GOLD RUSH!"

Kathleen "Kate" O'Day (Ann Savage), from San Francisco, arrives in Totem Pole to reclaim a hotel previously owned by her late father. But Horace Crossit (George Cleveland), the local judge, deems Jefferson Braddock (Tom Neal), the town's playboy, to be the rightful owner. Kate produces a deed to the property, thus demanding justice. Crossit agrees to help on the condition she acquire his legal services. At the ensuing trial, however, Kate discovers the judge to also be acting as Braddock's attorney. She declares the hearing to be a farce and vows to retake what is rightfully hers. Kate becomes flirtatious with Braddock in order to land a singing job at the hotel. Lita (Constance Worth), an established performer of the venue, becomes jealous of Kate's advances. "Sometime" Smith (Sheldon Leonard), Braddock's competitor, operates a saloon in Totem Pole. He conspires with Lita to acquire Braddock's hotel. A card game is scheduled between both men. The winner is to receive a heap of gold in addition to the other's place of business. Lita stacks the deck in Smith's favor. He wins the game, but Braddock discovers the marked cards. They prepare to take the conflict outside, but Kate intervenes. She confesses to Braddock that she planned to win the hotel using a method similar to Smith's, but did not act quickly enough. Later, Lita demands gold from Smith as compensation for her efforts. He attempts to kill her, but she shoots him dead. Braddock is subsequently framed for Smith's murder. Chaos erupts at the hotel. A fire is inadvertently started, thereby destroying the property. Kate and Braddock ultimately decide to venture out of state and acquire a hotel together.

Within the opening credits of Castle's film, the words "Suggested by the life of Kate Rockwell Matson, the original Klondike Kate" are presented to the audience. M. Coates Webster and Houston Branch assembled a script that was loosely based on the famous, attractive entertainer of the Yukon Gold Rush. Born in Kansas in 1873 as Kathleen Eloise Rockwell, she journeyed to Alaska in 1899. While there, she became romantically involved with Alexander Pantages, the soon-to-be entertainment mogul. Needless to say, the two made headlines. The character of Braddock is somewhat of a representation of Pantages. But the narrative, true to its title, evolves around Klondike Kate. Furthermore, Castle's film emphasizes a particular degree of independence amongst the women of Totem Pole. Molly (Glenda Farrell), an affable showgirl, proves herself to be quite shrewd when the circumstances are right. In addition, Lita and Kate are empowered with the skills necessary to outwit those of the opposite sex.

Molly is first seen upon the film's beginning as she arrives in Totem Pole with a performing troupe of young women, thus exhibiting an air of confidence while establishing herself as the group's leader. She refuses to be deterred by both Braddock and Smith, the most powerful men in town. As Braddock prepares a contract for the ladies, Molly does not hesitate to negotiate its details:

> MOLLY: You wouldn't be trying to hijack a bunch of poor defenseless girls, would ya, handsome?
>
> BRADDOCK (smiling): Yeah, Molly. Any objections?
>
> MOLLY: Depends on the deal.
>
> BRADDOCK: What was Smith gonna pay you?
>
> MOLLY: Twel... $15 a week.
>
> BRADDOCK: Okay. I'll double it. I'll give you $24 and all you can pick up.

The ladies rejoice at the outcome of the negotiations. Prior to sealing the deal, Molly comments on Braddock's good looks, thus boosting his ego. He is clearly flattered by the compliment, pausing to smile, but also maintain his composure. Molly, however, is in control. She begins to lie about the weekly rate Smith originally promised her and the ladies. Braddock realizes it. But Molly's charm has gotten the best of him. Despite her blatant deception, Braddock is willing to generously compensate the troupe. Later, when Smith becomes privy to the contract, he attempts to dissolve it. Yet, he is rendered powerless when Molly, who has reneged on their previous agreement, boldly proclaims, "A lady can change her mind, honey. This one did." Smith concedes defeat, but ultimately targets another woman for his own personal gain.

Sensing Lita is unhappy with Braddock, Smith attempts to exploit her weakness by recruiting her for his scheme, but she is not the vulnerable, pathetic woman he believes her to be. She essentially beats Smith at his own game. Lita makes preparations to depart Totem Pole before Braddock has a chance to learn of her role in the card game's outcome. Prior to leaving, she confronts Smith, demanding her cut of the winnings. But he begins to stall for time. Lita produces a firearm and holds Smith at gunpoint. It is clear she has foreseen his diversionary tactics and is preparing herself for the worst. Smith delays long enough to grab a knife and hurl it at Lita. He clearly misses his target. Lita seizes the opportunity to shoot Smith dead. She is not apprehended. Instead, in the aftermath of the murder, Braddock endures countless accusations. But the support of one woman, albeit hard-earned, is enough to carry him through the chaos.

Throughout Castle's film, Kate continuously thwarts Braddock's advances. She chooses to reciprocate his feelings only when it is convenient for her. During Kate's first night in Totem Pole, she is treated to a private dinner. Braddock and Duster Dan (Lester Allen), his close friend and confidant, use a designated room of the hotel, which also serves as Braddock's office, whenever the need to entertain a woman should arise. A glowing lamp is placed near its window in order for one to indicate to the other that the room is in use. Braddock makes Kate privy to the arranged signal as they prepare to dine in the room. Dinner eventually concludes, and he prepares to make his move. Braddock escorts

Kate to his bedroom, intending for the both of them to spend the night together. But she makes an impromptu request for water and locks the door the instant he leaves, thereby foiling his plan. Another night, Braddock arranges a midnight supper for Kate and him. But she suggests they go for a walk, despite his concern that the food will get cold. As they return to the hotel, the light from the office is visible. Kate suggests a second walk. Braddock is reluctant, but agrees on the assumption that the room will be available following their additional late night stroll. Yet, as they return, it becomes clear nothing has changed. The light continues to shine. Kate then seizes the opportunity to feign fatigue, claiming to have lost her appetite. Braddock bids her goodnight and, minutes later, chides Duster. But Duster claims he was not in the office, insisting to Braddock that he has been asleep in his bedroom. Castle then reveals that Molly, at Kate's request, went to the office and purposely lit the lamp. Hence, Braddock has been foiled again. He traditionally displays an air of confidence as he interacts with the town's inhabitants. And Braddock is frequently seen to be smiling throughout the narrative, but whenever Kate rejects his repeated advances, his smile disappears and a pent-up frustration becomes apparent. Finally, upon the film's conclusion, Braddock and Kate share a mutual affection for each other, but only because it was her desire to reciprocate his feelings.

Principal photography of *Klondike Kate* concluded on October 13, 1943. At the time, *The Chance of a Lifetime* had yet to be released to the American public, and Castle was unsure of how his first two films would fare with theatergoers. François Truffaut, the great director whose contributions to French cinema have inspired multitudes of artists, claimed that every filmmaker's first picture is a mad rush of ideas, while the second is an exercise in style. Despite the eventual disparagement Castle endured from critics, he was becoming acclimated to an industry that is sometimes cutthroat and thankless. *Klondike Kate* was released on December 16, 1943. Castle did not concern himself too much with the film's impending reviews, as the so-called failure of *The Chance of a Lifetime* had taken its toll. Nevertheless, the New Year was upon him, and along with it came a stroke of good luck.

CHAPTER THREE
THE WHISTLER (1944)

After two films, William Castle's career appeared to be going nowhere. Critics were harsh, and people of the industry were aloof. But Harry Cohn paid no attention to the criticism. Instead, he lectured his young protégé on the pitfalls of show business, declaring that "if a script is bad, no director, no matter how brilliant, can make it into a good picture." Castle never forgot this, and for the remainder of his career, he refused to let the critics get the best of him. Immediately after the pep talk, Cohn retrieved a script from his desk and handed it to Castle, who took it home to read. The story, entitled *The Whistler*, was quite different from *The Chance of a Lifetime* and *Klondike Kate*. Castle was so impressed that he read the script three times before making a late night phone call to Cohn, informing his boss that *The Whistler* "was one of the most terrifying screenplays [he'd] ever read."

Richard Dix as Earl Conrad.

Columbia Pictures, similar to other studios of the 1940s, produced many B films in order to occupy the bottom halves of double features. It was sometimes challenging for writers to conceive of original material for these films. Therefore, Columbia secured the rights to *The Whistler*, a radio program that thrived on the element of mystery. Based on a concept by writer J. Donald Wilson, the show provided a suitable setting for low-budget, film noir adaptations. Each episode began with the whistling of an ominous tune, followed by the title character's narration, which declared, "I am the Whistler, and I know many things." Following the opening monologue, the story would commence. The Columbia films traditionally began the same way, but the Whistler's face remained invisible to the audience, as only his shadowy figure could be seen. Although the Whistler maintained a low-key presence, he oversaw the narrative, and sometimes intervened with the film's characters when trouble was at hand.

The interior of The Crow's Nest.

Earl Conrad (Richard Dix), a successful businessman, is on a boating vacation with his wife when she mysteriously disappears. The authorities suspect death by drowning. Conrad returns home to a not-so-warm reception from his friends, who believe him to be responsible for his wife's disappearance. Feeling alone and helpless, he decides to end his life, and quickly makes arrangements for his own elaborate murder. Lefty Vigran (Don Costello), a shady criminal hired by Conrad to oversee the job, recruits an anonymous assassin. Shortly after the plan is set in motion, Vigran is killed during a shootout with police detectives. To complicate matters further, Conrad eventually learns that his wife is alive. Instilled with a reason to live, he attempts to call off the assassination, but cannot do so because Vigran is dead and the identity of the killer is unknown. Conrad immediately embarks on a mission to prevent his own murder. He encounters Antoinette "Toni" Vigran (Joan Woodbury), Lefty's widow. She blames Conrad for her husband's death. Toni's attempt to kill him goes awry, resulting in a car accident. Conrad survives, but Toni does not. He believes her to be the one Lefty hired for the job. But it eventually becomes clear that the real killer (J. Carrol Naish), who purposely shadows Conrad as a means to prey on his nerves, is still on the loose. The two eventually come face-to-face. Conrad tries to reason with his would-be murderer, but all attempts are futile. Meanwhile, Conrad's picture is printed in the newspaper because he has been reported missing and is believed to have become a victim of amnesia. He is apprehended at the city docks. The killer arrives on the scene and attempts to finish the job, but is shot dead by a port authority sergeant.

Castle became ecstatic upon learning he would direct *The Whistler*, but had reservations about working with Dix and Naish. The two were seasoned actors. Castle was only twenty-nine years old and barely had any experience. Nevertheless, he was encouraged to be creative and test out any ideas that came to mind. His primary objective was to establish "a mood of terror." Various techniques in the use of lighting and lenses were implemented. But location was important for Castle's film. The opening scene takes place at The Crow's Nest, a waterfront bar. The name is appropriate considering the circumstances. A crow's nest, serving as the lookout point of various ships, guarantees the best view of approaching obstacles or hazards. The Whistler is afforded the ultimate perspective. He observes the meeting between Vigran and Conrad, but remains untouchable. Furthermore, Castle uses the opening scene as a means to invite his audience into a

Richard Dix and Gloria Stuart.

horrifying world of secrets. Vigran, Conrad, and the killer are not privy to every detail of the arrangement.

Vigran gives the impression of a man who knows many things, but looks can be deceiving. He is neither completely aware of Conrad's plan nor his own unfortunate predicament. At The Crow's Nest, the two face each other from opposite sides of the table. Vigran unknowingly assists Conrad with the preparation of his own death:

> CONRAD: I've got a job for you.
>
> VIGRAN: Well, just what is it you want done, Mister...?
>
> CONRAD: Do you have to know my name?
>
> VIGRAN: No.
>
> CONRAD: I want to have a man . . . removed.
>
> VIGRAN: Oh. Well, um, what does this fellow do?
>
> CONRAD: Does that make any difference?
>
> VIGRAN: Yes, it makes a lot of difference. You see, if he's important, I won't touch him.

CONRAD: Just a small manufacturer.

VIGRAN: Oh, legitimate businessman. You see, murder of a chap like that will get a lot of publicity.

Vigran is completely unaware that Conrad is the "chap" to whom he is referring, partly because the latter refuses to provide his name. But the idea of a man arranging his own assassination is preposterous. There is no reason for Vigran to suspect Conrad as the intended target. The audience, too, does not make the connection. Castle does not reveal the plot twist until a later scene. Instead, the focus is kept on Vigran, who is incognizant of the police detectives waiting to arrest him. He eventually learns of the dragnet, and decides to escape through a rear exit. Castle's direction of the scene places the audience in Vigran's shoes. Like Vigran, we are unsuspecting of Conrad's motives and are also oblivious to the police presence lurking outside of The Crow's Nest. The detectives eventually close in on their suspect and are forced to kill him in an act of self-defense. Although the audience is afforded the opportunity to experience the events from Vigran's perspective, it is only for a brief period considering his demise takes place within the film's opening minutes. Castle's intention, however, is to place the emphasis on a more important character.

Conrad, the film's protagonist, continuously finds himself haunted by the unknown. Like Conrad, the audience is initially unaware of the killer's identity. The first time the assassin shows his face, he presents himself as a long-winded insurance salesman. He is perceived as annoying, but harmless. At the time, we do not realize that the so-called salesman, standing in Conrad's office, is the actual killer. Like Conrad, we are unaware of the "rough shadowing" experiment that is occurring. A short time later at Conrad's residence, the killer makes another appearance. He intends to strike, but his plans are thwarted when both Alice (Gloria Stuart), Conrad's secretary, and The Whistler arrive on the scene. It is at this point that the audience is afforded a clear look at the killer. Unlike before, his demeanor is serious. Yet, the conspicuous bowtie gives him away. The obnoxious, life insurance salesman is revealed to be the assassin. For a killer, he appears cool, calm, and collected. But aside from a couple of unexpected

J. Carrol Naish.

visits from The Whistler, his confidence in finishing the job is overshadowed by one crucial detail.

The killer, overly secretive to the point that his name is never revealed, does not realize that Conrad is the man who paid Vigran for the job. As he dines with Gorman (Alan Dinehart), an associate, the issue of the job's importance is raised. Gorman uses reason as a means to justify his point:

> GORMAN: Look! I think you're making a fool of yourself. You've been paid.

> The killer turns his focus to a nearby spoon, using the tablecloth to wipe it clean as Gorman continues to rant.

> GORMAN: Vigran's gone. His wife's gone. Who's there to know whether or not you go through with it?
> THE KILLER: The guy that paid Lefty'll know.

The irony is palpable. Conrad, the "guy" paying the killer's pricey fee, is desperate to prevent the job's execution. As the conversation with Gorman continues, it becomes clear that the killer has become obsessed with his psychological experiment. He will not stop until Conrad is dead. At various points of the narrative, the killer makes reference to life insurance and also touches upon the concept of death by fright (foreshadowing what is to come with *Macabre*). After his meal with Gorman has concluded, he returns to the flophouse where Conrad is resting. The killer decides to purchase a bed for the night, but refuses to provide his name to the desk clerk (Byron Foulger). He is subsequently registered under the pseudonym of John Smith. Earlier, the killer used the phony name of "Smith" while disguised as the insurance salesman. At the flophouse, he chooses to occupy the thirteenth bed, a number some consider to be superstitious (a recurring motif of Castle's films, appearing in the titles of *13 Ghosts* and *13 Frightened Girls!*). The choice is appropriate for his character. The killer is a superstitious man, occasionally perusing his book on necrophobia. Although he is unaware that he is working for Conrad, it does not matter. He pushes his experiment to its bitter end. Consequently, the killer is shot dead at the waterfront, the very location where Conrad's plan was first set in motion.

Castle celebrated the theatrical release of *The Whistler* during the spring of 1944. His film is remarkable for several reasons.

An experiment of the most unusual kind.

First, the performances of its key players are noteworthy. Gloria Stuart, an elegant actress of her time, is convincing as Alice, the frantic secretary who must control the emotions she harbors for Conrad. Stuart retired in 1946, but returned to her craft in the mid-1970s. She pursued her love of acting well into the twenty-first century, and even earned an Oscar nomination for her role in James Cameron's *Titanic*. Second, *The Whistler* serves as an example of effective film directing in regard to the art of contrast. Castle places an emphasis on contrast shortly before the story's climax. Conrad, on his way to the waterfront, does not realize that the killer is trailing him. Castle intercuts between separate pairs of suit pants. One pair, that of Conrad's, is significantly lighter than those of the killer, whose character is much darker by nature. Third, Castle places an emphasis on the concept of perspective. More often than not, the audience finds itself in Conrad's shoes. Towards the end of the film, as Conrad rests in the dock watchman's quarters, he peers out the window at the Diplomat, the ship that is about to set sail. The perspective is foggy because we are viewing the ship in the same manner as the weary-feeling Conrad.

Finally, *The Whistler* is remarkable for its reference to the pop culture of the 1940s. At The Crow's Nest, Castle's inclusion of the deaf mute's Superman comic book is noteworthy. Both The Whistler and Superman were popular fictional heroes of the era, especially within the medium of radio. In short, Castle's affiliation with *The Whistler* series proved to be successful.

Throughout his career, he worked on several film series for Columbia, including *Boston Blackie* and *Crime Doctor*. But *The Whistler* was the only series Castle had the opportunity to oversee from the beginning, having directed the saga's premiere film. Upon its release, multiple critics were impressed. One particular journalist by the name of Kate Cameron remarked, "Under William Castle's brilliant direction, the audience's attention is riveted to the screen throughout."

CHAPTER FOUR
SHE'S A SOLDIER TOO (1944)

On March 13, 1944, the United States achieved a momentous victory during World War II. The setting was Bougainville Island of the Pacific Theater. American troops defeated Japanese forces and retook control of Hill 700, a prime location considered to be the heart of the island. Thousands of miles away, on the same day, William Castle began work on his next feature, *She's a Soldier Too*. Its plot did not focus directly on the war overseas. Instead, Castle's film addressed a major phenomenon of domestic America. While many of the men were fighting abroad, women were welcomed to the workforce, hired primarily to manufacture war materials. But a variety of vacated jobs (i.e., switchboard operators, taxi drivers) also needed to be filled. Needless to say, *She's a Soldier Too* was advertised as a "SOCK DRAMA OF THE GALS WHO WEAR THE PANTS THESE DAYS."

In Philadelphia, Agatha (Beulah Bondi), Julia (Ida Moore), and Jonathan Kittredge (Percy Kilbride), all siblings, live together in peace and solitude. One rainy night, Tessie Williams (Nina Foch), a taxi driver, arrives at their doorstep in a panic. Her passenger, a pregnant woman, is in labor. Dr. Bill White (Jess Barker) arrives on the scene to help deliver the baby. Unfortunately, the mother dies while giving birth. Meanwhile, the bank threatens to foreclose on the Kittredge home. Much to Agatha's dismay, Tessie devises a plan to make a partial payment and stop the foreclosure. She and several other women, all of whom are working, rent the home's vacant rooms. Later, Charles Jones (Lloyd Bridges), the baby's father, arrives in search of his wife. Upon hearing of her demise, he abruptly departs. Tessie follows Jones and consoles him. But he remains hesitant to claim his child. Jonathan, an expert in the field of mechanics, loves to invent things. One such invention attracts the attention of Mr. Lucklow (Erik Rolf), a government engineer involved in the development of a top secret bomber. He takes out a patent with Jonathan's name on it. Lucklow attempts to present him with a royalty check, but to no avail. Jonathan does not want to be paid. He simply wants to help the soldiers come back alive. But Agatha, who wants to be rid of Tessie and the others, persuades him to accept the check. Consequently, the "working girls" leave. Jonathan, upset with Agatha, also vacates the premises. Shortly thereafter, Jones and Tessie, now newlyweds, arrive to take the baby into legal custody. Agatha, not wanting to be left in loneliness, invites everybody back to the house to live in joyous harmony.

The opening titles of *She's a Soldier Too* are cleverly embroidered (a technique that will later be seen with *Texas, Brooklyn, and Heaven* and *Homicidal*). As Castle invites us into the Kittredge estate, Agatha is revealed to be knitting a pine tree quilt. She speaks of the log cabin design that is to follow. Through her knitting, Agatha yearns for a life of solitude far from the confines of the busy city. Julia comments in regard to the street being full of trucks and people. Agatha replies, "As long as they stay there, I'm afraid there's nothing we can do about it." Yet, when Tessie arrives, Agatha is unwilling to help. Hence, the conflict begins. Beulah Bondi and Nina Foch are appropriately given top billing, because the narrative relies on the overall dynamic between their characters. The depiction of Agatha and Tessie's first meeting, a severe clash of their personalities, and the ultimate resolution of their conflict are indicators of the relationship's importance to the story.

When Agatha and Tessie meet for the first time, the rushed sequence of events sets the stage for the remainder of the film. Castle's portrayal of the cab's arrival purposely excludes the perspective of an important character. The character of Jonathan is significant to the narrative. His vibrancy and enthusiasm essentially keep the household together. Jonathan does all of the cooking. He keeps everything tidy. And when the doorbell suddenly rings late at night, he is the one to answer the call. As Jonathan opens the door, Castle does not reveal what transpires on the doorstep. Instead, we see Jonathan's face. After a brief glance, he moves away from the open door. Agatha approaches. As she peers through the doorway, Castle makes his audience privy to the arrival of the cab. Tessie, with her back to the camera, busily makes preparations for her pregnant passenger. Like Agatha, the audience looks on in confusion as the events unfold. Everything happens rather quickly. There is no formal introduction between

Agatha and Tessie simply because there is no time for one. Within the space of a single minute, the circumstances of the Kittredge household undergo a complete transformation. Yet, we are supposed to see things from Agatha's perspective instead of Jonathan's simply because Agatha and Tessie will eventually become the most important characters of the narrative. Naturally, first impressions are important. And the initial meeting between Agatha and Tessie, to which we bear witness, does not go well. Agatha becomes resentful, eventually referring to the newcomers as "outsiders" and "uninvited guests." Tessie, in turn, develops mutual feelings. Hence, Castle establishes conflict, and the narrative is formally under way.

A personality clash between Agatha and Tessie makes for an entertaining film. Their opposing philosophies are put to the test at the most inopportune of times. As Agatha approaches the kitchen to deliver news of the baby's birth, she can hear Tessie referring to the Kittredge home as an "old place" that is essentially devoid of life. Agatha, positioned outside of the kitchen behind a closed door, pauses before entering. As she makes her presence known, Jonathan apologizes because he is not sure how much of the conversation she has heard. Tessie, on the contrary, is not remorseful, as she appears hopeful that Agatha heard every detail. The latter replies, "I was reared never to hear other people's conversation." But Tessie counters with a saying of her father's: "Keep your ears open. The more you hear, the more you learn." Later, Agatha adheres to Tessie's philosophy as she eavesdrops on the conversation between Lucklow and Jonathan. A check in the amount of $15,000 is presented. Jonathan is reluctant. But Agatha intervenes, insisting he take the money. Tessie and the girls are subsequently evicted. The characters of *She's a Soldier Too*, in essence, adhere to their personal beliefs, but no philosophy is perfect. Agatha has her flaws, as does Tessie. But during a time of war, cooperation on the home front is vital. And at one point during the film, Tessie makes reference to a popular expression, declaring, "One hand washes the other." Consequently, Agatha's adherence to the age-old idiom ultimately proves beneficial.

As the conflict between Agatha and Tessie becomes resolved, Castle concludes his narrative. Both women are not entirely aware of their flaws until they come to a sudden, simultaneous realization. As the newlyweds depart the Kittredge home with the baby in tow, Tessie begins to ponder life from Agatha's perspective. A feeling of discomfort follows. Tessie did not express her gratitude to Agatha. Had it not been for the Kittredge home, life itself would be uneventful and devoid of meaning. Inside the house, at the same moment, Agatha begins to cry. Both women essentially come to understand the reality of their impending loneliness as it looms on the horizon. Tessie subsequently returns to the house, abiding by the very words she spoke to Jones earlier in the film: "People just have to have other people or they stop being human beings."

She's a Soldier Too was released on June 29, 1944. Castle's collaboration with Percy Kilbride is noteworthy. Years later, the release of *The Egg and I* would launch the popular *Ma and Pa Kettle* film series, with Kilbride starring as the dim-witted, but thoughtful, Pa Kettle. Coincidentally, *She's a Soldier Too* features a Benjamin Franklin sculpture created by Kilbride's character. It is a kitchen accessory and whistles like a "kettle" every time an "egg" has finished cooking. At the time of production, Castle was already good friends with Marjorie Main, the future Ma Kettle. He essentially enjoyed a special camaraderie among Hollywood notables. In addition, Castle was becoming a well-liked protégé of Harry Cohn, and slowly but surely, word of his diligence and versatility began to spread beyond the confines of Columbia Pictures.

CHAPTER FIVE
WHEN STRANGERS MARRY (1944)

During the early 1940s, brothers Frank, Maurice, and Hymie King migrated from Chicago to California with the hopes of launching their own film production company. Back home, they owned and operated a vending machine business. Following their arrival in California, the brothers made a living manufacturing film projectors. It was not long before King Brothers Productions was formed. During a meeting with Harry Cohn, the brothers were treated to a private screening of *The Whistler*. They were impressed with William Castle's style of direction, and inquired about using him to direct an upcoming picture of theirs. Cohn agreed to loan his protégé to the King brothers, but at five times the amount of Castle's weekly salary at Columbia. Money was not an issue for the Chicago natives, as confidence was running high. And with the ideal script, the gamble appeared to be worth it.

Mildred "Millie" Baxter (Kim Hunter), a newlywed waitress, travels to New York to visit Paul Baxter (Dean Jagger), her husband. She arrives at the hotel where he is supposed to be staying, but cannot find him. Instead, Millie encounters Fred Graham (Robert Mitchum), an ex-flame. The two become wary, as Baxter cannot be found. Graham convinces Millie to report her husband's disappearance to the authorities. Lieutenant Blake (Neil Hamilton), a homicide detective, agrees to help, but only because the opportunity may provide a lead towards another case he is investigating. Coincidentally, Baxter's most recent telegram to Millie was sent from Philadelphia. Around the time of its composition, Samuel Prescott (Dick Elliott), a wealthy entrepreneur, was strangled to death at the Philadelphia Hotel. Millie reveals that she saw Baxter only three times prior to marrying him, leading some to conclude she married a stranger. Eventually, Millie comes into contact with Baxter when he summons her to an apartment he is renting. He behaves discreetly, as if he has something to hide. His demeanor becomes frantic after a newspaper reports that Jacob Houser (Lou Lubin), a bartender at the Philadelphia Hotel, can identify Prescott's killer. Baxter eventually admits to being at the hotel on the night of the murder, but maintains he did not kill Prescott. The police apprehend Baxter a short time later. Millie seeks out Graham and soon learns that he, too, was in Philadelphia at the time of the murder. Blake authorizes a search of Graham's hotel room. A large sum of cash, originally belonging to Prescott, is discovered. Baxter is exonerated and Graham is arrested for murder.

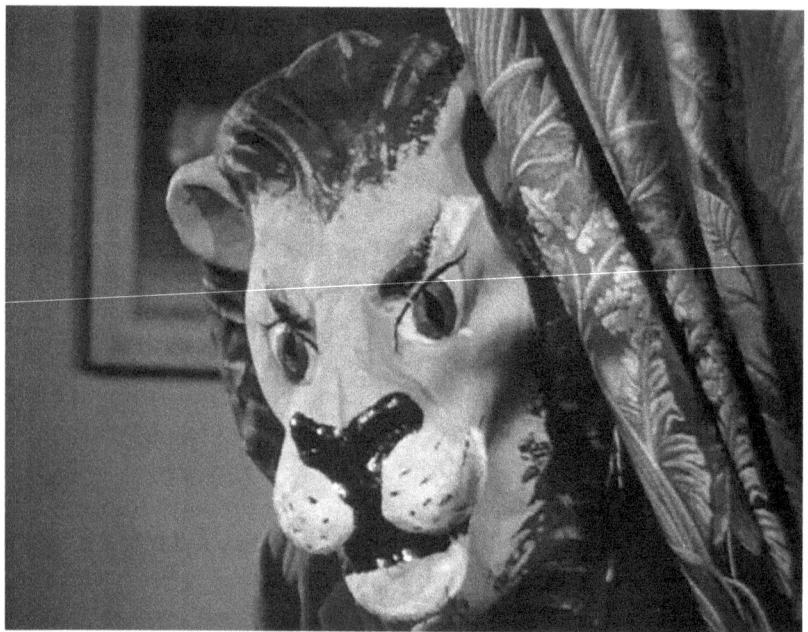

Prescott makes an entrance.

Traditionally, when a motion picture is favorably received by audiences, it becomes difficult for its director to respond with an equally successful film. *The Whistler* had met with astounding success upon its theatrical release. Castle wanted to prove to the King brothers, as well as the American public, that his success would not be short-lived.

In retrospect, his direction of *When Strangers Marry* is noteworthy because it is somewhat comparable to the works of Alfred Hitchcock. A particular scene, transpiring shortly after Millie arrives at Baxter's apartment, features Castle in a cameo role. It is neither a speaking nor walk-on role. Castle, suggested to be the apartment's previous renter, simply appears within a photograph of himself. Hitchcock, well known for his own clever cameos, had recently done something similar for *Lifeboat*. He, too, appears in a photo. Included in a newspaper, the picture boldly advertises Reduco Obesity Slayer, a weight loss product featuring "before" and "after" images of Hitchcock. Castle wanted to make his mark in the industry, even if it meant emulating one of the greatest film directors of the period.

But there was more to Castle's approach than the inclusion of a well-timed cameo. Hitchcock's films usually contained a plot device known as the MacGuffin, which represented a desired object, tangible or intangible, pursued by the main characters. The protagonists and antagonists of the story generally consider the MacGuffin to be important, whereas members of an audience may not. It merely serves as the backdrop to a more important plot. Arguably, the most famous MacGuffin in a Hitchcock film is featured in *Notorious*, as Cary Grant and Ingrid Bergman's characters stumble upon a supply of uranium hidden in several wine bottles. Their discovery, although important to them, is secondary to the audience. We are concerned about other aspects of the plot, particularly the fate of their relationship. In regard to *When Strangers Marry*, the identity of the Silk Stalking Murderer is similar to a MacGuffin in that it serves as a pretext to the narrative's central idea. The United States has often been referred to as a "melting pot," a metaphor for the assimilation of different cultures and concepts. At first, Castle's depiction of 1940s America appears to reflect the nature of the melting pot with its not-so-subtle references to worldwide organizations and methods of cleansing. But as the narrative progresses, a deeper meaning takes shape, especially when Baxter and Millie happen upon a vibrant establishment nestled in its distinct location.

Following the opening credits, the first image of *When Strangers Marry* presents the Philadelphia Hotel sign as it welcomes members of Lions Club International (LCI), a global organization working to serve many purposes, including the promotion of cultural awareness amongst its affiliates. A transition to the hotel's interior, complete with clever sound effects and fast-paced camerawork, reveals Prescott to be entering its deserted bar. The unmistakable growl of a lion is distinct. And a dolly shot is implemented as the camera moves rapidly towards Prescott. He wears the mask of a lion's head, a direct symbol of the club that

Kim Hunter as Millie Baxter.

takes pride in "doing something for somebody else." Prescott helps Baxter, a complete stranger, to acquire a room for the night. Philadelphia, also known as The City of Brotherly Love, was a place where people of different backgrounds, regardless of economic status or ethnicity, were given the opportunity to join together in their pursuit of happiness. The city quickly became a melting pot of various cultures. It is appropriate that, for purposes of Castle's film, LCI would host its convention in a metropolis such as Philadelphia. Furthermore, by the early 1940s, the organization had established its presence in several nations across the globe. Many more would become affiliated with LCI over the course of the following two decades, including a particular Middle Eastern country rich in cultural values.

The Republic of Turkey has made numerous contributions to American society, including the ever-cleansing Turkish bath that is present in the basement of the Sherwin Hotel. When Blake visits the hotel in search of Millie, he instead finds himself bathing and relaxing with Graham. A Turkish bath is known for its sauna-like setting. Bathers are initially exposed to a steady flow of hot air. In time, a stream of cold water is splashed across the body, considered by many to be the culminating point of the cleansing process. Castle's depiction of the Turkish bath is somewhat brief, lasting less than a minute. We bear witness to its climax as Blake and Graham douse themselves with buckets of cold water. Yet, the scene remains detached from the rest of the film. It is not necessarily specific to the plot. The two discuss random topics, such as the game of baseball and the institution of marriage (the latter of which is a reflection of the film's title). But Blake does not disclose his intentions for visiting the hotel until he and Graham arrive at police headquarters a short time later. Castle's inclusion of the Turkish bath, however, is indicative of America's status as a melting pot of cultural ideas and contributions. Although the scene remains prominent in the minds of select theatergoers, it is not as memorable as another to be revealed later in the film.

As Baxter and Millie seek refuge at Big Jim's, a popular Harlem nightclub, it immediately becomes clear that the cultural differences in American society have the potential to divide instead of unite. Castle's deliberate foray into terra incognita is arguably the most significant scene of the picture. The joyous patrons of Big Jim's pay little attention to Baxter and Millie. After a series of brief glances towards the unexpected visitors, the revelry continues unabated. Not a single person is deterred. Many years after the

Castle's cameo (When Strangers Marry was reissued in 1949 as Betrayed.)

release of *When Strangers Marry*, the model of the melting pot came under fire from social critics. An alternative idea, which came to be known as the salad bowl, continued to place an emphasis on the integration of various cultures in America. However, instead of cultures merging, or melting, into a supreme culture, the so-called ingredients of the salad are placed in close proximity to one another, similar to what is seen with Baxter and Millie's attempt to integrate with the patrons of Big Jim's. Proponents of the salad bowl model suggest that cultures will mix, yet remain distinct so that one's heritage may be preserved for future generations. In his memoirs, Castle wrote that he wanted his film "to express the melancholia of being troubled and lonely in a strange city." For Baxter and Millie, this could not be truer.

The filming of *When Strangers Marry* transpired from late May to early June of 1944. Castle completed his project on schedule, and as a result, he was awarded an extra $1,000 from the King brothers.

His film contains several noteworthy scenes. For example, when Blake invites Graham to police headquarters, the latter is presented with a series of photographs. The first is of a cold-blooded killer named Albert Foster, portrayed by Byron Foulger. Foulger previously appeared in *The Whistler* as the flophouse desk clerk and would go on to appear in Castle's *Crime Doctor* thriller, *Just Before Dawn*. Years later, in *Zotz!*, Castle would pay tribute to the popular character actor by naming two of the film's characters after him: Captain Byron and Major Foulger. But the police headquarters scene of *When Strangers Marry* is not only significant for Foulger's cameo. Later, Blake presents a picture of Robert Fiske, a man murdered by Foster.

During the early 1940s, a performer named Robert Fiske worked in Hollywood as a B film actor. But on September 12, 1944, Fiske died suddenly of congestive heart failure. Coincidentally, the very actor whose name was used to portray a dead man met his demise in real life. He was fifty-four years old, missing the premiere of *When Strangers Marry* by a mere two months.

Castle's film is also remarkable for his directorial style. He was becoming skilled at his craft, especially through the effective use of transitions. The first transition, transpiring as Prescott's body is discovered, begins with a woman's scream and concludes with the high-pitched noise of a train whistle. Another scene features a newspaper's front-page headline of the "Silk Stalking Murder!" as it transitions to a pair of silk stalkings hanging from a chair. Seconds later, as Millie frantically waits in her hotel room for Baxter's phone call, Castle presents a combination of loud music and flashing lights (the latter of which is featured in *Macabre* at Quigley's Funeral Parlor) emanating from a nearby dance hall.

When Strangers Marry essentially foreshadows several of Castle's later works. Approximately forty minutes into the film, Millie approaches a tunnel. The setting is eerily similar to a scene from *Homicidal*, as Miriam happens upon the dark, closed door of a sinister house. In regard to *When Strangers Marry*, Millie reluctantly enters the tunnel, and it is not long before she encounters a group of floating heads, a popular Castle motif that will later recur in films such as *It's a Small World* and *House on Haunted Hill*.

Upon the conclusion of *When Strangers Marry*, Graham attempts to push Millie to her death from atop the hotel. *The Houston Story*, *The Busy Body*, and the aforementioned *Zotz!* are additional Castle films to include a tense, rooftop setting.

When Strangers Marry premiered in San Francisco on November 2, 1944. Two weeks later, it premiered on the east coast at the Brooklyn Strand Theatre. Castle was able to attend, as he

Kim Hunter and Robert Mitchum.

had already been in town to direct *Meet a Body*, a Broadway play of the macabre. The Brooklyn landmark was packed, and critics were in awe. James Agee, the so-called "dean of critics" who wrote for *Time* magazine, reported that the film provided "a heart lifted sense of delight in real performance and ambition which I have rarely known in any film context since my own mind and that of moving-picture making were sufficiently young."

CHAPTER SIX
THE MARK OF THE WHISTLER (1944)

F. Scott Fitzgerald, the "great" novelist, once said, "Genius is the ability to put into effect what is on your mind." This was true for William Castle, especially as he traversed through the latter part of his career. But the aforementioned quote also applies to Cornell Woolrich, a writer and admirer of Fitzgerald's. During the early 1940s, the genre of film noir became increasingly popular. And several of Woolrich's original works were subject to film noir adaptations. *Dormant Account*, his short story, attracted the attention of Harry Cohn. Columbia Pictures was in the process of brainstorming ideas for another *Whistler* picture, and Woolrich's tale of crime and suspense appeared to fit the bill. Screenwriter George Bricker was hired to provide the adaptation, thus naming it *The Mark of the Whistler*.

Lee Selfridge Nugent (Richard Dix), a derelict, learns of a dormant account containing funds that have been unclaimed for many years. It was established in the name of Lee Nugent, an individual who cannot be found. Selfridge visits the bank. Based on the credibility of his name alone, he pretends to be the account holder, but the bank chooses to conduct a formal investigation before parting with the money. Several days pass, and Selfridge is allowed to collect the funds. The amount totals close to $30 thousand. Upon leaving the bank, he encounters Patricia "Pat" Henley (Janis Carter), a newspaper reporter. She publishes Selfridge's success story. Eddie Donnelly (John Calvert), a local socialite, takes notice. For reasons unknown, he intends to kill Selfridge, but is unaware that his target is not the real Lee Nugent. "Limpy" Smith (Paul Guilfoyle), a humble street peddler, becomes privy to Donnelly's plans. He warns Selfridge of the impending danger. An attempt to skip town is cut short when Donnelly intercepts Selfridge at the bus station. His motives are disclosed. Many years earlier, Donnelly's father owned a firm that became ruined due to the illegal activities of his business partner. In the aftermath, he went to prison. But his partner, the father of the real Lee Nugent, fled the country. Years later, Donnelly's father was finally released. But time had taken its toll, as he slipped into a catatonic state shortly thereafter. Donnelly tried to exact revenge on Nugent's father, but the latter had died of natural causes. Selfridge, facing death, attempts to reveal his true identity, but to no avail. Limpy comes forward, exposing himself as Nugent, the man Donnelly seeks. Donnelly is killed during a shootout with police. And the account's money is eventually returned to Limpy, the rightful owner.

Midway through Castle's film, Selfridge encounters Pat at the Club Royale. He intends to treat her to dinner and a show. But their evening is eventually cut short when it becomes apparent that Donnelly is in pursuit. Courtesy of an attendant (Willie Best), Selfridge escapes through a secret door of the men's room. A short time later, Donnelly enters the restroom. Unable to find Selfridge, he questions the attendant, who replies, "You must be looking for the Invisible Man, sir." During the latter part of the nineteenth century, H.G. Wells, the popular science fiction author, wrote *The Invisible Man*. By 1944, during the production of *The Mark of the Whistler*, Wells's creation had become quite popular with the American public. Several motion pictures, including *The Invisible Man Returns* and *Invisible Agent*, had been produced by Universal. In Castle's film, within the restroom of the Club Royale, Selfridge transforms into an invisible man of sorts. The concept of so-called invisible men is prevalent in *The Mark of the Whistler*. The Whistler himself is never seen. Yet, in a figurative sense, Limpy and Nugent's father are also somewhat invisible within the grand scheme of things.

Upon his escape from the Club Royale, Selfridge detects the presence of the Whistler, an unseen individual shrouded in mystery. The film's title character is clearly significant because he intervenes during key points of the narrative, but theatergoers do not see as much of him as they desire. As Selfridge walks down a dark street, he suddenly hears the whistling of a disquieting tune. The Whistler's shadow draws closer. He laughs prior to addressing Selfridge:

> THE WHISTLER: This is an amazing turn of events. Isn't it, Lee Nugent? You went to infinite pains to prove that you were the man to whom the money belonged. And now,

you are hunted. Is it by someone who may know of the fraud you perpetrated?

Again, the Whistler laughs. He resumes whistling as his shadow slowly retracts from whence it came. Like the ghosts of *House on Haunted Hill*, the Whistler can be heard, but not seen. He is a shadow without substance. In essence, he is an invisible man.

The Whistler, released just seven months prior to *The Mark of the Whistler*, left some theatergoers disappointed upon its conclusion. Although people were quite content with the overall narrative, a particular discontentment towards the title character was evident, as The Whistler was not to be seen throughout the entire picture. However, with the release of a sequel, some figured things would change. Alas, such was not the case, as The Whistler remained invisible yet again. But he made his presence known at key points of the story. His rendezvous with Selfridge is well-timed, as it establishes the following scene of the film.

As Limpy converses with Selfridge on an ill-lighted sidewalk, he assumes the form of an invisible man. Castle's use of low-key lighting casts the so-called street peddler in a different perspective. Seconds prior to the conversation, Limpy gestures Selfridge into the shadows, the very lurking grounds of The Whistler himself. Castle does not reveal Limpy's face. In fact, all that is visible of the peddler is his hat, and it appears to float in the air as Selfridge faces what appears to be an invisible companion. Castle intensifies the mood of the scene as he switches to alternating close-ups of both men. Selfridge's face is fairly visible. But Limpy cannot be seen. Aside from his hat, only two distinct pinpoints of light are visible, as the reflection of Limpy's corneas seemingly penetrates through the darkness. It is a chilling spectacle. Limpy, in a figurative sense, is invisible. Yet, in actuality, he is the real Lee Nugent. Therefore, his identity, like his physical presence of the scene, is subject to concealment. However, before Castle makes the revelation of Limpy's true identity, he transports his audience into the confines of the Donnelly home. And it is there that we learn the source of the narrative's conflict.

Donnelly speaks negatively of Nugent's father, a man who is not only responsible for the film's drastic chain of events, but is also an individual never seen by the audience. The scenario bears a striking resemblance to the narrative of *Homicidal*. In *The Mark of the Whistler*, theatergoers come to realize that, had it not been for the reckless nature of Nugent's father, the conflict of the story would be nonexistent. Instead of maintaining the ongoing charade of a street peddler, Limpy would have rightfully acquired the trust money as he came of age. And Selfridge most likely would have remained a derelict considering the newspaper advertisement would not have been published in the first place. Nugent's father does not appear in the film, but his malicious agenda inadvertently sets the story's events in motion.

In regard to *Homicidal*, it is discovered upon the film's conclusion that the plot is essentially driven by the selfish desires of Warren's father, a character who is never seen. An unseen character, be it male or female, is generally interpreted as mysterious. And a character of this nature is empowered with the potential to control the outcome of any narrative if it is so desired by the film's writer and director.

Principal photography for *The Mark of the Whistler* was completed on August 14, 1944. Shortly thereafter, Castle departed California to begin casting for his Broadway production of *Meet a Body*. Cohn reluctantly granted him an unpaid leave of absence.

While in New York, Castle was ordered to "look around" for another *Whistler* story. He eventually acquired the motion picture rights to *If I Die Before I Wake*, a suspense novel. However, both the story and Castle were not used for the next installment of the *Whistler* series. Instead, *The Power of the Whistler*, the third entry of the saga, was directed by Lew Landers. It was not until June of 1945 that Castle returned to the director's chair, and Cohn, in short, had new plans for his protégé.

CHAPTER SEVEN
THE CRIME DOCTOR'S WARNING (1945)

In 1945, Harry Cohn arranged for William Castle to direct an installment of the *Crime Doctor* film series, based on the popular CBS radio program of the same name. Four films had already been produced, and the saga was becoming a hit with the American public.

In *Crime Doctor*, the initial film of the series, we are introduced to a thief named Phil Morgan (Warner Baxter). As a result of being thrown from a moving car, he suffers amnesia, and eventually becomes Dr. Robert Ordway, a well-respected criminal psychologist. Upon the film's conclusion, he regains his memory and apprehends those responsible for his accident.

The continuing adventures of Dr. Ordway are portrayed in *Crime Doctor's Strangest Case*, *Shadows in the Night*, and *The Crime Doctor's Courage*. Castle's film, *The Crime Doctor's Warning*, served as a test of his endurance. In such a short space of time, he had successfully undertaken several projects in collaboration with the top brass of Columbia Pictures. Nevertheless, despite Castle's hectic schedule, he showed no signs of fatigue.

Clive Lake (Coulter Irwin), a struggling artist, suffers from memory lapses and turns to Ordway for help. Connie Mace (Dusty Anderson), Lake's fiancée, is mysteriously murdered. Prior to her untimely death, she worked as a model. Ordway learns that another model was murdered just days before Connie. Lake is a suspect and seeks refuge at his mother's home. She believes her son to be guilty, but Ordway is reluctant and decides to hypnotize Lake in an attempt to uncover the truth. A flashback places Joseph Duval (Franco Corsaro), a fellow artist, near the location of Connie's murder. Ordway learns that the deceased models once posed together for a painting known as The Ring. In addition, a third model participated in the event, but Ordway cannot locate her. Duval appears at the home of Lake's mother with proof of her son's innocence. He claims to know the true identity of the murderer, but he is suddenly shot dead by a prowler lurking in the yard. It is determined that the third model has been missing since the days immediately following her wedding. Ordway exposes Frederick Malone (Miles Mander), the owner of a prestigious art gallery, as the husband of the missing model. The crime doctor discovers her body, covered in wax, hidden in a room below the gallery. A guilty Malone admits to murdering the other models because they were asking too many questions about the disappearance of his late wife. He attempts to kill Ordway, but is unsuccessful when Lake and the police arrive to take him into custody.

Columbia began production of *The Crime Doctor's Warning* on June 14, 1945. Years earlier, when Castle met Orson Welles for the first time, the former proudly declared that they shared the same astrological sign of Taurus. The Zodiac symbol for Taurus is that of a bull. *The Crime Doctor's Warning* is an intriguing murder mystery, but it is also a film with subtle and not-so-subtle Taurean references. This is evident through Castle's direction of the scene at Pancho's restaurant. Furthermore, the name of an apartment building and personality of the murderer are accurate reflections of the popular astrological sign.

Ordway interrogates Nick Petroni (Eduardo Ciannelli), a male model, at Pancho's, and their conversation, in addition to the restaurant's ambiance, is symbolic of Taurus. The crime doctor is determined to find Duval, but instead of aiding in the investigation, Petroni would rather proclaim his ongoing hatred of women. A dark quality of Taurus is that of jealousy. Petroni's contempt for the opposite sex, in retrospect, is his ravenous desire to covet what he does not have. His marketability as a male model is diminishing. Meanwhile, the demand for females remains popular. Throughout Petroni's cynical rant, the immense painting of a bull fight is prominently displayed in the background. It covers an entire wall of the restaurant and rarely escapes the viewer's sight. A few minutes later, "the bull" is visible yet again.

As Ordway comes closer to exposing the identity of his unknown nemesis, the symbol of the Taurus sign is subliminally presented to the audience. The crime doctor visits Jimmy Gordon (John Abbott), the silhouette artist, at The El Toro Apartments. Castle's portrayal of Ordway's arrival features an exterior shot of the apartment building, clearly revealing its title. El Toro is Spanish for "The Bull." But the sign's title is not its only noteworthy characteristic. Also visible is an arrow, which points the way to the truth. In Gordon's apartment, Ordway learns that The Ring, in Gordon's possession for a lengthy period of time, has been stolen. Hence, a turning point in the plot transpires, as the suspicion is no longer on Gordon. Consequently, Ordway comes face-to-face with the real killer.

Malone, like Petroni, is a man of the jealous type, but it is the former's uncontrollable possessiveness, another Taurean quality, that ultimately gets the best of him. His dominant personality drives him to commit murder. Malone's wife, days after the wedding ceremony, decided that their marriage was a mistake and needed to be annulled. Naturally, Malone was devastated. But he could not let her leave. Malone demanded to model her entire figure in wax, but this led to her accidental death by suffocation. Embarrassed to go to the authorities, and unwilling to part with his prized possession, Malone kept the tragic accident a secret. His mistake ultimately transformed him into a cold-blooded killer, thus attracting the attention of the illustrious Dr. Ordway.

The Crime Doctor's Warning was released on September 27, 1945. The film's alternate title was *The Paper Doll Murders*. Although creative, it was a misnomer. Throughout the film, the audience is led to believe that Gordon, the mysterious silhouette artist, is the prime suspect in the killings. Yet, during the film's conclusion, we learn that Gordon is innocent and Malone is guilty. If, in fact, the former had been guilty instead of the latter, the title would have been more appropriate simply because Gordon creates "paper dolls" for a living. Nevertheless, the original title of *The Crime Doctor's Warning* remained. Despite Castle's satisfactory direction of the film, he took a brief hiatus from the *Crime Doctor* series. It was time, courtesy of Harry Cohn, to return to familiar territory, as the *Voice of the Whistler* was calling.

CHAPTER EIGHT
VOICE OF THE WHISTLER (1945)

Following the success of *When Strangers Marry*, the King brothers tapped William Castle to direct another picture of theirs. The film pertained to John Dillinger, the notorious bank robber of the 1930s. Castle and Philip Yordan, a screenwriter best known for his work on *Anna Lucasta* and *El Cid*, collaborated together on crafting a fictitious account of Dillinger's life. The two had previously shared ideas with each other regarding the script of *When Strangers Marry*. But as the production of *Dillinger* drew closer, Castle opted out of the project in order to direct *Meet a Body* on Broadway.

Several months later, he returned to Hollywood to resume his career in the motion picture business. Castle always had a knack for writing, and although he contributed his ideas to several of the films on which he worked, he was not always given screen credit for his efforts. Yet, in 1945, Castle and a colleague, Wilfrid H. Pettitt, wrote the script for the next *Whistler* picture. Based on a story by Allan Radar, it was entitled *Voice of the Whistler*, and the film marked the first time Castle would be credited as both a director and writer.

John Sinclair (Richard Dix), a powerful industrialist, suffers from acute exhaustion due to a workaholic lifestyle spanning the course of many years. He is strongly encouraged to take a leave of absence. Sinclair travels by train to Chicago, where he intends to embark on a boat trip along Lake Michigan. But upon his arrival at the railway station, he faints. Ernie Sparrow (Rhys Williams), a cab driver, witnesses the ordeal and takes Sinclair to the local clinic. Wishing to keep his identity a secret, Sinclair uses the pseudonym of John Carter. His diagnosis is grim. He is encouraged to cancel the boat trip and make friends. Joan Martin (Lynn Merrick), a nurse at the clinic, takes an interest in Sinclair. She is engaged to Fred "Doc" Graham (James Cardwell), an intern and co-worker. He is eager to marry, but Joan wishes to wait due to financial hardship. Sinclair, believing the days of his life to be limited, plans a coastal vacation to Maine. He concocts a business proposition. Sinclair asks Joan to marry him, promising her his entire fortune following his soon-to-be passing. She accepts with the hopes of one day enjoying a prosperous life with Graham, who abruptly ends the engagement upon hearing the news. In Maine, Sinclair, Joan, and Sparrow move into an abandoned lighthouse. Months pass, and Sinclair falls in love with Joan. But she detests their life of isolation and considers divorce. Graham suddenly arrives from Chicago. Joan is happy to see him, but time has taken its toll, as she is unsure of where her destiny lies. Graham attempts to murder Sinclair, who turns the tables and kills his would-be assassin. Joan summons the police. Sinclair is later found guilty of murder. Joan inherits his fortune, but ultimately spends the remainder of her days living at the lighthouse in torment and solitude.

Rhys Williams and Richard Dix.

Voice of the Whistler and *When Strangers Marry*, in addition to being films directed by Castle, each feature a supporting character named Fred Graham. The similarities between both men are uncanny. They are unable to marry the women they desire, and they each resort to murder as a means of self-fulfillment. But neither is ultimately successful in life.

In specific regard to *Voice of the Whistler*, the narrative naturally does not feature any individuals with the same name. Yet, a comparison of two particular characters with different personalities reveals a striking similarity in regard to life experiences. Sinclair and Sparrow, a well-known industrialist and former lightweight boxing champion respectively, disappeared from the spotlight during the height of their careers. Both men struggled with trust issues and were occasionally lonely from time to time. The audience eventually learns that Sinclair and Sparrow share an appreciation for coastal living. In addition, they consider chess to be a favorite intellectual pastime (a theme later explored in *Drums of Tahiti*). Yet, Sinclair gives the impression of a man who would prefer to play the game alone, whereas Sparrow would gladly welcome any opponent simply for the benefit of pleasant company. Sinclair and Sparrow, at one time, were affiliated with a close knit circle of associates. Furthermore, they were patients of the East Street Clinic, which led to their admiration of Joan. But despite a series of similar experiences, Sinclair and Sparrow greatly differ from one another in regard to the conscience of humanity.

As Castle introduces Sinclair and Sparrow, albeit separately, to the audience, he presents them as men who are affiliated with their own close knit circle of associates. Yet, one group is portrayed as an executive team of confidants, whereas the other is depicted as a small coterie of neighborhood friends. In Sinclair's office, a brief film in regard to the highlights of his life is presented. Despite the enthusiasm of his employees, Sinclair takes little interest in the picture. Paul Kitridge (Douglas Wood), Sinclair's corporate counsel, is commended for his handling of a recent case. But he is all too familiar with the increasingly cutthroat nature of his superior:

> KITRIDGE: I had to win or you'd have fired me.
>
> SINCLAIR: Probably, very likely would've.
>
> Sinclair and Kitridge then approach a conference table, where a team of executives waits. Kitridge sits as Sinclair faces his confidants:
>
> SINCLAIR: In the future, I want one thing clearly understood. From now on, I want nothing, absolutely nothing, to interfere with my personal life.

Sinclair walks away from the table. Kitridge exhibits frustration and then proceeds to address a fellow colleague:

KITRIDGE: What personal life?

The audience eventually learns that Sinclair has no friends. The people with whom he associates are merely colleagues, and they are forced to respect him out of fear of losing their jobs. When Castle introduces Sparrow to the audience, it immediately becomes clear that the humble taxi driver is an honest, genuine individual. Unlike Sinclair, he enjoys lasting relationships with his neighbors. A tour of Sparrow's community features several of his good friends, and Sinclair is quick to take notice. He asks, "How does a person go about making friends?" Sparrow credits his camaraderie with the neighborhood folk to his ability to keep an open mind and always give people a chance. His philosophy, in essence, is what led him to Sinclair in the first place. As the tour of Sparrow's neighborhood concludes, he presents the most significant of landmarks.

The East Street Clinic and its medical personnel, having previously nursed Sparrow back to health, welcome Sinclair (Carter) with the hopes of curing his ailments, but Sinclair does not appreciate the benefits of such a facility. The issue of trust is of paramount importance. Prior to entering, Sparrow says, "If you're gonna trust people, Mr. Carter, you better start right now. We all have to learn to do that sooner or later. I did." It is evident Sparrow has overcome his trust issues, but the same cannot be said of Sinclair, who is deceptive to the point that he alters his true name. Once inside, Sinclair struggles to interact with the clinic's occupants. He eventually comments that he has "been to too many doctors." A repeat visit to the clinic, similar to the first, is uneventful. He departs in frustration, brashly ignoring the only employee of the facility who has taken a genuine interest in his well-being.

Joan is admired by both Sparrow and Sinclair, as is initially evident through the separate deliveries of flowers, but a fine line between compassion and lust can sometimes be problematic. Sinclair is a man of pride, intent on acquiring what he desires. He pursues Joan with little disregard for the consequences of his actions. At the lighthouse, several months pass. Sinclair's envy of

Joan has gotten the best of him. Everybody, including Sparrow, falls victim to the tragic events of the film's climax. Graham arrives and is subsequently murdered. Sinclair is incarcerated. Joan is left to wallow in despair. And Sparrow has essentially lost the companionship he once shared with Sinclair. To reiterate, the similarities between both men are evident. And their friendship, in essence, is able to flourish primarily without incident. But in the end, the man who ultimately chooses to be unjust pays the price, and the one who remains conscionable to the best of his ability becomes the least affected of the narrative's victims.

When Castle agreed to direct *The Whistler* in 1943, he essentially became one with the series. An early scene of the saga's premiere film depicts Lefty Vigran plotting his next move at The Crow's Nest, a seaside tavern. He attempts to get the attention of a deaf mute sitting at the bar. And dominating a wall of the tavern is the portrait of a lighthouse. It cleverly foreshadows *Voice of the Whistler*, which came to be advertised as "The Strange Case of the Haunted Lighthouse!"

The film was released on October 30, 1945, presented as a chilling, suspenseful tale for theatergoers to enjoy, albeit briefly, on Halloween. Little did Castle know that, many years into the future, his name would become synonymous with the annual festivities.

CHAPTER NINE
JUST BEFORE DAWN (1946)

Following his direction of the latest *Whistler* installment, William Castle began preparations for *Just Before Dawn*, the sixth *Crime Doctor* picture. Warner Baxter, unlike Castle, was concluding a five-month break from films. He was well-rested and ready to work, which was beneficial to Castle, as Baxter's most recent film was *The Crime Doctor's Warning*. Not only was Baxter stepping into the same role following his hiatus, he was also working with the same director. A solid rapport between Castle and Baxter was beginning to form. But much had transpired since their first collaboration. World War II had recently come to an end with the surrender of Japan. Domestic America was thriving. And the general public was eager to devour anything Hollywood had to offer. It was simply a momentous time for Castle and Baxter to be a part of the entertainment industry.

Dr. Robert Ordway (Baxter) is summoned to help Walter Foster (George Meeker), an unconscious diabetic. Ordway is provided with insulin and immediately administers it. Minutes later, however, Foster dies. But not before he mumbles, "...hath given you one face." It is soon determined that the insulin contained poison. Ordway learns of Foster's desperate need for money prior to his death. Foster's sister, Claire (Adelle Roberts), phones Ordway claiming that her brother was reciting a line from *Hamlet* as he died. Before Claire can explain its significance, she is killed by Casper (Marvin Miller), a local hoodlum. Later, Casper attempts to kill Ordway. Although the crime doctor is unharmed, he feigns blindness in an attempt to deceive his enemies. The police cannot find any trace of Casper's fingerprints, but an analysis of his handwriting indicates that he is, in reality, a parolee named Corcelli. With the help of a make-up artist, Ordway's appearance is altered to resemble that of a notorious criminal. In disguise, he visits Casper (Corcelli) on the pretext of inquiring about a reputable plastic surgeon. Ordway is redirected to Ganss Mortuary, but its owner (Martin Kosleck) attempts to eliminate the crime doctor upon learning that Ordway is not who he appears to be. However,

Casper and Ganss are soon apprehended. Ordway continues his charade as that of a blind man, consequently evoking a confession from Alec Girard (Wilton Graff), a plastic surgeon to criminals, but prominent real estate agent to the public. Foster knew of Girard's secret and was blackmailing him. Following his orchestration of Foster's murder, Girard also ordered the killing of Claire and another innocent woman simply because they knew too much.

Castle and William Shakespeare, aside from being entertainers with the same first name, did not have much in common. They resided on opposite sides of the world and lived hundreds of years apart from each other. A notable disparity, however, is that Castle and Shakespeare catered to different audiences. Yet, in *Just Before Dawn*, a powerful quote from Shakespeare's *Hamlet* unites the otherwise contrasting realms of fiction together. During the play, Hamlet states, "God hath given you one face, and you make yourself another." Hamlet is upset with Ophelia, a lord's daughter, because he believes she is forcing herself to be somebody she is not. The same can be said of multiple characters in *Just Before Dawn*. Castle, in borrowing a single line from the great playwright, sets the stage for the transformation of his main character. Ordway will alter his mood, vision, and face in order to catch a killer.

Ordway, in reality an affable gentleman, must maintain a serious demeanor in the line of duty. During a visit to the office of Allen S. Tobin (Charles Arnt), attorney and overseer of the Foster estate, the crime doctor reveals his true colors. Shortly after the interrogation begins, Tobin suddenly becomes anxious. He frequently looks at his watch and, at one point, peers into the building's hallway. It is then revealed that the cause of Tobin's anxiety is simply a matter of tardiness on the part of his servant. Castle transitions to a brief, but significant, shot of Ordway smirking at the absurdity of the situation. Seconds later, the crime doctor is forced to resume his solemn appearance. The interview with Tobin eventually concludes. And for the time being, Ordway has accomplished all that he possibly can. Nevertheless, he continues an investigation that becomes more dangerous by the minute, forcing him to make an alteration of the most peculiar kind.

In order to deceive his enemies, Ordway feigns blindness, thus modifying his appearance with a pair of dark sunglasses.

Casper's failed attempt at the elimination of the crime doctor sets the latter's plan in motion. Ordway realizes that the closer he is to uncovering the truth, the greater of a threat he is to those responsible for Foster's murder. His supposed loss of vision puts his adversaries at ease. Ordway's charade continues until the final scene of the film, when Girard, who hides behind the facade of a successful businessman, unmasks himself as the mastermind of the killings. Girard, using the metaphor of a window blind when referring to his real estate company, becomes flabbergasted when Ordway reveals a special blind of his own. As the sunglasses are removed, the film's protagonist and antagonist come face-to-face without their disguises. The climactic scene makes for a fitting conclusion. But in order to obtain a means to an end, Ordway is willing to go a step further than his counterpart.

Ordway's greatest transformation of the film transpires when a new face is literally painted over his original one. He visits Harris (Byron Foulger), a make-up artist, in order to appear as Pete Hastings, a notorious bank robber. Hamlet was figuratively speaking when accusing Ophelia of making a new face for herself. But Ordway assumes a completely new identity. With the exception of his eyes, the crime doctor looks and acts like a different person. Instead of hiring another actor, Castle decided to have Baxter assume the role of Hastings, despite countless hours of time spent in the make-up trailer. In short, the end result proved to be successful.

Just Before Dawn was released on March 7, 1946. It is considered to be one of the better *Crime Doctor* pictures. Eric Taylor's script features an intriguing storyline, and a solid cast of supporting and lead characters effectively support the narrative. Dr. Steiner (Charles Lane), a character that is rarely seen in the film, discovers "just before dawn" that all three victims were killed by the same poison. It is a turning point of the story, thus providing a significant boost for Ordway. Without the narrative's supporting characters, its leads would be unable to flourish. But the director is ultimately responsible for the quality of that which appears on the screen.

With the exception of Eugene Forde, Castle became the only individual to direct multiple films of the *Crime Doctor* series. It was essentially a busy time in the young director's life. If he was not immersed in the adventures of Dr. Ordway, he was most likely working on a *Whistler* picture. Coincidentally, after a short two weeks of rest, the latter would be the focus of his next project.

CHAPTER TEN
MYSTERIOUS INTRUDER (1946)

William Castle's hiatus from the *Whistler* series did not last long. In his absence, Lew Landers directed *The Power of the Whistler*, the saga's fourth installment. Coincidentally, Landers's involvement with the series ended upon the film's release. But he was not the only director to depart after one picture, as George Sherman (*The Secret of the Whistler*), William Clemens (*The Thirteenth Hour*), and D. Ross Lederman (*The Return of the Whistler*) each followed suit.

In December of 1945, Castle, the only filmmaker to direct multiple installments of the saga, began production on *Mysterious Intruder*. It was to be his fourth *Whistler* picture, and he sought to make it his best yet. The film's tagline declared, "A WOMAN SCREAMS! A KILLER STRIKES! AND 'THE WHISTLER' STALKS HIS PREY!"

Edward Stillwell (Paul E. Burns), the elderly proprietor of a music store, seeks out a young lady named Elora Lund. In order to find her, he enlists the services of Don Gale (Richard Dix), a private detective. Three days later, the missing woman appears at the store. Stillwell makes reference to valuable heirlooms donated to him by her late mother. However, before additional details can be disclosed, Stillwell is murdered by Harry Pontos (Mike Mazurki), a known criminal. Furthermore, Freda Hanson (Helen Mowery), a woman hired by Gale, impersonated Elora in order to obtain information pertaining to the valuables. Following Stillwell's murder, she is taken to Pontos's house and is subsequently released. Later, Freda guides Gale to the home. Police detectives Taggart (Barton MacLane) and Burns (Charles Lane) suddenly arrive on the scene. Pontos is shot dead while resisting arrest, and Gale is eventually apprehended for breaking into the house. Meanwhile, the real Elora Lund (Pamela Blake), curious about the identity of the impostor, comes forward. Gale is eventually released from jail. He confronts Freda at her apartment, accusing her of sending the police to Pontos's house. She admits to it, and also reveals her association with the deceased hoodlum. Freda's doorbell rings. Gale hides. While waiting, he discovers a newspaper clipping Stillwell had given Freda just prior to his demise. Gale learns of two cylindrical records, each worth $100,000. Freda mysteriously disappears. Gale leaves and discovers Elora to be at his office. He makes her privy to the clipping. Elora wishes to notify the police, but Gale insists on searching Stillwell's store himself. Freda is found dead in her apartment. Witnesses, including James Summers (Regis Toomey), manager of the apartment building, report to authorities that Gale was in the area at the time of Freda's death. But Summers, eventually caught in the act of stealing the records from the store, is exposed as Freda's killer, having earlier joined forces with her and Pontos in order to accumulate the fortune. Gale kills Summers during a shootout. Taggart and Burns happen upon the chaos. Gale, unaware of their identities, fires at them. Both men shoot back, destroying the records and killing Gale in the process.

The production of *Mysterious Intruder* began on December 6, 1945, and concluded exactly two weeks later on December 20, 1945. Prior to the film's release, its working title was *Murder Is Unpredictable*.

Several aspects of the narrative are indeed unforeseeable. Upon its denouement, Gale slowly descends into the basement of Stillwell's music store. He discovers a pair of mysterious intruders, eventually revealed to be Summers and his accomplice. But despite being incognito, albeit for a brief moment, both men are not the subject of the film's title, as the words "mysterious intruder" clearly make reference to one, specific trespasser. Furthermore, the subject of Castle's picture is not limited to a specific individual. Select members of an audience will conclude that *Mysterious Intruder* refers to Freda, as she pretends to be somebody she is not, thus arousing Elora's curiosity. But the film's title is potentially applicable to Pontos, Gale, and The Whistler.

Pontos is initially seen lurking outside of Stillwell's store, and his unwelcome entrance into the shop shortly thereafter brands him as a mysterious intruder. His importance to the narrative, however, is minimal. Pontos murders Stillwell. Freda screams. Pontos then makes as if he is going to assault her. They depart, and the audience is left guessing at the intruder's significance to the narrative. Pontos is presented as mysterious not just because his identity is unknown. His cold-blooded murder of Stillwell, a defenseless old man, is despicable. Few would commit such an act. Pontos, however, is unexpectedly killed minutes after Stillwell's death. We then learn he was notorious for being "a very mean man with a knife." But any threat he poses is short-lived. Upon his exit from the picture, a greater danger becomes apparent to the audience. Yet, the shootout at Pontos's home remains noteworthy.

As Gale escapes from the house, Taggart and Burns pursue what they believe to be a mysterious intruder. In his desperation to break free from the premises, Gale is easily perceived as a criminal on the run. He collides with a row of garbage cans and loses a shoe in the process. He is then discovered by an elderly couple. The wife declares, "There's one of 'em!" Her husband proceeds to fire a couple of rounds at Gale, clearly missing the detective. But the elderly lady's choice of words is noteworthy. She speaks as if Gale is a criminal. He is a prowler, but his morality is more humanist than that of the recently deceased Pontos. Nevertheless, to the elderly lady, Gale is a mysterious intruder. As he makes his way to the street, Taggart takes notice and yells, "There he goes! Stop!" Again, shots are fired at Gale, but to no avail. Taggart and Burns, like the elderly couple, are on their guard, fully prepared to expose the intruder's identity. And it is not long before the missing shoe is reunited with its owner, thus solving the case of the mysterious intruder at Pontos's house. In regard to Castle's direction of the scene, the cinematography is significant. As Gale initially lurks outside of the home, he poises himself to enter. His shadow is thrown by the light. And like most detectives, he wears a fedora, thus producing an eerily familiar silhouette.

The Whistler is only visible when audiences are afforded a glimpse of his shadow, and of all the film's characters, he is the true mysterious intruder of the film because he travels beyond his realm of mystery into the foreboding atmosphere of Castle's narrative.

Mysterious Intruder is different from the saga's previous films in regard to its inclusion of the virtually unknown protagonist. Naturally, within the medium of radio, the Whistler can only be heard. On film, he has the potential to be seen, albeit partially. Every *Whistler* picture begins and concludes with a brief spectacle of his dark shadow. In addition to *Mysterious Intruder*, Castle directed the first, second, and fourth installments of the series, and for each of these films, he does not limit the Whistler's appearances to the narrative's introduction and conclusion. The Whistler's shadow, in essence, becomes visible to the audience at random, yet crucial, points of the story. Landers, director of *The Power of the Whistler*, chose to reveal the title character only upon his film's beginning and end. Castle's direction is different.

In addition to the introduction and conclusion of *Mysterious Intruder*, the Whistler's silhouette can be seen on three separate occasions, reminding an audience that a supreme being, visible only in shadow, is always present. Sherman followed suit with his direction of *The Secret of the Whistler*, the next installment of the series. It is best for an audience to be reminded of the Whistler's existence as frequently as possible. He is our guide. Although he is not always present, we experience the narrative with him. The Whistler is the most important of all characters, insomuch that a majority of the films in the *Whistler* series contain his moniker. Such is not the case with the title of *Mysterious Intruder*, but chances are it pertains to our indistinguishable hero.

Mysterious Intruder was released on April 11, 1946. Paul E. Burns's portrayal of the doomed Stillwell is noteworthy. Years later, when the opportunity arose for Castle to direct and produce his first feature, *It's a Small World*, he contacted Burns. The veteran character actor was ultimately cast as an Italian truck farmer. Mike Mazurki, the other male performer of the Stillwell murder scene, appeared in two of Castle's later films: *New Orleans Uncensored* and *Zotz!*

In regard to *Mysterious Intruder*, it served as the final *Whistler* picture to be directed by Castle and is considered by many to be the best of the series. The saga formally came to an end in 1948, when its final installment, *The Return of the Whistler*, premiered in theaters across the country. In 1954, a television series, appropriately titled *The Whistler*, aired in the living rooms of many Americans. Although the program was short-lived, J. Donald Wilson's creation continued to flourish over the course of many years.

CHAPTER ELEVEN
THE RETURN OF RUSTY (1946)

In 1945, Columbia Pictures produced *The Adventures of Rusty*, the first in what would later become a series of eight motion pictures. The films were geared towards younger audiences, as each narrative evolved around a lovable German Shepherd with an abiding affection for children. During the 1940s, national pop culture trends favored the likes of Lassie and Rin Tin Tin. Columbia countered with the character of Rusty. *The Adventures of Rusty*, despite its status as a B film, was favorably received by the American public. Harry Cohn gave the green light for a sequel, appropriately titled *The Return of Rusty*.

William Castle, tapped to direct the picture, was making a transition of sorts. The film was unlike any he had directed. *The Return of Rusty* lacked the noir ambiance of which Castle had become acclimated. Furthermore, in addition to working with younger children, he faced the obstacle of collaborating with a tireless canine for the mere benefit of his film. Yet, on March 15, 1946, Castle duly accepted the challenge as the first day of production transpired.

Loddy Bicek (Mark Dennis), a Czechoslovakian boy instantly orphaned when his parents are killed during a German air raid, is befriended by an American serviceman. Sergeant Jack Beals (Robert Stevens) smuggles the orphan across the Atlantic to the United States. But Loddy is discovered by the authorities upon his arrival in New York. He flees, but becomes separated from Beals. Loddy hitches a ride to the sergeant's hometown. He meets Danny Mitchell (Ted Donaldson), a boy whose best friend is a dog named Rusty. Beals remains absent, giving the boys ample time to become acquainted. Among Danny's circle of friends is Marty Connors (Mickey Kuhn), a taller boy whose father was killed during the war. Consequently, Marty dislikes "foreigners." Loddy soon learns that Beals is being held under military arrest pending an investigation. An inquisitive detective (Fred F. Sears) comes to town. Marty abruptly informs him of Loddy's whereabouts. But the orphan evades capture. Shortly thereafter, Loddy catches

Marty in the act of offering Rusty to a father and son passing through town. He attempts to prevent the transaction, but is too late. Marty then falsely informs Danny that Loddy skipped town with Rusty in tow. Meanwhile, Loddy rescues the canine and promptly returns him to Danny. But the boys argue over the truth behind Rusty's disappearance. Loddy confronts Marty, and a chase ensues. The latter falls into a deep ravine and injures his leg. Loddy also becomes trapped. The boys send a message to Danny, with Rusty serving as the courier. The note is successfully delivered. Danny and the gang come to the rescue, thereby extracting Loddy and Marty from the ravine. Beals is eventually exonerated. He files an application to adopt Loddy, and it is subsequently approved.

In 1938, Ace the Wonder Dog, a German Shepherd with a penchant for adventure, made his big screen debut in RKO's *Blind Alibi* as a trusty guide dog. Years later, he appeared as the title character in *The Adventures of Rusty*. However, by early-1946, Ace was nearing the end of his film career. And for reasons unknown, he was unable to reprise the role of Rusty as Castle became involved with the series. Nevertheless, a replacement was summoned. And on Castle's set, the newcomer was ultimately addressed as Rusty both during and in between takes. Mickey Kuhn later referred to the replacement as "one of the greatest dogs." Under the guidance of a devoted animal trainer, the faithful canine was "absolutely magnificent" for the story.

Early in the film, as Loddy dines with the Mitchell family, Castle places the camera just below the dinner table. The audience, like Rusty, finds itself looking up at the table's occupants. Castle offers his viewers a different perspective of the action, never for a moment underestimating the importance of his title character. But he also gave earnest heed to the well-being of the film's child actors. And because of his noteworthy selection of the film's cast, infinite compassion for kids, and implementation of a fun work environment, Castle's direction of *The Return of Rusty* served as a memorable experience for those involved in the film's production.

As casting for Castle's picture transpired, Kuhn was deliberately handpicked from a group of interviewees due to his stature. One method of establishing conflict within the medium of film is to ensure that the heavy, the primary source of such conflict, can assume the role of antagonist based on physical appearance. Kuhn recalled going to Castle's office for the interview. He looked around and discovered that he was, by far, the largest kid of the group. Kuhn questioned the invitation to audition considering his appearance in comparison to that of the other children. His stature became apparent as Castle asked everybody in the room to stand. The decision was quickly made to cast Kuhn in the role of Marty. He ultimately had a great time portraying the heavy, as the experience of performing in *The Return of Rusty* led to lasting friendships with fellow castmates.

But aside from the likes of Ted Donaldson, Dwayne Hickman, and several other child actors of the picture, another individual also had a positive impact on Kuhn's participation in the film.

Castle was always known to be compassionate with the children who worked for him. The key to his success was that he patiently welcomed their feedback and was never condescending. "Working with kids is difficult because attention spans sometimes aren't the greatest and you get restless if you work too long," Kuhn said. "But Castle was very patient. He was not the type of person to say, 'This is what I want you to do.' Instead, Castle would suggest, 'Why don't you try this?'" Kuhn recalled that the strategy worked quite well with the cast. Child actors were treated with respect. Naturally, they were significant to the narrative, more so than the adult talent. And Castle's underlying philosophy ultimately led to Kuhn's favorite memory of performing in the film.

Castle wanted his actors to have fun while they were working, and when it came time for Kuhn and Mark Dennis to execute the scene during which their respective characters fight one another, they were allowed to do it their way. Ample time for rehearsals was made, and filming was not rushed. Of the memorable experience, Kuhn said, "We did the scene ourselves and worked on it for a couple of days. We were taught how to throw punches among other things. Neither one of us got hurt."

Following the memorable fight scene, the narrative's conclusion reveals Rusty and company to be visiting Marty in the hospital as he recovers from his injuries. Loddy is present, and Marty eagerly inquires about the orphan's initiation into the club. It is clear the two have reconciled as they shake hands.

The film's final scene is noteworthy because fiction, in essence, reflected reality. As the production of *The Return of Rusty* concluded, the formation of a special bond became imminent. "Afterwards, Mark and I became fast friends," Kuhn reflected. "It was a lot of fun, and I will always remember the experience."

The Return of Rusty was released on June 27, 1946. Despite Castle's solid rapport with the young cast, it was his first and only involvement with the series. Consequently, six more films were produced. The saga concluded in 1949 with *Rusty's Birthday*.

In addition to Castle, *The Return of Rusty* also marked Kuhn's lone involvement with the series. Nevertheless, it was an unforgettable time in the young actor's life. In regard to working in the entertainment industry during the mid-1940s, Kuhn remarked, "It contributed very nicely to the family income. My father was a meat cutter. My mother took care of me. Whatever I made went towards our lifestyle. I was in awe of working with great people such as John Wayne, Jimmy Stewart, and Bette Davis. I learned a lot from them. However, because of great directors like Howard Hawks, Elia Kazan, and William Castle, I ultimately became empowered to hone my craft."

CHAPTER TWELVE
CRIME DOCTOR'S MAN HUNT (1946)

In May of 1946, William Castle began production on *Crime Doctor's Man Hunt*, the seventh installment of the series. It was also the third *Crime Doctor* film to be directed by Castle, and with this motion picture, he would supersede Eugene Forde as the primary director of the saga. *Crime Doctor's Man Hunt* is similar to *The Crime Doctor's Warning*, the film that began Castle's involvement with the series. In both pictures, the story begins at a populated carnival, and the opening scene evolves around a man troubled by lapses of memory. But as the narrative of *Crime Doctor's Man Hunt* progresses, it becomes evident that Dr. Robert Ordway is up against the ultimate adversary.

Philip Armstrong (Myron Healey), a war veteran suffering from shell shock, absent-mindedly wanders to the same carnival night after night. He consults Ordway (Warner Baxter), but does so discreetly for fear of discovery by his fiancée. One evening, the crime doctor encounters a pair of goons carrying Armstrong's corpse near a boarding house. Ruby Farrell (Claire Carleton), an occupant of the house, runs a shooting gallery at the carnival. Ordway questions Farrell about the gallery's air pistols, as Armstrong was killed by a gunshot wound to the head. Further investigation uncovers an old, boarded-up house within close proximity to the boarding house. Ordway is knocked unconscious during a brief search of the former. Gerald Cotter (Francis Pierlot), owner of the old house, maintains it has been vacant for years. Cotter's daughter, Irene (Ellen Drew), was Armstrong's fiancée. Aside from mourning the death of her lover, Irene constantly yearns for the day when she will reunite with Natalie, a long-lost sister who has been away for three years. Later, a mysterious blonde, in cahoots with the two men who disposed of Armstrong's body, murders her accomplices. Ordway believes the woman to be Natalie, but matters become complicated when Natalie's husband comes forward, claiming she has been dead for months. Hoping for a break, the crime doctor asks Irene to help him conduct a final search of the old house. But Irene, suffering from a personality disorder, exposes herself as

Natalie. She attempts to kill Ordway, but is quickly apprehended. She confesses to killing Armstrong, claiming he had discovered her disorder and was planning to inform her father.

To Castle, *Crime Doctor's Man Hunt* was just another B picture destined for the archives of Columbia Pictures. Nevertheless, he put forth a modest effort, keeping his film suspenseful from beginning to end. Midway through the narrative, the element of fire is used for a key transition. The audience watches as Natalie (Irene) lights a gas heater, preparing a slow death for her accomplices. The picture fades to black and slowly unveils a restaurant waiter to be igniting a different kind of heater (used as a means to keep food warm). Ordway's world, in essence, is constantly in motion. Furthermore, his situation is grim. But Castle, benefiting from the witty dialogue of Leigh Brackett's script, made *Crime Doctor's Man Hunt* more entertaining for its comic relief than its suspense. Instances of dark, dry, and zany humor provide a break in the tension at all the right moments.

Dark humor, a concept that evolves primarily around death, makes light of a tense moment early in the film. Ordway unexpectedly stumbles upon Armstrong's lifeless body, thus setting the stage for what is to follow. In an attempt to placate Natalie's goons, the crime doctor feigns inebriation. Instead of distancing himself from the situation, he puts his life at greater risk by striking up a conversation with both men. They are under orders to dispose of the corpse, as it is their top priority. Nevertheless, despite their malicious agenda, the goons put their plans on hold to graciously see Ordway, whom they believe to be severely intoxicated, safely home. But the humor does not stop there.

Dry humor, traditionally presented with little body language and emotion, is prevalent a short time later when police are summoned to the neighborhood where Armstrong was killed. Police Inspector Harry B. Manning (William Frawley), upon entering the boarding house, conducts a sometimes-comical interrogation of its occupants. The boarders are cooperative for the most part, but Marcus Le Blaine (Olin Howland), a conspicuous phrenologist with wavy hair, attempts to be droll. Just as Manning is about to knock on Le Blaine's door, it suddenly opens. Ordway, also present, is somewhat surprised by the method of which Le Blaine presents himself:

ORDWAY: Well, you must have been expecting us.

LE BLAINE: Your presence has been fairly well-advertised.

MANNING: Are you, uh, Marcus Le Blaine?

LE BLAINE: Yes. Have you an appointment?

MANNING: We're from Homicide.

LE BLAINE: Oh, I have a license to practice phrenology. Have you a search warrant?

MANNING: Do you want to be technical?

LE BLAINE: Oh, no. No, it's only I dream of someday finding a policeman that has one.

Ordway and Manning enter Le Blaine's quarters and ask him some procedural questions. The ensuing interaction between inspector and phrenologist quickly becomes a barrage of subtle insults and witty retorts. Furthermore, very little body language and emotion is apparent during the exchange. Later, as Le Blaine heads back to bed, he turns to Manning for a final, parting shot:

LE BLAINE: Well, goodbye. You know where to find me, if you want me.

MANNING: Good night, Curly.

William Frawley's portrayal of the hard-nosed inspector is memorable, and his deadpan deliveries are concrete examples of dry humor. By 1946, Frawley had been a comedian for over thirty years, and his talent is not only apparent at the boarding house, but during other scenes as well.

On the verge of catching a killer, Ordway and Manning find themselves in a bind, thus creating a tense situation that is eventually disrupted by an unexpected display of zany humor. Mr. Harrera (Leonardo Scavino), claiming to be the husband of the late Natalie Cotter, arrives at the police station to confront Manning. The hostilities lead to an amusingly heated discussion between the two. A belligerent Harrera becomes more aggressive as he threatens to sue for slander:

HARRERA: Is my poor wife to be accused of murder...

Harrera's maniacal expression oddly transforms into one of bliss as he pauses to look up at the ceiling.

HARRERA: ... while she's up there among the angels?

He assumes his original demeanor and approaches Manning, getting in the inspector's face.

HARRERA: Am I to receive this insult?

MANNING (perturbed): Listen! From what we know, Natalie Cotter isn't sitting around with any angels! And she'd just love to have us think she's dead...because then we'd stop looking for her!

HARRERA: Are you calling me a liar?

ORDWAY (intervening): No, wait a minute...wait a minute. The inspector may seem a little blunt, but he has to make sure you're telling the truth.

HARRERA (to Manning): I will make you pay for this! I will make you pay and pay....

MANNING: Bradley!

HARRERA: ...and pay!

MANNING (shouting): Bradley!

Castle's camera quickly pans to the right. Police Sergeant Bradley (Jack Lee) enters to take Harrera away. The argument, culminating with the rapid camera motion, is eccentric and goofy to the point that one cannot help but relish the amusement.

In the history of comedy, many films and sitcoms have thrived on these types of arguments. Ironically, in 1951, Frawley would go on to star alongside Lucille Ball and Desi Arnaz in *I Love Lucy*, a sitcom that is not only considered by many to be the best of all time, but one that features its share of humorous arguments.

Crime Doctor's Man Hunt was released in October of 1946. Audiences basked in its surprise ending and enjoyed a few laughs along the way. But Castle's twelfth film also introduces a major motif, old dark houses, often seen in his later films. The climax takes place within the dark, "boarded-up" house, conveniently located next to a "boarding" house filled with suspicious, yet interesting, characters.

Coincidentally, Castle's life outside of Hollywood would soon intertwine with characters of the outlandish sort. It would be well over a year before he would direct another picture. Instead, he would serve as the associate producer on *The Lady from Shanghai*, spending countless days aboard Errol Flynn's yacht, where a significant portion of the shooting transpired. Castle's autobiography provides a detailed, day-by-day account of the experience. Needless to say, it was unforgettable.

CHAPTER THIRTEEN
THE CRIME DOCTOR'S GAMBLE (1947)

After recovering from a near-fatal bout of amebic dysentery, William Castle returned to Columbia Pictures and was eventually handed the script for *The Crime Doctor's Gamble*. He was at a point in his career where he sought more of a challenge, and believed Columbia was assigning him films he could direct with his eyes shut. Nevertheless, an adamant Harry Cohn demanded Castle do the picture. Although Castle would ultimately concede to Cohn, it was evident that the tension between the two was coming to a head. Castle had become one with the *Crime Doctor* saga, having directed its fifth, sixth, and seventh installments. But in his absence, the eighth film, *The Millerson Case*, had been assigned to veteran director George Archainbaud. Some questioned whether Castle could effectively resume control of the series considering his waning interest in the studio.

Dr. Robert Ordway (Warner Baxter) is in Paris to give a series of lectures on criminal psychosis. While there, an old friend, Inspector Jacques Morrell (Marcel Journet) of the Prefecture of Police, asks him to investigate a homicide. Henri Jardin (Roger Dann), an acquaintance of Morrell's, is accused of killing his father during a fit of rage. He claims to have blacked out around the time of the murder and is unsure of his innocence. Mignon (Micheline Cheirel), Jardin's wife, believes her husband is above suspicion. Anton Geroux (Maurice Marsac), an artist who specializes in the replication of oil paintings, is not only a good friend to Jardin, but is also Mignon's former beau. He tries to convince Ordway that Jardin is insane, but also coaxes the crime doctor into the purchase of some paintings. The two agree to meet later in the day at Chabonet's art gallery, where Geroux is employed. But when Ordway arrives, he discovers the artist to be dead from several blows to the head. Later, the will of Jardin's father goes to probate, and Jardin inherits everything. At Ordway's request, all items are put up for auction. One item, an extremely valuable painting that once adorned the living room of the Jardin residence, is rendered to be a fake upon closer inspection. But

Jules Daudet (Steven Geray), Jardin's attorney, purchases it for sentimental reasons. Ordway later deduces that Daudet killed Jardin's father while in the process of robbing the original, and then purchased the fake in order to wipe out any possible trail that could lead to his incrimination. Daudet, who also murdered Geroux, originally planned for Jardin to plead guilty by reason of insanity, thereby eluding his own capture.

The *Crime Doctor* radio program came to an end in 1947, the same year *The Crime Doctor's Gamble* was released in theaters. A different format was presented on the radio. Traditionally, the events of the crime would transpire throughout the first half of the show. Dr. Ordway would then spend the remainder of time analyzing the evidence. But midway through the show, listeners were privy to the identity of the culprit as well as the method in which the crime was committed. Ordway essentially spent the second half of the show determining the mistakes that led to the criminal's capture. Castle's film takes a different approach, as Daudet is not unmasked until the end of the story. Sometimes, when an original work of art is redone in another form, the result can be just as enticing. Frequent references to "originals" and "copies" appear in *The Crime Doctor's Gamble*. At one point, Geroux lectures Ordway on "the art of making a good duplicate." In Castle's film, a copy tends to be more significant than its original source, as is the case with Geroux's philosophy, a key selection of French text (evident through the method of translation), and the debacle at the auction.

Geroux maintains ethical standards in regard to his profession as he diligently paints duplicates in order to make ends meet. The artist confesses a somewhat harsh truth to Ordway during the crime doctor's visit to the studio. Geroux speaks of selling his duplicates as originals, but concludes that to do so would be unethical. Ordway proceeds to question the artist's reasoning:

> ORDWAY: Well, if you're that honest, you mind telling me why you spend your time making copies when you could paint originals?
>
> GEROUX: You are an American…are you not?
>
> ORDWAY: That's right.

GEROUX: Then you will understand. For many years, I paint originals and I starve. Now, I paint copies and I eat.

During the conversation, copies of select paintings dominate the scene, as they are clearly visible throughout the studio. A duplicate of Mignon's portrait catches Ordway's attention, prompting the crime doctor to ascertain the extent of Geroux's feelings for his best friend's wife. Mignon, translated into English, means darling. Castle does not make his audience aware of the translation simply because it is already implied. A majority of the dialogue in *The Crime Doctor's Gamble* is spoken in English, and translations are only made when absolutely necessary.

Warner Baxter as Dr. Robert Ordway.

The film takes place in Paris, and naturally, many of the signs that adorn particular landmarks are printed in the French language, but Castle translates (or copies) only the most crucial of signs into English. Shortly after arriving at the front entrance of Chabonet's art gallery, Ordway finds himself in a peculiar situation. The door is locked. As the crime doctor peers through the showroom window, he sees nothing but darkness. Then, a sign near the window catches his eye. Printed in capital letters are the words "LES LIVRAISONS SE FONT PAR LA PORTE DE DERRIERE." Atop the text is a long, slender arrow pointing to the left. Seconds later, the picture fades to the same sign providing instructions in English. Castle's translation reveals the words "DELIVER ALL GOODS IN REAR." French text is frequently seen throughout the duration of *The Crime Doctor's Gamble*, and Castle rarely does anything to alter it. Theatergoers, particularly those who do not understand a word of French, are expected to use their imaginations. Translations, for the most part, are unnecessary. The scene at Chabonet's, however, is the only time Castle provides an English translation for his predominantly-American audience. It is crucial, but not just because the sign is wordy. The stage is being set for Ordway's clash with Daudet. And due to the latter's obsession with fine paintings, our hero is afforded an opportunity to set the perfect trap.

A painting's timely exposure, rendering it to be a copy instead of an original, creates a stir amongst the patrons of the Jardin auction. Brown (Wheaton Chambers) and O'Reilly (Emory Parnell), the so-called connoisseurs of fine art, interject a note of caution as curiosity begins to wane. Initially, as the item is presented for bidding, nobody seems to take notice, despite it being introduced as a "beautiful piece of art." Brown places a staged bid in an attempt to garner additional bids, but to no avail. The auction patrons are simply not interested in "la pièce de résistance." Ironically, it is not until O'Reilly's revelation of the fake that people begin to take notice. Again, in what appears to be an ongoing trend throughout *The Crime Doctor's Gamble*, more attention is paid to a copy than its original. Fortunately for Ordway, the copy was the perfect bait in order to lure Daudet out of hiding.

Principal photography for *The Crime Doctor's Gamble* wrapped on July 26, 1947. Before the film was released in theaters, Cohn made arrangements for Castle to direct *The Crime Doctor's Secret*, which was to be the next installment of the series. Castle refused.

Time passed, and on November 27, 1947, Ordway's "spree in GAY PAREE" had its theatrical release. But three days later, Castle was suspended from Columbia for refusing *The Crime Doctor's Secret* (a project that was eventually canceled altogether). His relationship with Cohn had finally reached a boiling point. For the first time in his career, Castle was without a studio he could call home. In short, he was on his own.

CHAPTER FOURTEEN
TEXAS, BROOKLYN, AND HEAVEN (1948)

All things considered, 1947 marked a dismal time in the life of William Castle. He began the year as a patient at Cedars-Sinai Medical Center (formerly Cedars of Lebanon Hospital) in Los Angeles. A severe infection threatened his life. Earlier, Castle had contracted amebic dysentery in Mexico while serving as the associate producer of *The Lady from Shanghai*.

Following his release from the hospital, it took longer than expected for him to get back into the swing of things. Castle did not return to the director's chair until July of that year. And by late November, he found himself suspended indefinitely from Columbia Pictures.

Yet, with the arrival of 1948, exciting prospects began to appear on the horizon. Because just a few days into the New Year, Castle was hired by United Artists to direct the first comedy of his career: *Texas, Brooklyn, and Heaven*.

Eddie Tayloe (Guy Madison), a reporter for the Fort Worth section of the Dallas News, inherits $6 thousand from a recently deceased grandfather. With aspirations of becoming a playwright, he quits his job and departs for New York, intending to complete an unfinished play. But Tayloe's car stalls just outside of Dallas. He encounters Perry Dunklin (Diana Lynn), a runaway. Based on her experiences of operating a gas station, she is able to fix the car. Perry is headed for Birmingham. She hopes to get a job, make enough money, and return to Texas in order to buy a ranch. Tayloe persuades Perry to accompany him to New York. They arrive shortly thereafter, but she expresses a desire to live in Brooklyn. Perry gets a job performing as a water nymph in a Coney Island sideshow. During a performance, a spectator becomes unruly with her. Tayloe intervenes. However, it costs Perry her job. Tayloe eventually finishes his play, but it is rejected. Down on his luck, he meets Mike (James Dunn), a bartender who introduces him to a riding academy. Tayloe appeals to its proprietor, Mr. Gaboolian (Michael Chekhov), with the hopes that Perry might be hired to help run the establishment. He believes her to be the ideal manager considering her love of horses. Gaboolian initially refuses, but Tayloe offers to secretly pay Perry's salary. He agrees, thus setting the plan in motion. Perry meets Mandy (Florence Bates), an older woman who claims that a lady's purpose in life is "to make a man think he's successful." She eventually adheres to Mandy's beliefs. In time, Gaboolian sells the academy to a confident Tayloe. As the business begins to build clientele, a substantial increase in revenue follows. Tayloe and Perry make enough money to return to Texas. And together, they purchase a ranch.

During the film's opening minutes, the audience finds itself within the city room (or newsroom) of the Dallas News. A copy boy enters. He moves quickly, as many journalists depend on him to deliver their stories to the copy editors. His screen time, although brief, is significant. The copy boy is played by Audie Murphy, who, at only twenty-two years old, was making his big screen debut. As his character walks through the newsroom, a particular journalist, without looking up from his work, calls out, "Boy!" The copy boy stops in his tracks, collects the journalist's recently completed story, and continues his errands. But the journalist, too, is significant. He is not only the newspaper's drama editor (an appropriate role for the individual portraying him), he is also Castle in a cameo appearance.

With United Artists, Castle experienced a sense of freedom. The studio, it appeared, was willing to grant him creative control over his work. *Texas, Brooklyn, and Heaven* was adapted from Barry Benefield's novel, *Eddie and the Archangel Mike*. Yet, the circumstances of the film's characters (i.e., Perry, Mandy, and Tayloe) are eerily similar to some of the events of Castle's early life.

Following the deaths of his parents, Castle, like Perry, ran away from home. The living accommodations of both individuals were instrumental in their decisions to leave. When Castle was very young, his mother suddenly died of pneumonia. A year later, his father succumbed to a coronary. In the aftermath, Castle went to live with his sister, Mildred. She was eleven years his senior and had just become married. Castle, feeling alone and frustrated at such an early stage of his life, spent many lonely nights sleeping on Mildred's living room couch. He eventually ran away from home. Although the fate of Perry's parents is never fully explained, her situation is quite similar to that of Castle's. Living with her brother and his wife, she feels "sort of unnecessary." Instead of "crowding the place," Perry escapes from the confines of her brother's home, only to find her way into Tayloe's life. But the aspiring playwright is not the only one to have a significant impact on her life.

Mandy, presented to the audience as a devious pickpocket, adopts the mannerisms of a young Castle as she stealthily raids Perry's handbag for loot. Yet, in both situations, a mutual respect between culprit and victim was (is) evident. On more than one occasion, Castle targeted his sister's purse for cash. Immediately prior to his aforementioned escape, he stole $30. However, like Mandy, he was eventually discovered. Although Castle robbed Mildred of her money, he did not loathe her. She was, after all, his sister and closest living relative. Mandy harbors similar emotions. She attempts to steal from Perry, but is caught in the act. In time, Mandy comes to love Perry as if she were her own daughter. In Castle's case, he continued to take money from his sister's purse so that he could attend a stage production of *Dracula* (featuring Bela Lugosi in the title role). But it was all for the love of the performing arts.

Castle had two things in common with the fictional character of Tayloe: a generous inheritance and a passion for the theatre. Both men essentially took high risks with the money that was bequeathed to them. Like Castle, Tayloe used his inheritance to pursue a theatre career. But instead of Tayloe's $6,000, Castle received an astounding $30,000 from his father's estate. Some have argued that Castle was hopelessly idealistic when it came to the spending of his inheritance. The Stony Creek Theatre, in Connecticut, was owned by Orson Welles. He used the venue as a means to test his plays before sending them to Broadway. Castle learned that Welles was closing the theatre because of the latter's imminent departure for Hollywood. With the hopes of one day becoming a Broadway producer, Castle leased the theatre for $5,000. His autobiography goes into detail regarding the turmoil that ensued following the acquisition. It was a gamble, but Castle's love for the theatre never died. Years earlier, he was persuaded, albeit unsuccessfully, to abandon the performing arts and join his sister in, of all cities, Dallas. Mildred and Allan, Castle's brother-in-law, had recently left New York for a different lifestyle. Allan worked in the dress business and was willing to provide

Castle with a job. Yet, had the invitation been accepted, Castle's film career most likely would have been nonexistent.

Texas, Brooklyn, and Heaven was the only film Castle directed for United Artists. It was warmly received by audiences across the country. A majority of the film's characters compose the driving force behind the narrative's success. Margaret Hamilton, of *The Wizard of Oz* fame, turned out an excellent performance as one of the Cheever sisters (she would later appear as Elaine Zacharides in Castle's 13 *Ghosts*). Particular characters of *Texas, Brooklyn, and Heaven*, however, are underdeveloped. For example, although Mike is the teller of Tayloe's story, very little information pertaining to their relationship is disclosed. But the shortcomings of Castle's film were secondary to his personal life. Months before the nationwide release of *Texas, Brooklyn, and Heaven*, he was fixed up on a blind date with Ellen Falck, an attractive young lady. Upon meeting her, Castle instantly fell in love and the two were married on March 21, 1948. It was simply a joyous time for the young director, as he was having the best year of his life. But little did Castle know that a reunion of sorts would soon be in order, because Columbia, Warner Baxter, and Harry Cohn were about to reenter the picture.

CHAPTER FIFTEEN
THE GENTLEMAN FROM NOWHERE (1948)

As a wedding gift, Harry Cohn lifted William Castle's suspension from Columbia Pictures. Life was good, but considerable uncertainty in regard to the future remained. Castle was clearly ecstatic about being married to Ellen, the woman of his dreams. He was unsure, however, of Cohn's business agenda. Castle was continuously intent on directing films with A-list actors. But before long, the idea for another Warner Baxter B picture quickly became a reality, and *The Gentleman from Nowhere* began production on May 3, 1948. It was to be the thirteenth film Castle would direct for Columbia. The number thirteen, a motif first introduced in *The Whistler,* carries with it an aura of superstition. Castle questioned whether appeasing Cohn was a step in the right direction or not.

In New York, Earl Donovan (Baxter), the night watchman of a storage warehouse, is hospitalized after attempting to apprehend a group of thieves. Meanwhile, F.B. Barton (Luis Van Rooten), an insurance fraud investigator, has spent years trying to unravel the mystery behind the death of Robert Ashton, previously employed as a chemist for the Los Angeles-based Wilshire Chemical Corporation. Ashton was suspected to have embezzled a fortune from the company prior to his car accident. Barton believes an accomplice was involved in the heist. He soon discovers a striking resemblance between Donovan and the late Ashton, thus devising a plan to lure the accomplice out of hiding. Donovan undergoes a complete makeover in order to appear as Ashton. In character, he travels west and surrenders to authorities. Bail is raised. Catherine Ashton (Fay Baker), Ashton's widow, plays a part in Barton's scheme, albeit reluctantly. Meanwhile, she maintains her husband's innocence. Barton learns of a formula Ashton devised shortly before his death. It ensures the creation of a food substitute product. With hopes of newfound success, Wilshire's executives are desperate to obtain the formula. Vincent Sawyer (Noel Madison), a company employee, is killed while attempting to discover the truth behind Ashton's death. The suspicion falls on Larry Hendricks (Wilton Graff), head of the purchasing department. He is rumored to have been in love with Catherine. Later, Barton is murdered, but not before Donovan reveals himself as Ashton, having assumed the identity of a watchman through the years specifically to remain in hiding. Ashton, alive and well, seizes the opportunity to expose Edward Dixon (Grandon Rhodes), chairman of the board, as the true embezzler of the company.

In essence, the character of Donovan is truly a "gentleman from nowhere." The audience initially perceives him to be a humble watchman when, in fact, he is Ashton, an esteemed chemist who is thousands of miles from home. Barton, too, accepts the pseudonym as reality. But he and the audience eventually learn that Donovan never existed. Donovan is essentially the most fictitious of characters within Castle's film. Yet, we know more about him than others who are central to the plot. Wilshire's corporate counsel, presented only by his last name of Fenmore (Charles Lane), frequently exhibits the characteristics of an enigmatic personality. His job is to protect the company. But Fenmore's awkward association with Barton, dismissal of Ashton's formula, and deception of Dixon upon the film's conclusion paint the picture of a man with shadowy intentions.

Fenmore describes himself as "cryptic" when visiting Barton's hotel room, and his intentions are not entirely clear. He wants to preserve Wilshire's image as that of a stable corporation, but his discreet nature hints at the possibility of an ulterior motive. Fenmore comes to the point shortly after his arrival:

> FENMORE: Reviving the Ashton scandal is going to be very damaging. A good name means everything to an old, established firm like Wilshire.
>
> BARTON: Well, that can't be helped.
>
> FENMORE: You know, the company made a great deal of money during the war. We'd be happy to refund the money you paid us on the loss.
>
> BARTON: Why should you want to do that?
>
> FENMORE: You want it back, don't you? That's why you've been looking for Ashton all these years.
>
> BARTON: That's one of the reasons.

FENMORE: By doing it my way, you'd recover the full amount.

BARTON: But ... without Ashton.

FENMORE: Naturally, you'd have to forget about him.

Fenmore makes his way to a nearby chair and sits down.

BARTON (approaches Fenmore): You surprise me, Mr. Fenmore. As an attorney, you should know that any reputable insurance company would never consider such a deal.

FENMORE (pointing at Barton): I'm not talking to the company. I'm talking to you.

BARTON: Has Wilshire authorized you to do this?

FENMORE: Well, not exactly.

Fenmore gives the impression of a man who could be acting alone. He undoubtedly wants the Ashton scandal to disappear. To Barton, the truth is more valuable than any form of monetary compensation. Moments later, Fenmore becomes livid when presented with the theory that Ashton is Donovan. Like the audience, he does not yet realize the reality of the situation. Nevertheless, Fenmore wishes to avoid a trial. He claims to be acting in Wilshire's best interests. But his secrecy is baffling, especially when it is maintained within the confines of the company.

During a board meeting, Fenmore becomes mysteriously quiet when the topic of discussion shifts to Ashton's long lost formula. He does not want Wilshire's executives to detect and expose the so-called impostor of Donovan, but his anxiety is extraordinary because, as the company's attorney, he does not have much to lose should the "gentleman from nowhere" be discovered. On more than one occasion, Fenmore insists that Barton will be on his own if anything goes wrong. When asked by his colleagues for his opinion of the formula, Fenmore brashly advises them to "stay clear of it." During the following scene, he and Barton engage in their second private discussion of the film. Fenmore appears to be worried about the masquerade. He wants to preserve Wilshire's integrity. But the formula has the potential to revive the stockholders' interest in the company. Yet, Fenmore wishes for it to remain a secret. One can only question the reasons behind his decision, as it remains unclear if he truly has the best interests of the company at heart.

Upon the film's conclusion, Fenmore feigns ignorance when Dixon desperately seeks validation of Donovan's existence. His deliberate lie, claiming he "never heard of Donovan until this minute," leads to further ambiguity. Although the finale establishes that Dixon framed Ashton and murdered Sawyer, it does not provide any insight into Fenmore's motives. Perhaps, Fenmore's reason for lying was to ensure Dixon's incarceration. But his demeanor is cause for suspicion, especially due to the scene's preceding events. His third and final meeting with Barton, transpiring a short time before the film's conclusion, is different than the previous two. They meet at a public bus stop, and Fenmore is not his usual self. He is intent on sending Donovan back to New York, providing Barton with specific directions to the airport. It is a trap, but there is no indication that Fenmore is acting under orders. He is essentially guilty of orchestrating Barton's death. Yet, his crime goes unpunished. In short, the character of Fenmore is contradictory and ambiguous. And, perhaps, one could argue that the same is true for the film's script.

The Gentleman from Nowhere marked the fifth and final collaboration between Castle and Baxter, who died just three years after the film's release. Coincidentally, both men are interred at Forest Lawn Memorial Park in Glendale, California. Following the production of *The Gentleman from Nowhere*, Cohn announced that he was sending Castle and Ellen on an all-expense-paid vacation to Europe. It was to be a belated honeymoon for the newlywed couple. But the trip did not go as planned. Castle's autobiography goes into explicit detail about the entire ordeal. Upon his return to the states, Cohn sensed disappointment in his young protégé, and ultimately offered him the chance "to try another studio." For the second time in as many years, Castle, filled with emotions of overwhelming sorrow, departed Columbia.

CHAPTER SIXTEEN
JOHNNY STOOL PIGEON (1949)

Life is full of passages, and William Castle's second departure from Columbia Pictures was a passage of risk and ambivalence. Universal-International, his new employer, featured an environment of "peace and tranquility" with its "rows of bungalows surrounded by flowers and manicured lawns." William Goetz, head of the studio, was perceived as the antithesis of Harry Cohn with his "soft-spoken" and "gentle" demeanor. Universal was essentially a symbol of hope and resurgence.

Castle, however, was uneasy as he prepared for his first assignment, *Johnny Stool Pigeon*. Principal photography began on March 21, 1949. But despite Castle's anxiety, the day was to be a joyous one, as it marked the one-year anniversary of his marriage to Ellen.

George Morton (Howard Duff), a federal agent, intends to expose a major narcotics ring. But in order to begin the process, he must go undercover. Morton enlists the help of Johnny Evans (Dan Duryea), a prison inmate with ties to the mob. Both men travel to Vancouver in order to meet with William McCandles (Barry Kelley), a suspected dealer. Morton and Evans feign interest in making a sale. McCandles refers them to an associate in Tucson. Terry Stewart (Shelley Winters), McCandles's assistant, accompanies Morton and Evans to Arizona. Nick Avery (John McIntire), manager of a Tucson dude ranch, reveals himself to be the head of the syndicate. He speaks of an important shipment that is to be hauled across the Mexico-United States border. Morton confides in Terry, thus identifying himself as an agent. Prior to departing for Mexico, he pleads with her to contact the authorities in case something goes wrong with the transaction. At the border, Morton learns that Evans has betrayed him by exposing his true identity to Avery. Terry, under close surveillance, successfully completes her task. In Mexico, Evans disobeys Avery's orders, as he refuses to kill Morton. The shipment, concealed within a coffin, makes its way into the United States. Morton and his fellow agents descend on the ranch. Avery attempts to evade the authorities. With Terry in tow, he boards his private plane, intending to cross the border.

Morton drives towards the runway as Avery prepares for takeoff. The plane collides with the oncoming vehicle, but Morton is able to escape seconds before impact. Avery is apprehended, and simultaneous raids put an end to the narcotics ring. During the ensuing trials, Evans and Terry serve as star witnesses for the government.

The opening minutes of *Johnny Stool Pigeon* are set in San Francisco, a location where Evans, among other characters, is presented to the audience. Although the plot of Castle's film does not become engrossing until the action shifts to Vancouver, the terrible predicaments that transpire beforehand are somewhat noteworthy. Because in order for Evans to be introduced into the narrative, a series of events must occur. An innocent sailor is murdered, and his killer is subsequently eliminated. Morton begins to realize that the probability of illegal narcotics "floodin' in all over the country" is rather high. His only lead is the Arctic World Trading Company, an "outfit" in Vancouver. But before Morton can leave for Canada, he will need a traveling companion with enough mafia clout to ensure the success of his undercover operation. He heads to Alcatraz, the famous San Francisco landmark. Evans, upon reuniting with the man who sent him to prison, expresses nothing but contempt for Morton. An inherent uncertainty persists throughout the film, because it is unclear if Evans will purposely blow the operation in an act of revenge. But it is his weakness of the opposite sex that ultimately prevents him from doing so. Evans becomes emotionally distraught upon learning of his wife's death. In addition, his first encounter with Terry reveals a sympathetic side to his supposedly gruff personality. Yet, it is Evans's passion for his late wife, as well as the film's heroine, that instills in him the strength to see the operation through to its successful end.

Evans, upon seeing his wife's lifeless body in the morgue, appears to temporarily abandon his tough-guy demeanor, as he is clearly devastated beyond belief. He does not fully understand the evils of narcotics racketeering until Morton puts things in perspective:

> MORTON: They killed her for the few bucks they could squeeze out of her every week to get the stuff she needed.

The certificate lists "narcotics addiction" as the cause of death, but Morton believes she was murdered. Although Evans is a reputed mobster, he has not had any previous dealings with the infamous narcotics rings. He mourns for his late wife, and gradually motivates himself to aid Morton in tracking down the individuals responsible for her death. The two depart for Vancouver, and it is only a matter of time before Evans seeks to fill the void left behind by his deceased spouse.

At the Frontier Club, Evans exhibits a "gallant" demeanor during his first encounter with Terry. But she takes an immediate interest in Morton, and Castle's portrayal of the ensuing events reveals more than a petty jealousy radiating from the ex-con. After Morton rejects Terry's advances, Evans invites her to the dance floor, where they engage in casual conversation:

TERRY: Who's your friend?

EVANS: Just a business partner.

TERRY: He's nice. I mean...he seems kind of different than the usual bunch of crumbs that hang around an outfit like this...if you know what I mean.

EVANS: Yeah, I know what'cha mean.

TERRY: Not that there's anything wrong with you either. What's your name?

EVANS: Johnny Evans.

TERRY: Where ya from, Johnny?

EVANS: The states... California.

TERRY: Oh, California. You mean there's still a place where it's warm and they got palm trees... and you can lie out in that lovely hot sun all the year round?

EVANS: I guess so. You know California?

TERRY: Uh-uh. Ah, I was brought up in Tucson, Arizona. I wish I'd never left it. Been in this dump for two years. The only time I've ever been warm was once I went to sleep with a cigarette and I set the bed on fire. When you going back?

EVANS: Depends.

TERRY: Is, uh, your friend going with you?

EVANS: Listen, sister. If you're figurin' on makin' a fast switch, count him out. I'm tellin' ya for your own good.

Terry slaps Evans across the face. He grabs her arms.

TERRY: I'm sorry. I shouldn't have done that. Lately, I've been . . . I'm just nervous.

Their exchange is noteworthy. It is obvious that Terry is unhappy living in Vancouver. But Evans does not want her to become involved with Morton for several reasons, primarily because of the danger that lies ahead. He is essentially cautious of Terry's potential involvement in the operation. Shortly thereafter, as Morton prepares to leave the club, she halts his departure. Terry expresses a desire to accompany him "back to the states." During their conversation, Castle frequently transitions to Evans, who watches the two from atop the staircase. Evans is envious, as Terry appears to have more of an interest in Morton than him. But as the plot thickens, it becomes clear that his mild jealousy will not disrupt any attempts to destroy Avery's syndicate.

Evans's love for his deceased wife, in addition to his growing affections for Terry, ultimately empowers him with the determination to put an end to the villainous narcotics ring. But his only chance at success is to deceive Morton. Evans and Terry become friendlier during the rail trip to Tucson. Morton takes notice, and privately questions their loyalty to the operation. One evening at the ranch, Evans feigns jealousy:

EVANS: She wants you! Don't 'cha know that yet?

MORTON: Me?

EVANS: Yes, you! Ya think I brought her along for myself?

Unbeknownst to Morton, Evans is setting his plan in motion. He makes it clear that he cares for Terry, but he does not disclose that she is the motivating factor behind his decisions. The morning after the argument, Avery commends Evans on his "great idea." And the audience, like Morton, is unaware of the plan. Evans's supposed idea to smuggle the narcotics via funeral procession, and kill Morton in the process, is eventually exposed. But Avery becomes the victim of a sham. Morton eventually realizes that

Evans never intended to turn against him. He later remarks, "I can understand why he played it that way, but it sure looked bad at the time." As *Johnny Stool Pigeon* concludes, immediately following the last of many convictions, Evans and Terry lock hands as they depart the courtroom together. A so-called stool pigeon has avenged the death of his wife, and has also attained closure so that he might begin a new chapter in his life.

Many years after its release, Castle referred to *Johnny Stool Pigeon* as a "big disappointment." He did, however, acknowledge the casting of Tony Curtis as the film's "claim to fame." In one of his first ever screen roles, the young actor appeared as the mute Joey Hyatt (credited as Anthony Curtis), Avery's triggerman. The character of Hyatt is somewhat similar to Helga Swenson of *Homicidal*. He sees and knows much, but has a difficult time expressing his thoughts. Ironically, the next time Curtis collaborated with Castle, he made effective use of his voice, portraying the unseen Donald Baumgart of *Rosemary's Baby*.

In regard to *Johnny Stool Pigeon*, Castle had hoped for a better reception. His primary reason for transferring to Universal was because he wanted to be taken seriously. Yet, the title of his film alone was enough to draw laughter from the critics. But as far as Castle was concerned, his tenure with Universal had just begun, and he was determined to press forward with confidence.

CHAPTER SEVENTEEN
UNDERTOW (1949)

Once upon a time, a young woman by the name of Peggy Varnadow, barely twenty-one years of age, signed a contract with Universal-International after showcasing her talents on *Your Show Time*, a short-lived television program that featured dramatizations of popular stories. Like Varnadow, William Castle, too, was a newcomer to the studio. The two faced a particular degree of uncertainty in regard to the future, as it had yet to be determined if Universal could nurture their success. Castle had recently undertaken and completed the lukewarm *Johnny Stool Pigeon*. Varnadow (later to be billed as Peggy Dow) was making her big screen debut in Castle's next film, *The Big Frame*. The story centered on the all too familiar premise of a man who is wrongly accused of murder. Prior to its theatrical release, the film's title was changed to *Undertow*.

Tony Reagan (Scott Brady), recently discharged from the Army, invests in a mountain lodge along the Sierra Nevada. Before he settles into his new home, he flies to Chicago with the hopes of marrying Sally Lee (Dorothy Hart), his longtime girlfriend. But upon Reagan's arrival, he is apprehended by police due to an anonymous tip. Rumors abound that "Big" Jim Lee, a wealthy casino magnate who is also Sally's uncle, ran Reagan out of town years earlier. The tip warns that Reagan may attempt to kill Big Jim. However, due to insufficient evidence, Reagan is released from custody. He visits Big Jim in order to discuss the impending marriage proposal. But before Reagan can make it to the front door, he is knocked unconscious. Later, he awakens only to discover a recently fired pistol within his grasp. And it is not long before Reagan learns that he has been framed for Big Jim's murder. He attempts to seek refuge with former acquaintances, but they are subject to questioning by the police. Instead, Reagan contacts Ann McKnight (Dow), a schoolteacher whom he accompanied on the flight to Chicago. Ann allows Reagan to hide in her apartment. She also helps him get in touch with Sally. Reagan asks Sally if she can locate Danny Morgan (John Russell), an old friend who may be able to provide a lead to the real murderer. She does, but it is soon revealed that Morgan, in love with Sally, murdered Big Jim in order to frame Reagan, take over the dead man's casino empire, and accumulate a mass fortune. Morgan attempts to eliminate Reagan, but Gene (Daniel Ferniel), a devoted employee of Big Jim's, intervenes. Morgan is killed. Ann quits her job and departs Chicago with Reagan.

Every motion picture contains its share of story elements, ranging from the fundamentals of character development and dialogue to the essentials of conflict and resolution. In addition, a film's setting is just as important. For *Undertow*, Castle engaged in extensive location shooting as a means to liven the noir ambiance. Famous landmarks, such as the Reno Arch and Chicago's Buckingham Fountain, are featured throughout the film. Furthermore, The Palmer House serves as the starting point of a foot chase between Reagan and Detective Cooper (Charles Sherlock). From beginning to end, the scene is completely devoid of dialogue. The absence of a key element, like dialogue, is sometimes necessary in order for a film's narrative to flourish. On occasion, the most crucial of story elements are unseen, or unheard, by an audience, and these factors often have the power to guide, or direct, a character towards a particular goal. In the case of *Undertow*, we are not exposed to Reagan's past, Mile High Lodge, or Big Jim.

Despite having served in World War II as a soldier of the United States Army, Reagan is presented to the audience as a "smalltime businessman" instead of a decorated war veteran. It is his time overseas that strengthens his character. After helping Ann to win big at the craps table, Reagan is confronted by Morgan:

MORGAN: The old Reagan hunches, huh? (chuckles) What's the big idea?

REAGAN: Oh, just givin' the girl a thrill, Dan.

MORGAN: Uh-huh. Never figured you for the wrong side of the table. You have changed.

REAGAN: Yeah, I guess I have. You know, you gotta be away for a while to realize how little this all means.

Reagan has been away for seven years, having stayed in the army "for an extra hitch." His past experiences have enabled him to grasp the big picture of life. As the film's protagonist, Reagan is quite likeable. During the affair at the craps table, Ann becomes attracted to him. However, Reagan is slow to reciprocate because he initially desires Sally. But Chicago is no good for him. The events of Reagan's war-torn past ultimately lead him to abandon the city in search of an entirely different style of living.

Mile High Lodge, Reagan's "home from now on," is not seen in the film. Yet, it is significant for many reasons, specifically because it is symbolic of those who are close to him. Larry, an old friend who often spoke of the lodge, was killed in the South Pacific. Castle's film begins in Reno. And as the audience gets its first glimpse of Reagan, he leans against a vehicle that features a Mile High Lodge placard. A man and boy soon enter the picture, but their relation to the film's plot is unclear. Minutes later, we learn that they are Larry's father and kid brother. Although Reagan has lost a dear friend, the memories flourish not only within the deceased's next of kin, but within the lodge as well. Yet, Mile High Lodge is a memento of the past as much as it is a representation of the future, and Reagan is willing to invest seven years of army savings (in essence, everything he has) towards its completion. On the flight to Chicago, the lodge is the highlight of his conversation with Ann. Reagan produces some photographs, which contain people, trees, and mountains. The lodge, however, remains unseen. Nevertheless, it is significant. Reagan believes Mile High Lodge is a destination where he and Sally will spend the remainder of their lives. But a particular figure of the film serves as an obstacle to his agenda.

Big Jim, a character on which the plot depends, is a mystery to the audience simply because, dead or alive, he does not make a single appearance in the picture. He alone is the focus of Reagan's first meeting with Sally. There is talk of the wedding as well as the controversy it will cause:

SALLY: Tony, you might as well know this. Uncle Jim still doesn't like anything about us. I can't even mention your name to him.

REAGAN: I can understand that. You're like a daughter to him. Me, I'm just a kid from a river road gambling joint with wedding bells on my mind.

SALLY: A kid from one of his places, starting the way he started, doing exactly what he'd done.

REAGAN: And I'm starting clean. Now, I'll talk to him.

It has been "seven long years" since Reagan and Sally have seen each other. The two have much to discuss. Yet, the subject of Big Jim dominates their conversation. It is clear to the audience that Sally's uncle is important. And we anticipate our first glimpse of Big Jim as Reagan arrives at the former's home. But things do not go as planned. The murder is committed, and thus, the character of Big Jim remains a mystery. Nevertheless, his mere existence, although a puzzlement to the audience, is crucial. Because without Big Jim, there is no conflict. And naturally, without conflict, there is no story.

Undertow was released in December of 1949. The film is noteworthy for a brief scene that is not particularly central to the plot. Almost an hour into the narrative, Detective Reckling (Bruce Bennett), the boyhood friend of Reagan, is seen leaning over a desk in his office. He is flustered because he does not have any leads in the case. Just then, another detective enters the office. The character itself is relatively unimportant as far as the story is concerned, but the actor who portrays him, appearing in only his second film, would go on to have a storied career for the remainder of his life. The actor is Rock Hudson, and although his screen time in *Undertow* is severely limited, he was gradually beginning to make a name for himself. Fortunately for Castle, it would only be a matter of time before another opportunity to nurture Hudson's budding career would arise.

CHAPTER EIGHTEEN
IT'S A SMALL WORLD (1950)

William Castle departed Columbia Pictures with the hopes of attaining more control over his films. But following the release of *Undertow*, he was still at the mercy of studio executives. It did not matter that he was now under contract to Universal-International. His situation had not changed.

In an attempt to gain more autonomy, Castle formed a small production company by the name of Motion Pictures, Inc. He and a colleague, Otto Schreiber, penned *It's a Small World*, a screenplay centered on the trials and tribulations of a midget. The film's production came and went, leaving Castle in search of a distributor. His quest throughout Hollywood led him to Poverty Row, which did not refer to a specific location, but instead, to a collection of B picture studios. One such studio was Eagle-Lion Films, originally formed with the sole intention of releasing British productions in the United States. However, during the late 1940s and early 1950s, Eagle-Lion was responsible for the distribution of many American films, including *It's a Small World*.

Twelve-year-old Harry Musk (Paul Dale), frequently mistaken for a six-year-old, lives a life of constant harassment because he is a midget. He lives with his father (Will Geer) and younger sister, Susan (Jacqui Snyder). Sensing that he is reluctantly accepted at home, Musk finds friendship with Janie (Lora Lee Michel), a local girl four years his junior. They eventually become the best of friends, spending most of their adolescence together. But when Janie becomes an adult, she moves away to get married. Musk, now twenty-one, joins a traveling carnival. It is not long before he ditches Jackson (Thomas Browne Henry), the carnival's obnoxious owner, and finds a job shining shoes. Musk proves to be quite the attraction, causing business to prosper. He makes enough money to rent his own apartment, and inadvertently meets Buttons (Lorraine Miller), a woman across the hall. Later, she introduces Musk to Rose Ferris (Nina Koshetz), a stout lady who operates a pickpocket ring. Buttons wants Musk to join the syndicate, deducing that a midget would be stealthier than a person of average size. He agrees, primarily because he is attracted to her. But when Buttons later rejects Musk because he is a midget, he decides to inform the police of Rose's operation. After the arrests are made, Musk learns of an opportunity to join a circus in Florida. He eventually embarks on a nationwide trek to begin a new life. Shortly after his arrival, he meets Dolly Burke (Anne Sholter), a circus performer and fellow midget. In addition to physical appearance, the two share many commonalities. Musk finally achieves happiness when he and Dolly get married.

Castle draws a parallel between the narrative of his film and that of Jonathan Swift's Gulliver's Travels.

The opening seconds of the film reveal its title, *It's a Small World*, to be projected across the screen in big, bold letters. Just above the title are the words, "A William Castle Production." Castle was intent on proclaiming his independence. As a writer, director, and producer, he could express himself in ways that were not previously possible. Some might argue that, due to Castle's creative control over the production, the film is a reflection of his early life. Like Musk, Castle endured constant rejection by his peers. It was not until a nine-year-old Castle realized he could touch his feet behind his neck that people began to treat him with respect, as he could accomplish things they could not. Musk, too, relies on his physical appearance as a means to earn the approval of others, which becomes evident as people line up in order to have a midget shine their shoes.

Another commonality was the cross-country journey that both Castle (New York to Los Angeles) and Musk (Santa Paula to Florida) undertook in order to find success. But despite these similarities, a deeper meaning is embedded within the narrative of *It's a Small World*. Following the film's opening statement that calls for "a greater and deeper knowledge of all humanity," specific examples (i.e., a reference to *Gulliver's Travels*, Musk's short-lived stint with Jackson's Traveling Carnival, and his transition from a rural to urban setting) indicate that the production is essentially a satire on human nature.

Gulliver's Travels, the classic novel by Jonathan Swift, has been adapted many times since its publication in 1726, and Castle's brief reference to the story is logical considering the film's satirical plot. As Janie reads a passage from the novel to Musk, the latter eventually loses interest. There is mention of Gulliver's encounter with the six-inch-tall natives. The novel's protagonist quickly comes to the realization that there are no other people like him. Musk, clearly aware of the irony, becomes disengaged and falls asleep. Satires have been created to serve multiple purposes, namely to make people laugh. But satires also identify issues in regard to societal flaws. Although the setting of Gulliver's world is unrealistic, the setting of Musk's is not.

Midgets are often treated like outcasts due to their physical appearance. *It's a Small World* sought to raise awareness of the issue. *Gulliver's Travels*, originally written as a satire on society, has been adapted for different forms of media such as radio, television, and music. It has been presented within different genres, especially those of fantasy and science fiction. But Castle's reference to the age-old novel acknowledges the tale for what it really is. Aspirations for improvements in society are never-ending, especially since human nature frequently rears its ugly head.

Musk's brief experience as a member of Jackson's Traveling Carnival proves that people are not always who they seem to be. Jackson, initially praising his line of work as "a great life," reveals his true colors at a diner. He treats Musk like a sideshow freak, ordering him to puff on a cigar as a means of entertaining the

"Your boy will grow no bigger than he is right now."

restaurant patrons, who look on in disgust. Not wasting any time, Musk makes his escape via the restroom window. On the run and as lost as a ball in the high weeds, he continuously encounters oversized images of Jackson's laughing face. Musk immediately retreats from the images, which represent gateways to a darker future and will most likely lead directly back to Jackson. Musk will do what is necessary to seek out the good in humanity. His escape from the diner is a step in the right direction, but it leads him into a different kind of world.

Musk's transition from the rural setting of Santa Paula to the urban setting of Los Angeles reveals that, regardless of age, human nature has its flaws. The flaws are evident within the mannerisms of particular adults. At a dance hall, a loud, repugnant woman approaches Musk and pinches his cheek, proudly referring to him as "a cute little man." He reacts by throwing a beer in her face. A short time later, Musk meets Rose, whose criminal activities clearly do not help his situation. The tagline of *It's a Small World*, touting the film as "the amazing story of a man forced to live in a child's world," could not be more appropriate. One of the reasons Musk departs Santa Paula is to rid himself of the degradation and cruelty that is often encountered with the children and

Paul Dale and Todd Karns.

adolescents of his community. Yet, shortly after his arrival in Los Angeles, it becomes clear that some adults can be just as insensitive and obnoxious as the children he left behind.

It's a Small World, released in June of 1950, was one of the final films to be distributed by Eagle-Lion. Coincidentally, it was the only film to be produced by Motion Pictures, Inc. Castle's production company quietly folded a short time later, leaving him no choice but to return to Universal, where he was still under contract. Another seven years would pass before Castle would once again enjoy the power of independence over a film's production, which transpired with *Macabre*. Coincidentally, both films contain the Castle motif of buttons.

In regard to *It's a Small World*, the object of Musk's affections, Buttons, is so obsessed with the circular objects that they have become her nickname. A blind Nancy Wetherby of *Macabre*, dazed after her tryst with Jim Tyloe, grasps at the air within her world of darkness as she chants, "Who's got my buttons?"

Aside from motifs, *It's a Small World* explores the theme of exploitation. Musk is frequently taken advantage of because he is a midget. We, the audience, look on as he is forced to think, feel, and act through pressing situations. These are, in essence, the very actions that define human nature. Castle aimed to foster a greater knowledge of humanity, and although his film was not very popular during its theatrical run, it has not been forgotten by film enthusiasts of today.

"They call me Buttons!"

CHAPTER NINETEEN
THE FAT MAN (1951)

Following the release of *It's a Small World*, William Castle began making preparations for his next feature with Universal-International. The studio, in "trying to compete with the other majors," had recently withstood a succession of failures. Castle, like Universal, was vying for recognition in the industry. He was eventually given the script for *The Fat Man*, a film noir based on the popular radio drama of the same name. J. Scott Smart, known by many as the "Lon Chaney of Radio," had starred as the program's title character since the show's inception in 1946. Much to the delight of his fans, Smart agreed to play the lead in Castle's film. Hence, *The Fat Man* was given a tagline of "Radio's Great Detective... NOW the Screen's Super Sleuth!"

Dr. Henry Bromley (Ken Niles), a prominent dentist, is murdered by an unknown assailant. His death is made to look like suicide. Jane Adams (Jayne Meadows), Bromley's nurse, suspects foul play. She contacts Brad Runyan (Smart), an elite detective affectionately referred to as The Fat Man. It is soon determined that an x-ray was stolen from Bromley at the time of the murder. It contained the dental records of Roy Clark (Rock Hudson), a new patient. Jane speaks of a duplicate image, but it, too, is missing. Runyan's only lead, Clark's supposed phone number, brings him to the posh estate of Gene Gordon (John Russell), a suspected racketeer. But Clark is said to have vacated the premises awhile back, having pursued an out-of-state job offer. Runyan seeks out Pat Boyd (Julie London), Clark's ex-flame. She and Clark were married, but he vanished a few days after the ceremony. Pat provides Runyan with a photograph of Clark. It is eventually determined that Clark also went by the name of Ray Chevlin and is discovered to have been incarcerated for robbing a race track. Ed Deets (Emmett Kelly), a former cellmate of Clark's who was imprisoned for a separate offense, spends his post-prison days performing as a circus clown. He meets with Runyan, disclosing every detail he can remember in regard to Clark's supposed version of the heist's events. Runyan begins to suspect that Clark was eliminated by his fellow accomplices. Following Jane's untimely murder, Runyan reflects back on the significance of the x-ray. He becomes suspicious of a recent truck accident, which transpired around the time of Clark's disappearance. The vehicle contained items belonging to Deets, as well as a corpse burned beyond recognition. Furthermore, Deets cannot be found. Runyan follows a hunch and confronts Gordon, who claims he did not kill Clark. He then encounters Deets, who has launched his own circus. It is determined that Deets, released from prison before Clark, decided to obtain his ex-cellmate's share of the stolen loot. He visited Gordon, the mastermind behind the caper, and made a deal to collect the fortune on the condition that he eliminated Clark following the latter's release. Deets, Runyan learns, then used the money to fund his circus. He staged the truck accident so that Clark could not be identified. But the existence of the x-rays complicated matters. Hence, to avoid discovery, Deets murdered Bromley and Jane. Within an abandoned circus tent, Runyan attempts to refrain from a tragic altercation with Deets, but Gordon arrives on the scene and attempts to kill them both. A shootout ensues. Gordon is wounded, and Deets is shot dead by Runyan.

The character of The Fat Man was created by Dashiell Hammett, the celebrated author of many works, primarily detective fiction. And his contributions to the radio program helped propel it to great success. Castle, in bringing Hammett's creation to the silver screen, faced the challenge of presenting Runyan (spelled Runyon in the radio version) in a completely different setting. For years, the great detective had been heard, not seen. The medium of radio enables people to enjoy select works of fiction by means of using their imaginations. Motion pictures are fairly limited in scope, as spectators are presented with a setting modeled on the director's vision. But Castle understood that radio also had its drawbacks. Because of the limitation, in addition to the inclusion, of specific elements, his direction resulted in a noteworthy radio-to-film adaptation. Castle stayed true to the show's original concept, but also featured the best of both mediums. The face of Deets, in addition to Runyan's overall screen time, are somewhat restricted by Castle's camera. Yet, J. Scott Smart and his long-standing reputation as Runyan, the quintessential detective, worked wonders for the film itself.

The face of Deets, although somewhat visible to spectators, remains unfamiliar throughout most of the narrative. Yet, it is the removal of his clown makeup upon the film's conclusion that proves to be a grand revelation of sorts. Hypothetically, if a murder is committed by an unknown assailant (as is the case with Bromley and Jane's murders) during an episode of the radio version of *The Fat Man*, the killer will naturally be unseen by listeners. Although Castle was working with the medium of film, he treated his narrative similar to that of a typical radio episode by severely limiting the screen time of Deets's true face, thus concealing the killer's identity. Shortly before Deets strikes for the first time, we see his silhouette as he walks into New York's Westbrook Hotel.

Seconds later, when Deets eliminates Bromley, his face becomes visible. Yet, he remains mysterious. Just prior to Jane's murder, Castle photographs Deets's entrance into another hotel (this time in Los Angeles, but with the same background music) in a somewhat similar fashion. Initially, all that is visible is a pair of feet. But as Deets enters the lobby, his entire figure, including his face, can be seen. In essence, as the story progresses, Castle gradually unveils his villain to the audience. Yet, the killer's identity remains a mystery. At the time of Jane's murder, we have been afforded one opportunity to see Deets in his circus attire, but it does not become evident that the mysterious hotel killer and overly-ambitious clown are one and the same until the film's climax.

Castle specifically cast Emmett Kelly, a veteran of the Ringling Brothers and Barnum & Bailey Circus, as the antagonist of his film. Although Kelly was well-known in America upon the release of *The Fat Man*, the general public was unable to recognize him when he was out of character. Hence, when he removes his makeup upon the film's conclusion, thus exposing himself as the ultimate villain, it is unpredictable and surprising. Castle knew the identity of his killer would be difficult for audiences to determine based on Kelly's specific notoriety. People were quite familiar with the "world famous clown," but they were unfamiliar with his true face. Similar circumstances could have applied to any radio episode of *The Fat Man*. For example, a famous individual with an easily recognizable face would most likely be successful in portraying a mysterious and unknown killer if listeners were unfamiliar with that person's voice. Hammett's creation was essentially meant for radio, and Castle took this into consideration as he progressed with the direction of his film.

Despite his status as the title character of *The Fat Man*, Runyan is afforded a limited amount of screen time. The film contains several flashbacks, none of which include him. Fans of the radio program were used to hearing Runyan instead of seeing him. And his continuous presence (which is nonexistent in the film) is unnecessary, because the narrative of Castle's picture pertains to Clark (a character seen only during flashbacks) and his mysterious disappearance.

To reiterate, within the medium of radio, one must rely on his or her imagination in order to enjoy a featured program. The most significant of flashbacks transpires when Deets goes into detail about the race track caper. It is, in essence, a flashback within the flashback (a rarity for motion pictures of the era). Deets, to a particular degree, must rely on his imagination because he was not present during the robbery. His method of accurately relaying the caper's events to Runyan is based on how well he understood Clark's account. The race track flashback is approximately five minutes long, and its details, in part, rely on Deets's ability to use his imagination and put himself in Clark's shoes. Upon the latter's demise, Castle shifts the focus of the film back to Runyan. And although The Fat Man is primarily considered to be a radio character, he is clearly worthy of motion picture fame.

As *The Fat Man* begins, the familiar notes of the radio program's theme music serve as a reminder of the character's inception, but it is J. Scott Smart's visible, albeit limited, presence and well-known voice that make Castle's film a successful adaptation. Runyan's initial appearance of the narrative gives meaning to the reason behind his nickname. He is first seen in "surgery," carefully carving poultry in the kitchen of a Washington Square restaurant. Moments later, as Runyan meets with Jane, he relishes a variety of food that is served to their table. She remarks, "I begin to see why they call you The Fat Man." A scene of this nature is clearly more entertaining when displayed on a screen as opposed to being heard on a radio. The luxuries of fine food and exquisite cooking frequently recur throughout the narrative.

Castle concludes *The Fat Man* with a line of dialogue that not only summarizes the nature of Runyan's character, but the scope of the film as well. Within the confines of their Los Angeles hotel, Bill Norton (Clinton Sundberg), The Fat Man's affable sidekick, asks his superior, "How's that hotel cooking, boss?" Without hesitation, Runyan replies, "It's murder...just murder!" He then chuckles as the picture fades to black.

A notable scene of Castle's film transpires when Runyan visits U.S. Trucking in order to inquire about the company's charred vehicle. He meets with Murray (Edwin Max), the manager. Runyan then asks to speak with the driver. Pinkie (Marvin Kaplan), Murray's brother-in-law, emerges from the back, thus beginning a comical exchange of sorts.

> "Eddie Max was such a good actor that I felt right at home playing the part of his brother-in-law," Marvin Kaplan told the author of this book. "He was very underrated. I had not met him prior to the production of *The Fat Man*. Eddie and I basically rehearsed the scene by ourselves. William Castle didn't come near us. In those days, directors trusted actors. Eddie and I were lucky because we were allowed to work by ourselves. We had established a relationship and it worked very well. Castle left us alone until he was ready to shoot. He had enough on his plate directing J. Scott Smart. Castle was a very nice man and I immediately took a liking to him. My role required only one day of work. If Castle didn't like what Eddie and I were doing, he would have told us. It was a great scene. The writing is important. Eddie and I had very good lines. Following the production, the two of us became great friends, and you usually don't get that with somebody you work with in one day. That's why Eddie Max was so terrific. Prior to filming, I didn't even read for the role of Pinkie. Castle must have seen me in some other production. I had done *Adam's Rib* with Spencer Tracy, Katharine Hepburn, and Judy Holliday. Working with those three was one of the greatest experiences of my career. The decision to cast me as Pinkie was most likely based on my appearances in previous films. The entire scene was filmed in about two takes. It was such a great comedic scene. I loved doing it. Comedy comes off stronger when

a dramatic story is being told. It's comic relief. We did it in 1950. I was twenty-three years old. I was as green as grass. I was a kid. Eddie and I were very minor characters in the film. But we were good characters, and funny characters, and it worked very well in a serious piece. Prior to being cast in *The Fat Man*, I had heard the radio show lots of times. On the set of Castle's picture, I didn't have much of a chance to interact with J. Scott Smart. Clinton Sundberg and Emmett Kelly were very nice people. Rock Hudson was a wonderful man. And William Castle was great. Years after *The Fat Man*, I had the opportunity to see some of his later films and considered him to be a very talented director."

Upon its theatrical release, *The Fat Man* was favorably received by fans of the radio program. Many had hoped for additional installments to follow, especially since the show itself was coming to a close. But Universal was not as optimistic. Castle later referred to *The Fat Man* as "a potboiler of little merit." He was, however, grateful that William Goetz allowed him to cast Emmett Kelly in the picture.

Although *The Fat Man* did not spawn any sequels, the title character's popularity caught on overseas. Because a few years after the release of Castle's film, an Australian version of the radio program took to the airwaves. It was not as superior as the original, but the new version kept the flame burning for a different, yet enthusiastic, culture of listeners.

CHAPTER TWENTY
HOLLYWOOD STORY (1951)

By 1950, William Castle was nearing the end of his first tenure with Universal-International. After directing a series of mediocre films for the studio, *Hollywood Story* was to be his next project. It was based on the real-life murder of William Desmond Taylor, a popular film director of the silent era whose killer was never found. Although Taylor's murder occurred in 1922, it was still fresh on the minds of many Hollywood figures in 1950.

Castle, striving for a nostalgic look to his picture, sought out the "stars of yesteryear" to comprise a portion of the cast. Francis X. Bushman, a well-known silent film actor once referred to as "King of the Movies," appeared as himself. Other notables of the era also made cameos, including Betty Blythe, William Farnum, and Helen Gibson. Furthermore, Joel McCrea, star of Alfred Hitchcock's *Foreign Correspondent*, briefly appeared in the film. In addition to the talent, Castle directed several of the film's scenes at the old Charlie Chaplin Studio in order to give *Hollywood Story* "a feeling of the past."

Franklin Ferrara, a respected director of silent pictures, is murdered in his bungalow. Twenty-one years later, Lawrence "Larry" O'Brien (Richard Conte), a New York producer, arrives in California at the request of his financier, Sam Collyer (Fred Clark). He investigates the Ferrara murder, intending to base his next picture on it. O'Brien seeks out Vincent St. Clair (Henry Hull), a former screenwriter of Ferrara's, and commissions him to pen the script of the proposed film. Collyer dislikes the picture's topic and threatens to cut financing. Sally Rousseau (Julie Adams), whose mother, Amanda, starred in several of Ferrara's films, pleads with O'Brien to cancel the picture, believing it will damage the reputations of many. Collyer, revealed to have been Ferrara's business manager, changes his mind and commits to the project. Charles Rodale (Peter Brocco), a secretary of Ferrara's whose employment was terminated a short time before the murder, contacts O'Brien to arrange a meeting. He is believed to have been the last person to see the famous director alive. But Rodale is killed before he can disclose what he knows. Ferrara supposedly had a younger brother, who is reported to have died in China. Others believe Rodale was Ferrara's brother. Roland Paul (Paul Cavanagh), an aging actor, is discovered to be Sally's father. He was married to Amanda, who was having an affair with Ferrara at the time of the murder. Hence, Paul arouses suspicion. Yet, due to mounting evidence, O'Brien believes Collyer to be the culprit. Paul, under pressure, confesses to the murders, copping a plea with the authorities. But O'Brien eventually discovers St. Clair to be Ferrara's younger brother and true killer, citing jealousy as the motive. Upon closing the case, O'Brien completes his picture and marries Sally.

Castle's film, true to its title, begins at the corner of Hollywood Boulevard and Vine Street, a famous Hollywood landmark. The opening credits commence, and a series of additional, notable sights follow. The headquarters of the American Broadcasting Company (ABC), National Broadcasting Company (NBC), and Columbia Broadcasting System (CBS) appear as symbols of television's growing popularity. Castle portrays Hollywood as a town that has undergone much change since the silent era, and with each day that passes, a new age gradually develops.

As the story begins, Castle includes a shot of the famous Hollywood Roosevelt Hotel. Like an elegant, contemporary superstructure, it looms in the backdrop of a dark, yet humble, abode. Franklin Ferrara's bungalow is the most significant locale of *Hollywood Story*. It inspires O'Brien to make his picture, and sometimes plays "tricks with his imagination." He becomes attached to the bungalow, finding it difficult to stay away. Numerous photographs, some of potential suspects like Amanda Rousseau and Roland Paul, adorn the walls. *Hollywood Story* features its share of suspicious characters, keeping many in the dark in regard to the killer's identity. A plot twist evolves around Philip Ferrara, the faceless, mysterious brother of the late director. And it eventually becomes clear that the brother and killer are one and the same, but not before O'Brien sacrifices much to expose the truth. Throughout the narrative, there is periodic mention of Ferrara's brother, and Castle prevents the character of St. Clair from escaping the minds of theatergoers on these occasions. O'Brien's initial recounting of the events leading up to the murder, as well as his phone conversation with Rodale, serve as solid examples. But the shocking denouement upon the film's conclusion is what draws the strands of the plot together.

Mary (Katherine Meskill), O'Brien's secretary, helps him recount the events leading up to the untimely murder, and as the focus shifts to Ferrara's anonymous brother, St. Clair is revealed to be snoozing in a nearby chair. Castle is selective with the series of images displayed throughout the scene. O'Brien walks over to the bungalow's player piano (foreshadowing the ghostly organ of *House on Haunted Hill*) and activates it as Mary reads her notes:

> MARY: Many believe that Rodale was actually a younger brother of Ferrara.

Immediately prior to the aforementioned snippet of dialogue, Castle transitions to a relaxed, dozing St. Clair. The camera remains on the writer-turned-murderer until the subject changes. But Castle purposely deceives his audience, presenting Ferrara's soon-to-be-discovered killer as a tired, aging has-been of the industry. Without realizing it, theatergoers are exposed to the missing brother (and killer) as Mary speaks of his existence. St. Clair, in essence, radiates an aura of innocence, whereas others do the opposite. Mary continues her dictation of past events, thus shifting the topic to Rodale's disappearance and subsequent, twenty-one-year absence. And his time in seclusion, although lengthy, is limited.

At the time of O'Brien's unanticipated telephone conversation with Rodale, and shortly after both men discuss Ferrara's supposedly reclusive brother, St. Clair makes a brief appearance. Although the conversation turns sour, Castle's transition to Sally's chance encounter with St. Clair is significant. As O'Brien and Rodale become acquainted over the phone, their exchange gradually becomes testy:

> RODALE: How ya fixed for brothers? Ferrara has one.
>
> O'BRIEN: There's a lot of doubt about that. Rumor has it he died in China...if there was a brother.

RODALE: The facts said that he didn't die in China and there was a brother. Still is . . . very much alive, very much kicking.

O'BRIEN: Hmm . . . you may have something there. Come around to the studio tomorrow.

RODALE: It's no good. You meet me tonight!

O'BRIEN: I'm busy tonight! We'll do it my way or not at all!

RODALE: I think you'd better listen to me, O'Brien.

Castle transitions to Sally, who is waiting for O'Brien near the studio entrance. St. Clair suddenly emerges from a building and stops dead in his tracks. He and Sally stare at one another for several seconds, and this is followed by his abrupt departure from the studio.

When we are first introduced to St. Clair, he is revealed to be frittering away within the confines of his decrepit Zuma Beach hovel. A picture of Amanda Rousseau is visible (he later comments about the "lovely" resemblance between mother and daughter). When St. Clair lays eyes on Sally for the first time, a feeling of nostalgia permeates through the air. He storms away, and O'Brien returns from the phone booth. Through the power of persuasion, Rodale has convinced O'Brien to make the trip to Ocean Park. It is somewhat miraculous considering the latter was determined to do things his way. Nevertheless, Rodale has, in fact, coaxed O'Brien into agreement. Yet, we are not afforded the opportunity to see exactly how the remainder of the conversation transpired because Rodale's powers of persuasion are not as relevant as Sally's chance encounter with St. Clair. The inclusion of Philip Ferrara into the telephone conversation remains important. Castle gradually keeps the character of St. Clair involved in the story as the mystery of Ferrara's missing brother intensifies. Prior to leaving for Ocean Park, Sally remarks about St. Clair's "sad face." If there is any idea in the minds of the audience that he could be the killer, such a notion quickly dissipates as O'Brien puts Sally's mind at ease, stating, "He'll brighten up on Wednesday. That's the day he gets paid." Yet, it is only a matter of time before St. Clair's true colors are revealed.

The film's denouement confirms that Vincent St. Clair and Philip Ferrara are one and the same. Castle delays before making his audience privy to the vital information O'Brien has acquired from the Church of the Good Shepherd. Earlier in the film, O'Brien makes a trip to San Juan Capistrano (prior to meeting St. Clair for the first time). At Franklin Ferrara's grave, O'Brien notices the medallion of a patron saint. Yet, its significance does not faze him until Collyer admits to finding a gold medallion in Franklin Ferrara's dead, clenched hand. With the church's help, O'Brien discovers the figure on the medallion to be that of Clare of Assisi (aka St. Clair), the patron saint of the Ferrara family. But he does not disclose this information to the film's characters, or the audience, until the time is right. During a moment of suspense and shocking revelation, O'Brien unmasks St. Clair as Philip Ferrara. A shootout ensues. And St. Clair, like his brother, dies on the floor of the infamous bungalow, clutching the medallion in his hand.

The production of *Hollywood Story* transpired during the winter holiday season of 1950. The shooting schedule provided Castle with an opportunity to integrate the Hollywood Christmas Parade (formerly known as the Santa Claus Lane Parade), a major attraction since 1928, into the film's narrative. From a distance, O'Brien observes Sally's interactions with Roland Paul as the parade comes to pass in the background. Another noteworthy scene of the picture involves Jim Backus (best known as Thurston Howell III of television's *Gilligan's Island*). He serves as the film's narrator and also portrays Mitch Davis, O'Brien's agent and childhood friend. With *Hollywood Story*, Backus was making the first of three appearances for Castle. Midway through the film, an ironic exchange occurs. O'Brien speaks of the potential dangers associated with making the Ferrara film. Davis chides him, saying, "I told you in the first place to leave it alone! I begged him! I said, 'Larry, make a Western!' You can't go wrong with a Western!"

Ironically, Castle's next film, *Cave of Outlaws*, was to be a Western. But above anything else, he eagerly anticipated the impending reception of *Hollywood Story*. Castle particularly sought the opinion of Harry Cohn, a man he had not seen for three years. A private screening was arranged for the infamous head of Columbia Pictures. In short, Cohn was impressed. Castle, however, was on his guard. Cohn then declared, "I want you back,

Bill. Sign with Columbia again and I promise you two things – money, lots of it – and you'll direct more pictures than you ever dreamed of." Castle was astonished. Although he was still under contract to Universal, he could not help but wonder if Cohn was true to his word. Only time would tell.

CHAPTER TWENTY-ONE
CAVE OF OUTLAWS (1951)

The setting of William Castle's next film, *Cave of Outlaws*, was unique to say the least. Interior shots of the cave were photographed at Carlsbad Caverns in New Mexico. Immediately following the opening credits, Castle acknowledges the cooperation of the National Park Service for providing the crew with access to the caverns. In his autobiography, he wrote of his experiences, claiming that everybody "lived underground like moles."

By 1951, very few film crews had dared to venture into the caves. *King Solomon's Mines*, another film to feature the monument, was released by MGM a year earlier. But what was once a well-kept secret was starting to become popular amongst the studios. As was the case for many of the films he directed, Castle strived for *Cave of Outlaws* to be different than the average picture, and Carlsbad Caverns was just the attraction to make this happen.

The year is 1880. The setting is the Arizona Territory. Armed men on horseback rob a train carrying a Wells Fargo payroll of gold. They flee into a nearby cave with the help of a teenage boy. A posse, hot on their trail, follows the robbers into the cave. There are casualties, and the boy surrenders. He is beaten for not disclosing the location of the gold. Fifteen years later, Pete Carver (Macdonald Carey), the grown-up boy from the cave, is released from prison. He finds solace in Copper Bend, the town closest to the cave. All merchants, figuring Carver will eventually find the hidden gold, deem his credit to be good. Dobbs (Edgar Buchanan), a Wells Fargo detective, watches Carver's every move. Elizabeth Trent (Alexis Smith), whose husband has been missing for months, needs help resurrecting her newspaper business. Carver comes to Elizabeth's aid and eventually learns of her plan to marry Ben Cross (Victor Jory), the wealthiest man in town. Garth (Hugh O'Brian), a henchman working for Cross, declares that Elizabeth's husband found the gold awhile back, but never exited the cave because Cross killed him. Garth's testimony is confirmed when Carver and Dobbs visit the cave and quickly discover the corpse and gold to be in close proximity to each other. Dobbs loses his balance and becomes injured. Carver foregoes the gold in order to transport the incapacitated detective to safety. The newspaper declares Cross to be guilty of murder. He finds Carver and challenges him to a duel. As victory appears to favor Carver, Cross suddenly demands a fair trial in a court of law. Carver and Dobbs return to the cave to retrieve the gold. Cross surprises them there, but Dobbs shoots and kills him.

Approximately one-third of Castle's narrative transpires in the cave, allowing viewers ample time to marvel at the ornate stalactites (hanging from the roof) and stalagmites (rising from the floor) of Carlsbad Caverns. The exterior shots of the cave were filmed at Vasquez Rocks, located just outside of Los Angeles. The landmark provided a refreshing change from the arid climate of New Mexico. The rustic town of Copper Bend was constructed on the back lot of Universal-International. But the most exciting parts of the film transpire within the caverns. An opening shot of the cave, manipulation of a random stalactite, and key flashback sequence essentially bring out the best in Castle's direction.

Minutes into the film, the Wells Fargo bandits evade their alleged captors by finding the perfect hiding spot, and Castle's opening shot of the cave provides a sense of depth that is riveting. Immediately upon their entrance into the caverns, the posse looks around to assess what is portrayed as an unfamiliar domain. Castle's camera slowly pans from left to right, revealing the vast interior of the cave. The shot lasts approximately twenty seconds, thus providing an audience with ample time to experience the action from the posse's perspective. The scenery piques our interest, as it is an astounding first impression of the very spectacle that most likely attracted theatergoers to the film in the first place. Castle's timing is precise, and it conveniently sets the stage for what is to follow.

Moments later, a random stalactite conceals the disturbing confrontation between the sheriff (Hugh Sanders) and a young Pete Carver (Russ Tamblyn). When the latter claims to be unaware of the gold's whereabouts, he is beaten. As the sheriff's skepticism grows, Castle directs his actors to slowly make their way behind the stalactite. The beating begins, and with the exception of two pairs of feet, our view is obstructed. The sheriff repeatedly strikes the boy, who sobs uncontrollably. Although the stalactite obstructs the action on the screen, the scene remains provocative, as it produces unpleasant sounds. Nevertheless, had theatergoers been afforded the slightest glimpse of the interrogation, it most likely would have aroused feelings of anger due to the level of child abuse involved. Instead, Castle relies more on sound than sight to tell his story. It is a strategy that will be revisited in a selection of his future films, specifically *House on Haunted Hill*. Yet, in regard to *Cave of Outlaws*, the technique is implemented more than once, thus recurring during Garth's testimony.

As Garth recounts the murder of Elizabeth's husband, Castle begins his flashback not only with a crafty camera shot, but also with an alteration of sound. The camera, like Garth's journey into the past, slowly moves backward into a different section of the cave, and a change in the pitch of his voice slowly becomes noticeable. An ominous mood is set with each second that passes. Garth's words start to echo within the deep and spacious surroundings. Indian folktales proclaim that the echoes of a cave carry the secrets of its past. Earlier in the film, a member of the posse warns the sheriff that the "Indians got stories about [the caves]." The belief is that those who venture in never come out, and the mystery behind the disappearance of Elizabeth's husband is consequently revealed through the chilling echoes of the cave.

In short, *Cave of Outlaws* is remembered primarily for its inclusion of Carlsbad Caverns. It also features a young Lee Marvin (of *Cat Ballou* fame) as the train conductor knifed in the back during the film's introduction. Castle would later reflect that "there was little excitement about the whole project." Nevertheless, his direction is noteworthy, because the scenery is exceptional, especially for its time. Towards the film's conclusion, Carver tells Dobbs, "It's a big world, and I haven't seen much of it." In the early 1950s, this was true for many Americans. People, in general, did not have the opportunity to visit spectacles like Carlsbad Caverns. With Castle's film, however, a single trip to the local theater worked wonders for the average person living in the average town.

CHAPTER TWENTY-TWO
SERPENT OF THE NILE (1953)

Following what seemed like a lengthy absence, William Castle returned to Columbia Pictures. Universal-International had offered to renegotiate his contract for another three years, but Harry Cohn had other plans, having made a promise he intended to keep. In addition to lots of money, he guaranteed Castle the opportunity to direct a supposedly innumerable number of pictures.

Enter Sam Katzman. He was a fixture at Columbia, having served as a producer of low-budget films for the studio since 1945. Katzman was known to work quickly, and several directors had difficulty adhering to his many demands. If a film's production fell behind schedule, there would be hell to pay. But Castle appreciated Katzman's will to persevere. *Serpent of the Nile*, their first project together, was presented as a story "all about that Cleopatra broad, Mark Antony, and that Julius Caesar guy." Castle sensed that working with Katzman was going to be memorable, later referring to the infamous producer as "a great showman."

Caesar, dictator of Rome, has been assassinated. His confidant, Antony (Raymond Burr), seeks vengeance. But leaders of the plot against Caesar sense their imminent defeat, and subsequently commit suicide. Captain Lucilius (William Lundigan), an operative of the rebels, is taken into custody. He and Antony argue over Rome's future. The latter plans to "conquer" Cleopatra (Rhonda Fleming), queen of Egypt and ex-wife of Caesar. Lucilius, in charge of Caesar's private guard at the time of Cleopatra's marriage to the dictator, accompanies Antony to his imminent meeting with the queen. She intends for her child, son of the deceased Caesar, to one day rule Rome. Cleopatra invites Antony and Lucilius to her palace in Alexandria. She privately seduces both men. Meanwhile, the queen's subjects feel dejected, as they go hungry everyday. But Cleopatra speaks of Egypt as a strong, rich ally for Antony's armies. Lucilius makes it clear to Cleopatra that he does not want her in Rome. Antony becomes enticed by the queen and so-called beauties of Alexandria. Lucilius is imprisoned by Cleopatra because he disagrees with her political agenda, but also because he rejects her advances. Octavius (Michael Fox), an adherent of Caesar's, assumes command of Rome. Antony provides Lucilius with the opportunity to escape from Egypt, but the latter chooses to remain. As a declaration of war, Octavius's army descends upon Alexandria. Lucilius fights alongside Octavius's troops. Antony hesitates to counter the attack, as he comes to realize Cleopatra does not love him. Lucilius discovers a dying Antony, suffering from a self-inflicted, fatal wound. Octavius and his troops gain a foothold in Alexandria. Cleopatra, choosing not to become a slave of Rome, commits suicide.

As the film begins, Castle presents its title with an animated serpent wrapped around the "S" of *Serpent of the Nile*. It becomes clear that the subject is Cleopatra, and the metaphor is apt to some extent. At one point, Lucilius compares Cleopatra with the predatory creature, telling her, "A serpent can be trusted more because we know how to defend ourselves against its venom. There is no defense against you." Lucilius makes reference to all of the men who have, at one time or another, had encounters with the seductive queen. Cleopatra is a temptress, and will often use her charm and beauty as a means to obtain what she wants.

In addition to the film's title, there is also a subtitle. It appropriately states, "THE LOVES OF CLEOPATRA." Indeed, there are those who merely serve as objects of the queen's affections, but one is more susceptible to her allure than the others. *Serpent of the Nile* chronicles the slow and unfortunate self-destruction of Antony. His dying faith in Rome, in addition to an indulgence of guilty pleasures, weakens his character. But Antony's doomed relationship with Cleopatra is what ultimately seals his fate.

Within the opening minutes of Castle's picture, it is somewhat evident that Antony's faith in Rome is not as strong as it should be for a man of his stature. He and Octavius, serving together in a triumvirate, clearly have their differences in regard to the future of the republic, and this is evident as the two rejoice in victory following a decisive battle:

OCTAVIUS: You, Mark Antony, and I, Octavius, sole rulers of the world....

ANTONY: ... of Rome.

OCTAVIUS: Rome is the world.

Unlike Octavius, Antony's love for Rome is waning. He no longer considers the city to be the center of civilization. Upon spending a considerable amount of time in Alexandria, Lucilius attempts to convince Antony that they belong in Rome. But the latter would rather delegate power to Octavius. Antony, of course, does not want to leave Alexandria. Later, as Roman forces prepare to storm Cleopatra's palace, Octavius ponders the whereabouts of Antony, his former comrade. He comes to realize that Antony no longer possesses the will to lead. Ironically, following Lucilius's capture at the beginning of the film, the audience is exposed to a completely different man, as Antony exhibits nothing but confidence while addressing his prisoner:

> ANTONY: Whatever I do, I do for two things: Rome and pleasure. I put Rome first.

Lucilius appears to be intrigued as he listens to his captor's rhetoric. Yet, it quickly becomes clear that words can be deceiving.

As Antony gradually loses interest in Rome, his tendency to indulge in an assortment of guilty pleasures becomes apparent. His passion for wine is evident, but he ultimately lacks the ability to control his intake of the intoxicating beverage. In Tarsus, prior to Cleopatra's arrival, the queen's servant provides Antony with an important message. It acknowledges the forthcoming meeting and hints at a strategic partnership between Rome and Egypt. Upon reading the message, Antony addresses Cleopatra's servant:

> ANTONY: Tell your queen, I'll be there. Tell her, also, it will take more wine than she can find in Egypt to make Mark Antony drunk enough to be fooled with words.

He returns the message to Cleopatra's servant, who quickly departs. Antony approaches Lucilius.

> LUCILIUS: I have heard that if a man has Cleopatra, he doesn't need wine.

But Antony's dependence on wine becomes stronger as he grows accustomed to the "beauty" and "sins" of Alexandria. At one point, Lucilius asks Cleopatra, "Does he yet change his blood into wine?" And she concedes that Antony is possessed not by her, but instead, by "pleasure."

Antony's relationship with Cleopatra is destined for disaster primarily because they do not share the same interests. Lucilius is able to interpret the queen's enigmatic personality, and he carefully monitors her manipulation of Antony out of concern for the Roman leader. Approximately thirty minutes into the film, Cleopatra compares her feelings for Antony with her ambitions:

> CLEOPATRA: Lucilius, as you love Rome, so do I love Egypt. Egypt must be my first love. The man who rules it at my side will be second. I have no choice, but the lover of my heart... must be last.
>
> LUCILIUS: And will you push Antony aside as easily as you push aside your heart?
>
> CLEOPATRA: No harm will ever befall Antony because of me. I promise you that.
>
> LUCILIUS: If I can, I'll make sure of it.

Lucilius attempts to prevent Antony's self-destruction, citing Cleopatra as the primary factor. He later claims, "She'll do to Rome what she's done to you." But Lucilius remains adamant that Cleopatra will not rule Rome. Castle hints at the existence of a possible love affair between the two during her marriage to Caesar. Lucilius is privy to the queen's manipulative nature, warning Antony to not "make Alexandria [his] tomb while Rome cries out in its need for [him]." But as Castle's film concludes, the audience is presented with a tragic ending. Upon Antony's death, Lucilius chides Cleopatra, stating, "You said once that no harm would come to Antony because of you." His words are the last of the film. Cleopatra kills herself, and Lucilius is seen exiting the empty, desolate palace.

Serpent of the Nile, a moderate success at the box office, was promoted by Sam Katzman as, "GIGANTIC! FANTASTIC! 2 YEARS IN THE MAKING!" In retrospect, Castle had different

Rhonda Fleming.

ideas for the film's promotion. The picture itself had been delayed in pre-production for a lengthy period of time. And Castle was quickly catching on to Katzman's style. He figured *Serpent of the Nile* should have been sold as, "2 YEARS IN THE TALKING! 12 DAYS IN THE SHOOTING!" But the film proved captivating to theatergoers. Raymond Burr's portrayal of Antony is remarkable, although the motives of his character are somewhat puzzling. For example, it is unclear why Antony is quick to befriend Lucilius considering the latter's involvement in the plot against Caesar. Furthermore, modern-day scholars of ancient Rome have disagreed with the film's storyline. In reality, Antony committed suicide because he believed Cleopatra, the love of his life, to be dead. The film's narrative clearly presents an alternative series of events that lead to his fate.

Nevertheless, *Serpent of the Nile*, despite its inaccuracies, was entertaining for its time. Rhonda Fleming offered a candid reflection to the author of this book, stating, "I have to admit, I was disappointed when I first saw the finished film. And I wasn't too happy with the way I played the role. There was not enough variety in Cleopatra's emotions for me to add to my performance. However, the Technicolor was beautiful and my costumes by Jean Louis were lovely. The distant painted scenes were definitely not good, very likely due to the low budget. Bill Castle, however, did an incredible job despite the limitations of the production. He was a wonderful man and a very good director. It was a treat working with him. I also enjoyed working with Bill Lundigan and Raymond Burr. They were two good actors who had some strong roles and helped to make the overall film stronger and get it a good rating."

Serpent of the Nile, although a B picture, appealed to theatergoers of all ages. And Castle was quick to discover Katzman's flair for making films that were loosely based on historical events of many years ago. In short, Harry Cohn was quite happy to have his protégé back at Columbia, remaining true to the promise he had made a couple of years earlier. Castle was paid a generous salary. And consequently, from 1952 to 1955, he directed an astounding average of six films per year.

CHAPTER TWENTY-THREE
FORT TI (1953)

November 26, 1952, marked a momentous revelation in motion picture history, as theatergoers were exposed to a cinematic phenomenon unlike any other. Arch Oboler's *Bwana Devil* celebrated its world premiere in Los Angeles. It was the first feature-length film to be presented in a three-dimensional format. Years earlier, William Castle pitched the same concept to the top brass of Universal-International, but he was strongly discouraged from making his vision a reality. The studio was simply unwilling to gamble on what was perceived as too risky of a commitment. Consequently, Oboler's film went on to gross millions, leaving Castle to wallow in his own grief. But Columbia Pictures was eager to reap the benefits of Oboler's success. Hence, Castle's next assignment was *Fort Ti*, a three-dimensional Western set during the French and Indian War.

The year is 1759. The setting is Albany, New York. Rogers' Rangers, under the command of Major Robert Rogers (Howard Petrie), represent the British in their fight against French and Indian forces. Raoul de Moreau (Louis Merrill), a French operative posing as a town proprietor, gathers intelligence from a local named Mark Chesney (James Seay). He seeks the most vital of information, as Lord Jeffrey Amherst (Lester Matthews), the British commander, plans an attack on the French settlement of Fort "Ti" Ticonderoga. But de Moreau believes Chesney will expose him as a spy. Using a band of Indians as "instruments of espionage," he orchestrates the kidnapping of Chesney's wife and children. Captain Jedediah Horn (George Montgomery), an elite ranger, is the brother of Chesney's wife. Determined to win the war and rescue the hostages, he assembles and trains a volunteer army. During the journey to Fort Ti, Horn encounters Fortune Mallory (Joan Vohs). She claims to have been a prisoner of the French, but Horn is hesitant to accept her story, believing her to be a spy. The rangers seek refuge at the farm of François Leroy (Ben Astar), a longtime friend of Horn's. Leroy assumes the role of a humble rancher, but secretly manufactures supplies for the

British. His spouse, Running Otter (Phyllis Fowler), harbors feelings for Horn. The emotions began years earlier. French troops attack Leroy's compound. Running Otter accuses Fortune Mallory of exposing the rangers' location. But Running Otter is eventually revealed to be the true conspirator, having made the accusation to keep Fortune Mallory away from Horn. She commits suicide as a means to escape her anguish. Horn overpowers the farm's captors and launches a full-scale assault on Fort Ti. Chesney's wife and children are set free.

Of *Fort Ti*, Castle commented that in order to achieve the full potential of his three-dimensional picture, he threw "every goddamn thing [he] could think of at the camera." The film begins with a British soldier firing a cannon directly at the audience. The opening credits are then displayed, during which time the cannon is promptly reloaded. As the words "Directed by WILLIAM CASTLE" appear on the screen, the cannon is fired for the second time. Castle essentially makes it clear from the beginning that the audience is his intended target. He was more concerned about throwing objects at the camera, whereas his screenwriter, Robert E. Kent, was more concerned about the structure of the story. *Fort Ti* offers a unique perspective of the French and Indian War, but the story was secondary to a majority of theatergoers. In fact, the narrative progresses at an unusually fast pace during specific scene transitions (i.e., from Albany to Calvin, night to day, and Fort Ti to Leroy's farm) that ultimately lead to conflict, thus providing Castle with ample opportunity to tap into his arsenal of three-dimensional effects.

Following the opening scene of *Fort Ti*, the film's setting quickly shifts from the city of Albany to the secluded settlement of Calvin. Horn speaks of the remote village (home to his sister and nephews) upon departing Amherst's quarters, and within the space of a single second, Castle transports his audience to different surroundings. Sergeant Wash (Irving Bacon), the captain's close friend and confidant, inquires into the specifics of Horn's agenda as the two exit the building:

WASH: How far did you say your sister lives?
HORN: About fifteen miles ... a settlement called Calvin.

Immediately following Horn's answer, the image on the screen changes to that of a hostile Indian, who wastes little time firing a flaming arrow at the audience. But the transition occurs so quickly that it is uncertain whether we are still in Albany or someplace else. It is eventually made clear that the locale has changed, as the arrow strikes its intended target (a sign on which the settlement's name of Calvin is carved). The following minutes entail the dreadful kidnapping sequence. Wrathful Indians and their flaming torches converge upon the audience. In short, the scene marks the introduction of Castle's three-dimensional spectacle. It is a moment eagerly anticipated by theatergoers, thus marking the beginning of the picture's special effects.

Midway through *Fort Ti*, shortly after Fortune Mallory makes her first appearance of the film, an unusually swift night-to-day transition helps to establish a memorable event of the narrative. A middle-of-the-night argument precedes an extraordinary morning stroll, thus leading to an unexpected ambush. As Horn prepares to sleep under the same tree as Fortune Mallory, it becomes apparent that the tension between the two is undeniable:

HORN: When you have anymore talking to do...do it to me.

FORTUNE MALLORY: If you were the last man in this camp, I wouldn't say another word!

Yet, during the following morning, they are together, away from the camp and isolated from the other rangers. As the picture transitions from night to day, the film's score becomes harmonious. Their stroll through the backwoods is somewhat surreal. But Castle deliberately interrupts the moment of serenity to startle his audience with the unexpected. A gunshot is heard, and Horn is almost hit. An Indian warrior, lurking behind a tree, threatens to fire again. Wielding a tomahawk, Horn hurls the weapon at his enemy, which, in essence, travels directly towards the audience. Castle places more of an emphasis on the conflict between Horn and the belligerent native than he does on that between Horn and Fortune Mallory simply because an action-packed, three-dimensional sequence is potentially, yet arguably, more entertaining to theatergoers if based on the former instead of the latter. After Horn successfully fends off his attacker, Leroy arrives on the scene. And it is at the Frenchman's farm where, perhaps, the quickest transition of Castle's motion picture concludes.

As Running Otter arrives at Fort Ti to expose the rangers' secret location to General Montcalm (Alphonse Martell), the picture quickly dissolves to Leroy's farm, where the traitorous matron is seen to be feigning ignorance as French soldiers storm the compound. The transition, composed of three shots instead of two, omits key events of the story in order to establish the grand finale of the picture. Running Otter is seen at Fort Ti, preparing to meet with the general. Castle then transitions to a shot of yet another "General," Leroy's golden retriever. The dog, severely wounded by a soldier's arrow, lies in agony near the farmhouse. The third and final shot of the transition brings the audience into Leroy's concealed workshop. Running Otter, having appeared just seconds earlier at Fort Ti, integrates with the hostages as she accuses Fortune Mallory of treason.

The sequence of events, beginning at the fort, composes less than a minute of screen time. Yet, a majority of the details leading up to the siege, including Running Otter's conversation with Montcalm, are omitted. To reiterate, Castle's priorities were not necessarily geared towards the film's dialogue, but instead, towards the three-dimensional effects of his picture. Approximately twenty minutes of *Fort Ti* remain at the time of Running Otter's accusation. Hence, through the omission of events that are significant to the story, Castle effectively sets the stage for his grand finale. Again, his target was the audience, and when it came time for the film's climax, theatergoers were treated to an impressive spectacle, complete with flying bats, thus capping off Castle's extravagant motion picture.

To cinematic historians, *Fort Ti* is probably best known as the first Western to be filmed in a three-dimensional format. It is also noteworthy for the originality of Robert E. Kent's script. The dynamic between humans, animals, and nature is emphasized at key points of the story. During a conversation with Fortune Mallory, Horn explains, "Everything in the forest kills something else to stay alive itself. Animals kill other animals for food. A large tree will kill a smaller tree to have more room for its roots. There's death all over the forest." On another occasion, Running Otter tells Horn that he has the "eyes of an eagle." It is a metaphor that will again be used as a means to describe George Montgomery's character in *Battle of Rogue River*.

In regard to *Fort Ti*, the creativity of Kent's writing is reflected in the naming of specific characters. Early in the film, Horn comments that the rangers do not get to take baths as often as they would like. Ironically, the last name of his companion is Wash. And just a short time later, the sergeant is revealed to be washing himself in a bathtub. Additionally, while on patrol, Wash frequently carries a powder horn, which is a direct symbol of Captain Horn, his superior officer and close friend.

Not only did *Fort Ti* mark the first of three collaborations between Castle and George Montgomery, it eventually became one of the highest-grossing motion pictures of 1953. But aside from its array of three-dimensional effects, the film's script should not be overlooked, especially in regard to its dialogue. Irving Bacon, for example, has the opportunity to recite what is arguably the best line of the picture. As the rangers prepare for battle against French forces, his character states a universal truth when claiming, "If everybody got drunk together, there'd be no more war."

CHAPTER TWENTY-FOUR
CONQUEST OF COCHISE (1953)

In 1848, upon the conclusion of the Mexican-American War, a boundary between the United States and Mexico had yet to be determined. Several territories were annexed by the victorious Americans. Mexicans living in these areas were given the choice to return to Mexico or remain in their homes. Those who chose to stay were granted American citizenship with full civil rights. A particular territory came to be known as the Gadsden Purchase, which was a designated area later comprising southern Arizona and southwestern New Mexico. But a majority of Mexicans remaining in this region became targets of countless Indian raids led primarily by the Apache and Comanche tribes. The United States sought to offer protection against the invasions, but it proved to be an expensive undertaking. William Castle's *Conquest of Cochise* offers a fictionalized account of the turmoil from varying perspectives.

John Hodiak as Cochise.

Major Tom Burke (Robert Stack) arrives in Tucson to meet with Cochise (John Hodiak), the chief of the Apache tribe. Tukiwah (Steven Ritch), Cochise's Lieutenant, explains to his superior that if they do not fight the Americans, they may have to fight the Comanche tribe. Cochise believes that war with the Comanches is better than war with the Americans. He and Burke agree to a peace treaty. Running Cougar (Joseph Waring), a Comanche warrior, raids a Mexican settlement. But Cochise and his tribe intervene to disrupt the attack. He kills Running Cougar. Tensions mount between the Apaches and Comanches. Cochise ponders the future with his wife, Terua (Carol Thurston). In Tucson, Sam Maddock (Robert Griffin), a prominent businessman, believes in lucrative profits "as long as there's Indians to fight." He orchestrates the assassination of Cochise with the intention of framing the Americans. Maddock recruits Don Felipe de Cordova (Rico Alaniz), a Mexican whose wife was murdered by Indians, to carry out the operation using an American firearm. During the attempt, Terua is killed. Later, Cochise orders Tukiwah to kidnap Consuelo de Cordova (Joy Page), Felipe's niece and daughter of a wealthy Mexican landowner. He is unaware of her relation to Terua's murderer. Cochise pledges to detain Consuelo until Burke can expose the assassin. Felipe is subsequently unmasked. During Consuelo's time in captivity, she becomes attracted to Cochise. Later, the Apache leader is captured and taken to the Comanche settlement. An American invasion is launched with the intention of rescuing Cochise. The Apaches join the fight against the Comanches. After Cochise is rescued, he requests that Consuelo return to Tucson with Burke. She complies, albeit reluctantly.

Conquest of Cochise was the fourth Western to be directed by Castle. He would go on to direct several more through the years. Yet, his picture pertaining to the famed Apache chief is somewhat atypical of his earlier and later Westerns. Much of this can be attributed to the narrative's supporting characters, especially in regard to the fate of an innocent victim. Furthermore, the circumstances behind the fates of the film's antagonist and heroine, too, are particularly worthy of attention.

Felipe, like his late wife, is an innocent victim of the bloodthirsty Indians, but an unusual fate awaits him. His growing intolerance of non-Mexicans ultimately leads to his demise. As Felipe dines with the family of his brother-in-law, Don Francisco de Cordova (Edward Colmans), he makes his feelings clear to those who are present. Consuelo attempts to pacify him:

> CONSUELO: Soon the American soldiers will be here, then things will be different.
>
> FELIPE: They are just as bad. Worse. When they kill and plunder, it is legal.
>
> FRANCISCO: The Americans are our only hope.
>
> FELIPE: Our only hope is to kill all of them on sight. They are no different from the others.
>
> CONSUELO: But they are here to make peace.
>
> FELIPE: Peace? On whose authority? The irresponsible opportunists in Mexico City? The word of President Pierce? Are they going to keep Cochise and his savages from killing and plundering below the border? Are they going to keep swine like Maddock from taking everything we have here?
>
> CONSUELO: It is possible.
>
> FELIPE: Not when you have seen what I have seen.
>
> Felipe directs his attention from Consuelo to Francisco.
>
> FELIPE: I am surprised at you, Francisco. Allowing your own daughter to speak this way. Between the Americans and Indians, they are slaughtering us off like cattle.
>
> Felipe bows his head in sorrow as he continues to speak.
>
> FELIPE: My wife, before my very eyes, and for no reason!
>
> Again, Felipe directs his attention to his brother-in-law.
>
> FELIPE: Can't you feel what I feel? She was your own sister!
>
> FRANCISCO: But we must be patient, Felipe.
>
> FELIPE: I will not listen to this kind of talk. I would rather die than hold out my hand to any of them, Americans or Indians!

Felipe throws his napkin on the table and storms out of the house in disgust. Although he is the victim of a heinous crime, his hatred of non-Mexicans is irrational. At times, Felipe cannot distinguish between good and evil. During *The Law vs. Billy the Kid*, Nita Maxwell's uncle is murdered by an overzealous deputy. She becomes a victim of the county government, but chooses to stay positive and not hold a grudge against those with ties to law enforcement. Like Nita, Felipe has been victimized. However, he does not listen to reason. Instead, Felipe goes to extremes in order to accomplish what he desires, and it is not typical for a character of his kind. Although he is a victim and initially garners sympathy from the audience due to his tragic loss, his ending is not a happy one. An irrational Felipe is killed as he attempts to murder Cochise. In retrospect, an analysis of the aforementioned dinner conversation reveals his misjudgment of the Apache chief. Cochise, in essence, is not a cold-blooded killer. However, Felipe's lingering suspicions in regard to the wrongdoings of another character are remarkably accurate.

Maddock, the driving force behind a majority of the film's conflict and, therefore, the story's true antagonist, is killed approximately forty-five minutes into the narrative. His death transpires when the audience least expects it. As Tukiwah and his men descend on Francisco's hacienda, their objective is clear. They are to take a hostage at Cochise's request. Yet, before Tukiwah can make it inside the home, his men happen upon Maddock and Felipe as the two are engaged in a private conversation regarding the assassination attempt on Cochise's life. But suddenly, within a matter of seconds, Maddock is shot dead by an Indian's arrow. It is unexpected, especially because the plot contains several loose ends. Ben Cross, the influential magnate of Copper Bend and antagonist of *Cave of Outlaws*, appropriately meets his demise during a climactic shootout at the caverns.

The film concludes shortly thereafter because, with his death, the conflict of the story has been resolved. Yet, in regard to *Conquest of Cochise*, Maddock is killed at a point of the narrative when much has yet to be accomplished. Immediately following the incident, Tukiwah prepares to take a hostage, and of the house's occupants, he chooses the ideal candidate.

Consuelo, the heroine of Castle's film, does not find happiness upon the story's conclusion. Throughout the narrative, it is unclear if her destiny lies with Burke or Cochise. The major, presented to

Robert Stack and Robert Griffin.

the audience as a compulsive womanizer, becomes enamored with Consuelo the second he lays eyes on her. Yet, she is a practical woman and does not submit to his will. Burke attempts to woo Consuelo with his boyish charm. He serves flat champagne (an action to be repeated as Frederick Loren offers the beverage to his less-than-enthusiastic spouse in *House on Haunted Hill*). But the major must compete with Cochise. During Consuelo's time in captivity, she is exposed to the customs of her Apache captors, and her attraction to Cochise becomes stronger with each passing day. Upon the story's resolution, a man and a woman do not live happily ever after. Such is not the case with Castle's *Jesse James vs. the Daltons*, as the film's concluding image clearly depicts Joe Branch and Kate Manning preparing themselves for the bonds of matrimony. Cochise, in contrast, does not wish to commit to Consuelo. He claims, "The laws of the Apache are very strict, and a chief above all else must live by them and marry within his people." As Consuelo departs with Burke, Tukiwah questions the reasoning of his superior, stating, "Cochise, there is no law that a chief must marry within his people." It is a certainty of which Cochise is mindful. Nevertheless, despite an earlier claim to the contrary, he does not appear to have accepted the reality of Terua's fate. Hence, there will be no happy ending.

The casting of non-Indian actors in Native American roles was commonplace during the 1950s. *Conquest of Cochise* is one of many examples, as people like John Hodiak and Steven Ritch were performers of European descent. Yet, despite his ethnicity, Hodiak's portrayal of Cochise is noteworthy partly due to Castle's direction. The Apache leader is first seen atop the summit of a towering rock. He appears miniscule primarily because of his distance from the camera. However, as Castle introduces Cochise into the narrative, it immediately becomes clear that the chief harbors a larger-than-life personality.

Hodiak, a popular stage actor, brought a certain charisma to the role. Sadly, he succumbed to a heart attack at the young age of forty-one just two years after the film's release. Following Hodiak's death, Hollywood remained lax concerning its stance towards the casting, or lack thereof, of Native American performers. Jay Silverheels, a Canadian Mohawk First Nations actor who appeared as Yellow Hawk in Castle's *Masterson of Kansas*, became an advocate for Indian rights. His fight was not easy. Although Silverheels was probably best known to television audiences as Tonto, the trusty sidekick of the Lone Ranger, film historians have acknowledged his establishment of the American Indian Actors Workshop. It served as a venue for Native Americans to practice and perfect the essential skills of the performing arts. For many, it was a challenge of perseverance. George Bernard Shaw, the illustrious playwright, once stated, "A Native American elder once described his own inner struggles in this manner: 'Inside of me there are two dogs. One of the dogs is mean and evil. The other dog is good. The mean dog fights the good dog all the time.' When asked which dog wins, he reflected for a moment and replied, 'The one I feed the most.'"

CHAPTER TWENTY-FIVE
SLAVES OF BABYLON (1953)

With *Slaves of Babylon*, William Castle believed he and Sam Katzman were invading Cecil B. DeMille's coveted territory. After all, the script was based on the Book of Daniel of the Old Testament, and DeMille was no stranger to the Bible. In fact, he would soon direct the classic remake of *The Ten Commandments*, a silent film he produced almost thirty years earlier. Castle's film, although quite different from DeMille's epic in many ways, is a remarkable costume drama. It provides some insight into the plight of Babylon's inhabitants. *Slaves of Babylon* also touches upon the value of religion, and offers a unique perspective of King Nebuchadnezzar and his relationship with the Prophet Daniel. Castle would later refer to the film as a "low-budget extravaganza."

Nebuchadnezzar (Leslie Bradley) rules over Babylon and the enslaved Israelites. Daniel (Maurice Schwartz), a slave skillful in all wisdom, stands in the king's palace as an advisor. At his request, Nahum (Richard Conte), a fellow slave, escapes Babylon in search of a shepherd named Cyrus (Terry Kilburn). Shortly after Cyrus is found, it is determined that he is the rightful king of Persia. He rejects the title until Nahum informs him that, as king, he can marry whomever he pleases. But Cyrus's grandfather, King Astyages (Robert Griffin), hinders his grandson's ascension to the throne. After a series of battles, Astyages is overthrown. Cyrus chooses Princess Panthea (Linda Christian) as his bride. Initially, she is uninterested, but changes her mind after Nahum entices her with the prospect of becoming a powerful queen. He is executing Daniel's secret plan, which is to coax Cyrus into invading Babylon. Determined to marry the princess, Cyrus presses forward with his army. Nahum stays behind to keep Panthea safe. The two become close. Nebuchadnezzar succumbs to a plague, thus establishing his son, Prince Belshazzar (Michael Ansara), as the new king of Babylon. Cyrus, unsuccessful in his initial attempt to defeat Belshazzar, retreats to safety. Panthea confesses her love to Nahum, but he rejects her advances. Cyrus, observing that his soon-to-be queen is upset, allows her to decide Nahum's fate. She delays. In Babylon, Daniel prays to God that his people be delivered from the evil of Belshazzar. Cyrus invades Babylon again, and Nahum kills Belshazzar just as the latter is about to kill Daniel. The Israelites, now liberated, depart for Jerusalem. Panthea becomes queen and orders the permanent exile of Nahum from Babylon.

Aside from appearing in many films, Maurice Schwartz was a popular stage actor. Friends and colleagues duly noted his pragmatic approach to life and the performing arts. A particular event that transpired during the filming of *Slaves of Babylon* was unlike any other Schwartz had experienced. In his autobiography, Castle fondly recollected his attempts to pacify Schwartz while shooting the scene with the predatory lions. The spooked actor "sounded like a frightened rabbit" and was hesitant to perform. Nevertheless, the scene was filmed without any casualties. In retrospect, Schwartz's overall performance is noteworthy, as the Prophet Daniel is one of the most important characters of the story. But equally important, perhaps, is Daniel's counterpart in King Nebuchadnezzar. Surprisingly, Castle's characterization of the king is fairly positive, as Nebuchadnezzar appears to occasionally sympathize with Daniel's cause.* The lions' den, fiery furnace, and entrapment of the departing Israelites essentially reveal Belshazzar to be the true antagonist of the film.

Although Nebuchadnezzar arranges for Daniel to be thrown into the lions' den, he does so reluctantly. The incident at the den is portrayed much differently in the Bible than it is within *Slaves of Babylon*, and this is due primarily to the presence, or lack thereof, of the king. In the film, Belshazzar's decree states that everyone must pray to the god, Bel Marduk, or be sent to the lions. Daniel is undeterred and, despite the plea of a fellow Israelite, continues praying to his own god. Belshazzar anticipates the act of defiance and does everything in his power to expedite the execution. Later, Nebuchadnezzar discovers that the lions have spared Daniel's life. It is a fate he accepts, thus allowing the prophet to live. According to the Bible, the king is not present at the lions' den to oversee the intended execution of Daniel. Instead, it is Darius the Mede, the man some scholars believe is the one to have succeeded Belshazzar as the ruler of Babylon.

---

* The narrative of *Slaves of Babylon* makes reference to more than one king. In order to avoid confusion, the word "king" will henceforth refer to King Nebuchadnezzar.

But there are claims that Darius never existed. In fact, a theory was proposed that Darius and Cyrus were one and the same. If Cyrus was to have been the authority figure present at the lions' den, Nebuchadnezzar would not have been in power because he would have long been dead. Yet, for purposes of Castle's film, Nebuchadnezzar is the one to oversee the execution and, consequently, spare Daniel's life. It is evident that Belshazzar desires the opposite outcome. Unsatisfied, he presses forward with his persecution.

As three of Daniel's companions are thrown into a fiery furnace as punishment for honoring their god, the king is not present, nor does he appear to have any involvement in the affair. Belshazzar is clearly responsible, and at this point of the narrative, Castle's audience sees more of the evil prince and less of Nebuchadnezzar. In the Bible, the king is the one to stand at the furnace and observe the preservation of the slaves as they miraculously emerge from the fire. In *Slaves of Babylon*, it is a shocked Belshazzar who gazes into the furnace and bears witness to the unfolding events. Nebuchadnezzar's appearances of the film are numbered. He gradually becomes insane and dies a short time later, but not before begging Daniel for forgiveness. Belshazzar assumes command of the throne and wastes no time executing his plans for the enslaved Israelites.

Following Nebuchadnezzar's departure from the picture, Belshazzar frees the slaves, only to send them directly into a fiery deathtrap. A celebratory feast presented in Belshazzar's honor is held at the time of the Israelites' peril, but a self-centered act of blasphemy serves as a reversal of fortune for the overzealous Babylonians. A few miles outside of the city, the marching Israelites are led by Belshazzar's soldiers onto a narrow path. They happen upon a confined, isolated section of the trail. Some of the Babylonian soldiers travel ahead of the group and light a fire, purposely sealing off a forward exit. Meanwhile, another group of soldiers positioned at the rear of the isolated section light a similar fire, thus entrapping the Israelites. Daniel, who has remained at the feast instead of joining his traveling companions, requests that a group of sacred vessels be returned to him. Belshazzar initially agrees, but instead of returning the vessels, he fills one with wine and drinks from it. He does not believe in Daniel's god and proves it to everybody with his act of blasphemy. Suddenly, an oversized, animated hand appears in the dining hall and proceeds to write a cryptic message upon the wall. Daniel interprets it, stating, "God has numbered your kingdom, and brought it to an end." Belshazzar is dumbfounded. Castle transitions to a shot of the trapped Israelites, who become liberated as it begins to rain heavily, thus extinguishing the fire. The feast, in addition to the timely appearance of the mystical hand, is included in the Bible. The entrapment of the departing Israelites, however, was added to the script. Castle's portrayal of Belshazzar is essentially darker than the Bible's characterization, and it paves the way for an effective, climactic scene during which Belshazzar is overthrown and killed.

Principal photography for *Slaves of Babylon* concluded on October 23, 1952. Another year would pass before its release to the public. Today, it is rarely shown on television and has received little attention through the years.

Upon the film's conclusion, Daniel tells Cyrus that his "name shall be remembered throughout the ages." Coincidentally, in 1957, a renewed interest in the historical figure of Cyrus the Great transpired. Donald Wiseman, a respected Biblical scholar, proposed the aforementioned theory of the eerie similarities between Cyrus and Darius.

Slaves of Babylon marked the final film appearance of Maurice Schwartz. The veteran actor returned to the stage and eventually moved to Israel. Tragically, he died of a heart attack at the age of sixty-nine. In retrospect, Castle's time with Schwartz, although brief, was essentially well spent.

CHAPTER TWENTY-SIX
DRUMS OF TAHITI (1954)

In the days following the New York premiere of *Fort Ti*, William Castle set forth to direct *Drums of Tahiti*, the next three-dimensional motion picture of his career. Set during the latter part of the nineteenth century, the film portrays the conflict between the native Polynesians and the "powerful arms of France" as both entities fight for control of the island kingdom. Early Tahitian history chronicles the trials and tribulations of the Pōmare Dynasty, a family of monarchs represented primarily by kings. Yet, Robert E. Kent's story centers on the reign of Queen Pōmare, the sole female ruler in the kingdom's history. Screenwriter Douglas Heyes, a newcomer to the industry, was hired by Sam Katzman to collaborate with Kent on the script. Together, the two were able to assemble an entertaining work of historical fiction.

Tahiti has become a protectorate of France, considerably reducing the powers of Queen Pōmare (Frances Brandt). Enlisting the help of the British, she plans an uprising against her conquerors. Commissioner Pierre Duvois (Francis L. Sullivan), a representative of France, suspects insubordination. He digresses with his "dearest" friend, Mike Macklin (Dennis O'Keefe), a local restaurateur. But Macklin is secretly loyal to the queen, and plans a voyage to San Francisco to obtain a slew of British rifles. Duvois becomes suspicious. Hence, Macklin is forced to travel under a false pretense. Upon arrival, he is to be married. Duvois demands to accompany Macklin on the journey, declaring himself as best man. In San Francisco, Macklin seeks out Gay Knight (Cicely Browne), an ex-flame. She rejects his proposal of marriage. But Gay's friend, Wanda Spence (Patricia Medina), agrees to play the part. Her motivation is money. Following the wedding, Duvois becomes incapacitated due to excessive drinking. Macklin seizes the opportunity to escape from San Francisco with Wanda and the rifles. Upon their arrival in Tahiti, Duvois is there to greet them, but he appears to be unaware of the contraband. The natives inform Macklin that a British fleet is on its way to launch an attack against the French. Duvois admits to Wanda that his ignorance has been a sham. He pleads with her to persuade Macklin to abort the attack. Wanda then warns her husband, as she has begun to develop feelings for him. Nevertheless, Macklin sets out to recover the rifles. But the fleet does not arrive, and a hurricane strikes Tahiti. Pōmare declares that "a stronger will than [hers] has spoken." Macklin restores his friendship with Duvois and publicizes his marriage to Wanda.

Drums of Tahiti is not so much about the conflict between the British and the French as it is about particular character relationships. The connection between Macklin and Duvois tends to dominate the narrative. It is a friendship of which the basis is deceit. At times, Duvois hints that he is well aware of what Macklin is planning. He also plays dumb, similar to the way a chess player may attempt to bluff an opponent. In fact, whenever Macklin and Duvois appear together on camera, a chessboard is usually visible in the scene. In a San Francisco hotel room, the latter asks, "Are marriages made in heaven, or are they just . . . just a part of a game of chess?" Duvois is clearly inebriated, but he is also intent on making his point. He compares himself with Macklin, as if they are opposing kings on a chessboard. Seconds later, Duvois passes out, and a so-called king is rendered helpless. But there are others who symbolize chess pieces (i.e., queens, knights, and pawns), and they, too, are a part of the game in the grand scheme of things.

The role of Queen Pōmare is similar to that of a queen on a chessboard. Her relationship with Macklin is an indicator of sustainability. As the two exchange views on how to fight the French, the sociology of gender dominates their discussion:

> MACKLIN: You've always been young and reckless, Queen Pōmare. You're a female! That's your trouble!
>
> QUEEN PŌMARE: Well, is it so odd for a queen to be a female?
>
> MACKLIN: That's the trouble with queens. They don't think like men. Any man would be a fool who thought of fighting France.
>
> QUEEN PŌMARE: Men are such fools.
>
> MACKLIN: Women make them so.

QUEEN PŌMARE: Oh no, my dear. How often does a woman take a fool and make a man of him?

Pōmare's words ring true, especially if Macklin is to be the representation of a "king" chess piece. On the chessboard, a queen is considered to be more powerful than a king, primarily because the former can move more than one square (step) at a time. A king, however, is limited to only one square per move. Pōmare clearly has more authority than Macklin. At one point, she asks, "Who wins at chess?" Macklin replies, "You do, sweetheart." But he does not heed her words of wisdom. Instead, he embarks on a so-called fool's errand and sails to San Francisco with Duvois in tow. Shortly after their arrival, and during yet another game of chess, the Frenchman remarks, "The queen is finished...unless, perhaps, the knight could help her? A good play, huh?"

Gay Knight, whose last name is a direct representation of the popular chess piece, becomes a part of Macklin's strategy to trick Duvois. The limitations of her role are made clear at the Golden Peacock, an entertainment venue in San Francisco. As Gay makes her first appearance of the film, she adorns the top half of a horse costume. In the game of chess, a knight is sometimes referred to as a horse because of its appearance, which is that of the popular equine mammal. Once Gay's costume is removed, Macklin makes his intentions clear. He wants her to fulfill the role of his fiancée and soon-to-be wife. Similar to a knight on the chessboard, Gay, an individual of multiple capabilities, is to be used for a special operation. She is a talented actress, and her versatility enables her to assume many roles. But Gay cannot marry Macklin due to her union with the traveling acrobat. Instead, Wanda agrees to participate in the supposed covert operation. Minutes later, Duvois classifies the knight as "helpless." Yet, if the game is to be won by Macklin, he will need to rely on the unlikeliest of pieces.

In order for one to succeed at chess, he or she will traditionally need to mobilize his or her pawns. The strategy of *en passant* (French for *in passing*), referring to a pawn's initial avoidance of confrontation, appears to be implemented by Duvois upon Macklin's return to Tahiti. As the boat makes landfall, not a single customs agent is present. Duvois avoids the use of agents (pawns), possibly as a means to prevent an immediate altercation.

En passant is an effective strategy if used at the proper time. Yet, it is unclear if Duvois favors the strategy. Earlier in the film, he states, "[The British] are forced to use pawns . . . too bad. A game may be lost by a pawn." Shortly thereafter, Macklin says, "You must remember [pawns] can win games too." Duvois replies, "I must remember that the next time we play." If Duvois did, in fact, implement *en passant*, his actions are irrelevant, because Mother Nature intervenes before the so-called game can be won.

Principal photography for *Drums of Tahiti* concluded on June 23, 1953. Two weeks later, Castle began production on *Jesse James vs. the Daltons*, the third (and final) three-dimensional picture of his career. Of *Drums of Tahiti*, Castle wanted theatergoers to feel like they were a part of the narrative. When Wanda, out of anger, hurled an empty coffee cup at Macklin, the audience ducked for cover. Because they, too, were Wanda's target. Castle saved many of his three-dimensional effects for the hurricane sequence of the film's climax. The theatrical poster for *Drums of Tahiti* advertises the film as "THE STORY OF TWO OUTCASTS." The tagline refers to Macklin and Wanda, as both characters appear together on the poster.

Castle's film is also significant for its portrayal of the relationship between Macklin and Duvois. Their love of chess is undying, and their conversations are memorable. On one occasion, Macklin remarks, "I often do things without thinking." To which Duvois retorts, "And I often think things without doing." Their friendship, in essence, is one for the ages.

CHAPTER TWENTY-SEVEN
CHARGE OF THE LANCERS (1954)

To say Sam Katzman was intense would be an understatement. The overtly keen producer was simply driven by a need to ensure big profits for Columbia Pictures. He was always in touch with current events and trends. If Katzman worked quickly enough, he could produce a film based on issues plaguing domestic America (i.e., *New Orleans Uncensored, The Houston Story*) and ensure the picture's release while its topic was still considered to be current in the minds of theatergoers.

Yet, in order to achieve results in a timely manner, Katzman relied on the diligence of particular individuals. Rapid screenwriters were summoned, usually at a moment's notice, and given strict deadlines in order to ensure the completion of their assignments. One such writer was Robert E. Kent, who sometimes penned scripts using the pseudonym of James B. Gordon. He and William Castle had the opportunity to collaborate together on a total of eight films. When Katzman presented them with the idea for *Charge of the Lancers*, both men willingly accepted. Fortunately for Kent, it was not imperative for him to work faster than usual in order to finish his script, as the film's narrative was not based on current events. But with Katzman at the helm, failure was not an option. Castle and Kent, quite aware of what was expected of them, stepped up to the challenge as they had done before on previous occasions.

At the time of the Crimean War, Czarist Russia plans to conquer Turkey. But England, France, and Sardinia form an alliance with the embattled nation to fight back against the aggressors. The allies attempt to overtake the Russian naval base at Sebastopol. Major Bruce Lindsey (Richard Stapley), en route from London, travels to the Crimean peninsula with an advanced, breech-loading cannon. Captain Eric Renault (Jean-Pierre Aumont), of the French regimen, accompanies the major. Upon their arrival at the British outpost, a demonstration of the cannon is successful. Lindsey is ordered back to London to acquire more of the prototype. But he is captured by the Russians shortly after his departure. The British stronghold is subsequently attacked. Renault escapes the assault and seeks refuge on a traveling caravan. He becomes attracted to Tanya (Paulette Goddard), a beautiful gypsy. Russian troops encounter the caravan and take its occupants to Sebastopol, where Lindsey, suffering from what appears to be a state of shock, is imprisoned. General Inderman (Ben Astar), the enemy commander, becomes convinced that Renault is a mind-reading gypsy. He recruits Renault to make careful observations of the catatonic Lindsey. Maria Sand (Karin Booth), a British nurse, arrives in Sebastopol after a temporary truce is negotiated. She and Renault tend to Lindsey, who admits to having feigned illness in order to avoid interrogation. Maria exposes her loyalty to the Russians and attempts to alert Inderman. But she is accidentally killed after being thrown from a horse carriage. Renault shoots Inderman dead upon rescuing Tanya from his clutches. He sends a coded message to the allies, thus enabling the lancer regiments to charge into Sebastopol and successfully overtake the base.

Jean-Pierre Aumont and Paulette Goddard.

Castle's direction of *Charge of the Lancers*, similar to that of several other Katzman-produced films, served as a learning experience for him. Although the narrative appears rushed at certain points, it remains entertaining. Upon the conclusion of Castle's picture, the allies prepare for battle. Renault speaks of a brief, seven-minute interval during which the Russian defenders are relieved of their duties by a rested conservation of troops. Believing it to be a risky, but ideal, time to attack, he remarks, "These are going to be the longest seven minutes in history!" Ironically, Renault's declaration comes at a point when seven minutes remain in the film. And much transpires within these final moments.

Aside from its climax, Charge of the Lancers is noteworthy for the character of Corporal Tom Daugherty (Charles Irwin). His love of poetry is noticeable on several occasions. Prior to the boxing match, Daugherty attempts to put Renault at ease. In reciting a verse from Henry Wadsworth Longfellow's Curfew, he says, "Darker and darker the black shadows fall; sleep and oblivion reign over all." Naturally, Daugherty's so-called words of encouragement do not necessarily help the situation. Curfew, however, was published in 1857, approximately one year following the end of the Crimean War. Nevertheless, it is not the only poem to which Daugherty makes reference. As he specifically cites the works of Joel Barlow, Richard Lovelace, and William Wordsworth, it becomes clear that Daugherty's additional citations are very much applicable to Castle's narrative.

The boxing match was shot day for night, an inexpensive production technique used in many films of the period.

A passage from Joel Barlow's Advice to a Raven in Russia, recited by both Daugherty and Renault within the film's opening minutes, evolves around the concept of war. The circumstances behind the poem's creation are somewhat similar to the context of the scene. In 1812, Napoleon made an attempt to conquer Moscow. He was not successful. Barlow, present during the battle, acquired the idea for his poem based on his observations of Napoleon's defeat. Upon the beginning of *Charge of the Lancers*, Daugherty proclaims, "War after war his hungry soul requires; state after state shall sink beneath his fires." He appears poised to continue when Renault interjects, stating, "Yet other lands in victim smoke shall rise, and other Moskows suffocate the skies." His recitation is a slight modification of Barlow's poem, as the word "lands" is substituted for "Spains." Nevertheless, the verses are a direct reference to Russia's dominance of the continent. Seconds later, Daugherty and company are attacked, as Russian forces launch an assault on the carriage. At the time of the poem's conception, Barlow himself was in a similar predicament. He and his traveling companions were also pursued by militant Russians. Yet, in Barlow's case, temperatures were extremely cold. Unfortunately, he contracted pneumonia and died a short time later. But Barlow, like other poets, left a lasting legacy.

Around 1642, Richard Lovelace wrote *To Althea, from Prison*, a poem appropriately referenced as the occupants of the gypsy caravan are taken to the Sebastopol prison. Renault's spirits are low, but Daugherty recites poetry as a means to lighten the mood. The corporal proceeds to quote Lovelace, stating, "Stone walls do not a prison make, nor iron bars a cage; minds innocent and quiet take that for an hermitage." Daugherty speaks of a dwelling where people are empowered to live in peace. Renault believes "the pigs on [his] uncle's farm have better quarters than [the prison]." But through the power of poetry, the corporal is not deterred. He is the only optimistic prisoner of the cell. As Daugherty attempts to continue with his recitation of Lovelace's poem, Asa (Tony Roux), the gypsy leader, makes a request for "no poetry." The corporal immediately acquiesces. Asa is understandably concerned about the well-being of his wife, Keta (Fernanda Eliscu), as well as that of Tanya. Both women have been taken to General Inderman's quarters. Despite Asa's request, however, the ongoing absence of Keta and Tanya eventually triggers Daugherty to cite the work of yet another poet.

A reference to William Wordsworth's *She Was a Phantom of Delight* is made as the corporal and company eagerly await the return of the women. Renault's continued pessimism is evident as the others are quick to remind him of Tanya's will to persevere.

A new weapon designed to bring an end to the war (a theme later explored in The Gun That Won the West*)*

The men have been transferred from their prison cell to more-than-adequate living quarters. But Renault feels guilty about Tanya's perpetual servitude to Inderman. Asa reminds him of her cleverness. Had it not been for Tanya, the men would have remained in prison. Daugherty seizes the opportunity to quote Wordsworth, thereby building upon Asa's optimism. He says, "A perfect woman, nobly planned, to warn, to comfort, and command; and yet a spirit still, and bright with something of angelic light." The recitation of Wordsworth's poem is perfectly timed, as Tanya and Keta reunite with the men just seconds later. Consequently, Daugherty does not recite poetry for the remainder of the film. As the narrative's conflict builds, his predicament, as well as that of the allies, becomes dire. During the film's final battle, Lindsey asks the corporal, "Where's your poetry now?" And Daugherty, clearly on edge, simply replies, "How can I think of poetry without getting indigestion?"

Robert E. Kent completed the script for *Charge of the Lancers* rather quickly, and the subsequent production of Castle's film transpired over the course of only eleven days. Hence, Sam Katzman was content. Yet, it is a known fact that B movies of the era were filmed using the quickest, least expensive method possible.

Castle frequently worked with select individuals more than once because his pictures were produced with contract talent. And on several occasions, he found it difficult to embrace his status as a contract director. Nevertheless, there was an ongoing need to make ends meet, and Castle would essentially direct whatever project Katzman desired. Assignments were typically accompanied by strict deadlines.

Upon the completion of a film, Castle would simply move on to the next project. He did not have a say in the matter. But deep inside of him was the burning desire to continue what he started with *It's a Small World*. Castle not only wanted to have creative control over the stories of his films, he wanted to produce and direct his own motion pictures. Although he did not know it at the time, the resurgence of his career was just a few years away.

CHAPTER TWENTY-EIGHT
BATTLE OF ROGUE RIVER (1954)

Unlike *Charge of the Lancers*, which takes place on the Crimean peninsula during the mid-1800s, William Castle's next film, although set around the same time, returns to the distant, yet familiar, setting of the American Old West. As was the case with most of his Westerns, the script evolved around real life events and locations. The setting for Castle's twenty-eighth film was the highly coveted Oregon Territory. Union forces, along with several Native American tribes, fought for the region's control just prior to the outbreak of the Civil War. The Rogue River, which flowed westward through the territory, served as the site of many battles. Hence, Castle had the ideal premise for his next film, appropriately titled *Battle of Rogue River*.

The Rogue River Indians, led by Chief Mike (Michael Granger), constantly outwit the army troops sent to defeat them. Stacey Wyatt (Richard Denning), a civilian, recruits local volunteers to join the fight against the natives. Major Frank Archer (George Montgomery), a no-nonsense soldier with orders to relieve the unit's commander, arrives in the territory with new artillery. Archer spars with Brett (Martha Hyer), daughter of the well-liked Sergeant McClain (Emory Parnell), over the cancellation of a ceremony honoring his arrival. But their heated discussion quickly subsides when Archer's reasoning puts Brett at ease, and she becomes attracted to him. Chief Mike deems Archer to be an honest man. They both agree to a thirty-day truce, requiring all of the chief's warriors to stay on the north side of the river, leaving Archer and his troops to remain on the south side. The rules are broken when Wyatt, declaring that Indians have attacked the unit's settlement and kidnapped Brett, persuades McClain to cross the river. Wyatt stays behind as the sergeant leads his soldiers into battle. McClain is injured and taken prisoner. The cavalry is unable to locate Brett. Instead, she and Archer remain at the settlement awaiting the arrival of McClain's squad. It is eventually determined that Wyatt lied about Brett's capture in order to prolong the fighting. Local businessmen, seeking to benefit from the ongoing battles, compensate Wyatt generously. Chief Mike deems the truce to be dead and prepares for war. But when McClain makes it back to the settlement alive, Archer discovers the truth. Wyatt attempts to kill the major, but he is shot dead by Chief Mike. Peace is achieved, and the Oregon Territory is admitted to the Union.

"I'm beginning to think maybe you are human after all."

The theatrical poster for *Battle of Rogue River* boldly announces that "ALL SIX WINNERS OF THE NATIONAL INDIAN BEAUTY CONTEST" are featured in the film. The women appear approximately ten minutes into the narrative. But their cameos come and go in the blink of an eye. The following scene, however, is of the utmost significance because it foreshadows what is to come for Chief Mike. When Castle introduces the Indian leader to the audience, he is seen lying on a cot in his teepee. Two natives enter with important news about "the new White leader of the soldiers." The camera retracts and slowly pans upward, but not before revealing a blanket with the words "U.S. Army" stenciled on it. It is symbolic of Archer's arrival. For the first time in his life, Chief Mike will face a counterpart unlike any other. A mutual degree of respect will quickly evolve. *Battle of Rogue River* is not about the battle as much as it is about the similarities between Chief Mike and Major Archer. Aside from being realists with the instincts of predatory animals, they are mere human beings underneath the guise of invincibility.

Throughout the film, both leaders conduct themselves with the physical and mental characteristics of predatory animals. The eagle is a symbol of their stature. During the aforementioned meeting in the teepee, Chief Mike immediately detects fear emanating from his men, similar to the way a predatory animal would sense fear within its prey. "Do you run here like frightened antelope to stand and stare at your chief with antelope eyes," he asks. Eagle feathers, once belonging to a bird of prey, adorn his headdress. Meanwhile, at the settlement, a soldier makes reference to Archer's "eagle eyes." In Archer's office, an antelope sculpture rests on the fireplace mantel, helplessly watching the major ponder and execute his next moves. The fearless nature of both leaders essentially enables them to approach their day-to-day lives pragmatically.

Matt Parish (Charles Evans), a local businessman, commends Wyatt's pragmatism for balking statehood, but Chief Mike and Major Archer are the true realists of the film. To them, patience is a virtue, and theories abound logically. When the chief first receives word of Archer's "new and terrible weapons," his men speak of a great disaster in which forests fall and tribes perish. Instead of panicking, Chief Mike takes a realistic and logical approach to the discussion:

CHIEF MIKE: All this you have seen?

INDIAN #1: My own eyes have beheld it.

CHIEF MIKE: You saw a tribe perish?

INDIAN #1: No.

The chief then turns his attention to the other warrior.

CHIEF MIKE: You saw a forest fall?

INDIAN #2: No, but I did see a tree fall. This, I swear.

CHIEF MIKE (looking to his right): And you . . . you saw a forest fall?

INDIAN #1: No, but I also saw a tree fall.

INDIAN #2: And I, also.

CHIEF MIKE: Each of you, then, has seen a single tree fall.

The two immediately nod in agreement. Chief Mike pauses briefly to ponder the situation.

CHIEF MIKE: Then, perhaps, many eyes having seen one tree fall have multiplied it into a forest.

The chief listens patiently, but is unwilling to jump to the same conclusions as his men. Archer, too, is a believer in practical reason. Later in the picture, when the major arrives at the Rogue River, Castle films the south shoreline from a specific perspective. We see what Archer sees: the prints of cavalry horses, and nothing more. He astutely observes that the natives did not, at any time, cross the river. Yet, McClain has gone missing amidst reports of fighting. This ultimately leads to Archer's deduction that both sides are fighting in self-defense, and he becomes aware of a political faction that opposes statehood for Oregon. Chief Mike and the major eventually join forces to eradicate the growing threat and are subsequently victorious. But underneath the supposed guise of invincibility, the two are mere mortals.

George Montgomery and Michael Granger.

As Chief Mike boldly declares to his men that Archer "is not a demon, but a man like ourselves," his rhetoric sets the stage for what is to follow. Throughout most of the film, Castle depicts the major as a tough leader with metaphorically thick, impenetrable skin. Following Brett's initial encounter with Archer, her curiosity becomes piqued. She wants to crack the secret code of his personality. At one point, Wyatt tries to pacify her with the simple explanation that the major is "only a man." But it does not satisfy her. Gradually, the layers are unpeeled to reveal what lies beneath. A turning point in the relationship between Archer and Brett occurs when she realizes that, underneath his complex aura, he is "human after all." Upon the film's conclusion, Archer has earned the respect of Brett, his men, and the audience.

Castle's tale of the Oregon Territory and its admittance to the Union was released in March of 1954. Like most B Westerns of the time, it did not remain in theaters for too long. Steve Ritch, a character actor who portrayed Tukiwah in *Conquest of Cochise*, appears as an Indian in *Battle of Rogue River*. Coincidentally, in 1995, he passed away in the city of Rogue River, Oregon, at the age of seventy-three. The aforementioned poster advertises *Battle of Rogue River* as a "FIGHT TO THE DEATH...WHILE A WOMAN WAITS." However, with Castle behind the camera, the narrative goes a little deeper than a routine battle between cowboys and Indians.

CHAPTER TWENTY-NINE
JESSE JAMES VS. THE DALTONS (1954)

Following the nationwide release of *Fort Ti*, producer Sam Katzman was given the green light to begin production on another three-dimensional film for Columbia Pictures. Like several other William Castle-directed Westerns before it, Jesse *James vs. the Daltons* was to be shot in lavish Technicolor. Throughout motion picture history, many films pertaining to the legendary outlaw have been produced. Yet, in *Jesse James vs. the Daltons*, the title character is nowhere to be seen. Instead, those with ties to the outlaw come together to represent him in their fight against the notorious Dalton Gang. Equipped with his Technicolor camera, Castle set forth to portray the events that led to the famous shootout in Coffeyville, Kansas, on October 5, 1892.

Kate Manning (Barbara Lawrence), accused of murdering a prominent Coffeyville citizen, is rescued by Joe Branch (Brett King) seconds before she is to be lynched. Branch, determined to find his long-lost father, believes he is the son of the famous Jesse James. He enlists Kate's help because of her father's ties to the notorious outlaw. She claims that James is dead, but Branch dismisses the idea. He concludes that the Daltons, a group of bandits wanted in seven states, will know where to find James. In an attempt to garner the Daltons' attention, Branch robs a train carrying an army payroll. The newspapers offer a reward for Branch's capture and predict that he will most likely head to Bartlesville. Bob (James Griffith) and Grat Dalton (John Cliff) discover him to be there, but are soon taken as his prisoners. Branch speaks of a hideout cabin in the mountains belonging to James, claiming that $100,000 was stashed there years earlier during the Civil War. The Daltons accompany him to the hideout with the hopes of acquiring the fortune. But James is not there. Instead, Bob Ford (Rory Mallinson), the man who killed James, arrives at the cabin. The money is discovered, but Ford deems it to be of the Confederate brand, rendering it worthless. The Daltons, angered at the situation, kidnap Kate and head to Coffeyville with the hopes of robbing two of its banks. Branch and Ford give chase and arrive just as the robberies are taking place. A massive shootout ensues, during which Grat is shot dead. Branch and Kate, free of the Daltons, marry in the local church.

Castle does not, at any time, reveal the year during which the events of *Jesse James vs. the Daltons* take place. The audience is afforded several glimpses of newspapers from time to time, but many do not contain a publication date. Perhaps, only history buffs of the American Old West may be privy to the film's time frame due to its climactic shootout, taking place on that fateful day in October of 1892.

Castle knew he was catering to a broad audience. Some purchased tickets only to experience the visual effects of a three-dimensional picture. Others may have been in attendance simply to see an entertaining narrative transpire before their eyes. With *Jesse James vs. the Daltons*, Castle was not concerned about conveying a specific time frame for the film's events, but he does present a setting in which the times are changing, thereby ushering in an uncertain new world. Storey's Saloon in Bartlesville, the cabin hideout of Jesse James, and the closing shot of the film offer significant reflections of this world.

Character interactions, taking place within Storey's Saloon in Bartlesville, are indicative of a deceptive, late-nineteenth century world. The saloon's bartender (Ray Kellogg) has a memorable encounter with Branch, but a much different one with Bob and Grat Dalton. Branch enters the saloon in a conspicuous manner, demanding an entire bottle of liquor. Attracting more attention than he already has, Branch pays with a $500 bill. The bartender reluctantly makes change. An arrogant Branch then gathers his belongings and leaves without another word. When the Daltons arrive just hours later, their exchange with the bartender is as pleasant as can be. After learning that Branch is staying in the hotel, the brothers take their final sips of whiskey and prepare to exit:

BOB DALTON (placing a coin on the counter): Thanks, friend.

BARTENDER: Like I said ... we aims to please.

They all laugh as the Daltons exit the saloon. The bartender exhibits sincere admiration as he watches them leave.

BARTENDER (to himself): Aw. Nice fellas!

The irony is riveting. In a changing world, people are sometimes not who they appear to be. Branch is dismissed as a misfit, whereas the Daltons are practically treated like saints. And the plot simply thickens when Branch and the Daltons find themselves in a situation where they have no choice but to cope with each others' presence.

Branch and the Daltons, stuck together in the hideout cabin awaiting the supposed arrival of Jesse James, eventually come to realize how cruel and fickle life can be in a post-war environment. The concealed fortune, which is what attracted everybody to the cabin in the first place, serves as a harsh reminder. Grat Dalton exhibits rage upon the discovery of the Confederate money, presented as a symbol of falsity. At the time of the Civil War, the boundaries of the Confederate States of America (CSA) were not clearly defined. Some territories were claimed by the CSA without formal secession. Although Castle does not specify the actual state in which the cabin scene takes place, it is most likely Oklahoma. Prior to reaching the hideout, Branch, Kate, and the Daltons visit Muskogee, Adair, and then Bartlesville. Not only are these cities in Oklahoma, they also follow a south-to-north pattern, indicating that everybody is ultimately traveling north to Coffeyville. During the Civil War, Oklahoma was claimed by the CSA without formal secession or control. In the aftermath of the war, the livid Daltons stare at the useless Confederate bills with contempt. A territory that many people fought and died for appears to have lost its validity. A changing world is sometimes symbolic of the perils of hardship, but it can also represent the opposite.

Within the concluding shot of *Jesse James vs. the Daltons*, Branch informs Father Kerrigan (Nelson Leigh) that he and Kate have decided to get married, and the action that follows alludes to the beginning of a new era for women. Just as Castle's camera reveals Branch to be removing his hat, we see that Kate is simultaneously placing hers on top of her head as they disappear into the church. Her lone action represents a step towards the independence of women. In 1892, only men were granted the right to vote, but ongoing efforts were being made to reduce these limitations. Just two years earlier, the National American Woman Suffrage Association (NAWSA) was formed to obtain voting rights for women in every state. Progress was being made one step at a time, and on August 26, 1920, the ultimate goal was reached with the Nineteenth Amendment to the United States Constitution.

Principal photography for *Jesse James vs. the Daltons* was completed in July of 1953, but the film would not be released to the public for another nine months. This was due, in large part, to the demanding preparations of a three-dimensional picture. In addition to coordinating the film's special effects, Castle worked with cinematographer Lester H. White to create vivid depictions of the American Old West. An example can be seen early in the film as the horse-bound Daltons rise from a distant hill, similar to the way fire ants might emerge from an anthill. In short, *Jesse James vs. the Daltons*, although forgotten by many, is an entertaining film worthy of at least one viewing.

CHAPTER THIRTY
THE IRON GLOVE (1954)

James Francis Edward Stuart, known to historians as the former Prince of Wales, lived a life of controversy from the moment he was born. His father, King James II of England, angered Protestants over his strict adherence to Catholicism. Because of his faith, the king was deposed from power shortly after his son's birth. James II died in 1701, inspiring the thirteen-year-old Stuart to lay claim to the thrones of England, Scotland, and Ireland. But Stuart's ascension was rejected primarily because of his religious beliefs and family history. Instead, the German-born George I was recognized as the rightful king. Stuart became known as the pretender to the throne. Thus, the people were divided. Once Stuart came of age, he sought a bride. George I knew that a marriage would ultimately produce heirs to Stuart's claim to the thrones. William Castle's *The Iron Glove* chronicles the prince's quest for holiness and supreme royalty in the sacrament of matrimony.

Captain Charles Wogan of Rathecoffey (Robert Stack), an Irishman, fights for Prince Stuart (Richard Wyler) and his cause. At a tavern, the Duke of Somerfield (Leslie Bradley) speaks out against the Crown and engages in a scuffle with the king's agents. Wogan is there and rushes to the duke's aid. He finds himself outnumbered and is forced to surrender. The duke is seriously wounded, and both are taken as prisoners of King George I (Otto Waldis). But Wogan is unaware of the circumstances behind his capture. The duke, secretly loyal to the king, faked his protests and injuries in order to trap Wogan. The beautiful Ann Brett (Ursula Thiess) becomes the Duchess of Somerfield upon an arranged marriage to the duke. She is to be a spy for the king. The duke, as he pretends to die, begs Wogan to escape with his wife and bring her into Stuart's care. Shortly thereafter, Wogan and Ann arrive in Paris, where the prince is staying as a guest of King Louis XIV. Wogan develops feelings for the duchess, but eventually learns that the duke is alive and well. He questions Ann's loyalty, but she appears to be genuinely sympathetic to Stuart's cause. Meanwhile, Princess Maria Clementina Zobieska

(Rica Owen) journeys through Austria. She travels to Paris with the intention of marrying Stuart. The duke attempts to intercept the princess before she can make it to her destination. He forces Ann to accompany him. Wogan, however, goes to great lengths to rescue Clementina. He engages in a duel with the duke. As the latter appears to gain the upper hand, he is shot dead by Ann. The prince and princess are married. A short time later, Charles "Charlie" Edward Stuart, the new prince, is born.

Some have referred to *The Iron Glove* as a costume drama. Others have classified it as a swashbuckler, a genre which first became popular with the Douglas Fairbanks silents of the 1920s. Whatever the classification, it is doubtful that contemporary audiences will take Castle's film at face value.

The Iron Glove is not particularly remembered for its semi-daring sword fights or its typical baroque costumes. In 1901, *Clementina*, a novel by Alfred E.W. Mason, was published. It centers on Wogan's adventures in protecting the princess. Coincidentally, the narrative of *The Iron Glove* becomes progressively engaging once the rescue of Clementina is under way. Prior to Wogan's travels within Austria, the threat of imminent danger, stemming primarily from a supposed emissary of King Louis XIV, lacks suspense. But upon Wogan's arrival into terra incognita, a reunion of sorts, in addition to an unexpected transformation, succeed in taking the story to the next level.

Count DuLusac (Louis Merrill), a guest of Louis XIV and, essentially, the film's antagonist while the duke is in hiding, is not a formidable adversary and, therefore, does not pose too serious of a threat to Stuart's cause. His final encounter with Wogan has its shortcomings. Tempers flare as the count is escorted out of the province:

> WOGAN: The way lies clear before you, DuLusac. Take it!
>
> DULUSAC: What? Am I to be deprived of your company so soon?
>
> WOGAN: The king ordered me to give you safe conduct out of his province. Were it for me to say, I'd hang you for a spy.

The two continue to trade barbs until DuLusac challenges Wogan to a duel. After a brief and lackluster display in the art of swashbuckling, the former appears to be defeated. DuLusac confesses the details of the duke's malicious agenda, but also identifies the duchess as an accomplice. Wogan is caught off guard, and the count seizes the opportunity to kill his opponent. But DuLusac cannot capitalize. Wogan is victorious. But the duel's culmination, unfortunately, is pathetic. Wogan's sword, in delivering its final thrust, clearly misses DuLusac. Yet, the count keels over and dies, and the audience has no choice but to accept the scene's outcome. DuLusac, however, did not pose too serious of a threat prior to his demise, which transpires just five minutes after a "resurrected" duke reenters the picture. Wogan's true nemesis, alive and well, is determined to succeed where DuLusac failed. The film's setting eventually switches to Austria, and it is at this point that the duke goes to extremes in order to ensure a momentous victory for George I.

With Princess Clementina's life in peril, Wogan chooses to reunite with Timothy O'Toole (Charles Irwin) and Patrick Gaydon (Alan Hale Jr.), two of his closest comrades, in an attempt to stop the duke. As proud Irishmen, their undying bond is not entirely evident until they venture into Austria. Although the film's opening minutes reveal a strong friendship amongst the three, the audience sees little of O'Toole and Gaydon following Wogan's departure, imprisonment, and subsequent escape to Paris. Approximately one hour into the film, the action shifts to a quaint Hofbräu in Austria, and it is there that the camaraderie between Wogan, O'Toole, and Gaydon becomes special. An Austrian lieutenant seated in close proximity to the three demands the "finest ale" from his waitress. Wogan takes immediate notice of the officer's attire, prompting a reaction from O'Toole:

O'TOOLE: What's in your head, Captain Charlie?

WOGAN: I'm thinking that uniform is just about my size.

GAYDON: I see your point, sir. And it'll be my pleasure to get it for you.

WOGAN: Discretion, man! We can't risk violence when the princess's safety is in our hands!

The waitress arrives at the lieutenant's table and serves the ale.

LIEUTENANT: Bring another! I can drink all you can carry!

WAITRESS: Yeah.

Wogan turns from the direction of the lieutenant to face O'Toole.

WOGAN: The lieutenant fancies himself a drinking man, O'Toole.

O'TOOLE: Aye, that he does.

WOGAN: And I wager you could drink him right out of that uniform.

O'TOOLE (smiling): Is that a question you're asking, Captain Charlie?

WOGAN: It's an order I'm givin', O'Toole.

O'Toole is only too happy to oblige. Although he is following orders from a superior officer, his actions are based solely on loyalty and friendship. O'Toole, in his attempt to subdue the Austrian lieutenant, makes a request for Irish whiskey. Like Wogan and Gaydon, he is clearly proud of his ancestral roots. And Castle's film essentially places an emphasis on Irish heritage. For example, the names of select historical figures are modified. In reality, O'Toole's first name was Edward (instead of Timothy), and Gaydon's first name was Richard (instead of Patrick). Yet, of all things Irish, it is the whiskey and its inebriating effects that set the stage for what is to follow, offering a touch of comic relief when it is most vital to the narrative.

Following the lieutenant's loss of consciousness, Wogan, in what is arguably the most memorable event of the film, orders Gaydon to transform into a woman. The scene's placement in the story predates the timing of select gimmicks seen in several of Castle's later films. For example, in order to experience the effects of EMERGO! (*House on Haunted Hill*), or, perhaps, the vibrations of PERCEPTO! (*The Tingler*), theatergoers had to wait for over an hour until the gimmick was unveiled. With *The Iron Glove*, Gaydon's transformation takes place approximately one hour into the narrative. To some, it was worth the wait.

Today, if one refers to Castle's film as a swashbuckler, he or she may be doing so under a false pretense. Because people are more likely to recall Alan Hale Jr. (fondly remembered as The Skipper on *Gilligan's Island*) dressing in drag than they are to recall the numerous swordfights, which are not to be taken too seriously in the first place.

In his memoirs, Robert Stack claimed to have accepted the role of Charles Wogan because he had reached "a low ebb in his career." There were two options. The first was to give up acting altogether and become a used-car salesman. The second was to work for Castle and someday "rise to greater glory." *The Iron Glove* did, in fact, serve as a stepping stone to Stack's eventual success. But the film is also noteworthy for its introduction of a significant Castle motif: curtains and concealment. When DuLusac's agent attempts to assassinate the prince, he does so from behind a curtain. The motif recurs in *Masterson of Kansas*. Curtains, in the case of the aforementioned films, are meant to serve as a safe haven for would-be killers. But as Castle's films become darker, so, too, does the motif. Curtains and concealment are also featured in *The Old Dark House* and *The Busy Body*, films in which the would-be killers have, in essence, become killers.

CHAPTER THIRTY-ONE
THE SARACEN BLADE (1954)

Frank Yerby, born in 1916 to an African American father and Caucasian mother, rose to literary fame in the late 1940s with *The Foxes of Harrow*. The novel's rights were later purchased by 20th Century Fox for screen adaptation. Many of Yerby's works evolved around historic events, prompting many critics to refer to him as a contemporary Alexandre Dumas. In 1952, he wrote *The Saracen Blade*, a tale about the life of a Sicilian commoner during the Crusades. It, too, attracted the attention of a major film studio, as Columbia Pictures secured the novel's rights and tapped William Castle to direct the adaptation. *The Saracen Blade* premiered in New York City in May of 1954. One particular *New York Times* review was unkind, claiming that many of the actors lacked "a sense of class and verve."

Pietro Donati (Ricardo Montalban), a peasant orphaned at a young age, suffers a great loss when his guardian, Isaac (Nelson Leigh), is savagely murdered by the dreaded Count Siniscola (Michael Ansara). A local baron, Rogliano (Edgar Barrier), offers employment to Pietro, who soon falls in love with Iolanthe (Betta St. John), the baron's daughter. But Rogliano has arranged for her to marry Siniscola's son, Enzio (Rick Jason), who plans to kill Pietro by means of a recreational hunt. One of the hunters is Frederick II (Whitfield Connor), the emperor of Europe. Coincidentally, he was born on the same day, and in the same marketplace, as Pietro. By chance, the two meet in the forest and become friends upon discovering their similarities. Frederick proposes an offer of knighthood to Pietro on the condition that they embark on a crusade together. He also encourages Pietro to marry. But Iolanthe has married Enzio, and Frederick cannot do anything to dissolve the marriage. Instead, Pietro weds Elaine (Carolyn Jones), the count's reluctant cousin. Frederick's cavalry of soldiers, which includes Siniscola and Enzio, embarks on its crusade. Pietro is knighted. Frederick is injured a short time later and is transported to safety, but Pietro is captured by the Saracens. His foreign exile lasts for months, but he is finally released. Frederick declares Pietro to be the baron of the Rogliano estate. Elaine becomes attracted to her husband's sudden power. Siniscola murders her out of jealousy. Pietro vows to avenge her death, although Frederick strongly advises against it. A battle ensues, in which Siniscola and Enzio are killed. Frederick strips Pietro of his prestigious titles, but the latter rejoices as he and Iolanthe depart for Venice to begin a new life.

The aforementioned New York Times review implicitly states that "Ricardo Montalban's rise from Italian serfdom to consorting with the ancient nobility is traced with standard precision." With The Saracen Blade, Sam Katzman yearned to produce an above average picture. He wanted to add a touch of authenticity to his production and requested that filming take place entirely in Italy. But Harry Cohn had the final say, opting to keep the budget to a minimum. Instead, principal photography transpired on a Columbia sound stage. Exterior scenes were filmed at nearby locations.

Screenwriters George Worthing Yates and DeVallon Scott adapted a script that was quite different from Yerby's original story. Castle's retelling of The Saracen Blade not only omits the hatred, anti-Semitism, and violence that is prevalent throughout the novel, it also places more of an emphasis on adventure than it does on historical context. Pietro's birth, the predicament of Isaac, and Castle's portrayal of the beautiful slave, Zenobia (Pamela Duncan), provide in-depth examples of the underlying disparities.

The birth of Pietro is a significant event in both the novel and the film, but the former depicts a darker characterization. Maria, Pietro's dying mother, is filled with hatred and contempt for her newborn son. Upon her first glimpse of the child, Yerby describes the baby as being "tiny and wizened." Maria cannot bear to look at Pietro, claiming he is ugly. "I hate him! I hate him! Take him away from me please," she cries. Castle's depiction is almost the opposite, as he limits the dialogue of Maria (Nira Monsour) to the bare minimum. When her character is first introduced into the narrative, she frequently smiles, but rarely speaks. As Pietro is presented to Maria, she turns away not in hatred, but in pain from the surging fever that will eventually claim her life. In time, Isaac looks after the orphan, and he, too, meets his demise earlier than expected. But his death is drastically different than that of Maria's.

Castle's depiction of Isaac's fate is less graphic and less theological than that of Yerby's. He omits the novel's horrendous details of Isaac's hanging corpse, and also avoids any mention of the religious faith to which the dead man adhered. In the film, when Pietro first discovers the body, the audience's view is limited. Several corpses, each one fully clothed, hang from the trees. Isaac can be seen from the shoulders down, with his back to the audience. In the novel, and after presenting the victim in a naked, upside down position, Yerby writes, "His belly was ripped open, so that his entrails dangled." Furthermore, Isaac's faith is an issue in the novel, but not in the film. He is introduced as "the Jew" before his name initially appears in print. During the Crusades, the Jewish people often found themselves subjected to attacks by Christians and Muslims. Yerby essentially made it a point to expose the anti-Semitism of the era. With Castle's film, discrimination amongst its characters is apparent primarily due to social class. Anti-Semitism is avoided altogether, as the word "Judaism," or any other form of it, is never spoken. Actions sometimes speak louder than words. But such is not the case with Yerby's writing.

In the film, Zenobia's physical assault on her master, Haroun (Leonard Penn), is not as violent as it is in the novel. The incident occurs around the time of Pietro's capture by the Saracens. As punishment for the assault, a guard is ordered to whip Zenobia. Haroun, looking on, is more surprised than angry when Pietro, who cannot bear to watch, tackles the guard to the ground:

> HAROUN: Why do you interfere when this is nothing to you?
>
> PIETRO: What has she done?
>
> HAROUN: This.
>
> Haroun points to a scratch on his cheek, so minor that it is barely visible.
>
> PIETRO: Aw. My heart is touched. A man could die of a great wound like that.
>
> HAROUN: I am not any man. I am Haroun, and the wound was to my pride.

According to Yerby, Pietro is present at the time of Zenobia's assault on Haroun (named Abdullah in the novel). The author writes, "Zenobia's left hand, moving with incredible stealth, closed over the handle of his poniard. She jerked it from the scabbard, and whirled, slashing. Abdullah's dark face opened in a great red line from eartip to the point of his chin." The depiction is graphic. In contrast, Castle's retelling of *The Saracen Blade* is specifically intended for a wide range of theatergoers. And when Zenobia reveals her scarred face to the audience, the imagery simply does not compare to Yerby's vivid description.

From its opening, Disney-like credits (within a colorful storybook) to the closing shot of Pietro and Iolanthe riding towards their new destiny, Castle's picture is essentially a romantic adventure that is not to be taken too seriously. It is quite different from Yerby's original story, which is, among many things, more cerebral than the film. The author infers that Pietro's brain is as "keen as the edge of a Saracen blade." Several details (i.e., historical events, additional characters) were excluded from Castle's film. As was the case for many of his novels, Yerby included extensive footnotes in *The Saracen Blade*. He was not just a novelist; he was an historical novelist whose attention to detail was precise. It is unknown if Yerby saw Castle's film. *The Saracen Blade* was the last of his novels to spawn an adaptation. The issue of discrimination, especially in regard to race, was considered to be a sensitive one by the author. In fact, Yerby was so displeased with the level of racism taking place in the United States that, only a year after the film's release, he moved to Spain and remained there until his death in 1991.

To Castle, *The Saracen Blade* was just another Katzman production. Yet, he described his adherence to the film's production schedule as a "Herculean task." But upon completion of the project, he and his wife, Ellen, were invited to a celebratory dinner at the Montalban residence. The occasion turned out to be rewarding in more ways than one. Because it was there that Castle and Ellen decided to name their firstborn child (a girl) after Montalban's wife, Georgiana.

CHAPTER THIRTY-TWO
THE LAW VS. BILLY THE KID (1954)

The Golden Age of Hollywood was, perhaps, the greatest period in the history of motion pictures. But it was marred by the Hollywood blacklist, a list of entertainers denied employment in the industry based on their association, direct or indirect, with the American Communist Party. It reached its peak in the early 1950s, irrevocably damaging the careers of many. The House Committee on Un-American Activities (HUAC) conducted aggressive investigations on the notion that communism could potentially permeate throughout Hollywood and beyond. Screenwriters, in particular, were a popular target of HUAC. A writer by the name of Bernard Gordon, blacklisted in 1952, fought back when he discreetly accepted an assignment for Columbia Pictures. Using the pseudonym of John T. Williams, Gordon crafted a story about the notorious William H. Bonney, aka Billy the Kid. His script would be the basis for William Castle's next film, *The Law vs. Billy the Kid.*

Bonney (Scott Brady), having killed a man in self-defense, flees to Lincoln County, New Mexico, with his friend, Pat Garrett (James Griffith). A short time later, the two encounter John H. Tunstall (Paul Cavanagh), an English cattleman who is at odds with Tom Watkins (Steve Darrell), the local sheriff. Weeks pass, and Bonney grows close with Nita Maxwell (Betta St. John), Tunstall's niece. Bob Ollinger (Alan Hale Jr.), a hired hand on the ranch, violently attacks Bonney out of jealousy. He is discharged, and quickly reports to Watkins that his former employer is harboring a fugitive wanted for murder. The sheriff's posse confronts Tunstall, who is mistakenly killed by a deputy. Watkins attempts to conceal the truth behind Tunstall's death by claiming that the deputy fired his weapon in self-defense. But Bonney is a witness to the incident. He quickly tracks down, and kills, the deputy. Governor Lew Wallace (Otis Garth) appoints Garrett as the new sheriff, believing it will increase the chances of taking Bonney safely into custody. He does not intend to punish Watkins, but he will pardon Bonney if the ensuing trial results in a conviction. Nita persuades Bonney to surrender so that they may have a future together. He agrees, but soon encounters Watkins and Ollinger at a local cantina. Bonney kills Watkins in self-defense, and then flees to a remote cabin. Garrett apprehends his old friend following a brief shootout. But Bonney eventually escapes from jail. He immediately confronts and kills Ollinger at a nearby hotel, then flees to Nita's home. The two make plans to escape from New Mexico by crossing the border into Mexico. But Garrett arrives on the scene and kills Bonney, thus ending the manhunt.

In order to complete his script, Bernard Gordon enlisted the help of Janet and Philip Stevenson, friends who had also been blacklisted by the government. The Stevensons had recently written a play about Billy the Kid, and it was their ideas on which Gordon's script was based. As a result, the story is set entirely in New Mexico and focuses on the latter part of Bonney's life. Its inclusion of John Tunstall is noteworthy, as historians have often debated his existence. Some claim he was just a myth. Many films pertaining to Billy the Kid have been produced, but Castle's was the first of several to include Tunstall. The Englishman's presence is significant because of its impact on the narrative. Through Tunstall, Bonney is unexpectedly introduced to different people and is subsequently exposed to different situations. In essence, *The Law vs. Billy the Kid* is a love story. And Nita Maxwell, an elegant ring, and Bob Ollinger validate Castle's portrayal of Bonney as a hapless romantic.

The character of Nita Maxwell is purely fictitious, and without her, the audience would most likely regard Billy the Kid as nothing more than an impassioned killer. Based on her relation to Tunstall, she is the representation of a prosperous future. After living on the ranch for several weeks, Bonney is presented with an offer:

> TUNSTALL: I've never seen a man work so hard, or take so many chances. You're ambitious, aren't you?
>
> BONNEY: Well, maybe it's just I found a place to hang my hat.
>
> TUNSTALL: Yes, of course.
>
> Bonney observes Nita approaching from the distance. She walks up a hill towards the ranch as Tunstall continues to speak.

TUNSTALL: But, you know...you could raise a loan to start a small ranch. I might be able to help, if you'd make up your mind about the future.

BONNEY (watching Nita): That's what I keep thinking about, Mr. Tunstall. The future.

The following scene depicts Bonney and Nita riding on a pretend, horse-drawn carriage along an imaginary New York City street. It is clear that, contrary to the historical Billy the Kid, the ultimate goal of Castle's protagonist is to attain love. In reality, Bonney was not much of a romantic, although he was rumored to have been friendly with several Latinas during his time in New Mexico. In regard to the film, his ties to the Latin American culture are evident not through its women, but instead, through his relationship with the local business owners.

Miguel Bolanos (Martin Garralaga), a jeweler affectionately referred to as "Tio," provides Bonney with a ring that is intended for Nita. During the Christmas celebration at the Maxwell residence, the audience is afforded the opportunity to see the ring serve its true purpose. Courtesy of Garrett, Bonney is given a minute alone with Nita. She is of the belief that he desires a gun in order to escape, but he is not looking to acquire a firearm. Bonney simply wants Nita to love him. The ring, having been in his possession for a lengthy period of time, is finally placed on her finger, and it fits perfectly. Bonney's rejection of the gun, and subsequent presentation of the ring, romantically uplifts an otherwise gruff figure of the American Old West. The historical Billy the Kid was rarely seen without a firearm and was not often seen with women. To reiterate, the ultimate goal of Castle's protagonist is Nita, and the ring is a direct symbol of their bond. But even the strongest of relationships occasionally happen upon unforeseen obstacles.

Ollinger will stop at nothing to ensure that Bonney and Nita are kept apart from each other. The clear motive for his actions is jealousy, and a drastic chain of events begins with Ollinger's pummeling of Bonney. Tunstall wastes no time in discharging the former. But Ollinger complains to Watkins. The posse arrives and Tunstall is killed, thus setting the stage for the remainder of the film. Set on revenge, Bonney gradually digs himself into a deeper hole. Garrett, as sheriff, forms a group of deputies. Ollinger, still angry about his lost opportunities with Nita, demands to be deputized so that he may have a chance to kill his so-called rival. He becomes a deputy, but is unable to fulfill his objective. In short, Bonney and Nita's love cannot be deterred by Ollinger's jealous nature. Yet, in order to thrive, every love story needs its share of conflict. And without Ollinger, Castle's film would simply be devoid of such conflict.

At the time of his portrayal of John Tunstall, Paul Cavanagh was sixty-five years old. The historical Tunstall, however, was only twenty-four years old when he was killed. Yet, Castle may have started a trend, because later films such as 1958's *The Left Handed Gun* and 1988's *Young Guns* also featured older actors in the role of Tunstall. In regard to *The Law vs. Billy the Kid*, an older Tunstall is ideal. If he were much younger, Nita would either be an infant, or not exist altogether.

Betta St. John's performance as Nita Maxwell marked the final time the actress would appear in a Castle picture. Just a few months earlier, the two had worked together on *The Saracen Blade*. Scott Brady and Alan Hale Jr., too, would perform for Castle for the last time in *The Law vs. Billy the Kid*. Both went on to have amazing careers. Brady made his final big screen appearance, ironically, as a sheriff in 1984's *Gremlins*. The film's director, Joe Dante, grew up idolizing Castle. And his collaboration with Brady was, perhaps, a simple twist of fate.

CHAPTER THIRTY-THREE
MASTERSON OF KANSAS (1955)

A couple of months after Columbia Pictures wrapped production on *The Law vs. Billy the Kid*, William Castle began work on yet another Western. Again, the main character of the film was to be based on a real-life figure of the American Old West. However, unlike an immoral Billy the Kid, Castle's new protagonist, William Barclay "Bat" Masterson, would find himself on the right side of the law serving as a Kansas sheriff. Along to join the battle were a couple of gunfighters with all too familiar names. *Masterson of Kansas*, released in January of 1955, marked the first time that the historical figures of Masterson, Doc Holliday, and Wyatt Earp were portrayed together in a film. Their onscreen presence would aim to electrify audiences across the country.

Masterson (George Montgomery), sheriff of Ford County, stands his ground as Holliday (James Griffith), his longtime nemesis, arrives in Dodge City to do some gambling. Before either can fire a shot at the other, Earp (Bruce Cowling), a federal marshal, intervenes. Masterson and Holliday put aside their differences upon learning that Amos Merrick (John Maxwell), a peacemaking friend of the Indians, is wanted for the murder of a high-ranking military officer. Merrick is eventually tried in a court of law and sentenced to death. Earp takes him into custody. They depart for Hays City, where the execution, only two days away, is to take place. Charlie Fry (William Henry), a powerful cattleman who is the true murderer, framed Merrick because the latter was planning to grant a sizable chunk of land to the Indians. Fry, deeming the land to be valuable for grazing purposes, persuaded an accomplice, Clay Bennett (David Bruce), to lie at the trial. Bennett testified that he saw Merrick pull the trigger, thus firing the fatal shot. Masterson believes Merrick to be innocent and embarks on a quest to prove it. Fry becomes privy to the operation and unsuccessfully persuades Holliday to kill Masterson. He then forms a vigilante committee to attack the stagecoach in which Merrick is traveling. Holliday decides to follow Masterson on his quest. Shortly after the stagecoach is ambushed, both men arrive on the scene to quell the attack. Masterson tracks down Bennett in the nearby town of Quolari. Fry's plan is exposed. In Hays City, Merrick prepares to be lynched. But Masterson, Holliday, and Earp enter town to stop the execution. A gun battle ensues, and Fry is killed in the process.

As *Masterson of Kansas* begins, an unseen narrator makes reference to three specific Native American tribes of the Midwest: Comanche, Kiowa, and Cheyenne. An informal doctrine, sometimes referred to as the "rule of three," proposes that things (i.e., people, states of being) presented in a quantity of three are more powerful than any other number of things. Perhaps, it sometimes rings true, because the narrator then speaks of the tribes' success in achieving a peace treaty with the Whites. But the rule also tends to have negative connotations. As Castle shifts the focus to Dodge City, the mood becomes tense. Masterson, arguably the city's most popular inhabitant, tells Merrick's daughter, Amy (Nancy Gates), that a man in his boots is one of three things: hard, fast, or dead. Yet, Holliday and Earp essentially add strength to Masterson's fight against the malicious Fry. And together, the three are a powerful force. However, the beginning, middle, and ending of the film reveal that the mere presence of Wyatt Earp is vital to the narrative's success.

Curtains and concealment.

Earp's first appearance, transpiring shortly after the film begins, is perfectly timed as he abruptly breaks the tension between Masterson and Holliday. Castle's earlier inclusion of

Earp's brother, Virgil (Donald Murphy), is effective in developing the federal marshal's character. Immediately following the opening narration, Virgil is seen pleading with Masterson to avoid a confrontation with Holliday. He speaks of his brother's impending arrival. There is talk of Earp's rapport with Holliday. It is also made clear that Earp served as the local sheriff prior to Masterson, who admits that his predecessor is "as fine a man as ever wore a badge." But Masterson, determined to stop Holliday, eventually leaves Virgil standing in the road with a dumbfounded look on his face. Although their conversation is brief, the audience becomes privy to Earp's influence over Dodge City. Minutes later, when Earp prevents Masterson and Holliday from killing each other, a sense of reason is temporarily attained. It soon becomes clear that the three have other fish to fry. Merrick is convicted of murder, and the true killer remains on the loose. Furthermore, issues of a more serious nature arise shortly after Merrick's stagecoach departs for Hays City.

Halfway through the film, the mystery of Earp's location abounds as Fry's gang of vigilantes closes in on Merrick. Castle's direction of the ambush evokes suspense primarily due to the portrayal of earlier events. Although Earp is present when Merrick prepares to leave for Hays City, it is uncertain whether he boards the stagecoach or not. Castle shifts the focus away from the federal marshal as Amy approaches her father to kiss him goodbye. He then transitions to a wide shot of the Dodge City street as the stagecoach gradually makes its exit. Earp is nowhere to be seen. Instead, a group of people, including Masterson and Amy, look on as Merrick is taken away. The average theatergoer might conclude that Earp boarded the stagecoach. However, from the point of departure to the height of the ambush, there are several scenes centered on the traveling caravan, and Earp is notably absent from all of them. Later, as the vigilantes launch their attack, Castle transitions to a close-up shot of Merrick. He appears to be the lone occupant of the cabin. Earp, in actuality, is sitting next to Merrick, but Castle does not reveal this to the audience. If we believe Merrick to be without the protection of a powerful and well-respected federal marshal, thus placing him in an extremely vulnerable state, the film's suspense will increase. The stagecoach narrowly evades the barrage of gunfire, and a dramatic chase ensues. The pursuit concludes at Ransom Pass a short time later. It is at this point that Earp finally makes an appearance as he emerges from the cabin to fight the vigilantes. The mood of the film quickly swings in a different direction. Especially since, seconds later, Masterson and Holliday arrive on the scene to join Earp in his battle. Both men appear graceful as they fire their guns at Fry's vigilantes from atop the mountain, while Earp fights to control the situation from the bottom of the pass. Many of the fighters stare at Masterson and Holliday, who are known to be each other's sworn enemy, in awe. The image is quite a spectacle, but it is not the only time of the narrative that the two join forces.

During the film's climax, Masterson and Holliday find themselves in a dire situation, but a helping hand from Earp validates the aforementioned "rule of three." Castle's productive use of a backward-tracking shot captures the trio with eloquence, thus making it the most vivid image of the film. At the gallows of Hays City, a mob forces Merrick closer towards the rope's noose. They abruptly pause as Masterson, Holliday, and Earp can be seen approaching from a distance. Castle then transitions to a backward-tracking shot of the three as they press forward with confidence. It is an intimidating sight, not just for the audience, but for those who remain on the gallows. Although the vigilantes clearly outnumber their opponents, most of them, along with Merrick, run for cover. A gunfight ensues. In the aftermath, only those foolish enough to challenge the powerful trio, namely Fry, are dead.

Doc Holliday, Bat Masterson, and Wyatt Earp establish their presence in Hays City.

Masterson of Kansas marked the third and final collaboration between Castle and George Montgomery. Three years after the film's release, a television series entitled *Bat Masterson* premiered on NBC. Gene Barry, who played the lead in Castle's *The Houston Story*, was cast as Masterson. The show's outlook was not as serious as that of the film, often relying on humor to support the storylines of select episodes. It is fondly remembered by many.

In regard to *Masterson of Kansas*, Montgomery's portrayal of the hard-nosed sheriff was not to be forgotten. On a spring afternoon in 1985, he made a special appearance at the Civic and Cultural Center in Brea, California. Montgomery was there to sign autographs for those he considered "old friends." Many in attendance reflected back on the nostalgia of his Westerns, fondly remembering a period of time when the Saturday matinee held a special meaning for theatergoers. Fortunately for Castle, he, too, was able to contribute to what many consider to be a special era in film history.

CHAPTER THIRTY-FOUR
THE AMERICANO (1955)

In July of 1953, Budd Boetticher, an acclaimed director of Westerns, journeyed to Brazil's Mato Grosso Plateau to shoot his next picture: *The Americano*. Murphy's Law, which states, "Anything that can go wrong will go wrong," was in full effect as the film crew encountered one problem after another. Weather conditions were unfavorable as well as untimely. Local financiers began to lose faith. And after two months of mediocre progress, the production shut down and most of the crew returned to the United States. But there was no set date as to when shooting would recommence. A majority of *The Americano* had yet to be filmed, and many wondered if the project would ever be completed.

RKO Radio Pictures eventually took over the reins of the production. It was not until the summer of 1954, however, that filming resumed in the states. Consequently, Boetticher decided to abandon the project in favor of a new medium, as television's *The Public Defender* was in need of a talented director. RKO searched earnestly for his replacement, and it was simply a matter of time before William Castle was hired to finish what Boetticher had started.

Sam Dent (Glenn Ford), a Texas cattleman, travels to Brazil to deliver three Brahman bulls. Upon arrival, he discovers Barbossa, the intended recipient, to be dead of a gunshot wound. Dent decides to deliver the bulls to the ranch of Bento Hermany (Frank Lovejoy), Barbossa's business partner. Manuel Silvera (Cesar Romero), a local "detective," accompanies Dent on the long journey to the ranch, but disappears en route during a stampede. Hermany encounters Dent a short time later and agrees to purchase the bulls for the original sale price of $25 thousand. As the "Americano" embarks on his return to Texas, he is ambushed and robbed of his money. Hermany believes the missing Silvera to be the culprit. He orders his foreman, Cristino (Rodolfo Hoyos Jr.), to storm the hut of Tuba Masero (George Navarro), a known associate of Silvera's. Dent happens upon the raid. Cristino murders Masero. Later, Silvera comes out of hiding. He and Marianna (Ursula Thiess), Masero's employer, meet with Dent to expose

Hermany as a criminal. Key information is disclosed. Cristino, under orders, robbed Dent. Hermany murdered Barbossa, and he intends to amass a significant amount of land, targeting Marianna's ranch as his next acquisition. Dent is reluctant to accept what is true. Despite becoming intimate with Marianna, he returns to the employment of Hermany. Brazilian authorities charge Dent with Masero's murder. In love with the "Americano," Marianna fights to ensure a fair trial, even if it means losing her ranch. Dent learns that Hermany concocted the false murder charge. Cristino confesses to killing Masero. The authorities storm Hermany's estate. Gunfire is exchanged, and Dent shoots Hermany dead.

Glenn Ford and Cesar Romero.

The Americano features its share of picturesque scenery (i.e., majestic sunrises, cascading waterfalls), as approximately one-third of the filming transpired in Brazil. To reiterate, Castle was not hired until the production relocated to the United States, making it somewhat difficult for viewers to determine which scenes were filmed under his direction. But Frank Lovejoy and Ursula Thiess were also hired as replacements. Coincidentally, the characters they portray, Hermany and Marianna, are introduced into the narrative within minutes of each other. Hence, any scene including one (or both) of them, in theory, was directed by Castle. And it soon becomes clear which of the two characters warrants more attention. Of Marianna, Hermany remarks, "Que mulher," meaning "much woman!" The women of *The Americano*, although characterized as sex symbols, possess an empowering nature, as seen with Marianna's emergence from a lake, the serving and consumption of alcoholic beverages, and the most enchanting of tunes.

As Marianna bathes in a lake, she uses her sex appeal as a means to deceive Dent. Manipulated by the element of suspense, he has no choice but to temporarily abandon his morals. Marianna is able to convince Dent, who assumes the role of voyeur, that she is naked underneath the surface of the water:

MARIANNA: Please turn your head while I get out.

DENT: Asking me to be a gentleman, huh?

MARIANNA: I ask too much?

DENT: You're asking quite a lot.

MARIANNA: Listen, I have no intention of staying in this pool all day while you ogle. I warn you . . . I'm coming out.

DENT: I'm ready if you are.

MARIANNA: Sure?

DENT: Sure.

Just then, a sulphur-crested cockatoo, which has borne witness to the entire exchange, emits a raucous call in eager anticipation of what is to follow. Marianna slowly emerges from the lake in a cream-colored bathing suit. And it quickly becomes clear to the devastated Dent that she has had the upper hand all along. Marianna's independent stature is what enables her to succeed in a male-dominated society. But she is not the only empowering woman of the film.

The beautiful Teresa (Abbe Lane), a supposed employee of Hermany's ranch, exhibits a high degree of control when serving beer to Dent and Hermany. Her actions essentially suggest that she is insusceptible to Hermany's influence. He makes the request for beer, specifically asking for "two glasses." A short time later, however, Teresa returns with three glasses of the frothy libation. She quickly serves Dent and Hermany, then takes the third glass for herself and exits the scene. Teresa's confident demeanor is an indicator of what is to come. Because it is soon revealed that she is loyal to Silvera, posing as Hermany's servant in order to

The director with Sam Wiesenthal and Ursula Thiess.

discover the truth behind Barbossa's murder. And her character is significant to the narrative in more ways than one.

Later, Teresa entrances Dent with her singing. The title of the song, which is that of Castle's film, alludes to a sexual magnetism between men and women. Dent, instantly intrigued by the tune, leafs through an English-Portuguese dictionary in order to understand the lyrics. Teresa puts him at ease, explaining that the song is about a homesick "Americano" who visits Brazil. According to the lyrics, the traveler meets a beautiful Brazilian girl, falls in love, and no longer yearns to return home. Dent fantasizes that it "could happen," and Teresa confidently assures him that everybody will "fall in love someday." Shortly thereafter, we learn that Teresa and Silvera are lovers. Again, she sings the same song. But this time, she directs her attention to Silvera. Dent, who is nearby, becomes captivated by the music. He sets his sights on Marianna. Teresa begins to dance. The mood becomes exotic, and Dent's attraction to Marianna intensifies as they kiss. For the Americano, fantasy has essentially become reality.

After seeing the production of his film through to the end, Castle celebrated the premiere of *The Americano* in New York City on January 19, 1955. The film's script is entertaining for several reasons, but specifically because it keeps the audience in suspense. Initially, we tend to question whether Silvera is Dent's ally or enemy. But as the narrative progresses, Silvera's role becomes clear. Naturally, the contributions of Budd Boetticher should not go unrecognized, as his initial direction of Glenn Ford and Cesar Romero is what most likely established a dynamic connection between the two performers in the first place.

In regard to music, Xavier Cugat, the famous Spanish-American musician, composed and supervised the film's score. He was married to Abbe Lane at the time of production (although the two would later divorce in 1963).

For Castle, the overall experience was noteworthy. *The Americano* marked his second, and final, collaboration with Ursula Thiess. It was also the only film he directed for RKO. A couple of months after production wrapped, Castle was back with Columbia Pictures. But this time, he was on location in The Big Easy, preparing for a challenge unlike any other he had ever faced.

CHAPTER THIRTY-FIVE
NEW ORLEANS UNCENSORED (1955)

In 1943, shortly before directing *The Chance of a Lifetime*, William Castle was summoned by the United States Office of War Information (OWI) to work on a special project. During World War II, the OWI was established as a means to promote patriotism through radio broadcasts, posters, and documentary films. Castle's assignment was to direct *Black Marketing*, a propaganda short warning Americans against the purchase of illicit goods. Throughout his career, he rarely affiliated himself with documentaries. But in 1954, he was approached by Columbia Pictures to direct *New Orleans Uncensored*, an exposé into the longshore workers' struggles with organized crime. The film is similar to a documentary in that it depicts a true story. In addition, prominent New Orleans figures, such as Fire Chief Howard L. Dey, appear as themselves. A narrator, in typical documentary fashion, presents the waterfront city to the audience within the film's opening minutes. *New Orleans Uncensored* has often been categorized as film noir, but its documentary-style qualities set it apart from the rest of Castle's films.

United States Senator Allen J. Ellender, of Louisiana, cautions the audience against "waterfront felons," encouraging "public-spirited citizens to root them out" before the felons' infiltration becomes widespread. Meanwhile, ex-Navy man Dan Corbett (Arthur Franz) arrives in New Orleans to purchase a boat and start a timber hauling business. As a means to earn supplemental income, he becomes a stevedore under the supervision of Joe Reilly (William Henry), the dock foreman. Before long, Corbett's suspicions arise, as select cargo is purposely misplaced and concealed. Reilly follows orders from Floyd "Zero" Saxon (Michael Ansara), a powerful racketeer whose stevedore operation is a front for his criminal activities. Corbett becomes acquainted with Reilly's wife, Marie (Beverly Garland). She expresses deep concern over her husband's growing involvement in his work. Reilly aspires to launch his own stevedoring company. But Saxon has him killed because he knows too much about Saxon's racketeering business.

Later, Corbett discovers a group of government-impounded crates to be engulfed in flames. He makes an arduous attempt to save the cargo, but fails. Saxon, looking to benefit from the incident, publicly hails Corbett as a hero and offers him Reilly's old job. Scrappy Durant (Stacy Harris), Marie's brother, attempts to warn Corbett against Saxon. But he, too, is killed. Corbett arranges a private meeting with Wayne Brandon (Judge Walter B. Hamlin), a chief administrator for the Port of New Orleans. A secret plan to trace Saxon's "lost" cargo is set in motion. The racketeering operation is exposed, and Saxon is killed during a shootout with Corbett.

New Orleans Uncensored is a clear example of film as propaganda, but it also offers a scenic look at the age-old city. Castle begins his film by presenting the audience with a map of New Orleans, which remains in the background as the opening credits are displayed. The subsequent narration speaks of a place that is rich in history, affectionately referring to New Orleans as the "Mistress of the Mississippi" and "Queen of the Gulf." Notable attractions of the past and present, such as Pontchartrain Beach and the French Quarter, are prominently featured throughout the narrative. But the city's inhabitants, in retrospect, are the force behind its appealing image. And the characters of *New Orleans Uncensored*, be they boxers, swindlers, or bureaucrats, are a symbolic representation of the city's storied history.

The film's opening scene, during which a group of stevedores literally fight for their jobs, is somewhat of a testament to the hard work and dedication of the region's professional boxers, and it also foreshadows Corbett's foray into the sport of boxing. But without the character of Durant, Castle's subplot cannot flourish. As coach of the longshoremen's union boxing team, Durant becomes a mentor to Corbett. A special bond between the two gradually forms. One particular scene, set within a boxing gymnasium at St. Mary's CYO, depicts an energetic Corbett pummeling a punching bag. Durant then approaches with a familiar companion:

DURANT: Hello, Danny.

CORBETT (smiling): Hiya, Scrappy.

Corbett immediately removes his right boxing glove and shakes Durant's hand.

DURANT: Danny, I want you to meet a friend of mine. Pete Herman. Pete's the ex-bantamweight champ of the world. Pete, this is Danny Corbett.

PETE HERMAN: Any friend of Scrappy's a friend of mine.

CORBETT: Glad to know you, Pete.

As Corbett finishes shaking hands with Pete Herman, Ralph Dupas, another boxer, enters the picture.

RALPH DUPAS: Hi, Pete. Hi, Scrappy.

Durant and Pete Herman greet Ralph Dupas in unison.

DURANT: Ralph, do you know Danny Corbett?

RALPH DUPAS: No, I don't believe I do.

DURANT: Danny, this is Ralph Dupas.

The two exchange pleasantries in what many would consider to be a memorable scene. At the time of production, Pete Herman was an established champion in the world of boxing. Ralph Dupas was an up-and-coming prospect who would go on to claim the light middleweight championship in 1963. Both men, in essence, were proud of their hometown. Yet, because of Durant, *New Orleans Uncensored* rightfully pays homage to a cherished pastime of the city. He is connected with the big time boxers, and he is also the one to guide Corbett in his newfound passion. But Durant's estrangement from his former boxing manager is what ultimately costs him his life.

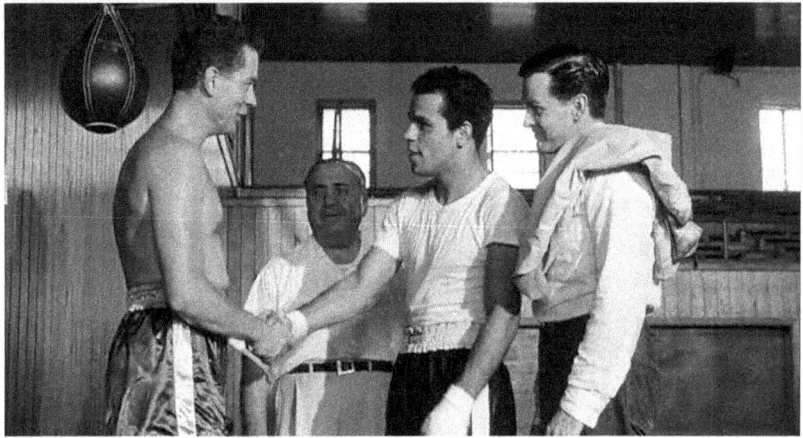

Arthur Franz, Pete Herman, Ralph Dupas, and Stacy Harris.

Saxon, portrayed as a modern-day Jean Lafitte, essentially continues the legendary pirate's tradition of plotting merciless killings and swindling hapless victims out of their belongings. Castle's picture contains subtle, as well as not-so-subtle, references to the French buccaneer of so many years ago. The opening narration lures the viewer into "the port of the legendary Jean Lafitte," and his name is mentioned from time to time throughout the film. But the name of Castle's antagonist is especially noteworthy because of its striking similarity to that of a prominent New Orleans writer. Lyle Saxon, who passed away several years prior to Castle's film, was well versed in the history of Jean Lafitte. And his novel, *Lafitte the Pirate*, is partially set in New Orleans. The city, also known as The Big Easy, essentially offered "an inevitable temptation to criminals" such as Zero Saxon and Jean Lafitte.

The focus of Castle's film is on waterfront crime, and where there are criminals, there are bureaucrats. Joseph L. Scheuering, Superintendent of the New Orleans Police Department, appears as himself. Appropriately enough, he enters the picture a short time after Reilly's death, which is a point of the narrative when the threat of Saxon's racket becomes critical. Scheuering is seen in his office with union president Al Chittenden, Wayne Brandon, and a longshoreman who is undergoing interrogation. Hanging on the wall is a map of New Orleans, the city Scheuering has sworn to protect. He acknowledges the impending danger to his forty-two mile waterfront, and is willing to summon an army if necessary. Instead, during a later meeting, Corbett becomes a

Michael Ansara, Mike Mazurki, and Frankie Ray.

self-declared whistleblower as he exposes Saxon's operation to Brandon. Naturally, Scheuering is present at the meeting, and it is his involvement that ultimately seals Saxon's fate. Sadly, the tenacious superintendent passed away in 1968, but his legacy continues to thrive within The Big Easy. Scheuering Security Service, Inc., founded around the time of the film's release, has persevered through the years due to its assertive stance against crime.

New Orleans Uncensored premiered in March of 1955. Coincidentally, the city's tourism sector underwent substantial growth in the years following the film's release. Castle, being on location, was able to capture the vibrant spirit of New Orleans, especially through his rhythmic montage of the city's nightlife.

The film is also noteworthy for the character of Alma Mae (Helene Stanton), Saxon's on-again off-again mistress. As a complicated and somewhat devious woman, she is the counterpart of Marie. The two women appear together in the film only once (shortly after Corbett is offered Reilly's old job) and do not engage in conversation with each other. But upon the narrative's conclusion, it is clear that Corbett has chosen Marie over Alma. And closure is essentially attained as the narrator proudly declares that an "ex-sailor, trying to buy a boat, happened to be the key to breaking the waterfront dictatorship of Zero Saxon, which had threatened the position of historic New Orleans as the second greatest port of the United States."

"Looks like my night to buy the drinks!"

CHAPTER THIRTY-SIX
THE GUN THAT WON THE WEST (1955)

From 1866 to 1868, an armed conflict known as Red Cloud's War occurred between the United States and several Native American tribes. A few years prior to its outbreak, gold had been discovered in Montana. The U.S., eager to construct an optimal route to the treasure, fought for control of the Powder River Country in northern Wyoming. Red Cloud, leader of a vast Sioux tribe, refused to surrender the territory. He served as such a formidable opponent that the U.S. would eventually name the war after him.

In William Castle's *The Gun That Won the West*, the story of the war is retold with an assortment of fictitious characters. Yet, some of the historical figures involved in the conflict, including Red Cloud himself, are also represented in the film. Castle's narrative evolves around the atrocities of the war, but also pays heed to important character relationships that develop throughout the story.

"Dakota" Jack Gaines (Richard Denning), the star of a prominent Wild West show, suffers from alcoholism. His wife, Maxine "Max" Gaines (Paula Raymond), struggles to keep him on his feet. Jim Bridger (Dennis Morgan), a friend with whom Gaines served in the army, is often forced to replace the troubled star so that the show does not suffer. One evening following a performance, Bridger is visited by two high-ranking military officers bearing important news. Colonel Carrington (Roy Gordon), the former superior officer of Gaines and Bridger, supervises the construction of forts along the Bozeman Trail in Wyoming and fears the Sioux may attack. Gaines and Bridger have had friendly dealings with the natives in the past, and Carrington believes both men may be influential in obtaining a new treaty with the tribe. In case negotiations become hostile, an advanced Springfield rifle has been developed to thwart any attack. Max convinces Bridger to abandon the show and go west, hoping that a change in lifestyle will lead to Gaines's permanent sobriety. But a meeting with Red Cloud (Robert Bice) goes awry when an inebriated Gaines, attempting to scare the natives, openly boasts of the rifle's power. The war begins. Carrington eventually orders Bridger to lead a cavalry of troops on an expedition deep into Sioux territory. A reluctant Gaines stays behind, but Max, who has lost faith in her husband, decides to accompany the men. She finds herself becoming more attracted to Bridger with each day that passes. He rejects her advances, deducing that a relationship between the two will simply complicate matters. To the surprise of many, Gaines becomes sober. Max proudly takes notice. The war continues. Max and Gaines eventually depart the fort to begin a new life together.

The first image of *The Gun That Won the West* reveals a map of Red Cloud's Country, indicating that Castle's forthcoming narrative will evolve around the famous war. However, the conflict is more infamous than famous, because it was one of the few wars during which U.S. forces were defeated. Hence, Castle faced a challenge with the direction of his film, because it was imperative that he avoid the alienation of his audience. In 1955, a majority of theatergoers did not want to watch Indians triumph over cowboys. Castle essentially placed more of a priority on character development than Red Cloud's War. The war is prevalent throughout the film, but its effect on Gaines, instead of its outcome, is central to the plot, as is evident through Gaines's assumed sobriquet, surreptitious friendship with Red Cloud, and life-changing transformation.

Castle's opening montage features a journey from one east coast city to the next, and the sobriquet of "Dakota," visible on numerous show posters, not only foreshadows what is to come with the westward trek, it also hints at Gaines's ties to the Sioux nation. Castle does not reveal how the nickname was earned, but Dakota was the name of a Sioux sub-tribe that fought against the U.S. in Red Cloud's War. Gaines's sobriquet is popular with his fans. And as *The Gun That Won the West* begins, the first line of dialogue, in which a Washington general declares that "West meets East," indicates that Gaines and his fellow cast members have roots elsewhere in the country. Not only does Gaines have strong ties to the West, he is much closer with the Sioux than we initially realize.

A twist in the film's plot is unveiled when we learn of a surreptitious friendship between Gaines and Red Cloud. The former allows himself to be captured by Afraid of Horses (Michael Morgan), Red Cloud's second in command, thus leading to a noteworthy reunion. A demonstration of the gun is displayed, and Red

Cloud then realizes that Gaines, his old friend, is trying to warn him of the potential bloodshed that is to come. Up to this point of the narrative, the audience is led to believe that Gaines, prior to becoming a showman, engaged in friendly encounters with the Sioux. However, there is never any indication of a personal bond between Gaines and Red Cloud. Furthermore, as both characters meet for the first time during the film, Gaines is belligerent and cannot stop shouting at his counterpart about the new gun that will supposedly "chase [Red Cloud's] whole nation into a hole in the ground." Yet, the alcohol is doing the talking, and Gaines is simply not himself. Their old friendship is eventually revealed to the audience. And the second meeting between the two is more positive in the sense that we see Gaines for who he really is.

"Did you come to warn me of this new gun because you once were my friend?"

Red Cloud's War forces Gaines to make a positive, life-changing transformation from an uncaring, passionless drunk to a thoughtful, likeable hero. As the war progresses, Max leaves Gaines in his miserable state, departing the fort to join Bridger and the rest of the cavalry. One evening, in perhaps the most memorable scene of the film, Max and Bridger converse in the moonlight:

BRIDGER: You should be sleeping.

MAX: It's like being home again. I think, perhaps, I thought the sky would've changed and the plains, and even the way the night smells so clean.

BRIDGER: Change? Even people don't change for the most part. Go a little deeper, they're what they are.

MAX: Even Jack? (eyes Bridger up and down) Do you think I was wrong to leave him?

Bridger does not reply, but instead, gazes towards the ground.

MAX: And that bothers you. Now, you don't want me around.

BRIDGER: We're not heading for the fort. We're going back into the woods. Some of the women might want to be going back to Laramie.

MAX: I won't be one of them.

BRIDGER: Max, what do you want? Do you want me to make love to you?

Max avoids eye contact, barely reacting to such a bold and forward question.

BRIDGER: That'd just mess up things worse. Go back now.

MAX: I'm sorry, Jim. Going back isn't going to make things work for Jack and me. It'll take more than that and maybe there is nothing. I don't know, but I'm going to find out.

BRIDGER: Alright. I said all I could.

Max has made up her mind. She will not go back to the fort in an attempt to win Gaines's affection simply because all efforts have been exhausted. It is the war that causes Max to follow Bridger, and hence, bring Gaines to the harsh realization that he is on the verge of permanent devastation. The war, however, offers Gaines a purpose in life, and with that, he summons the strength to rekindle his relationship with Max. Shortly thereafter, the film's narrative concludes without revealing the war's outcome.

Red Cloud's War formally came to an end with the signing of the Treaty of Fort Laramie in 1868, declaring the Powder River Country officially closed to all Whites. *The Gun That Won the West*, the final Western to be directed by Castle, does not specifically portray the defeat of U.S. forces. Instead, a closing shot of the film's final battle depicts Bridger and Afraid of Horses hammering it out in the river. The former clearly has the upper hand as he proceeds to defeat his adversary.

Castle then transitions to a cheering crowd of people at Fort Laramie as they celebrate the departure of Max and Gaines, two fictitious characters conceived as a means to complement the historical ones. Red Cloud and Jim Bridger are a part of history, but "Dakota" Jack Gaines exists only on celluloid. And without the character of Gaines, Castle most likely would not have been able to conclude the film, as well as his career in directing Westerns, diplomatically.

Red Cloud's warriors cross the river. Castle, like many directors, made extensive use of stock footage in order to ease the grueling demands of a tight production schedule.

CHAPTER THIRTY-SEVEN
DUEL ON THE MISSISSIPPI (1955)

Gerald Drayson Adams, an ambitious Canadian, found much success after moving to the United States. He broke into the entertainment industry as a literary agent, but eventually tried his hand at writing fiction. Many of his ideas were adapted for the silver screen. By the mid-1950s, Adams had provided the original narrative for over thirty motion pictures. One of his scripts evolved around the plight of the Louisiana sugar plantations during the early nineteenth century. Raiders and pirates, desperate to strike it rich, frequently stole from vulnerable planters. Black markets were formed in order to sell the purloined goods. "But a few courageous planters and their loyal overseers" fought to restore justice to the Mississippi River Delta. Adams's script, *Duel on the Mississippi*, provided William Castle with the opportunity to return to familiar territory. Only a few months had passed since the production of *New Orleans Uncensored*. Yet, with *Duel on the Mississippi*, Castle ventured away from the city and up the great river, directly into the heart of bayou country.

Jules Tulane (John Dehner), a planter, falls victim to a group of raiders known as "the delta men." Over a thousand bags of sugar are stolen from his plantation. Lili Scarlet (Patricia Medina), an accomplice to the crime, seeks redemption. Earlier, Tulane prevented her father, Jacques Scarlet (Ian Keith), from purchasing a local plantation due to his supposed ties to piracy. But Hugo Marat (Warren Stevens), Lili's business partner in the operation of a riverboat casino, is the true criminal. He is the established leader of the delta men. Tulane is in debt to Georges Gabriel (Louis Merrill), a refinery owner. Gabriel unexpectedly sells the loan note to Lili, who demands that Tulane immediately pay its entire amount. Unable to acquiesce, a five-year prison term becomes inevitable. But André (Lex Barker), Tulane's son, agrees to enter into a period of indentured servitude to Lili, thus suspending the sentence. If he loses his life at any time during his servitude, Tulane's debt and sentence will be cancelled. Marat becomes jealous of André, believing Lili will coax her so-called slave into proposing marriage, thus enabling her to become a lady. Later, Gabriel denies selling the loan note to Lili, claiming he had previously sold it to the bank. André suspects otherwise. Marat and Gabriel are eventually revealed to be co-conspirators in the region's thefts, as all stolen sugar passes through the latter's refinery. André discovers looted goods aboard the riverboat. Lili escapes to the Tulane plantation and declares the loan to be paid in full. Marat challenges André to a duel. Tulane and his overseers arrive on the scene and apprehend the delta men. The duel continues on the boat. Marat is dispatched, leaving André and Lili to live in romantic bliss.

The character of Marat, the accepted antagonist of *Duel on the Mississippi*, is intriguing. As he makes his first appearance of the film, he seizes the opportunity to engage in swordplay with a Tulane plantation overseer. Marat's opponent, clearly less experienced in the art of fencing, is defeated within seconds. Lili later chides Marat, claiming he enjoys the mere sight of people who fear his presence. She is aware of his priorities. Marat is more interested in weapons and duels than the day-to-day operations of the Lily Scarlet (the riverboat aptly named after the film's heroine). And his ruthless nature is evident on several occasions, especially during the cold-blooded murder of Gabriel, as the latter is senselessly shot in the back without a chance to defend himself. But despite Marat's reputation as a despicable swindler, he is not as intriguing as another character of the narrative, as Jacques Scarlet entertains from beginning to end. The first impression Scarlet makes on the audience, although amusing, is somewhat mysterious. In addition, the film's characters, especially Lili, do not necessarily appreciate Scarlet despite the extensive knowledge and advice he has to offer in regard to life and human behavior. Nevertheless, he is the only one who understands his daughter's complex personality.

As Scarlet enters the Tulane residence, thus marking his first appearance of the film, he amusingly presents himself as one with shady intentions, but looks can be deceiving. A reference to his immoral past simply adds to the uncertainty of his agenda:

> SCARLET: When President Madison granted full pardon to Lafitte's pirates for their services in the Battle of New Orleans, I left Bastille Bayou and became a lawful citizen.

Scarlet is clearly proud of his involvement in the famous battle that quelled British forces. But based on his overall demeanor, it is difficult to determine if he means well. Scarlet, helping himself to Tulane's brandy as if it is his own, is somewhat arrogant and over-confident in his determination to purchase the plantation. Despite being shunned by his so-called hosts, he is unfazed. The exchange is rather comical. Scarlet knows much about the details of Tulane's debt. In addition, he speaks of Bastille Bayou, the hideout of the delta men. Scarlet exhibits the characteristics of a potential antagonist, but as the narrative progresses, Marat is ultimately accepted as the film's villain. Furthermore, a different side of Scarlet is eventually revealed to the audience.

Lili does not necessarily appreciate her father's outlook on life, as valuable and enriching as it is. She pays little attention to him, and others tend to follow suit. In the courtroom, as Tulane is being sentenced, Scarlet pleads with his daughter to grant an extension to the "old and sick" plantation owner. But Lili ignores her father's advice, preferring to do things her way as she arranges for André to become her servant. A short time later, aboard the riverboat, Scarlet warns Marat that it "is not a good night to talk to Lili." The advice is ignored, thus leading to negative consequences. Marat becomes frustrated when Lili rejects his advances. She storms out of her cabin, heading for the boat's exit. Scarlet asks, "Lili, where are you going?" There is no reply. Scarlet then shrugs his shoulders and does not give the incident another thought simply because he is used to being shunned by his own daughter. But there are others who also pay him little attention. During the fight on the casino floor, Scarlet stands at the bar, casually fiddling with a deck of cards. Suddenly, a bottle of wine sails directly above his head and crashes against the wall. Scarlet barely reacts, pausing briefly to sample the wine's vintage as the melee continues to unfold inches from where he is standing. Regardless of the circumstances, people do not pay much attention to Scarlet, and he is quick to reciprocate such indifference. But when it comes to his daughter, a caring and compassionate nature resurfaces.

Scarlet is the only character of the film who has a general understanding of Lili's complex personality. He frequently compares his daughter with her mother, all while Lili's attraction to André grows stronger. Scarlet makes reference to a sensitive personality. André learns that Lili inherited it from her mother, and he is encouraged to use "extreme patience" at all times. At the Golden Rooster Inn, shortly after André's first duel with Marat, Scarlet fondly reminisces about the first time he met Lili's mother:

> SCARLET: Lili is very much like her mother. Ah, it seems like yesterday. I boarded a Spaniard off Panama, and in the cabin, I found her. Scarlet lips, red hair—
>
> ANDRÉ: —and a temper!
>
> SCARLET: Oh, it was unbelievable!

Scarlet proceeds to show André a set of bite marks on his neck, but Lili intervenes. She does not want to revisit the past. But the scene is significant because Scarlet is beginning to understand that Lili is slowly becoming attached to André. Later, while serving as Marat's prisoners aboard the riverboat, Scarlet helps his daughter escape to the Tulane plantation simply because he understands that the passion he once had for Lili's mother is the same passion André has for Lili. The remainder of the film's events transpires so there can, in fact, be a duel on the Mississippi. In the aftermath of Marat's death, Lili agrees to André's proposal for her to live at the Tulane plantation. Scarlet smiles as he watches the two depart together. He remarks, "Not at all like her mother." As Castle's film concludes, Scarlet comes to the realization that, while Lili has inherited some of her mother's characteristics, his contributions have been just as significant.

Duel on the Mississippi was released in October of 1955. Its opening narration features a voice that is distinctly familiar. Michael Ansara, a frequent collaborator of Castle's, appeared in several of the director's films (i.e., *Slaves of Babylon*, *The Saracen Blade*). But he sometimes served as Castle's narrator. Although Ansara was not officially credited for his narrating efforts, his commanding, majestic voice effectively set the stage for the story's subsequent events. It is fitting that he later engaged in voice acting during the twilight of his career. Despite being affiliated with many productions over the course of several decades, his contributions to Castle and Columbia Pictures remain noteworthy.

CHAPTER THIRTY-EIGHT
THE HOUSTON STORY (1956)

Lee J. Cobb, perhaps best known for his performance as Johnny Friendly in Elia Kazan's *On the Waterfront*, was cast as the lead in William Castle's next picture. Some of the filming took place on location in the "oppressive humidity" of Houston, Texas. The harsh weather took its toll on the cast and crew, and Cobb fatigued easily. One evening, he suffered a heart attack in his hotel room and was rushed to the hospital. A local cardiologist declared that Cobb would be unable to work for months. Sam Katzman decided to replace Cobb with Gene Barry, a relatively unknown television actor at the time. Production on Castle's film, *The Houston Story*, eventually recommenced once the unforeseen obstacle had been overcome. Although Castle did not want to lose the original star of his picture, Katzman's decision would later prove to be beneficial.

Frank Duncan (Barry), an oil driller, falsely identifies a corpse in the Houston morgue as Carrie Hemper, an up-and-coming chorus girl. His actions attract the attention of Gordie Shay (Paul Richards), a nightclub owner with ties to a crime syndicate. Duncan is summoned to the club and discovers that Carrie Hemper is now Zoe Crane (Barbara Hale), but his interest in the singer is trivial. Instead, Duncan persuades Shay to arrange a meeting with Paul Atlas (Edward Arnold), head of the mob's southwest territory. He then proposes a plan to secretly siphon oil from targeted wells in order to sell it at lucrative prices. Atlas accepts the proposal. At first, the operation proves to be successful, but Shay detests Duncan and devises a scheme to frame him. Under Duncan's orders, a supply truck carrying line pipe is hijacked. He specifies that nobody is to be killed. Shay handles the details, but arranges for the deliberate murder of an innocent driller. Emile Constant (John Zaremba), head of the syndicate, becomes livid over the killing because it leads to a full-scale investigation by the authorities. Shay blames Duncan, who then turns the tables when a secret tape recording exposes the former as the culprit. Constant ousts Shay from the organization. Chris Barker (Chris

Alcaide), Shay's henchman, attempts to murder Duncan, but is killed during the fracas. The police, tipped off by Duncan, apprehend Shay after the destruction of two key wells. Atlas is later shot dead while attempting to flee the country. Zoe warns Duncan about the pitfalls of his sudden rise to power. Constant sends two of his associates on a mission to eliminate Duncan. They kill Zoe, but are later shot dead by Duncan at a café. The police arrive on the scene and arrest Duncan before he can skip town.

Approximately thirty minutes into Castle's film, Zoe drives Duncan to his second meeting with Atlas and Shay. Duncan speaks of his imminent success and is unconcerned with those who may be hurt in the process. Zoe asks, "Doesn't anybody mean anything to you?" There is no reply. It is difficult for audiences to empathize with the character of Duncan because he is a callous individual. Lee J. Cobb, fresh off of his performance as the brash Friendly, would have been ideal for the role. And it is unfortunate that his health declined when it did. Nevertheless, Gene Barry's portrayal of Duncan is marked by unrestrained zeal and vehemence. Duncan, the main character of *The Houston Story*, is not a hero, but instead, a villain. And his survival-of-the-fittest mentality, demeanor towards the opposite sex, and deceptive relationship with a childhood friend are worthy of considerable attention.

"Out of all the docks in the world to jump off, she had to pick Houston!"

Duncan's determination to strike it rich is marred by his selfish ambition to climb the ranks of organized crime, regardless of who gets killed in the process. Regrettably, the supply truck hijacking results in the death of an innocent man. Minutes earlier, Duncan is jovial with the truck's occupants when they stop for coffee at the café. Their rapport with each other, undoubtedly formed over the course of many grueling hours together in the oil fields, is solid. Yet, Duncan knowingly puts his former co-workers in danger. He anticipates that Shay will incorporate murder into the operation, which is why the secret tape recording was made. A man is killed, Shay is banished from the combine, and Duncan is promoted. Duncan's survival-of-the-fittest mentality is shameful. But his former co-workers are not the only people for whom he lacks compassion.

Duncan, by nature, is a womanizer, and his lack of higher values when interacting with the opposite sex does not make him a likeable person. He takes much for granted, particularly Madge (Jeanne Cooper), his girlfriend. At one point, Duncan and his fellow drillers arrive at the café for lunch, and a co-worker dares to question his intentions:

> CO-WORKER: You gonna eat today, or play tag with Madge in the kitchen?
> DUNCAN: Watch your language, boy.
>
> A slight smile forms on Duncan's lips as he turns to face the others.
>
> DUNCAN: He's talking about *one* of the women I love!

His demeanor is blunt. Furthermore, the aforementioned scene marks the only time of the film when Duncan appears in his grungy uniform and hard hat, thus enabling the audience to see him as an emotionally hardened, working-class driller instead of the prudent businessman he cannot be. Once inside the café, the character of Madge is introduced into the narrative. She is but a humble waitress, and will do anything for Duncan. The feelings, however, are not entirely mutual. Shortly after his arrival at the café, the two make plans for the evening. But Duncan abruptly cancels on Madge once he learns Shay is out of town. She does not question the sudden change of plans. Madge essentially yearns for Duncan to be successful as long as she can be a part of his life. He is grateful, but his concerns lie elsewhere, as he eventually heads to Galveston in an attempt to seduce Zoe.

Their rendezvous is cut short when Barker catches them in the act. After Duncan is roughed up, he crawls back to Madge, who immediately nurses him back to health. Not only does he take her for granted, he frequently betrays her trust. But the pattern is consequently broken upon the film's conclusion. Because it is Madge who tips off Inspector Gregg (Roy Engel) as to Duncan's whereabouts, ultimately leading to the latter's arrest. Yet, another individual is equally responsible for Duncan's downfall.

Jeanne Cooper and Barbara Hale.

Louie Phelan (Frank Jenks), a childhood friend of Duncan's who is unknowingly lured into a web of deceit, does not waste any time informing Gregg about Constant's "gangsters." Presented as a genuinely honest man, he represents the opposite of his crony.

From the opening scene of *The Houston Story*, Duncan establishes himself as an accustomed liar who will cheat his way through life in order to get what he wants. A solid relationship, especially one that begins during childhood, is supposed to be based on trust. But Duncan establishes Phelan as a fall guy in case their racket is exposed. When the latter phones Gregg, he attempts to shift the focus on Constant, doing whatever he can to protect his friend. But Duncan generally treats Phelan in an inferior manner, distinctly referring to him as a "nice guy" who is "not too smart." Later, Phelan lectures a group of cabbies (former co-workers) about the secret of his success. He claims that those who study and read books can prosper in life. In the end, Phelan is unaffected by the chain of events that lead to Duncan's fate. Hence, an honest man earns a second chance at life, and a dishonest man goes to jail. It is not until Duncan is arrested and the words "THE END" appear on the screen that the audience can attain closure.

Trouble at the rooftop observatory.

The Houston Story is essentially a testament to the cliché that crime does not pay. Castle's direction is noteworthy, especially for a specific moment during the hijacking scene. As Barker creeps out of the bushes to surprise the unsuspecting drillers, a hand-held camera is used to intensify the attack. The camera, positioned at close range to Chris Alcaide's face, moves backward as his character of Barker sneaks towards us. The image is slightly bumpy, as if the audience, too, is treading through the undergrowth. Everything transpires in a matter of seconds, but the timing is accurate.

In addition to Castle's direction, the film's music is also significant. An early scene depicts an elegant and attractive Barbara Hale (of *Perry Mason* fame) as she sings "Put the Blame on Mame." The song pertains to a series of historical disasters. It first became popular with the 1946 theatrical release of *Gilda*, a film noir starring Rita Hayworth.

But direction and music aside, the most remarkable aspect of *The Houston Story* is derived from a single line of dialogue. When Duncan and Shay meet in order to plan the details of the hijacking, the former tells his visitor that he has "a new gimmick." The exchange is ironic considering Castle would later be dubbed as "King of the Gimmicks." Step by step, he moved closer to discovering an entirely different niche in the world of filmmaking.

CHAPTER THIRTY-NINE
URANIUM BOOM (1956)

During the mid-1950s, Sam Katzman launched Clover Productions, his B movie unit for Columbia Pictures. It was responsible for the production of many motion pictures, including William Castle's previous three films. After withstanding the topsy-turvy shooting schedule of *The Houston Story*, Castle returned to the studio just a few weeks later. His next project, *Uranium Boom*, was to be yet another Clover film.

Some of its background music, especially that which can be heard during the film's opening credits, is also featured in *The Houston Story*. Clover Productions sought to cut costs by any means necessary, even if it meant recycling a film's soundtrack for future pictures.

Uranium Boom, set in and around Glen Grove, a fictional Colorado boomtown of the Atomic Age, was advertised as "THE SHOUT THAT SET THE FUSE TO THE MOST EXPLOSIVE TREASURE HUNT OF MODERN TIMES!"

Ex-Navy man Brad Collins (Dennis Morgan) arrives in Glen Grove with high hopes of finding uranium. He encounters Grady Mathews (William Talman), a mining engineer with similar aspirations. The two become partners. Mathews speaks of a specific woman he intends to marry, but would prefer to wait until he can acquire enough uranium to fund a lavish lifestyle. A short time later, he and Collins make a grand discovery. Mathews chooses to guard the site of the uranium while Collins heads into town to register a claim. Jean Williams (Patricia Medina), the woman of whom Mathews spoke, arrives in Glen Grove. She cannot find him and becomes flustered. Instead, Jean encounters Collins. After a brief courtship, the two are married. A devastated Mathews dissolves his partnership with Collins. Determined to get revenge, Mathews recruits Floyd Gorman (Frank Wilcox), a San Francisco financier, to pose as a real estate investor and inquire about purchasing land near the discovered uranium. Collins, having established his own mine in the area, becomes curious. Gorman makes an offer to purchase Collins's mine, but to no avail. Gail Windsor

(Tina Carver), Gorman's secretary, meets with Collins privately and informs him of a railroad that is being constructed near the mine. All individuals with claims along the future train route would make a fortune because uranium could be shipped to consumers at half its price. Determined to beat Gorman at his own game, Collins takes out a loan from the bank and purchases every claim along the proposed route. But a proud Mathews informs him that the railroad was a hoax. Collins, now broke, eventually reconciles with Mathews. Both men, under Jean's so-called supervision, return to the badlands with the hopes of finding more uranium.

Uranium Boom *marked Castle's third and final collaboration with Patricia Medina.*

Around 1870, a stage play entitled *For Love or Money* was written by Andrew Halliday, a Scottish journalist. Since the time of his production, select forms of media (i.e., novels, films, and television shows) have addressed the age-old issue, thus implementing it as the ideal premise to a story. In *Uranium Boom*, Collins and Jean discuss the future shortly after meeting one another. He stresses to her that, due to other commitments, he is not ready to settle down. Jean appears flustered. Yet, her intentions are unclear. In retrospect, the main characters of *Uranium Boom* appear to place more of a priority on money than love, and there is a mutual misunderstanding between members of the opposite sex. Mathews does not understand Jean, who, in turn, does not understand Collins. And Collins, in essence, does not understand a majority of the women who come into his life.

Mathews incorrectly assumes he can read Jean's mind and, therefore, is not conscious of her true feelings. When he and Collins head to the badlands together for the first time, there is talk of an impending engagement:

> MATHEWS: Soon as we find uranium ... I'm gonna come back and ask [Jean] to marry me.
>
> COLLINS: Why didn't you do that before you came out?
>
> MATHEWS: Women like security.
>
> COLLINS: Did she say that?
>
> MATHEWS: Oh, no, not exactly. But I figure that's what she meant.
>
> COLLINS: What do you mean?
>
> MATHEWS: When she said she wasn't ready to marry yet. When I come back, she'll be ready, cause I'm gonna do it right. Flowers ... engagement ring ... the full treatment. She won't be able to say no.
>
> COLLINS: Never bet on what a woman's gonna say.
>
> MATHEWS: Ah, she'll marry me alright. I've been in love with her for years. And now I'm gonna have enough money to give her all the security she'll ever need.

Mathews does not understand the world from Jean's perspective. Shortly thereafter, she journeys from Denver to Glen Grove with the hopes of finding him. However, Jean is unaware that Mathews has discovered uranium simply because she has not been in contact with him for some time. One might argue that she truly cares for him. Jean was willing to travel over a hundred miles to look for Mathews, and members of an audience may conclude that her arduous trek was not motivated by money because she was not yet privy to his discovery. However, when Collins introduces himself to Jean as a millionaire, he does so by kissing her. And because of her eagerness to reciprocate in kind, she appears to forget about Mathews altogether. Hence, a new set of problems transpires.

URANIUM STOCK QUOTATIONS		
CALUTAH MINE	32.00	41.20
RUNNING WATER MINE	.35	.40
GREEN HILLS MINE	1.50	1.70
STONY CREEK MINE	.75	.95
HALLDALE CO.		
GLEN COE CO.		
BROWN ROCK MINE		
E. J. FORSYTH CO.		
SAN ROCCO MINE		
GAYNOR-ROSS CO.		
OLD BARB MINE		

As Collins arrives in Glen Grove, he takes note of the uranium stocks. One particular mine is named after Stony Creek, the theatre Castle purchased from Orson Welles many years earlier.

Jean's relationship with Collins gradually turns sour because he leads a dog-eat-dog lifestyle to which she cannot relate. A timely conversation between her and Mathews offers a broader perspective of her somewhat complex personality:

> JEAN: Look. Why can't you and [Collins] be friends?
>
> MATHEWS: Jean, you know how I feel about Brad. I don't like him.
>
> JEAN: That's childish. You used to be very good friends. What happened?
>
> Mathews gently grabs Jean's hands and looks into her eyes.
>
> MATHEWS: It's very simple. I want you back. I want us to be together the way we should have been.
>
> JEAN: That's impossible.
>
> She lets go of his hands and looks away from him.
>
> JEAN: I'm in love with Brad.
>
> MATHEWS: You're not happy with him.
>
> JEAN (turning to look at him): Yes, of course, I am.
>
> MATHEWS: You're not really happy.

Jean does not immediately reply. Instead, she stands up and walks away from Mathews.

JEAN: No one's ever really happy.

MATHEWS (approaching her): I don't mean that. I mean things like being lonely because you don't see him enough. Things like not having anybody to talk to about things that are important to you.

JEAN: I tell you, everything's alright.

Jean is uncertain about her future with Collins, but she will not admit her skepticism to Mathews. The conversation reveals her enigmatic nature. Yet, it also explains why, earlier, when dining with Collins at The Sorrento (a restaurant in Glen Grove), Jean does not speak of Mathews by name, despite having ample time to do so. Instead, she casually makes reference to a "fellow" for which she has no serious feelings. Jean, in essence, is unaware of what she wants in life. Her enigmatic personality makes for an entertaining narrative, and her reason for journeying to Glen Grove essentially becomes meaningless once Collins enters the picture. And he, too, chooses not to disclose his partnership with Mathews until it is too late. But his outlook on life is more complex than that of any other character of the film.

Navajo Charlie is the one individual of the narrative to value love and acceptance over money.

Collins, driven by a ceaseless quest to discover uranium, does not exhibit the patience that is necessary in order to appreciate the women who enter his life. His demeanor towards the opposite sex is evident from the moment Castle introduces him into the narrative. As Collins arrives in Glen Grove for the first time, he approaches an attractive woman to inquire about lodging. She offers to personally escort him to the hotel. Collins politely declines, as his mind is clearly focused on other prospects. The woman watches him leave, and then shrugs her shoulders in slight confusion. A short time later, as Collins and Mathews prepare to embark on their first outing to the badlands, a young woman approaches their jeep. She speaks specifically to Collins, expressing a desire to join his expedition and cook all of his meals. Again, he declines. Although Collins is a newcomer to Glen Grove, he has what Mathews refers to as an "enthusiastic following." By the time Collins is married to Jean, it becomes clear that his priority is money, not women. And Gail, during a series of so-called business negotiations with Collins, says it best when she declares, "I should've been a man. I don't understand women either."

With the release of *Uranium Boom*, Castle's association with Sam Katzman officially came to an end. In retrospect, both men worked together on a total of seventeen pictures. Katzman continued to produce B films through Clover Productions, whereas Castle departed Columbia altogether to pursue a new endeavor with Ziv Television Programs, Inc. Castle had the opportunity to direct thirty-minute episodes of select television shows, namely *Men of Annapolis*. Occasionally, he was granted permission to produce some of the episodes he directed. His career in television, although short-lived, was beneficial. Because Castle's dual responsibilities as a producer and a director helped to better prepare him for the ultimate stage of his career.

PART II
SHOWTIME!

CHAPTER FORTY
MACABRE (1958)

February 27, 1958, was a significant day in the life of William Castle. Harry Cohn, longtime president of Columbia Pictures, passed away at the age of sixty-six. Despite having to endure a sometimes-tumultuous relationship laced with insults and profanity, Castle was devastated upon hearing the news.

Prior to the death of his longtime colleague and mentor, Castle frequently happened upon a great deal of hardship and loss throughout his own life. And he struggled with his emotions, especially when it came to the deaths of his mother and father. Cohn's memorial service marked the first time Castle would actually cry at a funeral. It was an emotional release of grand proportions. Perhaps, Castle's momentous achievement was a sign that things were beginning to change, because his career was moving in an entirely new direction.

The clock adorning the façade of Quigley's Funeral Parlor is seen following the film's title. *Macabre* is devoid of opening credits, as the narrative begins immediately after the title is displayed. Castle's introduction was a rarity for its time.

A few years earlier, Henri-Georges Clouzot, the famous French film director, gained worldwide acclaim for *Les Diaboliques*, a horror film that evolved around a plot of conspiracy and murder. It was seen by millions, including Castle and his wife, Ellen. Audiences were horrified. Castle immediately came to the realization that many long for the thrill of being scared. He wanted to replicate the success of *Les Diaboliques* with a horror film of his own, but lacked experience within the genre.

After a lengthy search for the ideal story, Castle purchased the rights to *The Marble Forest*, a chilling novel of terror. Robb White, a writer with whom Castle had previously worked on television's *Men of Annapolis*, adapted a screenplay with its share of horrific elements. He intended to keep the novel's original title for the script, but Castle objected. White countered with the suggestion of *Gruesome*. Castle agreed, but primarily because of its French translation: *Macabre*.

Dr. Rodney Barrett (William Prince), a general practitioner in a small town, is frequently subject to animosity from the chief of police, Jim Tyloe (Jim Backus). The hard feelings began years earlier when Barrett's wife, Alice (Dorothy Morris), died from giving birth to their only child. He was not at her side because he was socializing with Sylvia Stevenson (Susan Morrow), an unmarried woman in town. Instead, Tyloe, Alice's ex-flame, was the one to be with her when she died. Years later, Nancy (Christine White), Alice's blind sister, dies mysteriously. Tyloe blames Barrett, claiming that a real doctor would have been able to save her. On the day of Nancy's funeral, Barrett's three-year-old daughter, Marge (Linda Guderman), goes missing. Polly Baron (Jacqueline Scott), Barrett's nurse, receives a mysterious phone call. An unfamiliar voice states that "Marge's funeral has just taken place, and now she's with the dead." Barrett and Polly conduct a search of the cemetery. Jode Wetherby (Philip Tonge), Marge's grandfather, frantically arrives on the scene. He struggles with a fragile heart condition. Later, during Nancy's funeral, Barrett uncovers a child's coffin. It contains a hideous, albeit fake, creature. An overwhelmed Wetherby suffers a fatal heart attack and plunges into Nancy's open grave. Ed Quigley (Jonathan Kidd), the town mortician, shoots Barrett, but then publicly confesses to helping the doctor kidnap Marge. In addition, Barrett purposely triggered Wetherby's heart attack in order to inherit the deceased's fortune. As the doctor dies, he reveals Marge's secret location to Polly. The child is discovered to be unharmed and sleeping soundly.

Jonathan Kidd and Jim Backus.

The Marble Forest, published in 1951, was written under the pseudonym of Theo Durrant, the name of a convicted murderer of the late nineteenth century who maintained his innocence until his execution. In reality, *The Marble Forest* is the work of twelve separate authors (thirteen including the pseudonym). In theory, the writers "recalled" Durrant to life so that he could use the novel as a means to proclaim his innocence to the world.

Castle was not only impressed with the story because of the collaborative effort behind its publication, he also believed it to be more frightening than *Les Diaboliques*. In the past, he directed films that were adapted from novels, but *Macabre* marked the first time he would oversee an adaptation while serving as the film's producer. Castle had more control than usual, and he and White made their own revisions to the story. But one particular aspect that remained unchanged was the race against time. The concept of time is the most crucial element of Castle's film. It evolves around the opposite realms of darkness and light, as seen within Nancy's world of shadows, the business of death, and the clock adorning the façade of Quigley's Funeral Parlor.

As Nancy is introduced to the audience, we see that she lives a life of ambiguity. The first of two flashbacks begins, and the screen appears blurry. A multitude of shadows spin together at a dizzying pace, and the sound of a speeding car becomes audible. The ever-changing kaleidoscope of distorted images remains visible until we find ourselves in the driver's seat, positioned behind the vehicle's steering wheel. The long stretch of country road rapidly disappears beneath us. And for the following seven minutes, we become immersed in Nancy's troubled life. Shades of darkness and light, appearing first along an abandoned warehouse and then among a residential swimming pool, establish symbolic boundaries of emotional feelings. But it is Nancy's blindness, the ultimate shadow of darkness, which determines her overall state of being.

Ellen Corby and Jacqueline Scott.

Nancy and Tyloe's rendezvous at the abandoned warehouse features a significant transition from darkness to light. Her emotions change as she crosses the building's threshold. Inside the warehouse, Nancy is in a state of terminal bliss. She feels comfortable, and the isolation is soothing. As Nancy emerges from the warehouse's dark interior into the brightness of a sunny day, the contrast of shadow and light serves as a metaphorical boundary that separates feelings of happiness from those of sorrow. Tyloe then proposes marriage, but Nancy rejects him. Their joyous escapade, transpiring within the confines of the dark warehouse, has concluded. As Nancy departs the building, she is transported back to the reality of her harsh world, remarking that "all men seem alike in the dark." Not only does she reject Tyloe's offer, but she also declares that he is "the last man in the world" she would marry. Yet, for Nancy, another suitor awaits.

Nick (Robert Colbert), the Wetherby chauffeur, approaches the family's fashionable pool as Nancy emerges from the shadows of her home, thus swimming into the light of day. The indoor-outdoor pool, like the warehouse, sets a boundary that determines Nancy's emotional demeanor. Prior to Nick's appearance, Castle begins the scene with an interior shot of Nancy removing her garment and sandals, and then slipping into the pool. She is alone and appears serene. By the time Nancy swims under the window and out towards the exterior of the house, Nick stands poolside awaiting her rise to the surface:

NICK: Hello, Miss Wetherby.

NANCY: You call me that one more time, I'll have you fired.

A slight smile forms along Nancy's lips.

NANCY: What are you doing here?

NICK: Nothing. You know something, Miss...Nancy? One of these times you're gonna dive in there, and there isn't gonna be any water.

NANCY (slapping the water with both hands): Kaboom!

Nancy is one who treats life with disdain. During an earlier scene of the film, she tells Nick she wants to "live fast, love fast, and die fast!" Whenever Nancy comes into contact with other people, it appears to bring out the worst in her. A life of solitude is

"Who is it, Polly? Who is it?"

the alternative. Nevertheless, she allows her physical impairment to become a hindrance to a productive and fruitful life.

Nancy lives within an immense shadow of darkness due to her blindness, a characteristic missing from the novel. At the time of her pregnancy consultation with Barrett, she appears hopeless. The doctor suggests that Nancy "go away somewhere for awhile." But she rejects the recommendation, claiming, "I just wanna be what I've been all my life: nothing." It is the last time the audience will see her alive. During the following scene, Barrett learns of Nancy's fate as Quigley, of all people, delivers the news. The lengthy flashback concludes. Incidentally, Quigley speaks of Nancy within the film's opening minutes, quoting Jode Wetherby as saying, "My daughter, Nancy, lived in darkness, died in darkness, and will be buried in darkness."

Quigley, employed as the town's mortician, is engaged in a peculiar business. *Macabre* emits death, as much of the narrative transpires at a mortuary and cemetery. Furthermore, Castle concludes his film with an animated funeral procession! Following *Macabre*, *House on Haunted Hill* begins with a pseudo-procession of its own, as Mr. Loren's guests arrive in separate funeral cars. In regard to *Macabre*, the business of death prospers amongst the opposing forces of darkness and light. Many events transpire

Philip Tonge as Jode Wetherby.

within the so-called marble forest both prior to and during Nancy's service. But the forces are also present at Quigley's Funeral Parlor.

Shortly after Barrett and Polly begin their search of the cemetery, the dark becomes darker. The two find themselves in a chilling situation while standing at the bottom of Nancy's open grave. In any work of fiction, a deserted cemetery is traditionally horrifying, but a deserted cemetery at night will simply intensify the setting. In the case of Barrett and Polly, the sky is gloomy. Both must rely primarily on the power of their flashlights, as the night is dark. They begin to dig within the open grave, but Hummel (Howard Hoffman), the gravedigger, arrives on the scene. He places a tarp across the grave's rectangular opening, blocking any natural, albeit minimal, light available to Barrett and Polly. The screen becomes pitch-black, ushering in the darkest part of the film. For a few brief seconds, nothing can be seen. The suspense is heightened, partly because the audience is not yet aware of Hummel's identity. Shortly thereafter, Wetherby arrives, and Barrett does not appear to be surprised. He does not even bother to ask his father-in-law how he learned of Marge's disappearance. Barrett most likely expected Miss Kushins (Ellen Corby), Marge's nanny, to disobey his orders by rushing to alert Wetherby of the crisis (which she does). As an indirect result, Hummel is accidentally killed by a strike from the old man's cane. Death is essentially in the air, and more is to come.

The darkness of night, accompanied by occasional streaks of lighting, is dominant at the time of Nancy's funeral. The setting is specific to Castle's vision, as he and White added a twist of the macabre to the original story. Early in the film, Tyloe comments that the funeral is the "strangest thing [he] ever heard of ... having [it] in the middle of the night." Although it is an oddity for a memorial service to be conducted on the cusp of midnight (Nancy is said to have passed at midnight), it is typical of Castle's world. A funeral does not transpire at any point of the novel, despite a majority of the story taking place within the town's graveyard. In the film, Nancy's service is marred by unforeseen events, including an outburst of gunfire. Barrett falls to the ground, clutching his stomach. Castle affords his audience an aerial glimpse of converging umbrellas. The image becomes a blur of dark shadows. Quigley soon exposes himself as the shooter and begins his confession. He reflects on many details, including the circumstances behind his staged scuffle with Barrett at the parlor.

The tryst concludes.

The greatest contrast of darkness and light is apparent at Quigley's place of business. Barrett, Polly, and Wetherby conduct their frantic search within the parlor's showroom. An unseen light source flashes periodically, illuminating the room in separate intervals. Following the inspection of several empty coffins, Wetherby pauses to look at a painting on the wall. It depicts a mother embracing her child. Wetherby exhibits sorrow, and despite the continuous pattern of flashing light, the portrait remains lit due to a nearby street lamp (Castle would later implement a similar technique regarding the painting of Dr. Zorba in 13 Ghosts). Just as the interior of Quigley's Funeral Parlor undergoes periodic illumination, so too does its exterior, primarily because of Castle's focus on one specific object.

The clock adorning the façade of Quigley's Funeral Parlor is significant to the film. It is frequently seen by the audience and serves as a reminder of Barrett's race against time. The steady pattern of flashing light is similar to the ticking of a clock, as the concept of time is the most important element of *Macabre*. The introduction and conclusion of Castle's film, in addition to its duration, place an emphasis on Quigley's clock. But a clever gimmick is also indicative of the importance of time.

Quigley's clock is prominently featured in the opening and closing shots of *Macabre*. On both occasions, an unseen narrator provides instructions to the audience. In the beginning, immediately after the film's title is presented, we are informed that "terrifying" images will be shown "for the next hour and

Nancy prepares to submerge beneath the water, and then swims into the light of day (below).

fifteen minutes." An emphasis on time is explicit. The narrator makes a special request of all theater patrons to "please set [their] watches" according to the time, which "is six forty-five in the evening." Upon the conclusion of *Macabre*, members of the audience once again find themselves looking at the clock, which now reads twelve fifteen in the morning. Again, we are provided with valuable instructions, which essentially state that the ending of *Macabre* is not to be revealed to those who have not yet seen it (Castle would later make the same request with *Homicidal*). In regard to the clock, it measures the five and a half hour ordeal that Barrett and company must endure. The measurement is detailed, especially because the opening and closing shots of the film are not the only times we see the conspicuous timepiece.

Christine White and William Prince.

Throughout Castle's film, Quigley's clock periodically appears as a reminder of the passage of time. *The Marble Forest*, containing over twenty chapters, is similar. The titles of select chapters are named after important characters of the story, but others are labeled with specific timeframes. For example, the opening chapter, prefaced with the name of the novel, is entitled *7:50 P.M. to 8:05 P.M.* Many others, including the final chapter, follow the same format. In the film, the clock is displayed to the audience at crucial intervals. A significant example is evident as Nancy's funeral begins. Quigley's clock informs the audience that the service is commencing at midnight.

When one is viewing *Macabre* for the first time, he or she will discover the element of time to be of the utmost importance, especially considering that Barrett's frantic search is believed to be genuine instead of concocted. Castle's request that theatergoers not reveal the film's ending is undoubtedly important. Of equal importance, however, is the narrator's warning to those who may become "uncontrollably frightened." Fortunately, Castle made preparations for such an emergency.

In order to promote *Macabre* to the general public, Castle made use of a creative gimmick that relied on a stringent time limit. In the rare case of death by fright, theatergoers were covered under an insurance policy that was only valid during the hour and fifteen-minute duration of the film. Castle described it as "a publicity stunt." If theatergoers were to unexpectedly die of

Several gather for Nancy's funeral.

fright, their beneficiaries would collect $1,000. It was a cinematic phenomenon. Excitement was in the air, as many bought their tickets in anticipation of the unknown. But the policy included a disclaimer, which stated that those with a known heart or nervous condition, similar to the fictional Wetherby, would not be eligible. In the film, Wetherby eventually succumbs to death by fright. But in reality, nobody ever collected on the policy, just as Castle had predicted. Nevertheless, the brilliance of his idea ushered in a new wave of audience participation.

Macabre, released in March of 1958, was made for $90,000. In order to finance the picture, Castle mortgaged his house. White

Many of the town's landmarks contain Wetherby's name.

also contributed a sizable chunk of his own cash. Allied Artists Productions, a Hollywood studio that specialized in low-budget motion pictures, agreed to distribute the film for 25 percent of the profits. *Macabre* ultimately grossed $5 million at the box office. Some have referred to it as Castle's directorial debut. *Macabre* is more of a rebirth of his career than anything else. Unfortunately, Cohn did not live to see the film, having missed it by one month. Whether or not he would have been interested in Castle's new-found passion is unknown. But Castle savored every moment of his success, celebrating the release of *Macabre* by climbing out of a coffin at the film's premiere. And after forty films, the prime of Castle's career was just beginning.

Macabre *concludes in style, as caricatures of William Castle and Robb White lead the animated funeral procession.*

CHAPTER FORTY-ONE
HOUSE ON HAUNTED HILL (1958)

Following the success of *Macabre*, William Castle and Robb White immediately began to craft a story for their next picture. Allied Artists was on board, eager for another profitable outcome. The finished screenplay evolved around a classic haunted house tale. Aside from landing Vincent Price for the starring role of *House on Haunted Hill*, Castle's main concern was to devise a gimmick that could top the insurance policy of *Macabre*. He did just that, dubbing his new attraction EMERGO! The idea was to have a plastic skeleton "emerge" from the screen and float above the audience during the film's climax. Although theatergoers had to wait for over an hour before the spectacle of EMERGO! was unveiled, the storyline leading up to the experience was worthwhile.

Frederick Loren (Price), a millionaire who has been married four times, rents a haunted house in order to throw a party for his current wife, Annabelle (Carol Ohmart). Instead of friends, he invites five strangers, promising each of them $10,000 should they survive the night. Watson Pritchard (Elisha Cook), the house's owner, attends the party and declares the estate to be haunted by ghosts. Annabelle, fearing for her life, makes it known to the others that Loren is determined to kill her. Nora Manning (Carolyn Craig), a guest who accepted Loren's invitation in order to support her family, decides to back out and forego the reward. But the caretakers lock the house earlier than planned, making it impossible for anybody to escape. Later, Annabelle commits suicide by hanging herself. Pritchard blames the ghosts. Nora has other ideas, especially after being attacked and left for dead. But Loren is soon revealed to be the intended victim of a murder plot concocted by Annabelle, who has faked her suicide, and Dr. David Trent (Alan Marshal), her lover. Consequently, they meet their demise instead of Loren, who waits "for justice to decide if [he is] innocent or guilty."

Prior to the production of *House on Haunted Hill*, Castle explained its plot to Price, who liked what he heard and gladly committed to the lead role. The central idea of the story, that a

Vincent Price and Carol Ohmart.

millionaire's wife is secretly plotting to kill him, is crucial because it provides the twist for a surprise ending. Therefore, it cannot be revealed to the audience until the film's final minutes. Both the *mise-en-scène* and narrative of *House on Haunted Hill* serve as the perfect distraction to lure us away from the reality of what is transpiring between Annabelle and Trent. Furthermore, Castle's direction, the supporting character of Nora, and Pritchard's sometimes-misleading "spook talk" are intriguing.

Following the post-production phase of *House on Haunted Hill*, the final print was established with a running time of seventy-five minutes. Although the film's duration is relatively short, much transpires within this space of time. The details of Castle's direction (i.e., intensity of his actors, omission of a significant event, and interior design of the house) enable the film to progress at a steady, yet exciting, pace, never allowing for a dull moment.

Castle's direction establishes a particular degree of intensity within the performances of his actors. From the beginning, when Pritchard warns us that "the ghosts are moving," it immediately becomes clear that *House on Haunted Hill* is not for the faint of heart. Throughout his entire opening monologue, Pritchard does not blink while addressing the audience. His face is projected

"It was my wife's idea to have our guests come in funeral cars. She's so amusing. Her sense of humor is, shall we say, original?"

against a dark background. He is alone, and quite skeptical about the house of which he speaks. As Castle makes his audience privy to Pritchard's character, he also sets the tone for the remainder of the film. We are soon introduced to the remaining guests as we watch them arrive, one by one, in separate funeral cars. Lance Schroeder (Richard Long), Ruth Bridgers (Julie Mitchum), and Nora nervously cling to the grab handles of their vehicles. Pritchard and Trent do not. Pritchard is obsessed with his ghosts, and therefore, is prepared for the evening's events. Trent is confident about his plan to murder Loren and feels no need to worry. The other three, however, have no idea what the night has in store for them. Castle does not reveal much, and he sometimes prevents his audience from seeing anything at all.

Courtesy of Castle, we are not allowed to see Trent's assault on Nora, and the omission simply makes for an exciting climax. A significant event, transpiring approximately halfway through the film, triggers the chain of events that lead to the missing scene. Shortly after Trent offers Nora a sedative (presuming she did not see a decapitated head, but instead, imagined it), the latter abruptly dismisses everyone from the room. Following her dismissal of the others, Nora is not seen by the audience for an extended period of time. And much transpires in her absence. Lance not only discovers Nora to be missing from her room, he

Julie Mitchum, Carolyn Craig, Elisha Cook, Richard Long, and Alan Marshal. Julie Mitchum was the older sister of Robert Mitchum.

also finds a "head" hanging in her closet. He proceeds to question Pritchard as to her whereabouts, but the interrogation is cut short when Annabelle concocts her fake suicide.

The narrative's focus shifts from Nora to Annabelle, thus distracting the audience from the reality of what is transpiring in another section of the house. It is during this chain of events that Trent attacks Nora, and Castle purposely omits the assault from his picture. He wants the audience, and Nora, to suspect Loren. In order for the narrative's plot twist to be effective, Trent cannot be unveiled as the antagonist until the film's conclusion. Had the audience been allowed to see the assault on Nora, the perpetrator most likely would have been partially, or completely, concealed from view (Nora herself was unable to positively identify her attacker when speaking with Schroeder a short time later). If the audience does not see Loren, but instead, a faceless figure, we are less likely to suspect him. Castle cleverly omits the attack, and instead of focusing more on Nora's disappearance, the audience becomes concerned about the "death" of Annabelle, instantly realizing that Loren is the only one in the house with the strongest motive for murder. To many, he becomes more sinister by the minute. Trent, however, is

Mrs. Slydes and Nora Manning.

portrayed as a conscientious individual. As the narrative's characters are cleverly developed, so too is the setting of the film.

Although most of the *mise-en-scène* in *House on Haunted Hill* evokes a feeling of dread, the interior design of the house leaves audiences marveling at its rooms and furnishings. As Annabelle presents Nora's bedroom to her, one of the first objects we see is that of a miniature spinning wheel. It is carefully placed in the center of the frame. As Annabelle walks towards the room's lone window, Castle's camera pans to the left, never allowing for the spinning wheel to leave its central position. The object is significant, as it is a representation of the room's intended occupant. According to the great philosopher Mahatma Gandhi, the spinning wheel is portrayed as a symbol of nonviolence. Nora is the most innocent of the film's characters, and hence, is the least likely to commit a violent act. It is not until she is pushed to the limit that she is forced to "shoot" Loren in self-defense.

Throughout the history of motion pictures, a supporting character has sometimes been so crucial to the plot of a film, that he or she had the power to control the course of the story, and the mere absence of such a character could weaken the overall narrative. Without Nora, the storyline of *House on Haunted Hill* lacks

The clock ticks closer to midnight.

creativity. Her fragility, apprehensiveness, and gullibility essentially propel the narrative to a new level.

Nora is the most fragile of the film's characters, a quality on which Castle relies in order to manipulate his audience. She loses all self-control when caught off guard. Although Nora's initial encounter with Mrs. Slydes occurs without incident (probably due to the physical distance between the two), the following encounter is quite the opposite. When Nora, standing in one of the cellar's storage rooms, knocks on the wall in order to produce a sound Schroeder can hear, Castle initially films her from a distance. We can see most of her body. As she kneels down, however, Castle cuts to a much closer shot of her head and shoulders. Seconds later, Nora turns to her left, and we suddenly see the face of Mrs. Slydes. Nora emits an ear-piercing scream, causing audiences to react with her. She is perfect for Castle's narrative. Had Mrs. Slydes surprised one of the other guests, such as Schroeder or Ruth, the reaction would not have been as intense (Ruth barely reacts to the "blood" the first time it drops from the ceiling onto her hand). Yet, because of Nora's fragility, she is easily frightened. And audiences react with her.

Because Nora is apprehensive of the house, the film's setting is presented as one of ambiguity and terror. The more she questions the safety of staying overnight, the more the audience realizes how frightening the house really is. When Nora and Schroeder remain in the cellar following Pritchard's brief tour of the property, she has second thoughts about attending the party, despite not being in any serious danger. However, as the clock ticks closer to midnight, and as the caretakers continuously play on Nora's nerves, she becomes more determined to leave. As her apprehensiveness grows stronger, it becomes clear that whatever is going on inside the house could pose a threat to its occupants. Yet, without a character like Nora, the film's setting may not seem as sinister. But her apprehensiveness of the house is not as strong as her apprehensiveness of Loren, thus making her an easy target.

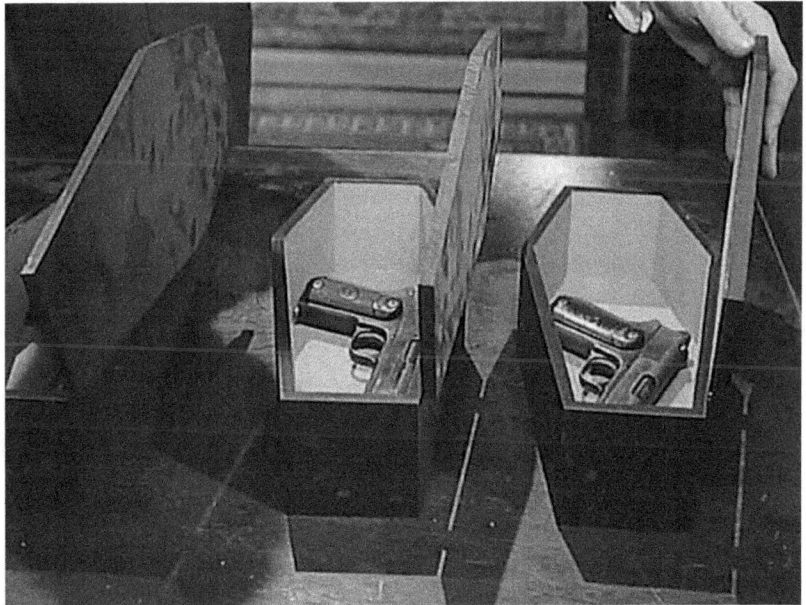

Party favors!

Nora's gullible personality, exploited by Annabelle and Trent, makes for an unpredictable ending. She is convinced Loren is trying to kill her, despite Schroeder's uncertainty. Schroeder presses Nora to reflect back on the mysterious attack, questioning whether or not it was their eccentric host who assaulted her in the darkness. Initially, Schroeder keeps an open mind, contemplating whether or not the attacker could be somebody else, but

Nora sticks to her theory that it was Loren. The more gullible she is, the less we suspect Trent of being the attacker, because all of the suspicion is on Loren. Hence, it is primarily because of Nora that the audience finds itself blindsided by the surprise ending of the film. After the dust has settled, and as the film nears its conclusion, Pritchard reminds us that the ghosts are still a threat, and "soon they'll come for you!"

Pritchard's "spook talk" tricks some into believing *House on Haunted Hill* is a classic ghost story instead of the tale of a millionaire's wife and the plot to kill her husband. The living versus the dead, a theme frequently seen in Castle's later films, is the only issue to preoccupy Pritchard's attention. Both the introduction and conclusion of *House on Haunted Hill* evolve around Pritchard and his ghosts. Yet, we do not see one at any time during the film. Von Dexter's score features its share of moaning and chain rattling, but seeing a ghost as opposed to hearing one offers a completely different perspective. Any individual viewing *House on Haunted Hill* for the first time is apt to perceive the ghosts as possible antagonists of the story, and thus, become distracted from the true conflict of the narrative. Nevertheless, Schroeder's debacle in the cellar, Trent's mysterious doorknob, and Pritchard's firm convictions suggest the house is haunted by unseen ghosts that establish a commanding presence.

As Schroeder "bumps" his head during the first excursion to the cellar, ominous phenomena (i.e., doors swinging shut, lights dimming) add credibility to Pritchard's theories. Trent is determined to prove that ghosts are creations of hysteria. He attempts to justify himself to Nora and Loren, but cannot simplify matters while tending to Schroeder's wound:

> LOREN: Nora, when you came in you said something about a ghost.
>
> NORA: There was something.
>
> LOREN: What did it look like?
>
> NORA: Well, it . . . it was wearing a black thing that went all the way to the floor.
>
> TRENT: Weren't you a little frightened at the time?
>
> NORA: Well, yes.

Trent turns his attention from Schroeder to Loren.

TRENT: That, Mr. Loren, is hysteria.

LOREN: Well then, doctor, how do you explain what happened to Lance? Was that hysteria, too?

Trent is unable to respond, and instead, turns his attention back to Schroeder. He immediately changes the subject. A short time later, we discover the "ghost" to be Mrs. Slydes, thus weakening the doctor's argument. But Pritchard has yet to lose the credibility that Trent has, especially since the mystery behind Schroeder's attack, among other things, goes unsolved.

An ominous organ accentuates the mise-en-scène *of the house's interior.*

The inexplicable back-and-forth rotation of Trent's bedroom doorknob does not appear to be the actions of a living being, especially since the doctor cannot determine the rotation's cause after a brief search of the hall. Similar to Schroeder's debacle in the cellar, the mystery of the rotating doorknob is never explained, thus leaving viewers to speculate on their own. Castle purposely films the door from Trent's perspective, never allowing us to see what could be lurking on the other side. The number of possibilities is limitless, and many would be reluctant to rule out the ghosts considering Pritchard's firm convictions.

Pritchard and his ghosts are never far from the minds of the audience, and the separate incidents involving Schroeder and Trent would lack intensity without Pritchard constantly preaching his beliefs to the occupants of the house. However, as the film progresses, we come to know Pritchard as a drunk and begin to detect the inaccuracies of his rhetoric around the time Nora goes missing. In the living room, Pritchard claims to Schroeder that Nora is gone because "[the ghosts] have taken her." Yet, it is only a short time later that Nora appears and demands that Schroeder hide her from Loren. Minute by minute, Pritchard gradually loses credibility. But it is not until the disastrous encounter with Loren that the audience begins to see Pritchard for the drunk that he is. Loren, thinking he is alone, quietly enters the room where Annabelle's body is laid to rest. He pulls back the canopy bed curtain and stares at her, openly ranting about her greedy, cold personality. Suddenly, a shadow envelops Annabelle, and Loren turns to find a dazed Pritchard gazing down at her. Loren, clearly angered by the intrusion, abruptly puts his hands around Pritchard's throat:

> MR. LOREN: What are you doing in here?
>
> PRITCHARD (gasping for breath): Wait! Don't we . . . .?
>
> MR. LOREN: What do you mean coming in here?
>
> PRITCHARD: I didn't want them to take her away!
>
> MR. LOREN: You're drunk!
>
> PRITCHARD: They will if you don't watch her!
>
> MR. LOREN: You're drunk! Alright! Out with it, Pritchard! Why did you come into this room?
>
> PRITCHARD: I'm the only one who understands!
>
> MR. LOREN: Understands what?
>
> PRITCHARD: Look! (gulps) Your wife isn't there anymore! She's already joined them!

MR. LOREN: Now Pritchard, I've had enough of your spook talk! Get out you sot and don't come back into this room again!

Loren pushes Pritchard towards the door, and the latter quickly exits. Although Pritchard appears convincing for a few brief seconds, it is quite evident that the liquor is doing the talking. He has humiliated himself to the point where he can no longer be taken seriously. If the ghosts did not take Nora, they will not take Annabelle. Nevertheless, Pritchard's "spook talk" is good for the narrative, as it has the potential to keep an audience on edge.

Shortly before *House on Haunted Hill* was released to the public, a sneak preview was scheduled for the press. Among the members of the audience was the notorious Louella Parsons, a gossip columnist whose favorite target was Hollywood. If there was anything about a film she did not like (i.e., acting, directing), it quickly became widespread news. Parsons had the power to influence the American public, and one negative review could ruin the careers of many. After viewing *House on Haunted Hill*, she wrote the following in her nationwide syndicated column: *"House on Haunted Hill is more frightening than a graveyard on a cold wet night, complete with blood dripping from ceilings, bodiless heads that talk, and the walking dead. Allied Artists has added the trick called 'Emergo,' which happens right in the theatre over your head at the most frightening moments. If you have a weak heart, don't see this. If you don't, you'll lap it up."*

For the second time in as many years, Castle had produced a hit. Low-budget horror films were becoming his specialty. Around the time the film was released to the public, Castle celebrated the birth of his second child, Terry. He attributed a great deal of his success to her, claiming she had brought him luck. Shows were selling out, box office returns were skyrocketing, and lines of eager spectators stretched for blocks. Castle was so ecstatic that, during the film's run at the Golden Gate Theatre in San Francisco, he distributed cigars to everybody, including underage theatergoers, as a way of celebrating the arrival of the family's new addition. Life was good, but little did Castle know that, at the time, his greatest hit was just around the corner.

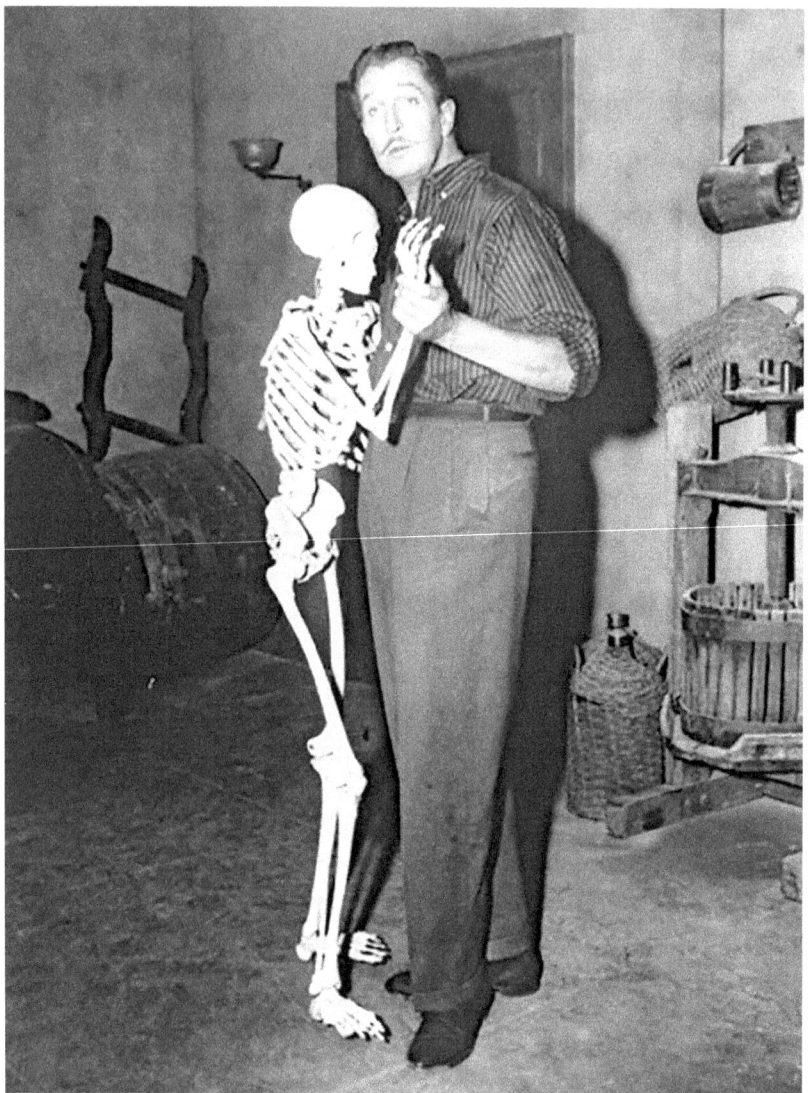

Vincent Price poses for the camera with his co-star.

CHAPTER FORTY-TWO
THE TINGLER (1959)

A little over a year had passed since the death of Harry Cohn, and Columbia Pictures was in the process of undergoing significant changes. William Castle was doing quite well for himself. The box office returns of *Macabre* and *House on Haunted Hill* were testaments to his success, and Columbia wanted him to return. But the studio's interest in Castle was not limited to the films he produced. Peculiar gimmicks of $1,000 insurance policies and flying skeletons encouraged audience interaction, thus boosting ticket sales. Castle ultimately decided that a return to Columbia was in his best interests. He was given complete autonomy over his films. Armed with more spending power than usual, Castle devised a clever gimmick known as PERCEPTO! Its purpose was to startle select members of an audience by delivering a buzzing, tingling sensation to random seats of the theater. Appropriately enough, Castle's film was titled *The Tingler*.

"I've been experimenting with this force for years. Never had a name for it until now. Now, I think I'll call it The Tingler."

Dr. Warren Chapin (Vincent Price), a pathologist, discovers a force within the human body that escalates when people become frightened. Potential victims can quell the force by screaming. Otherwise, their vertebrae will be crushed. Chapin dubs his new-found phenomenon "The Tingler." Oliver "Ollie" Higgins (Philip

Coolidge), operator of a silent movie theater, becomes acquainted with the doctor. His wife, Martha (Judith Evelyn), is a deaf mute. One evening, she is accosted by what appears to be a hideous ghoul. Lacking the ability to scream, she is killed by the tingler that lurks within her. Higgins transports Martha's body to Chapin's home, where the tingler is extracted from the corpse. The creature is confined to a cage. Higgins, intending to notify the police, departs with the body. Isabel (Patricia Cutts), Chapin's unfaithful and devious wife, seizes the opportunity to subdue her husband with a tranquilizer. Before leaving, she releases the tingler from its cage. It attacks the unconscious doctor, but Lucy (Pamela Lincoln), Isabel's sister, arrives before the situation becomes worse. Believing he has violated the laws of nature, Chapin decides to abandon his experiment and return the tingler to Martha's body. But when he learns that the police have no record of her death, suspicions abound. With the tingler in tow, Chapin confronts Higgins. A ghoul costume is discovered at the latter's apartment. Chapin correctly deduces that Higgins murdered his wife, using fright as a means to execute his plan. The tingler is reinserted into Martha's lifeless body. Chapin departs, leaving Higgins to ponder his future. Martha, resurrected by the force of the tingler, advances toward her husband to exact revenge.

Judith Evelyn, Vincent Price, and Philip Coolidge.

Television's *Men of Annapolis*, although short-lived, proved beneficial to Castle. Had it not been for the program, he most likely would not have become acquainted with a particular couple of talented individuals, and therefore, would have been unable to acquire their services for *The Tingler*.

The first was Robb White, a writer whose flair for his craft not only made him a favorite of Castle's, but also made him popular amongst his contemporaries in both the film and writing industries.

The second was Darryl Hickman, an established character actor who was specifically cast as David Morris, Chapin's devoted assistant and love interest of Lucy's. During the production of *The Tingler*, Hickman was the real-life fiancé of Pamela Lincoln.

Castle's onscreen pairing of the two was a tactic for widespread publicity. In fact, he pulled out all the stops to ensure the success of his film. With *The Tingler*, Castle reached the pinnacle of his career as a director of motion pictures. And the film's triumph was due, in large part, to an increased level of audience interaction, the inclusion of his trademark motifs, and a fitting tribute to the milestones of American cinema.

Around the time *Macabre* was being produced, Castle approached Sam Katzman to make what he believed to be a reasonable request. He wanted Columbia to distribute his film on the condition that he could serve as its producer and director. But Katzman had a policy that the producer and director of a film could not be the same person. Therefore, Castle eventually sold his film to Allied Artists. Later, when he returned to Columbia to make *The Tingler*, he was free of Katzman, and essentially set forth to establish a new connection with theatergoers. Castle's determination to interact with his audience is evidenced by his emergence from behind the camera. But Price's breaking of the fourth wall, in addition to the pulsating power of PERCEPTO!, also provide clear examples of Castle's will to "meet" the public.

With *The Tingler*, Castle ventured to the other side of the camera in order to personally address his audience. He appears in the film's trailer and also makes a noteworthy cameo during the opening scene of the picture. Despite having directed over forty films, *The Tingler* marked Castle's first appearance in a trailer. As the preview begins, a connection with the audience is established as the director introduces himself, reaching out to the average theatergoer by declaring that he or she will "play a part in the picture." During the film's introduction, and barring the traditional appearance of the Torch Lady of Columbia Pictures, Castle is the

Pamela Lincoln and Darryl Hickman.

first to be seen. He happens upon a familiar locale, which is that of a movie theater, and positions himself in front of its screen in order to interact with his audience. He speaks of "physical reactions, which the actors on the screen will feel." But Castle hints that "certain members" of his audience, too, will be susceptible to unknown sensations. Explicit instructions on how patrons can protect themselves are disclosed. Shortly thereafter, Castle's screen time concludes. And it eventually becomes the responsibility of another to guide the audience at just the right moment.

Vincent Price, upon the film's conclusion, breaks the fourth wall in an attempt to placate the crowd. It is important to note that two theaters are featured in the climax: the fictitious venue of the silent movie theater, and that in which spectators of *The Tingler* are seated. Castle's use of a plant deliberately exacerbated the mood of the real-life theater. An actress, playing the part of a ticket-holding patron, pretended to faint as the tension on the screen continued to mount. Medical personnel, also operatives of Castle's, were summoned to transport the "victim" to safety. Around the same time, Price turns off the lights of the fictitious theater. He states, "Ladies and Gentlemen, there's no cause for alarm. A young lady has fainted. She is being attended to by a doctor and is quite alright. So, please remain seated. The movie will begin again right away. I repeat, there is no cause for alarm." Price was not addressing the patrons of the silent movie theater, as there was no visual proof that any of them had fainted. Instead, he was speaking directly to the audience of *The Tingler*. And hence, the fainting of Castle's plant sparked a chain of events that ultimately led to interactive mayhem. As the tingler supposedly became loose in the theater, Price's voice was heard for a second time, and it was at this point that Castle seized the opportunity to present his audience with the icing on the cake.

"I know a wonderful psychiatrist with a perfectly divine straitjacket just your size!"

The gimmick of PERCEPTO! empowered Castle with the capability to literally reach out and touch theatergoers of all ages. Its popularity resulted in skyrocketing box office returns. To reiterate, the purpose of PERCEPTO! was to startle select members of an audience by delivering a buzzing, tingling sensation to random seats of the theater. Screaming, in theory, led to "immediate relief." And many of those who did not have the opportunity to experience PERCEPTO! upon an initial viewing of *The Tingler* returned to see the film for a second time. In fact, a majority of theatergoers bought their tickets primarily because of the excitement that transpired within the film's closing minutes. As Price commanded the crowd to scream for their lives, people were only too happy to oblige. The public, in essence, wanted to experience PERCEPTO!

Castle knew that the limited capabilities of some theaters would hinder the gimmick's effects. Therefore, he made accommodations. For example, an alternate sequence was created for drive-in theaters. As the tingler supposedly became loose amongst the parked vehicles, Castle, instead of Price, instructed motorists to turn on their headlights and scream for their lives. It was bedlam, but it was fun. And by the late 1950s, when people went to see a Castle picture, they counted on an entertaining gimmick, among other things, to accompany the presentation.

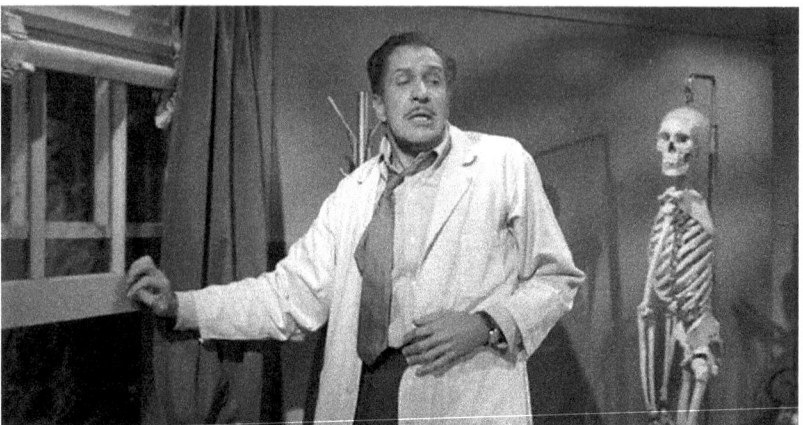

Chapin's experiment takes an unexpected turn.

The motifs of Castle's films, ranging from the gruesome décor of skeletons to the subtleties of ticking clocks, frequently recur from time to time. The cigar, arguably his most dominant motif, is an accurate reflection of the director's persona. Yet, in *The Tingler*, there are neither cigars nor any other smoking paraphernalia to be seen. And at the silent movie theater, the projectionist's sign boldly states that there is "positively no smoking." Nevertheless, *The Tingler* distinctively features the trademark motifs (i.e., death by fright, confined creatures, and a film within the film) that many would come to associate with Castle's earlier and later pictures.

Castle's death by fright motif, the very basis for the gimmick of *Macabre*, reaches its apex in *The Tingler*. Without it, the film's narrative would lack a solid foundation. During the opening scene, as Chapin performs the autopsy, he catechizes "the force of fear" and its effect on the human body. Higgins listens intently:

> CHAPIN: Many people die in fear. I wonder how many die of fear.
>
> HIGGINS: You mean . . . being scared to death?
>
> CHAPIN: Hmm . . . not on the death certificate. Fear causes tremendous tensions in the body. If you can't relieve those tensions, why can't they become strong enough to kill you?

Chapin's experiment and its purpose become clear to the audience. Hence, we anticipate its outcome and become immersed in a plot that evolves around death by fright. The motif first appeared in *The Whistler*, as the purpose of the killer's psychological experiment is to scare Earl Conrad to death. Coincidentally, the film, one of Castle's earliest, spawned yet another motif to be featured in *The Tingler*.

Confined creatures, first depicted as imprisoned mice (belonging to the killer of *The Whistler*), are commonplace within the confines of Chapin's humble laboratory. Castle creates a dichotomy between that which is visible and that which is mentioned in passing. The laboratory contains its share of containers, some large and adequate enough to quarantine a living creature. But that which occupies a container (or cage) is only visible to the audience when it is significant to the plot. As Morris makes his first appearance of the film, there is mention of a black cat he has recently captured, but it is never seen. Instead, Chapin assures Morris that they will eventually happen upon "something tangible, real." Later, a dog is acquired. But it, too, proves unnecessary for the experiment and, therefore, does not appear in the film. Eventually, the tingler arrives on the scene. Chapin's initial rendezvous with the creature culminates in its confinement to a partially wired cage. Hence, Castle transports his audience into a world where the most imaginary of creatures are, in fact, tangible and real. And common household animals like cats and dogs, although

A terrified Martha struggles to evade the unknown.

quite familiar to theatergoers, are insignificant and, therefore, unworthy of screen time.

Every showman, when presenting to an audience, boasts a main attraction. And the tingler, so significant that the film's title is derived from its classification, is Castle's crème de la crème. The cage proves flimsy. And for the first time in Castle's world of fiction, a creature that is confined to a cage breaks free to wreak havoc on the public.

The climax of The Tingler transpires during a screening at the aforementioned silent movie theater, thereby presenting a film within the film. Castle's motif was first implemented during his early years with Columbia and would occasionally recur in several of his other pictures. In Voice of the Whistler, executives view a short film in regard to the notable achievements of John Sinclair, the president of a company. In Hollywood Story, Larry O'Brien sits in a private screening room admiring Lon Chaney in The Phantom of the Opera. Later, he and Sally Rousseau watch one of her mother's films in the same theater. Following The Tingler, Castle's motif appeared in Zotz!, as Jimmy Kellgore takes Cynthia Jones to a drive-in theater (where the featured film is Castle's Homicidal). In The Busy Body, Charley Barker converts his boardroom into a temporary screening room so that he and his associates can scrutinize a gangster film. Yet, despite the motif's appearances in several of Castle's films, the underlying concept of motion pictures is dominant in The Tingler.

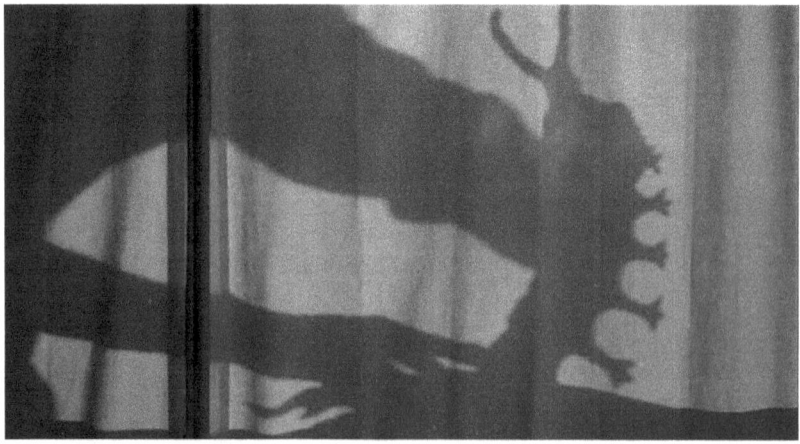

Castle's creature makes a grand introduction.

Shortly after Castle's address to the audience, we bear witness to a conversation between Chapin and Higgins upon their arrival at the silent movie theater. According to the latter, business is booming, as the "old pictures" tend to attract many. And people do not attend "just to make fun" of the films. A genuine interest exists. Later, Chapin urges Morris and Lucy to "go to a movie" so that he can conduct an experiment in private. But the suggestion is also made because the viewing of a film is a popular pastime. *The Tingler* contains several references, direct and indirect, to the pleasures of motion pictures. Hence, Castle's film is noteworthy for its unequivocal recognition of three cinematic milestones: the prosperity of the silent era, the benefits of synchronized sound, and the advent of color.

The Tingler pays homage to the silent era through its recognition of the period's defining characteristics. Castle's tribute evolves around the silent movie theater. Martha, a key figure of the story, owns the property. Her status as a deaf mute is noteworthy. David Skal, an esteemed critic of horror films, referred to Martha as "a character out of a silent movie." She is a direct representation of the venue she owns. The original Silent Movie Theatre, located in the Fairfax District of Los Angeles, was the real-life inspiration for the fictitious theater of *The Tingler*. Through the years, it has showcased the films of Buster Keaton, Douglas Fairbanks, and many more. In *The Tingler*, as Higgins prepares coffee, Chapin expresses an interest in a special performer of the era:

CHAPIN: I'd like to see some of the old Charlie Chaplin films again.

HIGGINS: Oh, we show them once a year. I'll let you know.

An appreciation of the period is evident. Chapin admires Chaplin, but he will have to wait for the annual retrospective to take place. The theater's current feature is *Tol'able David*, a 1921 classic of the silent era. According to Higgins, it is "just as good as the movies they make nowadays." Within its opening minutes, a rooster crows to announce the break of dawn. The image is aesthetically picturesque, despite the unavoidable absence of a key element.

"The Tingler is in the theater!"

Castle's use of synchronized sound, the very innovation to transform the realm of cinema, enhances the overall presentation of *The Tingler*. It creates a tense mood as Martha is accosted by her husband in their apartment. The chilling notes of Von Dexter's score can be heard, thus unnerving the audience. But the music alone does not carry the scene. A rocking chair moves in conjunction with an ominous squeaking noise. The bedroom door slowly closes, accompanied by the creaking of its hinges. And distinct clicking sounds are barely audible as the lamps deactivate. In essence, the beginning of the scene prospers through the efficacy of synchronized sound. Martha gradually finds her way to the bathroom, where more of the unexpected awaits both her and the audience.

The sudden flow of red blood, oozing into the sink and bathtub, is reminiscent of a momentous achievement in motion picture history: the advent of color. Castle went to great lengths in order to achieve a peculiar, unique image for the scene. First, the set of the bathroom was painted with black, white, and gray colors. Then, Castle equipped his cinematographers with color film stock. Finally, Judith Evelyn was given a complete makeover, covered from head to toe with various shades of gray. The cameras rolled, capturing the distinct brightness of the outpouring red liquid. What, at first, appears to be a scarcity quickly becomes a plethora. As evidenced by the spacious tub, Castle's fictitious bathroom contains as much blood as a blood bank. The birthplace printed on Martha's featured death certificate is Red Bank, an actual city in New Jersey. Hence, the film's traditional black-and-white setting is temporarily dominated by the intriguing shade of red. For the first time since *Duel on the Mississippi*, a color format was featured in a Castle film. To theatergoers, it was unexpected, but it was memorable.

A film within the film.

The theatrical release of *The Tingler* propelled Castle to great success. The film has developed a cult following over the years and continues to prove successful at revivals. It is especially notorious for PERCEPTO!, undoubtedly the most popular of Castle's gimmicks. *The Tingler* is also the first motion picture to feature LSD. In 1959, very few people were aware of the acid and its psychedelic effects. White's prior exposure to LSD warranted its inclusion in the story. Furthermore, his script made a significant contribution to the overall success of the picture.

The dialogue is memorable. Early in *The Tingler*, Chapin remarks, "Science is sometimes frighteningly impersonal." Upon the film's conclusion, he chides Higgins by telling him that "just because poison happens to exist is no excuse to commit murder with it."

The dialogue, however, has also been cited for its absurdity. At one point, Chapin tells Morris, "The Tingler is a solid mass extending from the coccyx to the cervices." Vincent Price and Darryl Hickman were faced with the daunting task of reciting their lines while maintaining a serious demeanor. Nevertheless, the two made the best of the situation and ultimately enjoyed making the picture.

Audiences, too, had a good time. And Castle wanted nothing less from theatergoers. *The Tingler* was, and continues to be, a hit with the American public. It had a profound impact on audiences, inspiring *The Saturday Evening Post* to officially designate Castle as "the master of movie horror."

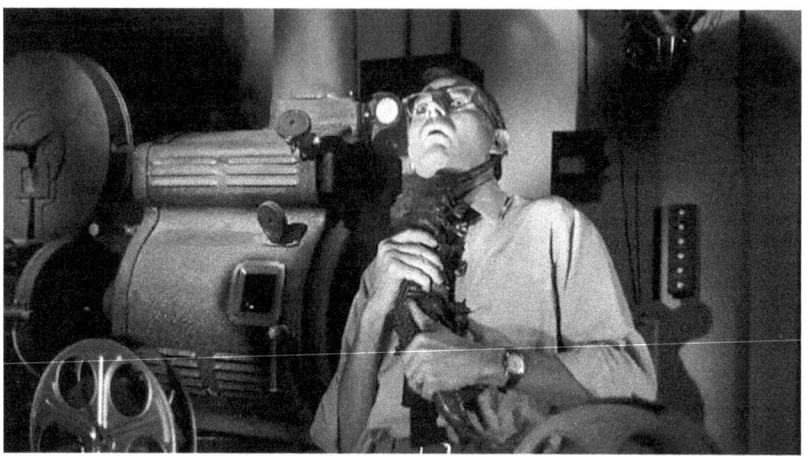

Dal McKennon as the theater's projectionist.

CHAPTER FORTY-THREE
13 GHOSTS (1960)

In 1960, William Castle was at the pinnacle of his career. Aside from the gimmicks of EMERGO! and PERCEPTO!, the mere presence of Vincent Price had strengthened the marketability of *House on Haunted Hill* and *The Tingler*. But as the production of *13 Ghosts* began, Castle had neither a clever gimmick nor a major star to accompany his project. He was more concerned about the former and was quite desperate for ideas.

This changed with a single trip to the doctor's office. An ophthalmologist, suspecting impaired vision, tested Castle's eyes with a series of metal frames and lenses. Eventually, the concept of ILLUSION-O! was born. Immediately prior to screenings of *13 Ghosts*, theatergoers were provided with cardboard glasses in order to view an intriguing collection of apparitions, considered by many to be the true stars of the film.

Cyrus "Cy" Zorba (Donald Woods), a Los Angeles-based paleontologist, lives paycheck-to-paycheck to support his wife, Hilda (Rosemary DeCamp), an older daughter, Medea (Jo Morrow), and a younger son, Buck (Charles Herbert). On the verge of losing his house, Cy is summoned to the office of Ben Rush (Martin Milner), attorney at law. Rush represents Dr. Plato Zorba, Cy's recently deceased uncle. Zorba's will grants Cy full ownership of a ghost-infested mansion. The family moves to the house, despite the uncertainties. During the family's first night in the new home, Cy encounters several ghosts, including a flaming skeleton. He discovers that the house contains a total of twelve ghosts, including Zorba's spirit. Furthermore, Cy learns of a mysterious thirteenth ghost that has yet to take form. Zorba's memoirs reveal that his assets were converted to cash and placed in an undisclosed location shortly before his death. Elaine Zacharides (Margaret Hamilton), Zorba's longtime assistant and housekeeper, questions the circumstances surrounding her employer's demise. In an attempt to communicate with Zorba's spirit, Elaine conducts a séance. She and the family learn that somebody will die. Meanwhile, Buck accidentally discovers the missing cash to be hidden in the home. He informs Rush, who is not only revealed to be Zorba's killer, but has also been secretly trying to frighten Cy and his family away from the house in order to steal the money. Rush attempts to murder Buck. But Zorba's ghost interferes, killing Rush and converting him into the thirteenth ghost.

"Do you believe in ghosts?"

During the months leading up to the premiere of *13 Ghosts*, Castle struggled with the film's apparitions. He faced the technological challenge of getting his ghosts to appear and disappear before the eyes of his audience. Much had been invested, and after approximately forty failed tests, Castle was beginning to lose hope. ILLUSION-O! was nearly abandoned altogether, but plastic lenses "of just the right density" were eventually devised by a team of experts. Cardboard glasses were produced at a high volume and sent to theaters nationwide. Fortunately, ILLUSION-O! was not discarded for some other gimmick, because it ultimately strengthened the film's narrative. Castle, in portraying the human world as dreary, establishes a fine line to separate it from the supernatural world. Some are unhappily earthbound, but the ghost viewer (and cardboard glasses), in addition to the portrait of Plato Zorba, foster hope by working to unite both realms together.*

More often than not, the supporting characters of Castle's films are skeptical of the world in which they find themselves. Significant examples include Watson Pritchard of *House on*

---

* In order to avoid confusion, the words "ghost viewer" will henceforth refer to the instrument used by the narrative's characters, whereas the words "cardboard glasses" will refer to the special eyewear of the audience.

Haunted Hill and Ollie Higgins of *The Tingler*. The trend does not change with *13 Ghosts*. Mr. Van Allen (John Van Dreelen), Cy's boss and curator of the Los Angeles County Museum, appears cynical of the world. But the ghosts and Buck share similar emotions.

As Van Allen makes his first appearance of the film, Castle begins his depiction of a dreary world in which some have given up hope. At the museum, Cy lectures to a group of students, but becomes sidetracked when approached by his boss:

CY: What's the trouble, Mr. Van Allen?

VAN ALLEN: Your wife's on the phone.

CY (gesturing to the students): But, I'm lecturing.

VAN ALLEN: I told her that.

CY: Will you take over for me then?

VAN ALLEN: Of course.

Van Allen starts in the direction of the students and then pauses to address Cy.

VAN ALLEN: Oh, Cy. Where are you?

CY: Explaining how man survived the Pleistocene Age.

Cy departs as Van Allen appears to process the instructions.

VAN ALLEN (to himself): How did he...and why?

Van Allen is not at all pleased with the world in which he finds himself. His reasoning, perhaps, is that humans went to great lengths to survive the icy conditions of the past only to find themselves in a situation that is not much better. Economic hardships appear to have befallen a select group of people, namely the museum employees who work to preserve their own history. Van Allen, supporting three children as opposed to Cy's two, earns little more than his underling. Throughout the film, the introverted curator rarely smiles and appears to be generally uninterested in the meaning of life. He is a skeptic in the truest sense of the word and does not appear to be motivated by anything, except when it comes to the translation of Zorba's diary.

The Zorba mansion.

The diary reveals that the ghosts, considered by many to be the main characters of the film, are frequenting a human world that is not to their liking. Zorba's notes provide a chilling explanation. Crimes are committed not by ghosts, but by "unscrupulous men" who must be stopped. Rush, succumbing to greed, has murdered Zorba. The ghosts cannot be released from holding the Earth until revenge is theirs. The perfect opportunity arises when Rush plans an elaborate death for Buck. Although the youngest Zorba escapes with the help of the ghosts, some might wonder how he would have acclimated to a different dimension had he, in fact, joined his uncle on the other side.

Throughout the narrative, Buck appears to lose hope in the human world, frequently yearning to discover the mysteries of the supernatural. His conversation with Elaine during the film's closing scene simply reinforces the feelings he has harbored since first being introduced to the audience:

BUCK: [The ghosts] haven't really gone, have they?

ELAINE: They'll be back. They'll be back.

BUCK (smiling): Real soon I hope.

Despite everything that has happened, Buck appears nostalgic. It is evident he was happier when the ghosts were lurking about the house, as they brought significance and meaning to his

Charles Herbert as Buck Zorba.

life. Castle's introduction of Buck to the audience reveals a young boy to be entering a house that is devoid of furniture. He lives a life that is lacking in substance and excitement. It is not until Buck receives the book of ghost stories that his demeanor changes for the better. The Zorbas eventually inherit the ghost-infested house, concealed items are discovered, and Elaine gives a rudimentary lesson on the ghosts' history. Step by step, Buck's fantasies and desires are gradually fulfilled, but it is the ghost viewer that ultimately brings him within reach of the supernatural world.

By providing cardboard glasses in order for his audience to experience the full effects of ILLUSION-O!, Castle put theatergoers into the shoes of the film's characters by bringing them as close to the action as possible. Within the narrative of 13 *Ghosts*, Zorba's unique ghost viewer establishes similar connections, thus creating a fine line between Buck's world and that of the ghosts. Buck's encounter with Shadrack the Great, Rush's visit to Medea's bedroom, and the initial appearance of Zorba's ghosts suggest that the mere presence of a viewing apparatus, or lack thereof, reveals more to the narrative than one might expect.

Buck's use of the ghost viewer brings him within arm's length of Shadrack and his feline sidekick. Shadrack's acknowledgement of the youngest Zorba reveals a mutual degree of trust and admiration, and Castle's depiction of the scene sets it apart from the remainder of the film. As Buck opens Shadrack's oversized trunk, Von Dexter's score departs from its ominous overtones and transitions to a cheerful, circus-like tune, thereby lightening the

A most ominous reflection.

mood of the scene. Buck playfully experiments with a bullwhip. Shortly thereafter, and with the help of the ghost viewer, he comes face-to-face with Shadrack, who then gestures for his amazed spectator to come closer. Buck does not hesitate as he immediately approaches the ghostly magician. During the following scene, however, Buck will display almost the opposite approach with Rush. When the latter offers his hand in acknowledgement, the former is hesitant to accept. With Shadrack, the trust is immediate. With Rush, however, Buck is unsure of how to approach the situation. Although he is unaware of the circumstances behind the earlier disturbance in Medea's bedroom, his hesitation is justified.

When Rush, disguised as a hideous ghoul, frightens Medea, a significant clue is presented to the audience, as Castle does not instruct us to use the cardboard glasses at any time during the scene. Rush's ghostly attire of cobwebs and old clothes, although convincing to some, differs from what we have seen up to this point of the film. By the time he accosts Medea, theatergoers have used the cardboard glasses on a frequent, steady basis. Perhaps, when looking at Rush, some in the audience might believe they are seeing a ghost despite an absence of the words "USE VIEWER" at the bottom of the screen (the process of retrieving and using the cardboard glasses has almost become habitual to theatergoers at this point of the film). Furthermore, the official trailer for *13 Ghosts* refers to a disguised Rush as "the evil ghost in the bedroom." Despite several indications that the mysterious figure in Medea's bedroom could be a ghost, there are some in the audience who

Rosemary DeCamp, Jo Morrow, Donald Woods, Martin Milner, and Charles Herbert.

will not be fooled, as Rush's costume does not appear genuine. In addition, his figure lacks the glowing, reddish color that comes to be associated with the true ghosts of the film. Later, when Cy informs Rush of the incident, the latter ironically questions if Medea was "wearing those glasses Zorba made" at the time of the attack. Had a real ghost been responsible, Medea would have been unable to see her attacker, as she was not in possession of the ghost viewer.

The cardboard glasses, in displaying the first appearance of the ghosts following the family's arrival, focus on the most significant adornment of the house. The oil painting of Zorba is the key link between the human and supernatural worlds. The first time "USE VIEWER" appears onscreen, we find ourselves facing Zorba's portrait as two of his ghosts gradually appear. A hanging woman flies up to the ceiling, scaling the very painting that defines her confinement to the house. An executioner then severs his already decapitated head with the graceful swing of an axe. It is an exciting moment of the narrative. Following a twenty-five minute wait, and barring Castle's introduction of his motion picture, theatergoers were finally allowed to make use of their cardboard glasses for the first time during the film. But despite the debut of the ghosts, one must not underestimate the attention given to the portrait.

Ancestral paintings, a major motif, appear in a selection of Castle's films, including *Duel on the Mississippi* and *The Old Dark*

House. During *13 Ghosts*, however, the motif constantly recurs from beginning to end. Halfway through the film, Buck, thinking he is alone, slides down the banister. The first traces of the hidden cash come to light. However, instead of noticing the money, Buck spots the ghost viewer lying on a nearby table. While examining it, he looks up, only to discover his late uncle staring down at him. The boy offers a polite "good morning" and then promptly leaves the room. Zorba appears to be watching when people least expect it. The portrait, which establishes a connection between the human and supernatural worlds, sustains an extraordinary source of energy not only through the power of observation, but also through reflection and physical force.

Zorba's observing spirit, a constant presence throughout the film, is paramount at the time of the séance. Castle's use of lighting develops the scene by shifting the focus towards a particular area of the house. In order to conduct the séance, Cy obliges Elaine's request by turning out all of the lights. Once completed, the portrait remains lit with a diagonal streak of light. The audience cannot help but notice Zorba, in the background, preparing to watch over the ceremony. Castle's frame of reference contains all of the necessary elements, because Zorba's ghost will soon

The ghosts assume control of the kitchen.

emerge from the portrait in order to connect with Cy. At the time of the spirit's release, Rush initiates his plan to kill Buck. But Elaine can sense that "the ghosts are restless, angry." The energy has been building, and Zorba is on the verge of revenge, as he has known of Rush's betrayal since long ago.

Early in the film, a reflection of Rush within the portrait foreshadows his own demise at the hands of Zorba. The position of Castle's camera is noteworthy. Zorba's arms appear to wrap around Rush's upper torso, while Medea, who is free from her uncle's grasp, innocently gazes at the portrait. Rush botches the details of his employer's death, claiming the ghosts left Zorba with his "back broken, face torn to shreds, [and his] lips ripped away." The reflection is symbolic of Zorba's astute nature. Despite Rush's attempt to cover up the truth with a story of his own, he is ultimately unable to fool his own victim. Zorba has the murderer in his clutches and will deal with him at the appropriate time. Consequently, later that evening, a stern proclamation is issued after Rush dines with the Zorbas.

The portrait exhibits Zorba's supernatural powers, and also foreshadows Rush's annihilation, with a sudden display of physical force. As Buck and Medea experiment with the ouija board, it makes bold predictions, but when the game is no longer able to answer for itself, an unexpected jolt of William Castle startles us when we least expect it. Through her interrogation, Medea learns that somebody is going to be hurt, but she commands Buck to present the ultimate question without touching the board. He asks, "Are [the ghosts] gonna kill any of us?" For the first and only time of the film, the portrait moves from its location on the wall, crashing down on the nearby coffee table. Buck is almost hit, but

As the séance begins, the portrait of Plato Zorba is visible in the background.

"Ask me no questions and I'll tell you no lies."

it eventually becomes clear that he is not the intended target. Zorba's determination to address Rush is best fulfilled through the portrait. The fact that neither Buck nor Medea is touching the ouija board is irrelevant, because seconds later, Zorba easily takes control of the *planchette* in an attempt to warn his niece. The rapid downfall of the portrait is symbolic because Zorba is descending upon Rush, thus continuing a process of bringing the beleaguered attorney to justice before the latter is consciously aware of it. At the beginning of *13 Ghosts*, Castle addresses his audience with the burning question, "Do you believe in ghosts?" It is evident that Rush does not, and his ignorance ultimately leads to his demise.

13 Ghosts was released in July of 1960. In its simplest form, the film is a classic rags-to-riches tale that keeps its audience intrigued from beginning to end. Furthermore, the narrative includes a selection of scenes with little or no dialogue, but the film continues to progress at a steady pace. Castle was on hand to attend the premiere of *13 Ghosts* at the RKO Pan Theater in Minneapolis, Minnesota. Days before the momentous event was to take place, he crossed paths with Cedric Adams, a local radio personality and newspaper columnist. Since the 1930s, both Castle and Adams had worked tirelessly to succeed in their chosen professions.

Prior to the release of *13 Ghosts*, Castle devised a plan to promote his film by conducting a séance with Adams and several others. A local pastor was summoned to serve as the medium. Castle was eager to know if *13 Ghosts* would enjoy a successful run. According to Adams's column, it was predicted that the film "would do better in the east and west than in [Minnesota]." But spiritualistic messages sometimes need to be taken with a grain of salt. Because the séance also predicted that Adlai Stevenson would become the next president of the United States when, in fact, John F. Kennedy would be elected only a few months later. Contrary to some reports, Castle went on to enjoy a successful run in Minneapolis. And a multitude of teenagers, serving as proud members of the National William Castle Fan Club, turned out for the chance of a lifetime to meet their idol.

Castle meets with his fans in Minneapolis.

CHAPTER FORTY-FOUR
HOMICIDAL (1961)

In addition to Minneapolis, William Castle also appeared in New York to celebrate the premiere of 13 *Ghosts*. The attendance was quite strong, as almost every seat in the auditorium had been filled. But nearby, at the DeMille Theater, a horde of people gathered to see Alfred Hitchcock's *Psycho*. The turnout was so great that a line of those waiting to gain entrance into the theater stretched clear around the block. Unlike Castle's film, *Psycho* had been showing in New York for close to a month, and it was still playing to sold-out crowds. Some critics claimed Hitchcock had beaten Castle at his own game. *Psycho*, in essence, was a modestly budgeted thriller, typical of Castle's recent successes. Hence, Robb White countered with a diabolical idea of his own. The title of his script, similar to that of *Psycho*, consisted of a single word: *Homicidal*.

"We know each other very well. Don't we, Helga?"

A mysterious blonde (Jean Arless), using the name of Miriam Webster, checks into a Ventura hotel and bribes Jim Nesbitt (Richard Rust), a bellhop, to be her husband. A local Justice of the Peace, Alfred S. Adrims (James Westerfield), presides over the ceremony. But "Miriam" suddenly stabs Adrims to death and flees to a secluded mansion just outside of Solvang. Helga Swenson (Eugenie Leontovich), confined to a wheelchair and incapable of speech, lives in the home. She becomes uneasy when told of Adrims's death. Later, the real Miriam Webster (Patricia Breslin) arrives with flowers for Helga. She addresses the blonde only as Emily. Karl Anderson (Glenn Corbett), a Solvang drug store owner, is in a relationship with Miriam. At work, he fills a prescription for Doctor Jonas (Alan Bunce), the local physician. The doctor speaks fondly of Helga. She used to be his nurse, but suddenly quit following the birth of a boy known only as Warren. Helga delivered the child, as Jonas was unavailable at the time. When Warren's parents died, Helga, having been a friend of the boy's mother, took him to her native Denmark. While there, Helga had a stroke. When Warren came of age, he asked Emily, a friend he met in Denmark, to bring Helga back to the states in order to take care of her. Warren, who is Miriam's half-brother, recently returned from Denmark himself. He will soon turn twenty-one and, therefore, inherit $10 million from his late father's estate. Helga frequently becomes anxious around Emily, thus arousing the suspicions of Miriam. Anderson, with Emily's photo in his possession, drives to Ventura to meet with the police about the Adrims homicide. Nesbitt is summoned. Upon seeing the photo, he positively identifies Emily as the killer. Warren and Miriam race to the mansion to make sure Helga is safe. Warren enters alone. After a moment's hesitation, Miriam follows. She discovers Helga has been murdered. Emily attacks Miriam, and then suddenly reveals herself to be Warren. Jonas happens upon the scene. In the confusion, Miriam shoots Emily/Warren dead. It is later determined that, many years earlier, Warren's father desperately wanted a son. His wife, not wanting to disappoint her spouse, concocted a masquerade by concealing the sex of their newborn child. In reality, Helga delivered a girl. Adrims, a county clerk at the time, signed the birth certificate and was paid to keep quiet about the baby's gender. According to the father's will, the entire estate was to go to a son on his twenty-first birthday. Otherwise, Miriam would collect the fortune. Adrims and Helga were murdered because they knew the truth behind Warren's existence. And the masquerade was continued in order to prevent Miriam from inheriting the estate.

Homicidal was the fifth and final script Robb White penned for Castle. It is intriguing, yet complex (the preceding synopsis is

Glenn Corbett and Alan Bunce.

the longest of this book). As the film begins, Castle addresses his audience, specifically making reference to White's earlier scripts. He states, "The more adventurous among you may remember our previous excursions into the macabre, our visits to haunted hills, to tinglers, and to ghosts." White's tale of homicidal mania, when compared with the other four that were written during his extended collaboration with Castle, is arguably the most entertaining. Thus, *Homicidal* is the type of film that cannot be seen only once. An initial viewing features a series of astonishing events. However, repeated viewings enable spectators to better understand Warren's sad existence.

The theatrical trailer of *Homicidal* lasts approximately twenty seconds. Very little of the film's premise is revealed. Castle's intentions were to heighten the mystery of the unknown. Prior to the nationwide premiere of his motion picture, he held a test engagement at the Palace Theater in Youngstown, Ohio. It was there that Castle famously said, "Ladies and gentlemen, please do not reveal the ending of *Homicidal* to your friends, because if you do, they will kill you. And if they don't, I will."

Aside from an unpredictable ending, the entire film features a series of astonishing events that, traditionally, would not be expected upon an initial viewing. The Adrims murder, prolonged fate of Helga, and Fright Break gimmick are abrupt, yet electrifying.

An eerie similarity exists between the two images. Miriam Webster and Millie Baxter (below, from When Strangers Marry*) each prepare to encounter what lies ahead.*

The killing of Adrims is unexpected, and therefore, is surprising to any audience. Seconds prior to knocking on the justice's door, Nesbitt makes a questionable decision. He leaves the keys in his car, and Emily takes notice:

EMILY: You're gonna leave the keys in it?
NESBITT: Who'd steal that heap?

Nesbitt faces Adrims's house and notices that all of its lights are out. The setting is ominous. Yet, Nesbitt is at ease. Minutes earlier, he refers to the impromptu engagement as "the strangest thing [he's] ever been through." However, upon arriving at the Adrims residence, he feels safe enough to the leave the keys in his vehicle. Furthermore, Emily does not give the impression of one who is about to make a quick getaway. She appears to be slightly concerned about Nesbitt leaving the keys in the car, but she does not resemble one who is overly protective. Yet, it is his decision that ultimately enables Emily to flee the scene of the crime. She is gone in a matter of seconds. Hence, because Nesbitt leaves the keys in his car prior to entering the residence, and because Emily does not appear as one who is anxious, there is no indication of the terrible events that are to come. Adrims is murdered in cold blood. Later in the film, Emily sets her sights on the next target.

"What do we really know about anybody?"

Helga's fate is prolonged, so much so that the audience is unsure of what to expect in regard to her future. Despite making preparations for an elaborate death, Emily is taken aback by Jonas's untimely arrival at the mansion, thus enabling Castle to send his audience on an emotional roller coaster of sorts. The very knife that was used to murder Adrims is sharpened. Emily takes the phone off the hook and closes the curtains. It is at this point that the audience realizes Helga is about to be killed, until a knock at the door eases the tension. Emily hides the knife in a magazine and answers the door. Jonas enters and, after many years, comes face-to-face with Helga. He greets her warmly. Jonas then inquires about Emily's passion for reading, not realizing how close he is to the concealed knife. Helga, with the help of a detached doorknob frequently in her possession, nervously taps on the arm of her wheelchair. Jonas becomes curious, and the audience becomes hopeful. But he does not notice the knife. As Jonas appears ready to leave, Castle transitions to a close-up shot of Helga's shuddering face. Much to the frustration of theatergoers, she cannot speak. However, the tension is partially diffused when Jonas notices the disconnected phone. Perhaps, many deduce that Helga will survive, but such is not the case. A suspicious Jonas leaves, and Emily makes her move. Although the thought of Helga surviving the ordeal is uplifting, we simply do not know what to expect when engaged in the cinema of William Castle. In short, the doctor is unable to save Helga, but his return to the mansion prevents Warren from killing Miriam. And it is around this time that Castle reveals his ace in the hole.

The Fright Break gimmick, although well-publicized throughout the promotion of *Homicidal*, manages to creep up on theatergoers at a key moment of the narrative. Haunting elements of sight and sound simply add to the suspense, and the audience is faced with the ultimate decision. Warren and Miriam arrive at the mansion. He enters, leaving her alone in the car.

Hugo Friedhofer's persistent score, coupled with the uneasy ticking of a clock, merely sets the scene for what is to follow. Miriam exits the vehicle and ponders her next move. The statue of a wyvern, featured prominently throughout the film, beckons her to live dangerously and follow Warren. Unsure of what to do, Miriam looks to the sky, only to discover the light of a full moon penetrating through the drifting clouds. Finally, Miriam decides to enter the mansion. As she gets closer, the sound of a beating heart (similar to what is heard when Warren Chapin of *The Tingler* removes the hideous creature from its habitat) gradually becomes audible.

> Hence, the stage is set. A forty-five second clock appears on the screen as Castle's voice declares, "This is the Fright Break! Do you hear that sound? It's the sound of a heartbeat... a frightened, terrified heart. Is it beating faster than your heart... or slower? This heart is going to beat for another twenty-five seconds... to allow anyone to leave this theater who is too frightened to see the end of

the picture. Ten seconds more and we go into the house. It's now or never. Five ... four ... you're a brave audience ... two ... one."

For theatergoers, it was the ultimate decision. Those who departed the auditorium were given a full refund. However, they were sent directly to the Coward's Corner, a designated area of the theater's lobby. These patrons were required to remain in the corner for the remainder of the film. Furthermore, as *Homicidal* concluded and the rest of the audience filed into the lobby, the so-called cowards had no choice but to be put on display. The Coward's Corner proved to be quite the attraction. But overall, a majority of theatergoers chose to remain in the auditorium. And it was clearly for their benefit, as they were treated to a spectacular ending.

Castle concludes *Homicidal* with a peculiar, yet thoughtful, image. The audience is taken back to the mansion's playroom, the very location where the story began. Miriam's doll is perched atop a windowsill. The window itself is open, and there is a slight breeze. Suddenly, a gust of wind sends the doll falling towards the floor of the room. It lands face down, directly onto the dreaded leather whip. Castle's concluding image is somewhat haunting. It not only signifies the end of *Homicidal*, but it also represents the termination of Warren's sad existence. In order to understand the meaning behind White's script, it is imperative to engage in repeated viewings of Castle's film. The opening scene, debacle at Miriam's flower shop, and character of Helga are all worthy of closer examination.

The opening scene, transpiring within the infamous playroom, is subject to a different interpretation when viewed more than once. It enables the random viewer to see Warren and Miriam's relationship from a unique perspective. Upon an initial viewing, members of an audience see a boy tormenting what appears to be his younger sister. Smiling, he casually takes her doll. However, the reality is that Warren is not only a girl, but he is also the younger sister. Naturally, he/she wants the doll because it is a feminine toy. Miriam, completely unaware of the circumstances behind Warren's birth, believes she is dealing with a younger brother instead of a

Richard Rust and Glenn Corbett (below), although similar in character, do not appear onscreen together during the film. Sadly, both men passed away during the 1990s at the age of fifty-nine.

younger sister. Over time, a specific type of jealousy develops, thus leading to a noteworthy event of the film.

Emily's vandalism of the flower shop is significant for many reasons, specifically because it is fueled by her envy of Miriam and Anderson's budding relationship. The destruction of particular objects offers insight into the sibling jealousy. At first, it appears as if Emily does not intend to do any damage. But upon seeing the miniature statues of brides and grooms, she becomes enraged. Hence, the havoc begins. Visions of an impending marriage are paramount, but Emily will do everything in her power to keep Miriam and Anderson apart. She eventually finds a photograph of Warren and smashes its frame. Emily is unwilling to

Patricia Breslin as Miriam Webster. The name of her character is strikingly similar to that of the publishing company, Merriam-Webster. The trademark was coined many years after the theatrical release of Homicidal.

accept the existence of her alter ego, a persona that was the source of her lost youth. Later, Anderson enters the vandalized shop. And Emily seizes the opportunity, inflicting harm upon the very individual who, thinking she was Warren, used to start fights with her in childhood. Anderson, of course, was paid by Warren's father, an unseen character ultimately responsible for the film's drastic chain of events. In short, Miriam did not have as traumatic of a childhood, and Emily/Warren has been resentful for many years. The jealous feelings eventually lead to homicidal tendencies. Once Adrims is dispatched, a single, remaining individual (with the exception of Emily/Warren) is privy to the horrific details behind Warren's existence.

The character of Helga is clearly an important part of the story, but after multiple viewings, it becomes clear that she is vital to the narrative's success. Castle's integration of Miriam's doll into the film's *mise-en-scène* is symbolic. As the opening credits come to a close, a young Warren is seen clutching the doll against his chest. It stares back at Miriam, helpless and unable to speak. Helga is in the same predicament. Her eyes, as well as those of the doll, have borne witness to many atrocious events through the years. Helga knows much, but cannot speak or write a single word. When Warren and Miriam revisit the playroom, key information is revealed:

MIRIAM: So long since I've been in here. I don't know whether I like it or not.

WARREN: Why?

MIRIAM: Well, the things it reminds me of. Helga would never let me in here. She was always trying to keep us away from each other.

WARREN: That was part of the system . . . toughen me up . . . keep girls out of my life . . . make me more of a man. All because of my father.

MIRIAM: I hardly even remember him.

WARREN: I do. I remember everything he did to make me as hard and ruthless as he was. Do you know that he even paid Karl to start fights with me when we were kids?

MIRIAM: I used to watch the two of you hitting each other. Then, I'd look at Father. He'd be smiling.

Warren walks over to a corner of the playroom and opens a chest of drawers. He removes the leather whip and cracks it against the chest. Facing Miriam, he holds it up for her to see.

WARREN: Remember this?

Miriam barely nods her head.

WARREN: Helga would come in here with this, all to make me strong.

Warren continues to crack the whip against his left arm. Miriam looks on in confusion.

WARREN: I'd learned to count on my back.

MIRIAM: I don't think I'll ever forgive Helga for that.

WARREN: She was only obeying orders...Father's orders.

In disgust, Warren throws the whip on the floor. It will remain there for the remainder of the film. The conversation indicates that Warren has compassion for Helga. But such is not the case with his alter ego. A psychological difference between the personas of Warren and Emily is evident whenever Helga is present.

Helga does not appear tense around Warren. However, when she is approached by Emily, she immediately becomes uneasy. Miriam, too, reacts in the same manner. She admires Warren, but despises Emily. As Miriam and Warren continue their conversation in the playroom, she discovers her doll.

> MIRIAM: Do you remember the only argument we ever had? It was over this.

> Miriam holds up the doll for Warren to see. He chuckles softly.

> WARREN: How you howled when I swiped it from you.

> MIRIAM: And you never gave it back to me either.

> WARREN: Keep it. Take it home with you.

Later that evening, as Miriam sleeps in the playroom, Emily makes a surprise appearance. It is an untimely visit. Emily is seen to be cradling the doll in her arms. Miriam demands that she leave, and even threatens to call Warren for help. Emily then clutches the doll against her chest, similar to what is seen with the younger Warren upon the film's introduction. She finally departs, leaving Miriam in a dumbfounded state of emotions. To reiterate, as *Homicidal* concludes, the doll comes crashing down onto the whip, thus signifying the end of Emily/Warren. But again, one cannot underestimate Helga's importance to the narrative, as it is her inability to speak or write that helps to conceal the best kept secret of the film.

On December 29, 1969, eight years after the theatrical release of *Homicidal*, something strange transpired. The location was Philadelphia. The setting was a small basement studio located in the KYW-TV building on Walnut Street. An episode of *The Mike Douglas Show*, a television program hosted by the "Big Band" era singer, was being recorded in front of a studio audience. The featured guests included James Brown (frequently referred to as "The Godfather of Soul") and Alfred Hitchcock. At one point, Brown asked the great director about *Homicidal*. Unaware that the film was directed by Castle, he proceeded with his question

Gilbert Green as Lieutenant Miller. He offers an explanation (below) in regard to Warren's history.

nonetheless. Brown asks, "Did you actually use a girl, or did you use a fellow?"

The question, clearly an inquiry into the supposed gender of Jean Arless, had been on the minds of Americans for many years. And Hitchcock, not even bothering to mention that *Homicidal* was directed by Castle, simply replied, "I wouldn't dare tell you." Why he did not give credit where it was due is unknown.

In truth, both Warren and Emily were played by one woman, whose real name was Joan Marshall. Overall, many of Hitchcock's fans were not enthusiastic about *Homicidal*, claiming it was an outright fabrication of *Psycho*. But others were able to keep an open mind. It has clearly stood the test of time and continues to jolt the average spectator of today.

CHAPTER FORTY-FIVE
MR. SARDONICUS (1961)

Following the release of *Homicidal*, William Castle and Robb White parted ways. Although the reason is not entirely clear, several theories of their disbandment exist. The most popular belief is that Castle did not provide his writer with adequate compensation for his efforts. White ultimately returned to television, penning a series of scripts for *Perry Mason*. But he also continued to make a living as a novelist. Many of his works, published both before and after his time with Castle, were set in the Pacific Theater of Operations during World War II.

Castle himself was vacationing in another region of the Pacific when he came across an idea for his next picture. In Hawaii at Honolulu's Kahala Hilton, he was relaxing poolside when a "macabre tale" in *Playboy* caught his attention. *Sardonicus*, a novella by Ray Russell, evolves around a man whose "face becomes permanently frozen in a wide, frenzied grin" upon seeing his father's rotting corpse. Castle knew the story would pave the way for an entertaining narrative, thus enabling him to implement yet another creative gimmick.

Arrival at the castle.

Sir Robert Cargrave (Ronald Lewis), a respected London physician, experiments with cures for paralysis. He receives a letter from Baroness Maude Sardonicus (Audrey Dalton), an ex-flame. Her husband, Baron Sardonicus (Guy Rolfe), has heard of Cargrave's research and expresses a desire to meet him. The doctor accepts the invitation and travels to central Europe. Upon arrival in Gorslava, the location of the Sardonicus castle, Cargrave takes note of certain peculiarities. He reunites with Maude, and then meets the baron. Much to Cargrave's consternation, Sardonicus conceals his face with a mask. The baron, formerly known as Marek Toleslawski, reminisces about the time his father, Henryk Toleslawski (Vladimir Sokoloff), purchased a lottery ticket prior to passing away. It remained in the pocket of the burial suit. The ticket, however, later proved to be a winning one. Marek (Sardonicus) sought to retrieve it by unearthing the coffin. When he came face-to-face with the decayed remains of his father, the shocking experience caused a severe paralysis of his facial muscles, thus producing a hideous, teeth-baring grin. Upon learning of the baron's plight, Cargrave agrees to treat him, but initial attempts prove unsuccessful. Sardonicus, aware of the doctor's history with Maude, threatens to punish her should further treatments fail. Cargrave conducts additional research. He then injects Sardonicus with a mysterious liquid. The baron's grin quickly disappears. Believing he is cured, Sardonicus annuls his marriage to Maude. She and Cargrave depart the castle together. But Krull (Oskar Homolka), the baron's servant, locates the doctor and informs him that Sardonicus cannot open his mouth. Cargrave confesses to injecting the baron with nothing but water. The research was a charade. Sardonicus's affliction, in essence, was psychologically induced. And the only way for him to make a full recovery is to be conscious of the healing power of his own mind. Cargrave instructs Krull to enlighten the baron. But Krull, having endured years of torment at the hands of his master, lies to Sardonicus upon returning to the castle, claiming to have "missed" the doctor. The baron wallows in despair at the mere thought of his imminent starvation.

Castle, impressed with Russell's story, hired him to pen the script of *Mr. Sardonicus*. Hence, the novella and screenplay are quite similar. A key difference, however, is evident in regard to the fate of Sardonicus's mother. In the film, she passes a year before her husband. But in the novella, she lives. One year after Castle lost his mother, his father, too, died suddenly. The

Ronald Lewis as Sir Robert Cargrave. The Sardonicus logo appears in the background. It is featured throughout Castle's film and Ray Russell's novella.

coincidence between Castle's parents and those of the film's title character is uncanny. In addition, as Castle personally introduces *Mr. Sardonicus* to his audience, he acts and speaks in a manner of which Russell had originally intended for Sardonicus himself. The film begins, a cigar is lit, and our host greets us. Castle then produces a dictionary with the intention of locating the definition of "ghoul." But first, he happens upon "ghoom," a word pertaining to searching for game in the dark. Castle eventually finds what he is looking for, and then takes pride in enlightening the audience on how "an evil being who robs graves and feeds on corpses" will be a theme of his film. In the novella, Russell presents the character of Sardonicus in a peculiar light. Cargrave arrives. Dinner is served. And following the meal, Sardonicus and Cargrave adjourn to the library.

Russell writes, "The smoking of the cigar made Sardonicus look even more grotesque: being unable to hold it in his lips, he clenched it in his constantly visible teeth, creating an unique spectacle." Sardonicus obtains a dictionary, briefly defines ghoom, and then presents Cargrave with a definition of ghoul. In defining the word through his title character, Russell uses the adjective of "imaginary." Castle, for reasons the audience will soon discover, does not. Furthermore, in the film, Sardonicus does not smoke a cigar, as this would have resulted in an awkward spectacle. But Castle's decision to stray from Russell's story and read from the dictionary himself is simply a frank reflection of his persona. Castle, to a particular degree, aligns himself with the title character of his film. He is enamored with Russell's concept, but also deems it necessary to take the story to the next level. The novella includes some of Castle's frequently-used motifs, which are significantly enhanced in the resulting adaptation. Furthermore, additional motifs are effectively implemented in accordance with Castle's personal vision. Yet, for purposes of audience engagement, *Mr. Sardonicus* features a villain that is far more loathsome than that of Russell's novella.

Castle's film, in addition to the story on which it is based, contains references to the works of William Shakespeare. At dinner, the likes of noteworthy personalities are the topic of conversation. Sardonicus speaks of Macbeth as an "evil character." And Cargrave counters, citing Iago (of *Othello*) as a tormentor of "ghoulish delight." The Shakespeare canon is a Castle motif first presented in *Just Before Dawn*. It will later recur in *Zotz!* But in regard to *Mr. Sardonicus*, there are additional motifs (i.e., coffins, skeletons, and keyboard instruments) contained in Russell's novella that are greatly enhanced for the film.

Oskar Homolka as Krull.

A coffin is one of Castle's most popular motifs and, although present in the novella, receives a considerable amount of attention in *Mr. Sardonicus*. During the flashback of Marek's past, and as he prepares to unveil his father's corpse, a special angle of the coffin is carefully photographed as a means to build suspense. A shovel is used to open the lid. Castle frequently intercuts between a winded Marek and the creaking coffin. A single shot of the lid, and nothing more, is then presented to the audience. Marek's hands, which have been visible throughout most of the scene, are missing from the frame, as the emphasis is clearly on the coffin and its opening lid. Then, a brief shot of the full moon dominates the screen for a split second. Finally, the rotting corpse is unveiled, and Marek's problems become drastically worse. In Russell's novella, there is more of an emphasis on the moon than the actual coffin. In fact, the chapter in which the graveyard events transpire is entitled, "The Moon His Undoing." Yet, in *Mr. Sardonicus*, a coffin is portrayed as a special object. Because the well-known motif, among many others, is a commonality in the cinema of William Castle.

Skeletons are dominant in several of Castle's later films, but in regard to Russell's story, the emphasis is on the skull, and a particular scene of *Mr. Sardonicus* greatly enhances the original conception of the motif. The illuminated windows of the baron's castle reveal a chilling image. Approximately thirteen minutes into the film, Krull and Cargrave arrive at their destination. As Castle presents the Sardonicus estate to his audience for the first time, the vision of a giant skull dominates the picture. Specific windows – two as a representation of a skull's eye sockets, one to depict the nose cavity, and several more to represent a sinister grin - are lit in a precise pattern. In the novella, Russell's second chapter is appropriately titled, "The Sight of a Giant Skull." It chronicles Cargrave's imminent arrival. Yet, in describing the illuminated castle windows, Russell writes, ". . . at the end of the rutted road, stood the castle itself – dark, save for lights in two of its many windows." Castle, however, presents a structure with at least ten well-lighted windows. It is prominently displayed to viewers as Cargrave arrives. Castle's depiction of the skull is essentially more vivid than Russell's original conception. A short time later, Maude enters the picture. And it eventually becomes clear to the audience that her character is significant to the narrative in more ways than one.

Contrary to Russell's novella, Maude is the only occupant of the castle to play the piano, and through her character, Castle is able to present his commonly recurring motif of keyboard instruments. A medley of beautiful music is what ultimately reunites Cargrave with his lost love. He listens intently as she performs a solo:

Guy Rolfe's mask enabled him to avoid the rigors of a cosmetic makeover, but when it became necessary for his character's disfigured face to be presented to audiences, he had no choice but to spend many grueling hours with the makeup department.

MAUDE: I love this music.

CARGRAVE: It's exquisite, but sad.

MAUDE: Yes, but there's strength under the sadness.

Maude finishes playing. Her gaze remains transfixed on the piano's keys. Cargrave approaches her.

CARGRAVE: That was very beautiful, Maude. You and your music are the only beautiful things in this place.

In what is, perhaps, the most serene moment of the film, Cargrave and Maude share a passionate kiss. Their ultimate reunion transpires at a crucial point of the narrative, and the piano is just the object to bring them together. Early in the film, Maude speaks fondly of "the most recent musical scores from Rome and Berlin" upon reuniting with Cargrave after many years. The piano, in essence, keeps her spirits alive as she lives under dreadful conditions. In Russell's novella, both Maude and Cargrave take turns playing the piano at a relatively early point of the story. But Castle saves the motif for an important moment of his film, as Cargrave prepares to deliver Maude from the evils of Sardonicus. The baron's castle is undoubtedly a treacherous place, especially for women.

Erika Peters as Elenka Toleslawski. Castle's motif of materialistic wives, evident in House on Haunted Hill *and* The Tingler, *recurs in* Mr. Sardonicus.

Shortly after Castle brings us into the confines of the Sardonicus estate, a gathering of sorts transpires. Five villagers, all women, await the baron in a private chamber. Sardonicus enters and specifically singles out the only blonde of the group. The others leave, and the lone remaining woman proceeds to remove the baron's mask. A scream is immediately heard throughout the castle, thus adding to the mystery of the film's title character. Yet, in regard to the chosen woman, it is no wonder Sardonicus picked her. The motif of blondes frequently recurs in Castle's films. But it, like others, is not present in Russell's novella. However, vivid depictions of select motifs are sometimes better portrayed within the medium of film. Hence, Castle's personal vision is evident as he integrates the motifs of floating heads, confined creatures, and materialistic wives into the story.

Floating heads, appearing individually, materialize in the air as Cargrave struggles with nightmares just hours after his arrival at the castle. The order in which the heads are displayed is noteworthy. First, the head of the stationmaster (Charles H. Radilak), a character previously seen upon Cargrave's arrival at the Gorslava train depot, floats above the bed. The suspended image, reiterating an earlier line of the film, says, "You would not understand. You are young. You do not yet have daughters." The stationmaster's remarks continue to puzzle Cargrave, even in his sleep. The image then dissolves into a second head, belonging to Anna

(Lorna Hanson), Sardonicus's maid. She speaks of a possible end to the mysterious experimenting that has transpired in the castle. The third head we see is that of Krull's, who takes pride in his work ethic and loyalty to the baron. Before Castle presents us with the fourth head, Anna's head reappears. But this time, she is seen to be writhing in agony. Maude then materializes before our eyes. She continues to emphasize that Cargave's presence at the castle is "most urgent" to her well-being. Finally, Sardonicus himself appears as the fifth and final head of the sequence. He alludes to having known a ghoul. Seconds later, Cargrave awakens in a cold sweat, thus concluding the phantasmagoric series of floating heads. With the exception of Anna's first appearance in the sequence, the characters are presented in the order in which Cargrave encountered them following his arrival in Gorslava. The stationmaster was the first person he happened upon, followed by Krull, and then Anna. Maude was next, and Sardonicus, appropriately, was the last of the characters to be encountered by Cargrave. Yet, of all the images, Anna's head is the only one to appear twice, and for good reason, because her second appearance of the sequence is noteworthy, as an unwelcome group of blood sucking beings is attached to her face.

Audrey Dalton and Ronald Lewis. Castle exhibits his motif of keyboard instruments.

Leeches, the confined creatures used by Krull as a means "to cure certain afflictions," are ever present as Anna struggles to maintain consciousness. The vile beings, which appear in only two of

Castle's films, contribute to one of the most memorable scenes of *Mr. Sardonicus*. Leeches first appeared in *Fort Ti*, as the villainous Raoul de Moreau flaunts his collection to the injured Mark Chesney. They swim within their confining container. De Moreau offers to apply his pet leeches to Chesney's bruised face, but to no avail. He is a firm believer in their healing powers. But others, namely Cargrave of *Mr. Sardonicus*, attest to the contrary, dismissing the use of leeches for medicinal purposes as "witch doctor's nonsense." Yet, unlike the leeches of *Fort Ti*, those of *Mr. Sardonicus* have been extracted from the container and placed onto a hapless victim, thus arriving in full force. When Cargrave sees Anna's leech-infested face for the first time, it marks an unforgettable moment of the film. And we, the audience, are just as appalled as the good doctor. Cargrave eventually confronts Sardonicus. And the baron responds by reflecting upon the time of his first marriage.

Elenka Toleslawski (Erika Peters), the materialistic wife of Marek (Sardonicus), is unhappy simply because she cannot have the things she desires. Her ongoing impatience ultimately gets the best of her, as she pressures her husband into becoming a grave robber. Shortly after the death of Marek's father, Elenka seeks freedom from their impoverished lifestyle:

ELENKA: You could get a good price for the farm.

MAREK: Sell my father's farm? No. And even if I did, what then?

ELENKA: We could go to the city and rent a big house.

MAREK: And the money would be gone in half a year.

ELENKA: The half a year of luxury? Yes! It would be better than this!

Just then, a knock is heard at the door. Janku (David Janti), a family friend, enters and produces a newspaper clipping containing a list of the winning lottery numbers. When it becomes apparent that Marek and Elenka are about to inherit a sizable fortune, joy ensues. But the celebration comes to a halt when it is determined that the lottery ticket, required in order to collect the winnings, was located in the suit pocket of Marek's deceased father at the time of his burial. Elenka, however, is not deterred:

ELENKA: Did you say the lottery ticket was in the pocket?

MAREK: Yes.

ELENKA: Uh-uh. Not *was*, Marek. *Is*! The lottery ticket *is* in the pocket!

MAREK: What are you saying?

ELENKA: It's as clear as daylight!

MAREK: What are you saying?

ELENKA: Marek! It's the only way!

MAREK: May God forgive you!

ELENKA: You have said that you loved me. This is your chance to prove it!

Under pressure, Marek tragically complies with Elenka's demands. Shortly after acquiescing, his morality ceases to exist. The once innocent Marek gradually transforms into the evil Sardonicus. At one point during the film, Cargrave speaks of Macbeth as being "pressed into evil by circumstance." His words ring true, as they are very much applicable to Sardonicus.

The early episodes of the Crime Doctor *radio program featured an ending similar to that of* Mr. Sardonicus. *Twelve lucky "jurors" were selected from a studio audience, and their job was to determine the antagonist's fate. Castle's Punishment Poll, too, encouraged audience interaction.*

Russell went to great lengths in regard to the development of his title character. The novella, although somewhat brief, contains vivid descriptions. The character of Sardonicus, upon being introduced into the story, makes a distinct impression on the imaginations of the readers. Russell writes, "A pallor approaching phosphorescence completed his astonishing appearance." Sardonicus is presented without a mask from the very page on which his character is introduced. Hence, there is an element of suspense contained in the film that is not necessarily present in the novella, as Castle does not reveal the face of the baron until midway through the picture. *Mr. Sardonicus*, in essence, features a villain that is not only more mysterious than the character depicted in Russell's story, but one who is also far more loathsome. In order to establish such malevolence within his antagonist, Castle incorporates the frightened villagers of Gorslava, as well as the characters of Anna and Krull, into the narrative.

From the moment Cargrave arrives in Gorslava, it becomes evident that those who inhabit the region are scared of Sardonicus. The aforementioned stationmaster does not risk speaking of the baron's unusual desires for the young women of the village. He becomes disturbed upon hearing the name of Sardonicus:

> STATIONMASTER: But there is no coach that will take you in the direction you speak of. The country up there is wild and mountainous. The roads are bad. Some places, there are no roads at all.
>
> CARGRAVE: I'm afraid you don't understand me. I was to be met by a private coach.
>
> STATIONMASTER (smiling): A private coach, from those parts? Nobody lives up there.
>
> CARGRAVE: But I assure you, somebody does. My host, Baron Sardonicus.

The stationmaster's smile quickly vanishes and is replaced by a look of genuine fear. A confused Cargrave attempts to ascertain why the mere mention of the baron's name is so disturbing. The stationmaster becomes paranoid, seeking reassurance that he did not speak ill of Sardonicus. He then proceeds to comment about

Cargrave not yet having daughters (words which will later haunt the doctor in his nightmares). Later, as Sardonicus meets with the young ladies in his private chamber, he compares the "wondrous bounty" of wine to that of women. By flaunting his wealth and abusing his power, he preys on the simple-minded villagers of Gorslava. Sardonicus is feared for many reasons. Those who have borne witness to his disfigured face, as is the case with the lone blonde of the group, are quick to spread the word (provided that they live to tell the tale). Yet, much to the dismay of those with daughters, the baron remains intriguing to the young women of Gorslava. His castle, in essence, serves as a symbol of opportunity. But for the few women who reside with Sardonicus, their lifestyle is one of entrapment.

As Anna makes her first appearances of the film, it becomes clear that she is a human "guinea pig" subjected to continuous torture on the orders of Sardonicus. The application of leeches to her face is merely the beginning of what is to come. Anna eventually finds herself hanging mercifully from a ceiling. She is perched on the tips of her toes as her body is painfully stretched from top to bottom. Krull questions Anna in regard to her discreet conversation with Cargrave, but she is not forthcoming. When Krull threatens to apply the leeches not just to her face, but her entire body, she submits to his will. Later, as Cargrave is about to begin treatment on the baron, Krull chides Anna because she slowly delivers a heavy pail of steaming water to the makeshift operating theater. Her misery, in essence, comes at the hands of Krull. But he is following orders.

Krull's "most commendable" work ethic is a clear indicator of his loyalty to Sardonicus, but the feelings are not necessarily reciprocated. The original servant-like character of Russell's story is significantly enhanced for the film, as it ultimately ensures the effective implementation of the Punishment Poll, Castle's gimmick. The novella briefly makes reference to "a taciturn fellow with Slavic features," but he is not referred to by name. Furthermore, Russell writes of a valet, butler, and coachman as separate characters whose involvement in the story is minimal. As Castle introduces Krull into the narrative, it becomes evident that the "humble servant" is a significant character. We learn that Maude's letter to Cargrave is to be personally delivered to the doctor. And Krull, instilled with fear, makes a desperate attempt to accomplish his objective. He pleads with Cargrave's head nurse (Mavis Neal Palmer), making her promise to place the letter "in Sir Robert's hand." Krull, in essence, fears his master. He fully understands that, should he fail to make contact with Cargrave, the consequences will be dire. Nevertheless, the message is delivered successfully, and the doctor journeys to Gorslava. But the audience, along with Cargrave, eventually learns that Sardonicus, upon having his authority questioned, removed Krull's eye in an act of pure evil. Hence, as the narrative concludes, Castle presents his audience with the Punishment Poll. Theatergoers were provided with glow-in-the-dark ballots in order to determine the fate of Sardonicus. Only one of two options, mercy (thumbs up) or no mercy (thumbs down), could be selected. Naturally, after repeatedly bearing witness to the baron's atrocities, audiences sentenced Sardonicus to further punishment. The final scene depicts Krull and Sardonicus together in the castle's dining room. A vast spread of food is noticeable. Krull purposely deceives his master in regard to having "missed" Cargrave at the train depot. He proceeds to indulge himself in fine food and drink. Castle intercuts between Krull's mouth and the baron's eyes. Although Sardonicus has the advantage of complete vision, a mouth and its accompanying muscles are essential for life. Hence, through the Punishment Poll, Krull's revenge is fulfilled as the baron suffers a slow, torturous death.

Mr. Sardonicus premiered in New York on October 18, 1961. Not only did the film mark Von Dexter's final collaboration with Castle, it was the last motion picture to be scored by him. Sadly, the talented composer developed an ailment of his hand and fingers, thus hindering his ability to keep pace with the grueling demands of the industry. But his efforts did not go unnoticed. *Mr. Sardonicus*, its haunting score, and the Punishment Poll were a hit with the American public. Columbia supposedly opted for "a more palatable ending and insisted [Castle] let Mr. Sardonicus live."

Some questioned whether an alternate conclusion existed in the first place. Nevertheless, theatergoers were quite content with their opportunity to interact with Castle, ultimately granting "no mercy" to the film's villain. In his memoirs, Castle fondly recalled, "The sheer joy of making *Mr. Sardonicus* made it one of my favorite films."

The above image, presented within the trailer for Mr. Sardonicus, *depicts the lynch mob of* Jesse James vs. the Daltons. *Castle borrowed footage from his earlier film in order to effectively promote the Punishment Poll.*

CHAPTER FORTY-SIX
ZOTZ! (1962)

One day during the early 1960s, William Castle ventured up to his attic in search of a book that had been in his possession for some time. Eventually, while rummaging through an old trunk, he came across *Zotz!*, a 1946 novel by Walter Karig. Castle acquired the rights a short time later.

The story concerns a man who inherits special powers with the help of an ancient relic. Castle was impressed with Ray Russell's work on *Mr. Sardonicus* and hired him to adapt a screenplay from Karig's satirical novel. But *Zotz!* was a comedy, a genre with which Castle had very little experience. At this point in his career, *Texas, Brooklyn, and Heaven* was the only comedy he had directed. Furthermore, Castle had established himself as a director who specialized primarily in horror films. A transition from horror to comedy would be quite difficult to make, but despite the skepticism of some, he pressed forward with confidence, describing the change of pace as "therapeutic."

Jonathan Jones (Tom Poston), a professor at Saracen Valley College and specialist in ancient languages, obtains a rare coin from an extinct civilization. After translating its inscription, a thunderstorm begins, and a naked woman appears in his front yard. He provides her with clothing and she leaves. Later, Jones discovers a newfound power that is attributed to the coin. A fellow colleague, Professor Kellgore (Jim Backus), dismisses Jones as strange and feels somewhat threatened by him. Dean Updike (Cecil Kellaway), head of the college, is retiring and has decided that either Jones or Kellgore will fill his soon-to-be-vacated position. Jones's life becomes more interesting when he is introduced to Professor Virginia Fenster (Julia Meade), the naked lady he encountered in his yard. She is to be his new colleague. After an experiment with the coin goes horribly wrong, the dean concludes that Jones is losing his mind. Determined to prove the coin's powers, Jones travels to Washington, D.C., and meets with the top military brass of the Defense Department. However, they reject him as delusional. The situation becomes worse when Russian spies, posing as U.S. government officials, kidnap Jones with the hopes of recovering the coin. Cynthia (Zeme North), Jones's niece, and Virginia are also captured. After a brief melee, the coin disappears down a storm drain, but not before Jones is able to outwit the Russians by using the coin to his advantage. The spies are taken into custody, and Jones's reputation is restored. He is promoted as the new dean of the college.

"Zotz!"

During the weeks prior to its release, Castle went to great lengths to promote *Zotz!* to the American public. Enormous billboards were erected, containing only the film's title in large letters. Random motorists decorated their cars with *Zotz!* bumper stickers. Plastic gold coins were manufactured and shipped to many cities. In short, the public's curiosity became aroused rather quickly. Castle kept theatergoers guessing up until the opening seconds of the film, when the Torch Lady of Columbia Pictures, the very figure to adorn the beginnings of many Castle films, asks the popular question that had been on people's minds for weeks. "What's Zotz?" Castle's modification of Karig's story, in addition to an illusion of predictability, reveals that there is much more to *Zotz!* than meets the eye.

Karig's novel was intriguing for its time. It even attracted the attention of Walt Disney, who offered Castle a large sum of money for the story's rights. Castle declined with eloquence, but spent the remainder of his life questioning his decision. At the time, it seemed like the best thing to do. Castle had a good understanding of Karig's original concept, and he believed he could produce a highly entertaining film based on it. *Zotz!* does not stray too far from the plot of the novel. Castle, however, made some noteworthy modifications, including an increase in humor, an absence of religious overtones, and the addition of Kellgore.

Mayhem at the Updike residence.

Karig intended for his novel to be a satire on the United States government during World War II, and its storyline is comical to a particular degree. But Castle's portrayal of the party at Updike's home indicates that the original story lacks much of the humor seen in the film.[*] When Jones releases the mice in an attempt to prove his theory, chaos ensues. A disaster of outrageous proportions, reflective of the slapstick humor seen in a typical *Three Stooges* short, has a domino effect on all of the guests. Nobody is safe, and when it appears that the commotion will subside, it becomes worse. The debacle at Updike's party is arguably the funniest, or craziest, scene of the film, and Castle's depiction of the events enables it to stand out in the minds of theatergoers. But despite the film's added humor, one particular element was removed from the original story.

Castle's picture is completely devoid of the religious overtones present within Karig's novel. In order to understand the key differences between both settings, one simply needs to look at the name of the college. In the novel, Jones teaches at St. Jude's

---

[*] Karig's novel includes a chapter that features a group of mice on the loose, but very few people are involved in capturing the rodents. In Castle's film, mice essentially wreak havoc on the many guests at Updike's home, which leads to a more comical scenario.

Theological Seminary and finds himself immersed in a conservative, religious environment. He even makes his residence with a prominent reverend and his wife. In the film, however, religion is not a factor, and the name of the school has been changed to Saracen Valley College. The moniker is more reflective of Jones and his field of study. In ancient times, a Saracen was considered to be a nomad of the Syrian and Arabian deserts. The very languages in which Jones specializes originated from both regions. Furthermore, the college, named after the fictional city of Saracen Valley, is an indirect reference to *The Saracen Blade*. Castle, in essence, had a natural tendency to borrow from earlier films of his.

The character of Kellgore, played by Jim Backus of *Macabre* fame, was created specifically for the film. He is immediately presented as the antagonist, leading the audience to believe that Jones is not in any serious danger because Kellgore, although a nuisance, is relatively harmless. Of course, we later learn that he is not the true antagonist of the story. Nevertheless, his presence is necessary. During Updike's farewell dinner, Jones utilizes the coin's power to hinder Kellgore's speech, providing yet another memorable and entertaining scene of the film. But the incident ultimately reveals a peculiar innocence within Kellgore. Shortly after Jones is abducted, we see Kellgore, still seated at the table, fondly reminiscing about the humiliating events of his speech. He is poking fun at himself and no longer seems to care about Jones.

Jim Backus as Professor Kellgore. Backus had previously performed for Castle in Hollywood Story *and* Macabre.

Kellgore suddenly ceases to be a threat. And the turn of events is somewhat unforeseeable.

Castle occasionally strived to deceive audiences, avoiding predictability at all costs. Throughout the history of motion pictures, there has existed a certain breed of theatergoers who pride themselves on the ability to predict a film's outcome, regardless of the genre. They are sometimes seen standing in line, eagerly awaiting entry into a theater. They can sometimes be heard chattering from the eleventh row of the auditorium. Castle, of course, thrived on the element of surprise and wanted to deceive as many theatergoers as he could. With *Zotz!*, he establishes an illusion of predictability that is triggered during Jones's psychological evaluation. The illusion continues during Jones's visit to the Pentagon and is also evident during his time in captivity.

As Jones is evaluated by Dr. Kroner (James Millhollin), the former is down on his luck, and Castle relies on Jones's loss of credibility in order to manipulate the expectations of the audience. Towards the end of the evaluation, an unconvinced Kroner demands proof of the coin's power. Jones is initially reluctant, but changes his mind. Members of an audience might be eager to predict that, considering Jones's unfortunate lack of credibility, the coin will fail and Kroner will get the last laugh. Traditionally, a fictitious scenario of this nature produces an outcome that is not in favor of the protagonist. But when Jones points his finger, the unexpected transpires as Kroner keels over in pain. It is a small victory for Jones and comes as a complete surprise to the audience simply because it is unforeseeable. Jones is at the beginning of his woes. Therefore, one would expect a demonstration of the coin's power to fail. Instead, Jones proves Kroner wrong and eventually travels to Washington, D.C.

Castle's illusion of predictability is best demonstrated upon Jones's arrival at the Pentagon. The coin causes nothing but trouble, beginning on the structure's ground floor and continuing all the way up to the office of General Bullivar (Fred Clark). Several people, including a captain and major, fall victim to the coin's power. A fire sprinkler system is accidentally triggered. And by the time Jones meets Bullivar, the audience has been exposed to one catastrophe after another, leading us to believe the coin's power will continue to run amok. Jones proposes his idea to the general and is not taken seriously. He then displays his hand to Bullivar, as if he is preparing for a demonstration. The general simply laughs and devises a way to dismiss his guest:

> BULLIVAR: Look, I'm afraid they've sent you to the wrong department. Now, what you want is the entertainment division of Special Services. I'll make one little phone call and settle this whole thing for you.
>
> Bullivar walks over to a phone on his desk. Jones watches in confusion.
>
> JONES: No. Wa... wait!
>
> BULLIVAR (picks up receiver): Now, get me Colonel....
>
> JONES: General, I can prove it!
>
> BULLIVAR (speaking into receiver): Never mind.

Just as Bullivar hangs up the phone, the figure of a window washer slowly descends into view. The supposed foreshadowing of what will happen next is almost blatant, because based on the chain of events that has transpired ever since Jones arrived at the Pentagon, one cannot help but think that this newcomer, too, will fall victim to the coin's power. But the window washer is left unharmed, and some would argue that he is left unharmed because an event of this nature would simply be too predictable. Instead, Castle throws his audience a curve ball. Not only is the window washer unaffected by the coin's power, he is also unveiled as Josh Bates (Carl Don), a Russian spy and, consequently, the true antagonist of the story.

During Jones's time in captivity, he finds himself at the mercy of the Russians, and through the use of a particular camera angle, Castle is able to deceive his audience with the element of fire. The flame of a Bunsen burner, utilized by Igor (Mike Mazurki) as a means to torture Virginia and Cynthia, provides an unexpected hope for freedom. Jones is rendered helpless when Bates and Igor tie his hands behind his back. The chances of using the coin as a means of escape become drastically slimmer. The Russians clearly have the upper hand, and the audience is left to ponder how the characters we have come to embrace will prevail. The camera, positioned behind and slightly to the right of Bates, reveals the flame of the Bunsen burner to be within inches of his body. Although nothing happens and the flame continues to burn, its mere presence provides a glimmer of hope because it appears as if Bates will catch on fire. But again, if an incident of this nature were to transpire, it would be too predictable. Instead, Jones finds another means of escape by simply making a run for it. But despite Castle's illusion of predictability, random moments of *Zotz!* contain events that, perhaps, might be foreseen by a select group of wary viewers. For example, following Jones's escape, he flirts with disaster as he teeters along the edge of a rooftop. And one might sense that he will plunge to the ground, only to utilize the coin's power of slow motion (which he does). But a turn of events such as this, predictable or not, simply adds to the film's

Too close for comfort.

dizzying climax.

    Zotz! did not perform as well at the box office as Castle would have hoped, and although the film was released during his prime, it does not garner much attention amongst contemporary film aficionados. It is usually omitted from the lineup of various William Castle retrospectives. Nevertheless, for its time, *Zotz!* proved successful with a different kind of audience, which was that of younger children. Those who could not bear to sit through the horrors of *The Tingler* or *Homicidal* were offered a pleasant alternative.

    In addition to its appeal to youths, *Zotz!* marked Castle's third and final collaboration with Mike Mazurki, an actor who had performed for Castle in both *Mysterious Intruder* and *New Orleans*

Uncensored. *Zotz!* also represented the first, but not the last, collaboration with Tom Poston. In fact, the two would later work together during the production of *The Old Dark House*. Like *Zotz!*, the film was to be another comedy, but in order to increase his chances of producing a successful picture, Castle would incorporate many of his ideas from the genre he knew best: horror.

CHAPTER FORTY-SEVEN
13 FRIGHTENED GIRLS! (1963)

For his next gimmick, William Castle decided on an international contest of sorts, pitting some of the world's most beautiful girls against each other in a well-advertised competition. There were to be multiple winners, each hailing from a separate country. Those fortunate enough to be victorious were rewarded with a role in *The Candy Web*, Castle's film of murder and espionage. Its opening sequence was shot at least thirteen separate times. Each winner, playing the part of a "teenage diplomat," was given the opportunity to introduce the film in her native language. Castle essentially created a different version for each represented nation. In the United States, Kathy Dunn, a young actress appearing as the primary character of the story, introduced the film in English. Furthermore, in an attempt to better market his motion picture to American audiences, Castle changed its title to *13 Frightened Girls!*

Candace "Candy" Hull (Dunn), on vacation from boarding school, travels to London with her fellow classmates. Their fathers serve as diplomats at the city's embassies. Candy is infatuated with Wally Sanders (Murray Hamilton), an attaché of the U.S. Embassy. Kagenescu (Walter Rode), the representative of a small country, is under surveillance, as he may seek an alliance with the East. His elusive nature flusters Sanders. But Candy spots Kagenescu at the home of Mai-Ling (Lynne Sue Moon), her friend "from Red China." Kagenescu's meeting with Kang (Khigh Dhiegh), Mai-Ling's uncle, unexpectedly concludes with the former's murder. Candy discovers the corpse. The murder weapon, a letter opener engraved with an American seal, is deliberately used as a means to frame the West. Using the pseudonym of Kitten, she sends the opener to Sanders and begins a stint in "the art of espionage." Through her classmates, she gains access to foreign embassies, thus implementing a strategy of eavesdropping on conversations, seducing men, and more. But Soldier (Joyce Taylor), Sanders's girlfriend, is later kidnapped. Kang is responsible and will only release his hostage upon acquiring Kitten. Candy seeks Mai-Ling's help, but is also taken prisoner. She exposes herself as Kitten.

Sanders comes to the rescue, informing Kang that Candy/Kitten was not under orders from the U.S. government. School resumes. Kang sends Spider, his secret enforcer, to eliminate Candy, as she is unknowingly in possession of a confidential microfilm. Mike (Charlie Briggs), the personal chauffeur for Candy's father, reveals himself as Spider. Again, Sanders comes to the rescue, shooting Mike/Spider dead before the latter can fulfill his objective.

Murray Hamilton, Kathy Dunn, Hugh Marlowe, and Charlie Briggs.

Castle's motif of the number thirteen is ever-present within *13 Frightened Girls!* Yet, with the inclusion of Candy and Mai-Ling into the story, the number of girls increases to fifteen. It is not until the closing seconds of the film that Castle presents the thirteen winning "diplomats" (and no other character) together in the same shot. The girls bid farewell to Candy and Mai-Ling, who prepare for the next chapter of their lives. The two have endured trying times. But for Candy, her recent adventures in espionage have been life-changing. *13 Frightened Girls!* exhibits a growing maturity within its lead character, as Castle's protagonist comes of age under the most unusual of circumstances. Candy's newfound confidence is the contributing factor to her overall success. It does not waver as she withstands constant rejection from Sanders. Furthermore, Candy's increased self-esteem is what ultimately enables her to evade a tragic death and boldly confront the enemy.

Candy's advances towards Sanders, a man many years her senior, are undeterred despite being met with constant rejection.

Soldier understands the situation from a female perspective and deems it necessary to explain such curious behavior to her long-time boyfriend. Shortly after Candy slips out of Sanders's office to begin work on the "South America" operation, he casually refers to her as a "funny kid." Soldier seizes the opportunity to present him with what is perceived by many as a foregone conclusion:

> SOLDIER: That funny kid is almost a woman . . . .and a woman in love.

She sympathizes with Candy because she, too, was once a sixteen-year-old girl. It is common knowledge that women mature quicker than men and, therefore, are more likely to approach life with the mindset of an adult despite not yet completing adolescence. Candy has discovered a growing maturity within herself, gaining the confidence necessary to confront the many obstacles of life. Soldier is not privy to Candy's private life, but she understands the feelings of a "woman" at sixteen years of age. Sanders, however, is one of several men who underestimates the determination of the film's heroine.

Joyce Taylor as Soldier.

Due to her resolute spirit, Candy evades a tragic death at the hands of Peter Van Hagen (Garth Benton), leader of the Soviet Student Party. In more ways than one, she makes it clear to him that he is not dealing with an inexperienced adolescent. Van Hagen attempts to explain why Candy should not accompany him to his supposed home country of Holland, citing her age as a factor:

> VAN HAGEN: You are only sixteen.
>
> CANDY: I'm a woman.

> Candy abruptly turns her back on Van Hagen and moves away from him. He slowly approaches, placing his hands on her shoulders.

> VAN HAGEN: That's true. Yes, that's very true.

Van Hagen kisses Candy's neck, but she rejects his further advances, instead asking for a glass of ginger ale. One thing leads to another, and the action shifts outside to the balcony of his hotel room. Candy does everything in her power to withstand the effects of the chemicals Van Hagen has placed in her drink. But he suddenly decides that scotch, an adult libation, is more suitable for the occasion. Van Hagen forces her to drink, but Candy resists. If she is to be successful in her transition to womanhood, it will be done on her terms, not his. Van Hagen eventually falls to his death, leaving Candy to face yet another individual who dares to doubt the drive and determination behind her fighting prowess.

Candy's confrontation of the malevolent Kang marks the beginning of a new era in the sixteen-year-old's life. Her undying confidence is apparent, and Castle symbolizes such confidence through a detailed montage. The height of Candy's success is depicted with a blending of various images. Castle begins his montage with a geographical globe rotating against a cloudy blue sky. A white kitten gradually fades into view. It appears to traverse across the spinning globe, constantly meowing as Castle inserts images of the Eiffel Tower, the United States Capitol, and more. Kitten, in essence, is successfully making the rounds in her relentless quest for growth. Later, at Kang's residential palace, Candy stands proud despite her capture:

> KANG: So you are the little American kitten, with two feet and the wings of an eagle. It is difficult for me to believe. You are only a child.

CANDY: I'm a woman!

Kang is taken aback by Candy's brash demeanor. She does not falter. Her confidence is displayed at the highest level, causing Kang to retort with an imperfect analogy:

KANG: Once the American government agent was Tiger... feared in all the jungle.

Kang walks over to Candy and grabs her chin.

KANG: Now, she is just a little pussycat.

His underestimation of Candy is apparent, as it ultimately leads to an American victory. Kang's analogy, albeit a false one, represents the exact opposite of what Castle's montage conveys to viewers. As the succession of images concludes, the meowing of the kitten suddenly becomes the growling of a large feline mammal, similar to that of a tiger.

"Latin is a dead language! A dead language is not worth dying for!" (The deceased Plato Zorba, of 13 Ghosts, wrote in Latin.)

13 Frightened Girls! was released in July of 1963. Its production transpired immediately following that of The Old Dark House. Yet, Castle's grisly tale of the sinister mansion and its eccentric inhabitants would not be released for another three months. Joyce Taylor fondly reminisced about the production of 13 Frightened Girls! to the author of this book, saying, "I was grateful to Mr. William Castle for casting me in the character of Soldier. As a director, he gave me the liberty to improvise in a way suitable

to fulfill the needs of each scene. We seemed to be a kindred mindset from the start, which is always reassuring."

In order to promote 13 *Frightened Girls!* to the general public, Castle attended the film's premiere in every represented nation, personally introducing each "teenage diplomat" to her home crowd. In addition to his overseas escapades, Castle appeared onscreen in select cities to present yet another gimmick to theatergoers. Patrons were provided with a small item known as The Danger Card. It read, "DON'T GET CAUGHT IN THE CANDY WEB." Castle heeded his audience to guard the item carefully, as he would return upon the conclusion of the picture to disclose the details of the card's significance. After the film, theatergoers were instructed to moisten the "printed" side of the card. Those whose cards revealed the word "DANGER" were awarded a prize from the theater manager. Castle essentially relished the theatrical release of 13 *Frightened Girls!*, later referring to the film's success as "an international holiday."

Kathy Dunn and Lynne Sue Moon. The thirteen winning "diplomats" are seen in the background.

CHAPTER FORTY-EIGHT
THE OLD DARK HOUSE (1963)

With *The Old Dark House*, William Castle journeyed across the Atlantic to produce his picture in Great Britain. It was there that he partnered with Hammer Films. The well-known production company was established in 1934. Over time, it had developed a reputation as a dominant force within the realm of horror films.

Naturally, Castle sought a spine-chilling tone for his motion picture, but he also recognized the potential of comic relief through his star, Tom Poston. *The Kine Weekly*, a trade newspaper serving Britain's film industry, obtained an interview with Castle at the time of production in 1962. Of *The Old Dark House*, he said, "This picture gives equal emphasis to horror and comedy. The days of the straight shockers have just about run their course."

Tom Penderel (Poston) is an American car salesman living in London. His flatmate, Casper Femm (Peter Bull), has purchased a convertible. He would like it delivered to Femm Hall, his family's estate in the country. Penderel obliges, but the vehicle becomes wrecked upon arrival. He enters the old dark house, only to find Casper dead from an apparent staircase fall. Cecily Femm (Janette Scott), Casper's cousin, kindly warns Penderel to leave. But before long, the eccentric residents of Femm Hall reveal themselves. Roderick Femm (Robert Morley), lord of the manor, claims the house was originally built as a fortress. He speaks of a distant relative known as Morgan the Pirate, who had accumulated a fortune prior to his demise. Morgan's will states that any descendants living in the house will inherit their share of his earnings, provided they are home every night by midnight. Should the "fortress" be destroyed, the entire fortune will be divided amongst its residents. Jasper Femm (Bull), Casper's twin brother, comes out of hiding to inform Penderel that Roderick killed Casper and will soon eliminate the others in order to collect the inheritance for himself. Later, Agatha Femm (Joyce Grenfell), Casper's mother, turns up dead. Potiphar Femm (Mervyn Johns), Casper's uncle, believes the ensuing rain will cause a great flood. He unveils a replica of Noah's Ark, intending for Penderel and

Morgana Femm (Fenella Fielding), Casper's other cousin, to board the ship and repopulate the human species. Others, including Roderick, are murdered. Cecily reveals herself to be the killer. She plants dynamite throughout the house to ensure her receipt of the fortune. But Penderel turns the tables, killing Cecily with her own explosives.

Tom Poston and Peter Bull.

The Old Dark House essentially tells the story of a stranger in a strange land. Years earlier, Castle explored a similar theme with *The Americano*, a film in which the protagonist travels from his familiar surroundings of Texas to the unknown landscapes of Brazil. Shortly after his arrival, he finds himself yearning for the very things he left behind. For example, on more than one occasion, the "Americano" requests American beer, but instead, is provided with Brazilian beer.

Of *The Old Dark House*, a similar sense of homesickness is evident with Penderel's journey into terra incognita, thus enabling Castle to "Americanize" his motion picture. Castle does not specifically acknowledge an earlier version of the film, and the overall presentation of his remake is laced with American inferences from beginning to end.

In 1932, Universal and its founder, Carl Laemmle, produced the first version of *The Old Dark House*. The legendary James Whale, known primarily for his horror films of the period, directed the picture. Although set in England, filming took place entirely in Southern California. To reiterate, Castle's production transpired

A partially concealed Femm Hall.

on British soil. Bray Studios, the River Thames, and additional landmarks of Great Britain were utilized in order to add a touch of authenticity to the final cut.

Naturally, the 1963 version is quite different than that of 1932. However, despite being shot on location in England, it is ironically more "American" in regard to content. Castle's film has no significant relation to the story (penned by British novelist J. B. Priestley) on which the earlier version is based. In addition, there is a clear distinction between the lead actors and motor vehicles of both films.

Priestley's *Benighted*, a novel that serves as the basis for the 1932 version, presents a story that is not at all similar to that of Castle's motion picture. Aside from the setting, as well as the names of particular characters, only one similarity is clearly evident between the two films. In regard to the 1963 version, seconds after his initial encounter with Penderel, Roderick declares, "We make our own electricity here!" The 1932 counterpart of Roderick Femm is Horace Femm. And during a similar situation, he states, "We make our own electric lights here . . . and we are not very good at it." One might be reminded of Thomas "Tom" Edison, the famous American inventor. And his nationality, among other things, is significant in regard to the 1963 version.

Tom Poston, having had the benefit of being addressed by his real name while assuming the role of Tom Penderel, is the main attraction of Castle's film. Yet, there is a stark contrast between him and the supposed lead actor of the 1932 version. The famous

"It's not every day that we have an American for dinner!"

Boris Karloff was given top billing for Laemmle's production, and many consider his character to be the most memorable of the story, but others might question such reasoning. He portrays a mad butler who sometimes intertwines with the film's characters. And prior to the opening credits, a producer's note pays tribute to Karloff's "great versatility." But he does not speak during the entire film. Furthermore, the narrative is able to progress quite smoothly in his absence. Among a mixed cast of American and British performers, Karloff (a native of London) definitely stands out from time to time. However, unlike Poston, he is not the true star of the film. When Castle assembled the cast for his version of *The Old Dark House*, all but one were naturalized citizens of Great Britain. Poston is not only the lead in Castle's film, he is the only American. And it is immediately clear from the opening scene at the Mayfair Casino that the story is very much about his character.

As Penderel departs the casino for Femm Hall, considerable attention is given to the "American" vehicle in which he travels. His automobile is a reflection of who he is, and it defines his very presence in England. Penderel is not just a car salesman. He is a salesman of foreign (American) cars. Casper's desire to own a vehicle of such prestige leads to the unlikely chain of events that follows. Penderel makes the arduous trek to Femm Hall in order to deliver his flatmate's latest acquisition. But it is no ordinary car. It is a convertible, an American invention dating back to the early 1930s. Other countries, such as England, have replicated the concept through the years. Castle depicts the convertible and Penderel as symbols of America. The vehicle, to a certain degree, is almost as significant as the film's main character. The opening minutes of the 1932 version, however, present a group of weary travelers arriving at an old dark house, and very little attention is given to their vehicle. Unlike the convertible of Castle's motion picture, it is a typical car that bears very little relevance to the plot. The directors of both films, in essence, had to pick and choose what they considered to be the ideal elements of their respective settings.

Joyce Grenfell as Agatha Femm. With the exception of Tom Poston, The Old Dark House *featured a cast that was entirely British.*

Castle took the original concept of *The Old Dark House* and essentially made it his own. A particular scene, transpiring shortly after Agatha's death, is noteworthy because of Jasper's unexpected reaction to her absence. She is not present at the midnight meeting. Therefore, she forfeits her share of the fortune. Jasper declares, "Mother never spent her money on anything but wool. She hoarded every penny." But pennies were, and still are, an American form of currency. In England, the shilling was the basic monetary unit in circulation. Incidentally, as Jasper is heard saying "penny," a closer examination reveals that he is clearly mouthing the word "shilling." In short, many modifications, some being politically pragmatic, are evident when comparing the 1932 version with that of 1963. Castle's picture, like its predecessor, takes place in Great Britain, but the 1963 version is loaded with American inferences from beginning to end. A comparison of the film's opening credits with its theatrical trailer, the beginning minutes of the picture, and the image that is displayed as *The Old Dark House* concludes are all implied endorsements of America.

A slight disparity between the opening credits and trailer of Castle's film reveal a possible bias in favor of the United States. The difference is evident when credit is given to those responsible for producing the motion picture. Will Hammer (born William Hinds), the founder of Hammer Films, died in 1957. Five years later, his son, Anthony Hinds, served as a producer of *The Old Dark House*, and he is listed as such in the trailer. Naturally, Castle is listed as the director. And as the trailer concludes, "A HAMMER-CASTLE PRODUCTION" is displayed across the screen. Months later, *The Old Dark House* was released to the public. But Anthony Hinds, a stalwart of the British film industry who would end up producing over sixty motion pictures throughout his career, is not listed in either the opening or closing credits. Furthermore, the primary names are switched, as "A WILLIAM CASTLE-HAMMER PRODUCTION" becomes one of the first titles seen by audiences upon the film's introduction. Judging by the credits presented in the trailer, Hammer Films appears to play more of a role in the production of *The Old Dark House* than people realize. As the film's opening titles wind down in preparation for the story to commence, the words "Produced and Directed by William Castle" are projected onto the screen. But an additional title remains before the sequence is to be concluded, and it is not a representation of Hammer Films. For the second time, the audience is presented

Roderick Femm, next to the painting of Morgan the Pirate.

with the words "Directed by William Castle," thereby setting the stage for what is to follow.

Within the beginning minutes of Castle's picture, the word "American," or any other variation of it, is spoken approximately ten times. Roderick makes his animosity of the United States quite clear as he acquaints himself with Penderel. As Cecily introduces both men to each other, tension is in the air:

RODERICK: Who is this?

CECILY (nervous): Oh, m-m-may I present my Uncle Roderick Femm. This is Mr. Tom Penderel. He was a friend of Casper's.

RODERICK (glaring at Penderel): Really? Casper had some very strange friends. Were you one of them?

During the exchange, Roderick, having recently spent a considerable amount of time in the rain, fiddles with a pair of wet rags that have been tied together.

PENDEREL: No, I'm not strange. I'm American...

In a minor fit of anger, Roderick yanks the rags in opposite directions, thereby tightening the existing knot. He looks as if he intends to strangle Penderel.

PENDEREL (perplexed): . . . from America.

RODERICK (looking at Cecily): It couldn't be.

Cecily simply shrugs her shoulders in response. Roderick, already suspicious of the newcomer, becomes further agitated upon learning his visitor's nationality. But his mood suddenly changes when the opportunity to "have an American for dinner" presents itself. During the meal, there is talk of the Femm family's mysterious confinement to the house. Roderick questions whether some wish to leave Femm Hall altogether. And Penderel cannot make sense of the situation:

PENDEREL: You mean you like it here? (chuckles) I mean, you like all this?

Cecily glances towards Roderick, who is clearly perturbed with the questions. Penderel's smile quickly disappears as he comes to the realization that he has offended his host.

PENDEREL: Well, maybe I didn't put it the right way.

RODERICK: Oh, but you have, Mr. Penderel. Very frank of you! Quite American!

An uncomfortable situation almost becomes unbearable. But the dinner conversation concludes shortly thereafter, and the action shifts from the dining room to the main hall. The first image we see is that of a leaking ceiling. The prior scene, depicting the dinner sequence, begins with a similar shot. The dark and gloomy atmosphere of the Dartmoor countryside literally seeps into the dreary confines of Femm Hall. And it is not until the threat of destruction is eradicated that a change in the weather becomes evident.

The concluding image of *The Old Dark House* depicts a crisp blue sky as the American flag is flown on the flagpole of Femm

"Tom, please, would you help us? What should we do? One of us is a murderer."

Hall. In comparison with previous scenes, it is nothing short of patriotic. Benjamin Frankel's score, composed primarily of haunting and sinister melodies, becomes positively uplifting as his rendition of John Philip Sousa's "The Stars and Stripes Forever" can be heard upon the film's conclusion. Earlier in the picture, Agatha comments that the "rain goes on as if it never wanted to stop." She is murdered a short time later, and the Femm flag, in what becomes a frequent tradition, is lowered to half-mast. The family logo is a representation of everything that is bleak and dismal. But Penderel eventually thwarts Cecily's plot to destroy the fortress, and an American establishes himself as the ultimate hero of Femm Hall. The rains cease and the sun emerges from the clouds. Hence, the American flag, unlike that of the Femm family, is a representation of everything that is appealing and hopeful. And Castle, the auteur, concludes his film in style.

The replica of Noah's Ark.

The Old Dark House was released in the United States on Halloween. Its trailer presents the film as "a mystery with murderous laughs" that is "based on J. B. Priestley's novel." Yet, aside from the setting of a house that happens to be both old and dark, there is very little relation between the original story and Castle's film.

At one point during the 1932 version, the counterpart of Tom Penderel (simply known as Penderel) makes reference to the novel's title, claiming, "This certainly is a 'benighted' household." James Whale's retelling of the original story is fairly accurate. But the 1963 version is not a reflection of Priestley's world. It is a reflection of Castle's, and this is evident from beginning to end. Charles "Chas" Addams, the popular cartoonist with a taste for the macabre, added his personal touch to the design of the opening credits. His hand, disguised to resemble that of a ghoul, can be seen gently signing (painting) his name across the screen.

In addition to Addams, Castle collaborated with screenwriter Robert Dillon. Both men, who also worked together on *13 Frightened Girls!*, assembled a script with a delicate balance of humor and suspense. Dillon's inclusion of the nursery rhymes *Humpty Dumpty* and *The Bells of St. Margaret's* pays homage to the customary English folklore of many years ago. Castle's recurring motif of tape recorders, beginning with *The Houston Story* and continuing in *Macabre*, culminates with *The Old Dark House* (it will recur in *Strait-Jacket* and conclude in *The Night Walker*) as we occasionally hear the sinister voice recite select verses of the rhymes. Despite its frequent references to Anglo-American themes, Castle's film was not released in England until 1966. Nevertheless, *The Old Dark House* made quite an impression on audiences, regardless of which side of the Atlantic theatergoers were based.

CHAPTER FORTY-NINE
STRAIT-JACKET (1964)

The setting of William Castle's next picture, *Strait-Jacket*, returned to the states. Robert Bloch, best known for his novel, *Psycho*, penned the film's script. Both men, engrossed in the pre-production stages of their picture, were abruptly summoned from California to New York at the urgent request of Leo Jaffe, Columbia's executive vice president. Bloch's script had piqued the interest of Academy Award winner Joan Crawford, and she immediately arranged for a lunch meeting to take place at her Manhattan apartment. Castle and Bloch figured it was best to acquiesce to Crawford's demands. Many dignitaries of the motion picture industry were constantly at her beck and call. And whatever Joan Crawford wanted, she usually received. Hence, shortly after the concept of *Strait-Jacket* was presented to her, she was cast as the lead. In order to effectively market the picture, Columbia produced *How to Plan a Movie Murder*, a four-minute featurette starring Castle, Crawford, and Bloch. Throughout its duration, select characters of *Strait-Jacket*, presented as potential victims, are introduced to the audience. Upon the featurette's conclusion, Crawford addresses her colleagues, declaring, "*Strait-Jacket* is our picture, so we can plan as many killings as we like." To those who did not know her, she presented herself as an effective collaborator. But many contributed to the film's production, and Crawford had every single one of them in the palm of her hand.

Lucy Harbin (Crawford) catches her husband in bed with another woman. During a fit of rage, she decapitates them with an axe and is subsequently sent to an asylum. Bill Cutler (Leif Erickson), Lucy's brother, adopts her young daughter, Carol (Vicki Cos). He and his wife, Emily (Rochelle Hudson), take Carol to the country and start a farm. Upon Lucy's release twenty years later, she is reunited with her grown daughter (Diane Baker) at the Cutler Ranch. Carol has become a talented sculptress. Her steady boyfriend, Michael Fields (John Anthony Hayes), attempts to meet Lucy. But he is not successful. Lucy, self-conscious in regard to her aging appearance, undergoes a complete makeover in order to appear younger. Furthermore, she is haunted by strange voices, and also has nightmares pertaining to decapitated heads and bloody axes. Michael eventually meets Lucy. She flaunts her beauty and puzzles him with her flirtatious behavior. Dr. Anderson (Mitchell Cox), of the asylum, makes a surprise visit to the ranch. He questions Lucy in regard to her nightmares, but she is not forthcoming. Anderson takes notice of her odd demeanor, believing she is trying to recapture a dangerous past. Upon insisting that Lucy return to the asylum, he is mysteriously murdered with an axe. Shortly thereafter, Leo Krause (George Kennedy), a hired hand on the farm, suffers a similar fate. Raymond (Howard St. John) and Alison Fields (Edith Atwater), Michael's parents, host dinner at their lavish estate. A disagreement pertaining to Carol and Michael's impending marriage puts a damper on the evening. Lucy abruptly departs and quickly disappears. A search ensues. Meanwhile, Fields is killed. Alison is then accosted by what appears to be an axe-wielding Lucy. But the real Lucy arrives on the scene and unmasks Carol, who has masqueraded as her mother in order to commit the murders. Carol knew Michael's parents would object to their marriage. She orchestrated a plan to convince everyone that Lucy maintained homicidal tendencies. In addition, Carol produced sinister tape recordings of haunting voices and sculpted a collection of prosthetic heads in order to intensify her mother's nightmares. She is sent to an asylum. Lucy ultimately commits herself to helping Carol cope with the setbacks of mental illness.

During the early 1960s, Castle attended a screening of *What Ever Happened to Baby Jane?* The film, a psychological thriller starring Bette Davis and Joan Crawford, triumphed at the box office. Castle took note of the picture's success and became determined to replicate the results with his production of *Strait-Jacket*. He figured the odds were in his favor considering Crawford's commitment to his project. And she did not hesitate to make her presence known to everybody. In fact, as the film's opening titles are displayed, the words "Starring Joan Crawford" precede those of "A William Castle Production." Star power is important concerning a film's marketability, but it can also serve as a distraction to any director.

The director poses for the promotion of his film.

Although Castle encountered several obstacles while working with Crawford, he maintained his composure and saw the project through to its end. The final cut is nothing short of entertaining, and audiences are kept guessing up until the shocking denouement at the Fields estate. Castle's portrayal of the events leading up to Carol's unmasking is noteworthy. The beginning of *Strait-Jacket*, particularly the haunting images presented within the film's opening titles, is especially important because it foreshadows what is to come with the remainder of the narrative.

The pre-credits sequence of the picture contains subtle clues in regard to the future. But the artwork, serving as a backdrop for the opening titles, depicts the tale of Lucy's incarceration and subsequent life following her release from the asylum. Furthermore, the images portray Carol's transformation from an innocent child into a maladjusted adult.

Strait-Jacket features the longest pre-credits sequence of any motion picture directed by Castle, and much transpires within these opening minutes. The film's beginning also marks the big-screen debut of Lee Majors, who plays Frank Harbin, Lucy's doomed husband. During the sequence, a select number of clues foreshadow the future. A jukebox is presented to the audience. Shortly thereafter, the intermittent whistling sound of Lucy's approaching train can be heard. And then, as Frank and his lover, Stella Fulton (Patricia Crest), meet their demise, Castle rhymes the face of a maniacal mother with that of a traumatized daughter, thus providing the greatest clue of the picture.

Lucy Harbin reunites with her daughter following a twenty-year absence. She continues to wear her wedding ring, an indicator that it is difficult for her to let go of the past.

A jukebox, one of the first objects presented to the audience, provides a subtle clue in regard to Lucy's future. Its featured tune, in addition to a visible record holder, is significant. An instrumental version of "There Goes That Song Again" (based on the 1940s hit by Russ Morgan, the "Big Band" era musician) can be heard as Castle introduces Frank and Stella to the audience. True to its title, the song will recur again, specifically at times when Lucy becomes the center of attention. Yet, in regard to the jukebox, Castle's emphasis on its contents is of particular importance. The audience is initially exposed to the spinning record. Seconds transpire, and Castle's camera slowly moves backward to reveal the jukebox, but not before a key number is presented to theatergoers. The record containing "There Goes That Song Again" belongs to the twentieth record holder, and the number "20" (engraved on a metallic label) is visible for mere seconds. The image symbolizes Lucy's forthcoming incarceration, as she will remain in the asylum for twenty years. Following his subtle presentation of the jukebox, Castle cuts to a shot of Frank and Stella as they prepare to depart for the final destination of their lives.

Diane Baker as Carol Harbin.

As Frank and Stella arrive at the Harbin farm, the distant whistling sound of Lucy's approaching train is symbolic of the immediate future. It becomes an intermittent reminder of the impending danger that is to come. Frank and Stella enter the house, thus awakening the younger Carol. A grown Carol, the scene's narrator, declares, "[Frank and Stella] made one mistake in thinking that the child was asleep." The whistling sound is heard again, and the ensuing narration states, "They made another mistake, too. Frank's wife, Lucy, had decided to come home on the evening train." Frank, in bringing Stella to his home, has taken the affair to the point of no return. And the first whistling sound essentially transpires as the fate of the young lovers becomes sealed. The whistling is intermittent, and it is simply a matter of time before Lucy's actions irrevocably damage the lives of everybody in the home. Frank and Stella are viciously murdered. In addition, the onset of Lucy's mental breakdown becomes evident. But perhaps, the fourth and final occupant of the home is affected more than the others.

The face of the young Carol is rhymed with that of Lucy's as the latter carries out the murders, thus foreshadowing a future during which a daughter will ultimately follow in the footsteps of her homicidal mother. The scene itself gives meaning to the film's title. As Lucy carries out the senseless murders of Frank and Stella, Castle invites his audience into the horrors of the asylum. We have no choice but to watch as Lucy strikes with the axe, but another image, blended with the first, depicts her confinement to a straitjacket. It marks a rare point of the picture when theatergoers are afforded a glimpse of the object of the film's title. The straitjacket, in essence, is symbolic of Carol's future. As Castle rhymes the faces of mother and daughter, he not only indicates that Carol will consequently become a killer. He also suggests that, twenty years into the future, she will be confined to a straitjacket at the asylum. As the sequence prepares to transition to the future, Castle blends the image of Lucy's confinement with the face of the young Carol. The camera zooms in towards the girl's eyes. Lucy disappears. Seconds later, Castle transitions to a second pair of eyes. The camera zooms out, and the audience

"Lucy Harbin took an axe, gave her husband forty whacks! When she saw what she had done, she gave his girlfriend forty-one!"

is introduced to the adult Carol. Twenty years have passed, and a daughter nervously prepares to reunite with her lost mother. Castle then seizes the opportunity to present his audience with the film's opening titles.

Academy Award winner Boris Leven, the production designer of *Strait-Jacket*, began his career as a sketch artist. Over the course of several decades, he served as the art director of many motion pictures. His design of *Strait-Jacket* is noteworthy, especially in regard to the film's opening titles. As an aged Lucy Harbin is first presented to the audience, she is seen disembarking from a train. It has been twenty grueling years since the murders, and her face appears haggard in comparison to her initial appearance of the film. She prepares to step onto the station's platform. The image freezes and dissolves to the first sketch of the credits. Both depict Lucy's face. Additional sketches, some of which portray the tale of Lucy's incarceration and subsequent life following her release from the asylum, are then presented as the opening titles adorn the screen. Through the drawings, we are exposed to Lucy's bewildered psyche, agonizing confinement, and gradual detachment from those who care about her.

The first sketch of the film's titles depicts Lucy's face, but the presence of hollow eye sockets is indicative of a bewildered psyche. Following the murder of Dr. Anderson, she exhibits a semiconscious demeanor. Carol discovers Lucy in the darkened living room of the Cutler home and proceeds to interrogate her:

CAROL: Where were you?

LUCY: Right here in this chair.

CAROL: Sitting in the dark?

LUCY: Must've fallen asleep.

CAROL: You've changed your clothes.

Carol walks over to a lamp and illuminates the room.

LUCY: I can't wear them. I've tried to do it, just to please you. Carol, I'd do anything in the world for you. You must know that. But I can't go back twenty years. It's wrong.

You've got to understand. When I put those clothes on, something happens to me, something frightening.

CAROL: You, y-you saw the doctor?

LUCY: Yes.

CAROL: What did he say?

LUCY: Nothing.

CAROL: You mean he didn't tell you?

LUCY: Tell me what?

CAROL: Where, where is the doctor?

LUCY: Well, he must've left hours ago.

Carol approaches the window and peers into the front yard. She sees the doctor's parked car. Carol then turns to face her mother.

CAROL: H-his car!

LUCY: Something wrong?

CAROL: I-i-it's still outside. Where is he? Where is he?

LUCY: The doctor's gone.

CAROL (whispering): Mother!

LUCY: The doctor's gone.

Carol grabs her mother's arms in frustration.

CAROL (screaming): Mother!

LUCY: The doctor's gone.

CAROL: Tell me! Oh my God!

Carol abruptly departs, thus leaving her mother in a continued state of bewilderment. Lucy is barely conscious of her surroundings. Her trance-like demeanor becomes puzzling as she repeatedly states, "The doctor's gone." Of course, Castle is placing all of the suspicion on Lucy so that the audience does not suspect Carol as the true murderer. Nevertheless, the aforementioned sketch and its featured, hollow eye sockets are indicative of

Lucy's detachment from reality. Unable to embrace a new life, she figuratively sees little of her immediate surroundings, especially when reminded of a troubled past.

George Kennedy as Leo Krause.

Lucy's agonizing confinement is represented not only with the asylum's straitjacket, but also within the second sketch of the opening titles. She is helpless in regard to Carol's transition from adolescence to adulthood. The sketch depicts a young girl crawling on the ground, and two decapitated heads are close enough for her to touch. More important, however, is the inclusion of a single eye. It dominates the image. The eye represents that of Lucy's. She is incarcerated and cannot avoid the aftermath of her actions. From behind an invisible barrier, she watches her young, traumatized daughter try to make sense of the unfortunate predicament. Lucy is helpless because she has been confined to the asylum. And according to the image, she can only watch as Carol's prolonged turmoil begins. Upon Lucy's release twenty years later, a different world awaits.

Another image of the film's titles reveals an isolated woman, possibly Lucy, reaching towards the sky as four separate faces, representing the additional four occupants of the Cutler Ranch, observe in astonishment and confusion. She relates more to the farm's animals than its people. As Lucy and Carol attempt to become reacquainted after twenty years, the latter offers the former a tour of the ranch. They approach the chicken coop:

CAROL: You see? Now you know where your eggs came from at breakfast.

LUCY: I never thought my brother would end up running a farm again.

CAROL: He started it right after we moved out here.

LUCY: Twenty years ago.

Lucy places her hands on the wired fence and stares into the coop. Carol immediately takes notice.

CAROL: What's the matter?

LUCY: Nothing. I just hate to see anything caged.

The popular motif of confined creatures frequently recurs in Castle's films. Furthermore, in *Strait-Jacket*, one of the creatures is human. Lucy was occasionally confined to a straitjacket while at the asylum, but she also feels trapped inside of her own body, and it pains her to look at the entrapped chickens.

Seconds later, Carol takes Lucy to the pig pen, where the latter takes note of the inadequate, dirty living conditions. Lucy, in essence, sympathizes with the animals while finding it difficult to relate to the people of the Cutler Ranch. And within the

Leif Erickson, Mitchell Cox, and Joan Crawford. Cox, an executive of the Pepsi-Cola company, was cast in the picture at Crawford's demand. Crawford was the widow of Alfred Steele, the former CEO of Pepsi.

sketch, she is clearly depicted as being reclusive from the others. However, a second look at the sketch offers a fresh interpretation.

Upon the conclusion of *Strait-Jacket*, we realize that Carol, instead of Lucy, is the true outcast of the Cutler Ranch. A significant clue is presented early in the film. Shortly after looking at the pig pen, Lucy expresses concern for her daughter, declaring, "[It] must be very lonely around here for someone like you." Carol then makes reference to "lots of friends." But we soon discover that she is referring to the inanimate objects of her art studio. Much has transpired over the course of twenty years, and the haunting sketches of the film's opening credits not only address the circumstances of Lucy's plight, the images also tell the tale of Carol's transformation from an innocent child into a maladjusted, homicidal adult. Her murder spree, dual personality, and masquerade are vividly depicted to the audience through the sketches.

The final image of the film's opening titles (barring a repeat appearance of Lucy's facial sketch) represents and reveals Carol's silhouette to be climbing a steep slope as three ghost-like faces, symbolized as the victims of her murder spree, observe in sheer horror. The circumstances behind Anderson's death, coupled with Van Alexander's score, are particularly noteworthy. As the doctor explores the farm, he is lured to his death by the sound of Lucy's jingling bracelets. Earlier, Carol's interest in the jewelry is revealed to be greater than that of her mother's. And she ultimately uses the bracelets to attract Anderson's attention. The doctor enters Krause's supposedly vacant shed and proceeds to clean his pipe. He glares at the wooden ceiling twice. Each time, Alexander's score intensifies, somewhat comically, as a means to evoke a sense of entrapment. Anderson, like the many chickens before him, is then decapitated upon Krause's stump. The doctor's murder is significant because it marks the beginning of Carol's spree. Shortly thereafter, Krause is killed (during a scene of the picture when Alexander's score is peculiarly absent). And finally, Fields is murdered upon the film's conclusion. Yet, in regard to the aforementioned image, the ghosts of Carol's victims, all men, look on in horror as she attempts to climb the mountain. Her ascent is symbolic of her quest for acceptance. But Carol's journey, like her sanity, proves to be short-lived, as she is ultimately sent to an asylum.

Lucy envisions a return to the asylum.

The eighth image of the film's titles depicts a dark, slender figure walking away from a kneeling one that is much lighter in contrast, thereby symbolizing the formation of Carol's dual personality. It resembles a key scene of the film's conclusion. Carol, standing in the entryway of the Fields home, reveals her motive for the murders. Michael looks on in confusion as she repeatedly stabs the mask of her mother. Meanwhile, Lucy, standing on the doorstep, listens from outside the home. Within the eighth image, and similar to several others, a pair of eyes is visible. Lucy can only wallow in the aftermath of her actions. Like the eyes of the sketch, she is confined. Carol grows up without a mother's guidance. Lucy is helpless, and cannot do anything to prevent the formation of Carol's dual personality. In regard to the aforementioned scene, a mother can only listen as a daughter struggles with the forces of good and evil. Carol becomes hysterical as she stabs, but appears to also console, the mask:

> CAROL: I hate her! Oh, oh, I'm sorry. Please. No, I didn't mean to hurt you. Please. I love you. I hate you!

Lucy listens from the doorstep. She begins to sob uncontrollably. The damage has been done, and Lucy blames herself for the carnage. Inside, Carol directs her emotions towards the mask, an object that is significant to the narrative in more ways than one.

Another image of the film's opening titles reveals a single arm reaching for a mask, thus signifying the beginning of Carol's masquerade. The events surrounding the murder of Fields offer clues in regard to the cunning disguise. The killing transpires within the walk-in closet of his master bedroom. As Fields reaches for a pair of shoes, Carol emerges from behind a row of hanging jackets. Castle's camera exposes her face and reveals the mask she is wearing. It is a brief shot, but the incident marks the first time of the film that select members of an audience will realize Lucy is not the axe murderer, as the featured face appears to be artificial. After Fields is murdered, his inquisitive wife, Alison, walks upstairs and enters the study. Immediately visible is the lone shadow of a head. Alison illuminates the room, thus revealing a bronze bust. The object is significant because it draws comparison to Carol's greatest creation. During the film's final scene, Cutler examines the notable bust of Lucy:

> CUTLER (to Lucy): She had everything worked out, didn't she? Modeling your head so she could make a mask from it that looked like you, even dressing like you.

Shortly thereafter, Lucy covers the bust with a sheet, thus signifying an end to the carnage and *Strait-Jacket*. Seconds later, Castle cleverly ends his picture with a unique image of the Torch

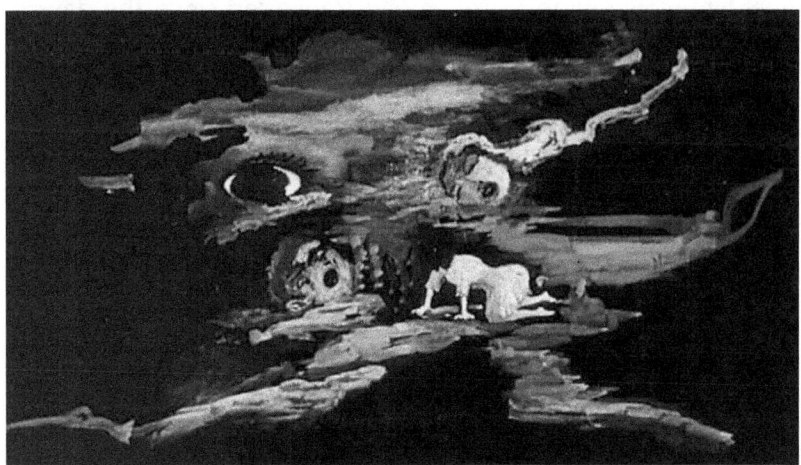

A sketch from the film's opening titles depicts the aftermath of Lucy's horrific crime.

Lady of Columbia Pictures. She has been decapitated, and her head, like a loyal pet, rests comfortably at her feet.

Upon its release, *Strait-Jacket* met with great success at the box office. Multiple sources, however, have acknowledged that Joan Crawford was very difficult on the set. But when it came time for the film's nationwide premieres, she went on tour with Castle to express her gratitude to multitudes of theatergoers. Over time, many have questioned the existence of a gimmick for *Strait-Jacket*. Some claimed it was Crawford herself. But Castle cited cardboard axes, bestowed on audiences across the country, as the true gimmick of the film.

Strait-Jacket, however, is noteworthy primarily due to its star power. In his autobiography, Castle stated, "All the rumors I had heard about Joan Crawford being difficult were false. She is truly a great artist. Directing her was one of the greatest experiences of my life." Mere speculation indicates he wrote this to appease her. But if he truly believed otherwise, he would not have chosen to work with her a second time.

Strait-Jacket was the first of two collaborations between Castle and Crawford. Both would later reunite for the production of *I Saw What You Did*. In regard to *Strait-Jacket*, the picture marked the end of an era for Castle, as it turned out to be his final film for Columbia. Much had transpired since the days of Harry Cohn, and through the years, the studio became a second home to him. By 1964, Castle had directed a total of thirty-eight films for Columbia, and although he may not have realized it at the time, the remainder of his career would be spent elsewhere. The fate of Crawford's affiliation with Columbia was similar, as *Strait-Jacket* marked her final stint with the studio as well. In fact, unbeknownst to anybody, the future beheld an eerie coincidence for both her and Castle.

Diane Baker, Joan Crawford, and William Castle.

CHAPTER FIFTY
THE NIGHT WALKER (1964)

Dona Holloway, once the executive secretary of Harry Cohn, served as William Castle's associate producer on several films, beginning with *The Tingler*. Her work ethic was invaluable to say the least. Following the success of *Strait-Jacket*, Castle returned to Universal. And Holloway, fiercely loyal, accompanied him every step of the way. Whenever Castle had an idea for a film, Holloway was usually one of the first to hear about it. Her feedback was important, and she had enough influence to reject a proposal if she deemed it unsuitable for motion picture production.

Castle had maintained contact with Robert Bloch since collaborating with him on *Strait-Jacket*, and when the award-winning novelist developed a script pertaining to recurring dreams and mysterious lovers, Holloway approved. Hence, shortly thereafter, Castle began production on his fiftieth motion picture, aptly titled *The Night Walker*.

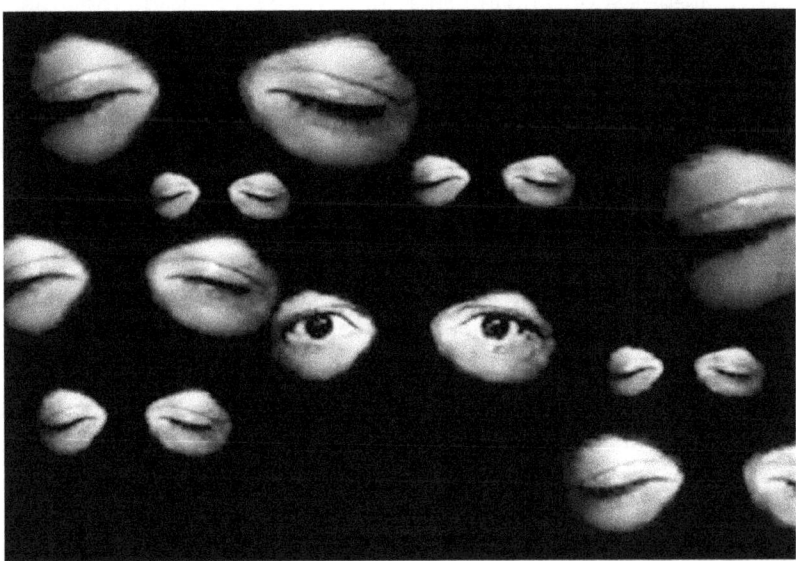

A haunting image from the film's opening sequence. Paul Frees, the popular voice actor, provides the narration. Vic Mizzy scored the background music. The original motion picture soundtrack of The Night Walker *was Mizzy's first.*

Howard Trent (Hayden Rorke), a wealthy blind man, becomes disturbed upon hearing his wife, Irene (Barbara Stanwyck), continuously talk in her sleep. She speaks of an unknown lover. Trent suspects Barry Morland (Robert Taylor), his attorney. Irene confesses to Morland that she cannot identify the man of her dreams, but admits that her late-night lover bears some resemblance to him. After Trent is killed during a mysterious explosion at home, Irene reluctantly continues to live in the house. Her dreams become nightmares, as she is haunted by the death of her husband. Irene eventually moves to an apartment attached to a beauty shop she owns. As she sleeps, a handsome man (Lloyd Bochner) appears to visit her in her dreams. One night, he takes Irene to a chapel. But its priest and few occupants are inanimate figures. Suddenly, a badly burned Trent appears. The priest then attempts to marry Irene and her late husband. She struggles to wake up, but finally does so. Later, Irene guides Morland to the chapel of which she dreamed, but the building is deserted and lacks furnishings. However, the handsome man of her dreams, revealed to be an individual of substance, is present and remains concealed. He phones Joyce Holliday (Judi Meredith), a beautician at Irene's shop, and informs her that he is changing their plan. Morland suggests to Irene that the man of whom she dreams might be George Fuller, a private detective previously hired by Trent to spy on her. Joyce is later stabbed to death. And her murderer appears to be the burned Trent. In search of answers, Irene and Morland go to her former home. They become separated. Irene ventures to a smoky area of the house, also the site of the explosion. Trent appears and proceeds to remove a mask from his face, thus revealing himself to be Morland. He confesses that the explosion was not an accident. Morland murdered Trent with the intention of accumulating the deceased's fortune. Aware of Irene's dreams, he conspired with Fuller, her late night visitor, to concoct a grand charade and eventually kill her. Morland prepares to fulfill his objective, but he is shot by Fuller, who is avenging the murder of his wife, Joyce. Fuller advances towards Irene, intending to eliminate her, but Morland, not entirely dead, intervenes. A struggle ensues, and both men fall to their deaths through a deep hole originally created by the explosion.

With *The Night Walker*, Castle makes subtle references to a selection of his previous films. Approximately one hour into the narrative, Morland tells Irene, "When you were married to Howard, you lived in his world of darkness." His declaration is reminiscent of *Macabre*, as Nancy, like Howard Trent, struggles to become acclimated to the absence of light. In addition, Irene lives at her beauty shop, appropriately named Irene's. Lucy Harbin, of *Strait-Jacket*, undergoes her cosmetic makeover at a place called Irene's Beauty Salon. With *The Night Walker*, Castle essentially revisits the past in more ways than one. In sometimes borrowing from his earlier films, he manipulates the audience into believing Morland is an honest, trustworthy individual. An important phone call to the beauty shop evokes frustration. Furthermore, particular scenarios of *The Night Walker*, similar to what is depicted in *House on Haunted Hill* and *Homicidal*, indicate that Morland is not the antagonist.

Rehearsing the church sequence. Barbara Stanwyck and Lloyd Bochner (credited as "The Dream") await further instructions from the director.

When Morland attempts to phone Irene at her shop, he is not successful because the call is intercepted by Joyce, thus evoking frustration from the audience. The events of the previous scene better enable Castle to portray Morland as a trustworthy character. He slowly enters the Trent estate. Voices are heard. Morland makes his way upstairs, discovering the source to be Trent's tape recording system. As he deactivates it, a knife is hurled at him, striking the nearby wall. Morland's assailant is unknown, but Irene's mystery man (aka George Fuller), having established himself as a conspirator at this point of the narrative, is the likely suspect. The attack gives audiences all the more reason to side with Morland. He has convinced Irene that he trusts her, and he appears genuinely concerned for her well-being. After Joyce intercepts Morland's phone call, she deliberately deceives Irene, claiming, "It was, uh, Mrs. Archer. She made an appointment for tomorrow morning." Hence, the audience becomes frustrated. Joyce, Fuller, and a possibly undead Trent all appear to be the cause of Irene's misery. Ironically, we want Morland, the true, yet unknown, antagonist of the picture, to make contact with Irene. He has undoubtedly played his part very well.

Morland is similar to Dr. David Trent of *House on Haunted Hill* because he essentially pretends to be somebody he is not.[*] Both men present themselves as conscientious and prudent, but secretly prey on the innocence and vulnerability of their victims. At one point, Morland meets Irene for dinner at a fancy restaurant. He speaks of his ability to put women at ease, claiming, "Sometimes [women] get so relaxed around me they just fall asleep." Irene appears content, but gradually becomes uneasy as her recurring dreams become the topic of conversation. Morland, the mastermind behind her nighttime escapades, feigns concern:

> MORLAND: Irene, you're not making sense. I think it's about time you talked this whole thing over with a doctor. Let me make an appointment for you.
>
> IRENE: Are you telling me you think I'm crazy?

In *House on Haunted Hill*, Dr. Trent, a psychiatrist, attempts to pacify a frantic Nora Manning by offering her a sedative. Like Irene, she becomes defensive. Yet, despite any other disturbances in the house, Dr. Trent is the primary cause of Nora's misery. He later prides himself on driving her to complete hysteria. Both Morland

---

[*] In order to avoid confusion, "Dr. Trent" will henceforth refer to the character of *House on Haunted Hill*, whereas "Trent" will refer to that of *The Night Walker*.

and Dr. Trent, in essence, wear a façade of legitimacy as a means to disguise their selfish, horrendous agendas. But a key difference between the two is that the former intends to eliminate his victim.

Upon the conclusion of *The Night Walker*, Morland convinces Irene that he will confront a supposedly murderous Trent by entering into the darkness of Trent's home, thus implementing a strategy similar to what is devised by Warren of *Homicidal*. The intended victims of both films are initially prevented from accompanying their partners. Irene expresses concern as Morland prepares to infiltrate the house. He assures her that he has company and produces a firearm. She is instructed to call the police from a nearby booth. Morland enters the home. But Irene quickly discovers that the phone line has been cut. Gunshots are heard. Irene takes the bait and follows Morland, who has set the perfect trap. He appears as Trent, and then unmasks himself before attempting to kill her. In *Homicidal*, Warren and Miriam Webster, like Morland and Irene, drive to a dark mansion in order to supposedly confront a killer. Despite her protests, Warren tells Miriam to wait in the car. He obtains a gun from the glove compartment prior to entering the mansion. Time passes, and curiosity gets the best of Miriam. She follows Warren, who reveals himself to be Emily. In essence, the murder plots of *The Night Walker* and *Homicidal* initially appear foolproof. But in the end, good triumphs over evil.

The Night Walker premiered in Los Angeles on December 30, 1964. During the aforementioned dinner scene, Irene questions Morland, asking, "Why haven't you ever married?" He replies, "Who says I'm not?" The exchange between the two is ironic. Barbara Stanwyck and Robert Taylor, the real-life counterparts of Irene and Morland, were married from 1939 to 1951.

And at the time of the production of *The Night Walker*, Taylor was married to Ursula Thiess. When asked if there were any objections to her husband co-starring with his ex-wife in Castle's picture, Thiess merely replied, "Not necessarily."

In retrospect, Stanwyck and Taylor played their parts convincingly, perhaps drawing upon experiences of the past in order to establish an added sense of realism for their roles. Castle, of course, did his best to make sure both were comfortable with each other. After all, the onscreen reunion of Stanwyck and Taylor made for good publicity, a concept on which Castle positively thrived.

Barbara Stanwyck and Robert Taylor.

CHAPTER FIFTY-ONE
I SAW WHAT YOU DID (1965)

Out of the Dark, a 1964 suspense novel by Ursula Curtiss, became the basis for William Castle's next film, *I Saw What You Did*. The story of an innocent prank and its severe repercussions had untapped potential for adaptation into a major motion picture.

During the 1960s, a telephone was considered to be one of the most popular items in the typical American household. And it became significant during Castle's appearance in a "world premiere" trailer for the film. During the advertisement's closing seconds, an onscreen telephone begins ringing. As Castle reaches for its receiver, the image freezes. An unseen narrator then commands, "Don't answer it! See it!" An additional trailer continued to warn the audience of the unknown dangers associated with answering a telephone. It was merely Castle's strategy to attract thousands of potential ticket holders to the nearest theater. As a result, his plan became a moderate success.

Libby Mannering (Andi Garrett), a girl in her late teens, is left in charge of babysitting her younger sister, Tess (Sharyl Locke), when her parents depart on an overnight trip. She invites Kit Austin (Sarah Lane), a good friend, to join them for the evening. Out of boredom, the girls begin making prank calls to random strangers. Laughter ensues until Libby phones the residence of Steve Marak (John Ireland), and the call inadvertently leads to an altercation between him and his wife, Judith (Joyce Meadows). In the heat of the moment, Marak murders Judith. Libby, unaware of what has transpired, hangs up the phone. Marak places Judith's corpse in a trunk and buries it in a shallow grave. Later, Libby decides to phone Marak for a second time. When he answers, she jokingly says, "I saw what you did, and I know who you are!" Marak becomes frantic after Libby ends the call. Out of curiosity and unaware of the prank's consequences, the girls drive to his home. Amy Nelson (Joan Crawford), Marak's mistress and neighbor, catches Libby lurking in the yard and orders her to leave. The girls subsequently return to the Mannering residence. Amy eventually confronts Marak, believing Libby to be a rival for his affections. She is also aware of Judith's murder, and attempts to blackmail him into marriage. But Marak kills Amy, too. Using the registration card Amy took from Libby's vehicle, he obtains the latter's address. Kit eventually departs, leaving Libby and Tess alone in the house. Marak appears and questions both girls in regard to the evening's events. When it becomes clear that Libby and Tess are privy to his agenda, he attempts to kill them. But the police, having already discovered Judith's body, arrive on a hunch and shoot Marak dead.

"I saw what you did, and I know who you are!".

The promotion of Castle's film did not come to full fruition by the time of its theatrical release. A gimmick to have theaters furnish seatbelts for the safety of all patrons (in order for them to avoid being "shocked" out of their seats) was eventually abandoned. In addition, the film's poster contained a tagline that declared, "WILLIAM CASTLE WARNS YOU: 'THIS IS A MOTION PICTURE ABOUT UXORICIDE!'"

But a majority of the general public did not understand the meaning of the word. Uxoricide pertains to the killing of one's wife. Nevertheless, when compared with the other motion pictures of Castle's filmography, *I Saw What You Did* has a relatively easy-to-understand plot. Furthermore, its characters are somewhat fascinating. Ellie Mannering (Patricia Breslin), Libby's mother, is particularly unique because she is the most altruistic character of the story. Naturally, the opposite can be said of Marak. People, in general, differ from one another in regard to their level of selflessness. Without Marak's egomaniacal personality, the film would be devoid of conflict. However, additional characters of the narrative are the source of such conflict. Dave Mannering (Leif Erickson), Libby, and Amy exhibit a selfish nature as they embark on quests of personal fulfillment, thereby triggering a drastic chain of events.

Mannering, a self-absorbed father who is more concerned with a career agenda than the welfare of his own family, inadvertently throws the evening off course by refusing to cancel the dinner date with Tom Ward (Douglas Evans), his business colleague. Libby is aware of her father's weakness and does not hesitate to exploit it. As the film begins, she and Kit converse via telephone:

LIBBY: Can you come for dinner, and then spend the night?

KIT: I don't know about all night. My father's awfully peculiar.

LIBBY: So is mine, but I can handle him.

A follow-up phone call confirms Kit's suspicions, as she is allowed to stay at the Mannering home only for the evening. Ellie then learns that the previously scheduled babysitter is unable to watch the girls due to illness. She pleads with her husband to cancel the date, but he would rather save face and continue as planned. In essence, he would prefer to risk his family's safety than endure an awkward situation with Ward. As Mannering and Ellie struggle to come to an agreement, Libby seizes the opportunity and interjects with a question:

LIBBY: Mother, when are you gonna realize I'm practically grown up?

Spot, the family dog, looks on in what might be construed as astonishment, then sneezes. Nobody appears to take notice. Mannering proceeds to address Ellie in regard to Libby's question.

MANNERING: You know she's got a point there?

Ellie stares at her husband with understandable reluctance, but he continues to plead his case.

MANNERING: No, no, she's very responsible.

Libby acknowledges the comment with a devilish grin as she rapidly nods her head. Mannering is so absorbed in his career that he lacks the ability to manage the manipulative measures of his daughter. Hence, he and Ellie depart for the evening, thus setting the stage for Libby's childish antics.

Libby, by means of several prank calls, attains personal satisfaction at the expense of others, but the festivities are taken to the extreme when she phones Marak. Her burning curiosity gets her into further trouble. After the first call to Marak's home leaves Libby unsatisfied, a follow-up call is made, but it goes unanswered. Nevertheless, she continues to pursue him. Although Judith's murder most likely would have transpired regardless of the initial phone call to Marak's home, the circumstances would have been different simply because Libby's prank complicates matters. As a result, Marak murders his wife perhaps sooner than planned. And Amy quickly becomes suspicious of his demeanor and actions. As Marak's phone rings for the third time, she desperately pleads with him to avoid answering it. But curiosity overtakes him, too. Libby, in uttering not only the most famous line of the picture, but also the film's captivating title, tells Marak, "I saw what you did, and I know who you are!" He becomes distraught. And consequently, a terrible situation soon becomes catastrophic.

Amy, in love with Marak, yet aware of his heinous crime, selfishly attempts to blackmail him into marriage, but her actions lead to an unfortunate demise. However, it is Libby (also known as Suzette) and her relentless pursuit of Marak that exacerbates Amy's jealousy. The repeated phone calls arouse the latter's suspicion. But Libby's late night jaunt to Marak's home unleashes a display of unbridled wrath. Amy becomes livid, thus presenting her so-called beau with an ultimatum:

AMY: We're going to get married, go away, and do exactly what you said: be together.

MARAK: You're crowding me again, Amy. I got things to do!

AMY: Sure, you have things to do, with Suzette! I heard you on the phone with her. I listened in the bedroom. I also know what happened here tonight to Judith.

Marak stares at Amy in disbelief, then looks away.

AMY: It's a simple choice, Steve. Life with me, or no life at all.

MARAK: You're blackmailing me into marrying you. You must want it awful bad, the ring with the missus in front of your name.

AMY: But only with you.

MARAK: What you're saying is I have no choice.

AMY: Not at all. Very simple, all I have to do is pick up the phone and call the police.

MARAK: Well, Amy. Maybe it'll work. Who knows? You might be just what I needed.

Marak then proceeds to make a drink for himself, but his concession of defeat is short-lived, as his plan to murder Amy is immediately executed. He eventually makes preparations for his visit to the Mannering residence. Marak uses Ellie's registration card, taken by Amy during a fit of jealousy, in order to reach his destination. Hence, Mannering's abandonment of his daughters, Libby's irresponsible antics, and Amy's selfish agenda each trigger the critical chain of events that ultimately leads to the film's climax.

Joyce Meadows spoke to the author of this book regarding her memorable portrayal of Judith Marak. Of her experiences, she said:

> "On the Universal lot, *The Alfred Hitchcock Hour* was in production. One day, I was performing for the show when a casting director approached me. He mentioned that a small part was available for a William Castle film. I agreed without looking at the script because this casting director, Ralph, used to bring me to Universal all the time to perform in different shows. It happened to be a short day of work on *The Alfred Hitchcock Hour* when the crew of *I Saw What You Did* whisked me over to the makeup department to prepare me for my scenes. While I was having my hair

done, I read the script and became horrified. I thought of *Psycho* and how women are sometimes portrayed negatively in films. I wasn't happy about performing in Castle's film, but I committed to the project because I said I would. The role was basically dumped into my lap during my lunch hour, and everything was completed in one afternoon. Despite the circumstances behind my involvement with *I Saw What You Did*, William Castle had a wonderful way of getting the most out of his pictures with not a very large budget. He made some excellent films on a smaller budget. I think, today, it's great that young people can make their own films due to so many advances in technology. Making a film in Hollywood costs millions of dollars. And Castle, bless his heart, was very instrumental in doing a lot with not a very large budget. Nevertheless, *I Saw What You Did* wasn't a good experience for me. In 1960, I did not go to see *Psycho* because of that horrifying scene, and then five years later, I'm cast in a role similar to Janet Leigh's. I obviously did not enjoy being chopped to death. In 1965, special effects were clearly not as advanced as they are today. Most of my time was spent in that shower that afternoon. In fact, the filming went on into part of the evening. The dialogue that was spoken prior to me entering the shower transpired smoothly. But once I was in that shower, there were no computerized special effects to ease the production of the scene. Castle's crew invented their own effects and integrated them into the picture as best as they could. The shower scene was very technical. There were times I had to fall into that horror of being slain in the way I was. Furthermore, my scenes were filmed on a different set from that of Joan Crawford's. Crawford, in addition to several older stars of the era, would not walk on a film set if a younger person was present. Crawford didn't mind the teenagers. But I was a young adult, and she wasn't about to enter the stage if I was anywhere in sight. Therefore, I had to be filmed on a completely different set. The crew wasn't sure how long my scenes were going to take, so I was placed elsewhere. Crawford wouldn't talk to me, but she wasn't the only one. My agent handled several older stars. Marlene Dietrich was one of them. I would be in the commissary having lunch with my agent. He was Dietrich's agent, too. And she would be out by the door standing there. My agent would eventually look over and see her, then say, 'Oh, she's here now. You'll have to leave.' Dietrich would not come over to the table and sit down until I left. She would refuse to be seen around a younger person. This is why I had no interaction with Joan Crawford. I didn't have any scenes with her, but if I did, she would've demanded that Castle cast a performer close to her age or, perhaps, someone a little older. Some of the older stars of the era simply didn't want to be compared with young adults in regard to appearance."

"Working with John Ireland was memorable. By 1965, he had done a lot of work. To me, he was a movie star. I became bashful around him and he picked up on my demeanor. During breaks, he would approach me and flirt a little bit. John didn't come on too strong, but he did flirt. For obvious reasons, we didn't really have a good experience filming the scene. But my time on the set of *I Saw What You Did* was very brief. I mentioned to John that I was performing in an episode of *The Alfred Hitchcock Hour*. The next day, I was back on that set. And John dropped by to visit. He watched me work. I was impressed and thought his gesture was very sweet. John was complimentary and encouraging. But he was a well-established movie star and I was not. Once my scene was finished, I walked over to where he was standing, gave him a big hug, and thanked him for visiting. Afterwards, I never saw him again. Those two days were the only connection I had with John Ireland."

On May 14, 1965, Castle celebrated the world premiere of *I Saw What You Did* in Minneapolis, a place of which he was no stranger. It had only been a few years since the city played host to the premiere of *13 Ghosts*. Although the times had changed, the devotion of Castle's fans remained consistent, as hundreds of spectators congregated together in boisterous revelry.

I Saw What You Did was a hit with the American public, and it also marked Joan Crawford's final appearance in a Castle film. Coincidentally, both entertainers shared an eerily similar fate. Crawford and Castle both died of heart attacks. They both died on a Tuesday. They both died during the month of May. And they both died in 1977. Crawford's sudden death transpired exactly three weeks prior to that of Castle's. In short, it was a sad time in Hollywood. But the memories of Crawford and Castle will live forever, because their notable and extraordinary accomplishments will never be forgotten.

Cary Grant visits the set of I Saw What You Did. He is pictured with Joan Crawford, William Castle, and John Ireland.

CHAPTER FIFTY-TWO
LET'S KILL UNCLE (1966)

June Skinner, a native of Vancouver, developed a knack for writing during adolescence. Yet, it was not until her late thirties that she celebrated the publication of her first novel, *O'Houlihan's Jest*. She wrote under the pseudonym Rohan O'Grady.* *O'Houlihan's Jest* centered on the Irish War of Independence.

In order to complete her novel, Skinner (O'Grady) relied primarily on her knowledge of Ireland and its storied history. Her extensive research of the island nation proved to be effective, as *O'Houlihan's Jest* met with moderate success. Coincidentally, O'Grady had never been to Ireland prior to, or during, its composition. Nevertheless, the settings of her novels eventually changed to her native British Columbia. The region's coastal islands served as the backdrop for her third novel, *Let's Kill Uncle*.

A short time after its publication in 1963, William Castle acquired the story's rights and hired Mark Rodgers, a television writer, to provide an adaptation for the silver screen.

Twelve-year-old Barnaby Harrison (Pat Cardi) becomes parentless following his father's death in an automobile accident. Frank Travis (Robert Pickering), a police sergeant, assumes temporary custody of the boy until the latter can be reunited with his next of kin. Major Kevin Harrison (Nigel Green), of the British Intelligence, is Barnaby's uncle and only living relative. He resides on Serenity Island. Traveling by steamer to his new home, Barnaby clashes with Chrissie (Mary Badham), another passenger close to his age. She plans to visit her Aunt Justine (Linda Lawson), another resident of the island. Upon arrival, Barnaby and Chrissie find their new surroundings to be eerie. Together, they encounter a haunted hotel, killer sharks, and more. After being delayed for a day, Barnaby's uncle arrives via self-piloted aircraft. Early the next morning, he hypnotizes his nephew and then coerces him to the highest cliff of the island. Just as Barnaby is about to plunge to his death, Justine happens upon the scene and disrupts the trance. The major, commonly referred to as Uncle, is nowhere in

---
* June Skinner was born in 1922 as June Margaret O'Grady.

sight. Travis, reluctant to believe Barnaby was hypnotized, delays his departure from Serenity Island nonetheless. Uncle privately informs his nephew that he will soon murder him and make it look like an accident. If successful, he will collect a $5 million inheritance. Chrissie suggests that she and Barnaby devise a scheme to kill Uncle before his plan can be executed. Both parties exchange blows, but neither is successful in eliminating the other. Uncle makes one last attempt at hypnosis, but to no avail. He declares the "game" to be "a tie," and expresses hope that Barnaby and Chrissie have learned "a little of how this world goes."

Pat Cardi as Barnaby Harrison.

The opening credits of *Let's Kill Uncle* feature an eclectic collection of tin soldiers. Medieval Muslims brandish their scimitars, and German troops of a later period stand poised to attack as Herman Stein's haunting score is heard in the background. A clear difference among the eras of world history is apparent, but within the mix of soldiers is a rebel group of fighters that is distinct. The band of misfits foreshadows what is to come with Barnaby and Chrissie's rebellion against the militaristic Uncle. In the novel, O'Grady's antagonist is characterized in great detail. At a relatively early point of the story, the reader discovers that "Uncle's eyes were quite mad." And during the hypnotism sequences of the film, Castle makes use of an extreme close-up to capture the intensity of Nigel Green's piercing blue eyes. But O'Grady writes that Uncle frequently wore dark glasses, a detail, among many others, that is omitted from the motion picture. Castle's depiction of the novel, especially in regard to the character of Uncle, is considerably lighter than O'Grady's original story. Uncle's relation to Barnaby, his passion for writing, and the film's general lack of violence reveal the disparities between both versions.

Nigel Green.

In Castle's picture, it is immediately established that Barnaby's deceased father (Castle in a cameo role) is survived by a brother, but O'Grady's concept of Uncle's relation to the family is quite different. During a key point of the novel, Barnaby reveals that his legal guardian is "not [his] real uncle." Instead, his late aunt, a blood relative, was married to Uncle at the time of her death. She was incredibly wealthy. According to her will, her entire fortune was placed in a trust fund for Barnaby, but he cannot access the money until he is twenty-one years of age. If he dies before he can collect, the inheritance will go to Uncle. Hence, the game is afoot. But the stakes are higher. Because in the novel, the inheritance is $10 million as opposed to the film's $5 million. Naturally, money has a tendency to bring out the worst in people. And the $5 million difference is simply one of several reasons why O'Grady's characterization of Uncle is darker.

Castle initially presents the major as a hero of World War II, thus establishing him as a contemporary author who avidly chronicles his triumph over the Germans. O'Grady presents Uncle as a man with more of a passion for reading than writing. In the novel, he is a devoted fan of the Marquis de Sade, a controversial author who gained notoriety during the late eighteenth century. The Marquis penned much of his literature in a French prison. He was an outspoken critic of the Catholic Church, and many of his works evolved around eroticism. O'Grady writes of the Marquis as Uncle's "favourite author" and "friend." Yet, there is no mention of the infamous French aristocrat in Castle's picture. The Marquis was notorious for integrating violence into his writings, which may account for his overall absence from the film.

"Barnaby, your uncle's trying to kill you, right? Well, let's kill Uncle first!"

The title of Castle's picture, clearly derived from O'Grady's novel, is somewhat misleading due to the narrative's lack of brutality and destructiveness. Uncle's fate differs greatly between what is portrayed in the film and what is printed in the novel. O'Grady writes of a gruesome death. Uncle is viciously attacked and killed by a cougar. Castle's ending is not as graphic. In fact, it is almost the opposite. A killer shark, residing in the swimming pool of an abandoned hotel, threatens to dispatch Uncle after the latter is pushed into the pool by Barnaby. But the threat is over in a matter of seconds. Uncle climbs out of the pool unscathed, and the mood of the film undergoes a complete transformation. The major leaves Serenity Island. Herman Stein's score becomes positively uplifting, and Barnaby stares at Uncle's departing plane with sincere admiration, proclaiming, "I'll miss you, Uncle Kevin. I really will." Perhaps, the greatest issue with *Let's Kill Uncle* is that the conclusion is rushed, not to mention bizarre. During one scene, there is extreme conflict. But only a couple of minutes later, Uncle, a would-be killer, flies off into the night sky. And Barnaby is left awestruck by the very man who tried to murder him.

"Bill Castle," Pat Cardi once told the author of this book, "was endlessly patient. He was as sympathetic to a child actor as a director possibly could be. A year earlier, I worked on a picture entitled *And Now Miguel*. Its director, Jim Clark, had ideas for how he wanted me to play the part, but he did not articulate exactly how he wanted this to happen. I walked off the set and started crying to myself. People became concerned, telling Clark, 'Oh, no! You've upset the star of the film!' Furthermore, living with my dad wasn't fun at all. During the production of *And Now Miguel*, he was with me on the set all the time. He went with me to New Mexico when the film was shot on location. My dad was great at playing head games. That made me nervous all the time. Regardless of the production, I would try to stay on the opposite side of the sound stage from where he was. But at some point in time, he'd always pull me into the dressing room and give me grief. It was as if he was trying to hold me back from reaching my full potential."

"Being in close proximity to Dad was always a problem, but on the set of *Let's Kill Uncle*, it never seemed to be. In fact, at one point, Bill Castle intervened, saying, 'Dad, let's

Linda Lawson and Robert Pickering.

move off the set for a while, okay? Let Pat figure it out for himself.' Bill was just fun to work with. I enjoyed going to the set every day. Shortly after we first met, during a conversation about my model planes, he asked me what my favorite aircraft was. I told him it was a Beechcraft Bonanza. He asked, 'How big is that plane?' And I said, 'It's a private plane.' Then, about a month later, I discovered a Beechcraft Bonanza was on the set. We were getting ready to do the scenes with the airplane. Castle lifted it by one wing, and I lifted it by the other. We didn't get it off the ground, but we lifted it off its shocks so that it actually rose. And we thought that was kind of cool. He was playing with me like we had this game going. Castle was very personable with kids. He liked having kids around. If things ever got hot and heavy on the set, he'd look at me like an uncle and say, 'Okay. It's going to get a little shaky here. You might want to go to the dressing room.' He was a good guy. One could see that he had an ego, but he was so friendly that it wasn't an issue. He didn't care if people knew he had an ego, not at all. He actually asked me one time, he said, 'Pat. You've worked with a lot of directors.

Am I not the greatest director you've ever been with?' I'd say, 'You're by far the best director I've ever worked for.' And he replied, 'I knew that.' Being a child, I wasn't sure how much of that was sarcasm or just being silly, or maybe he needed some affirmation from his cast. Children don't usually give back too much along those lines. They wouldn't necessarily tell a director, 'Gee, I really like working with you.' Adult actors will do that all day long. But children are generally on the set to get the job done and go back to their lives."

"The overall experience of *Let's Kill Uncle* was an interesting thing. I got to walk around in the old hotel. It was on Stage 12 of the Universal lot. Aside from the hotel, there were a couple of other sets in addition to the airplane, forest, and house. The boat was also on the set. That's why *Let's Kill Uncle* was filmed on Universal's largest stage. It contained the process projector. Back then, they didn't use a green screen. Instead, the projector showed footage of the ocean behind us. That projector synced up with the camera. I don't know how they did it, but back then, it was all mechanical. If one were to look at the

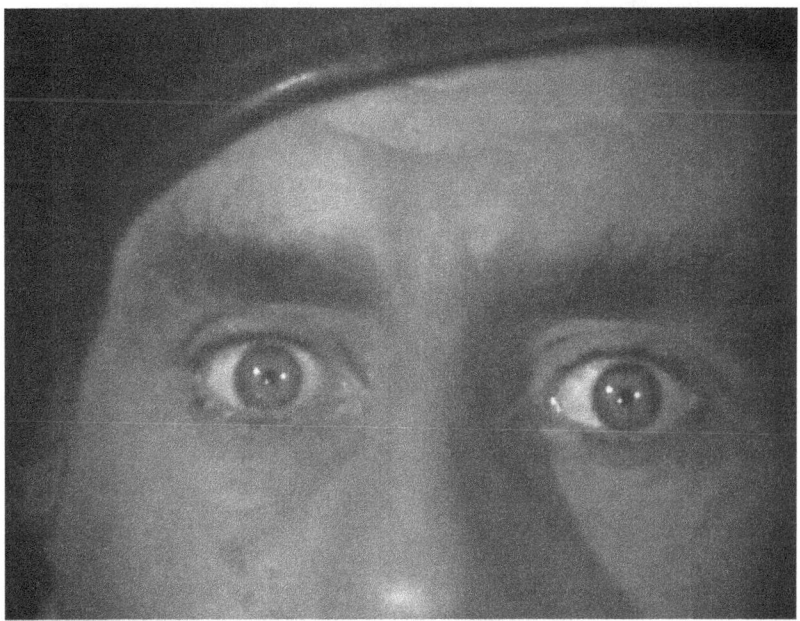

The madness of Uncle's eyes.

screen, he or she would be able to see it flickering. I loved being around that stuff because it was just neat how they do that. And the swimming pool was on that stage, too. They could just open up the floor. The swimming pool was under it. Water components are built into some of the sound stages. Grips go in and literally pick up sections of the floor and build around whatever the water structure is supposed to be for that particular production."

"Bill Castle and I were talking one day around Christmas time, and I asked him, 'What does somebody get a guy like you for Christmas?' And he says, 'I'll tell you what you can get me. Get me a box of Cuban cigars.' Castle then went off like Mark Twain talking about cigars. Later, I approached my dad and said that we needed to get some Cuban cigars. He said, 'How do you get Cuban cigars?' I replied, 'I don't know, but that's what we have to get him because that's what he wants for Christmas.' My dad was soon on task to find Cuban cigars. He couldn't find them. But my dad had just designed a hot lather dispenser. Its packaging was about the same size as a box of cigars. He had designed the dispenser for an engineering firm that his cousin owned. My dad told me, 'You just can't get Cuban cigars. It's against the law to have them in the United States because of the Cuban missile crisis and whatnot.' We eventually wrapped up the dispenser. I thought, 'Why is he going to want this?' I handed the package to Bill. His eyes went back and forth between me and the package. He said, 'I don't know how you got this. This is the best Christmas present ever! This is going to be perfect! I love this!' And I said, 'Mr. Castle, it's not what you think it is.' He opened it up and said, 'What is it?' And I said, 'It's a hot lather dispenser for shaving.' And he says, 'I love it! This is the greatest gift you could have given me!' And he totally went past it without skipping a beat. He thought for sure it was Cuban cigars. It was a disappointment, but he never would have let me know that. Yet, I walked away thinking he must be really disappointed. And then I set out trying to find Cuban cigars. Years later, when Castle was filming *Bug*, I finally obtained a box of them and made a special delivery. He was quite content. Not too long after that day, I saw him again. People said Bill Castle never drove a car. But he did. I was standing in line at a movie theater. Suddenly, I heard a lot of honking. Castle was driving a black Lincoln, or something similar to it. He was coming right towards the sidewalk and waving at me. Then, he turned the wheel at the last minute, hit the curb, and kept going. I watched him drive away, the whole time thinking he shouldn't be driving. His office was at Paramount, and I happened to be at a theater near the studio."

Barnaby and Chrissie venture towards the island's abandoned hotel.

"Lew Wasserman, the longtime head of Universal, became particularly involved with the production of *Let's Kill Uncle*. One day, he came on the stage and kind of looked at me. Then, he proceeded to watch the filming. Everything got really quiet. Castle and Wasserman were having a discussion. Somebody, possibly my dad, was trying to get me away from the area. But I think I was standing by the airplane, looking over the wing and watching both men. Bill just kept shaking his head, saying, 'No!

No!' And then Wasserman said, 'Change it to five million dollars, because for ten million, I'd kill the kid myself!' He walked off the set. Wasserman believed the original value of Barnaby's worth was exorbitant. The kid should not be worth ten million dollars. He should be worth less, like five million, or even a million dollars."

"There was another time on the set when they cleared the stage and Bill Castle had a problem with somebody, but I'm not sure who it was. I just remember the argument got very loud. There was yelling back and forth and I don't know who the other person was. But the entire cast, crew, and everybody else was outside, waiting in the street. The sound stage was shut down and the assistant director was standing in front of the door. Seconds before I exited the stage, I heard Bill yelling. He said something like, 'Okay! Let's get this straight! Who's in charge? Who's producing? Who's directing? Who's making this movie, you or me?' I never found out who the other person was. At the time, I thought Castle may have been fighting with the director of photography."

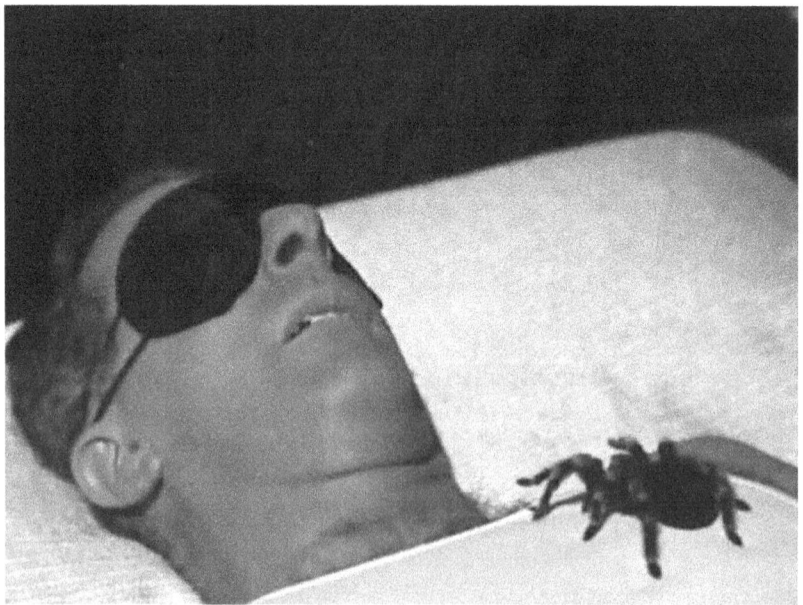

A tarantula inches closer to its target.

"I know Bill had problems with the Black Tower (the large building in front of Universal). It was called the Black Tower because it was the biggest thing in the San Fernando Valley. It could be seen from miles away. We all knew Bill had problems with the tower. He especially had a problem with the legal department because he wanted me to star in *Let's Kill Uncle*. Universal's lawyers fought him on this, but they couldn't take action because it was in Castle's contract that he could choose Barnaby. He was asked to use Mary Badham for Chrissie, but it was not a problem. I don't know if he had any other girls audition or not. I know he saw a slew of boys. They brought me in a couple of times. The first time I went, John Badham, the casting director and Mary's older brother, interviewed me in his office. While I was there, he called Bill and said, 'Bill? I've got Barnaby here in the office right now.' And I thought, 'Oh, that's a good sign.' John, of course, went on to become a famous director. He was just as personable as Bill Castle. For my second visit, I was brought into Castle's office. I read a couple of scenes and they called me back to read with Mary. Some stars were present. James Mason's son was there. They were trying to get him to read. But I could hear him through the door. He couldn't read. I think Stan Livingston was there. After reviewing the options, Bill Castle eventually said I was going to play the part. But there was a fight. Prior to *And Now Miguel*, I signed a seven-year contract with Universal. I was on staff. I had a school room and would go to the studio every day. But there was no work. I did *And Now Miguel* and that was it. Every day, the teacher and I would meet at the studio's school room. It was a huge, empty, white room that contained nothing but a table, the teacher, and me. Finally, I went on an interview because I was bored to tears. *It's About Time*, a television show produced by Sherwood Schwartz, was about two astronauts who went back in time to live with cave people. I was ultimately cast as Breer, a cave child. I did the pilot thinking there are hundreds of them and few ever get picked up. But it gave me something to do. Richard Donner directed the pilot, and the show got picked up. When I interviewed for *It's About Time*, it was beyond the scope of my contract with Universal. I wasn't supposed to go on any interviews without notifying the studio ahead of time. I basically did the interview and pilot without ever telling the Universal executives. They read in the trades that I had a television series on another network. Universal was affiliated with NBC at the time, and *It's About Time* aired on CBS. The executives had no idea at first, but when they found out, they sued my family right away to stop the contract. Sherwood Schwartz ended up fighting for me. While this was happening, I snuck onto the Universal lot to audition for *Let's Kill Uncle*. I got the part, and then Castle ended up fighting for me, too. Universal's legal department was trying to kill my acting career. We went to court. Universal lost the case. It didn't even go to trial. During the discovery phase, they noticed that my mom didn't sign the contract. My mother was asked, 'Do you want your son to be working at Universal?' She said, 'No.' The judge then replied, 'Okay. That does it. The contract is null and void.' The next fight was Bill Castle fighting with Universal about

Trouble amongst the clouds.

his contract allowing him to pick Barnaby. And he picked me. But his decision met with opposition. Castle eventually won the fight. Production was delayed. And then, we ended up doing the film. After *Let's Kill Uncle*, I returned to *It's About Time*. The pilot was shot before Castle's film, and the remainder of the series was filmed afterwards."

"During the production of *Let's Kill Uncle*, Nigel Green was great. His onscreen persona was that of an absolute gentleman. He was a warrior to the bone, a man's man. Aside from the fact that Nigel would never murder anyone, he was exactly the same when the cameras were not rolling. In regard to acting, he gave me hints of things I could do differently. In a way, Nigel introduced me to theater. When I found out he was doing stage productions in England with all of these other great actors, I couldn't believe it. He would say, 'Why don't you say this particular line a certain way? I'll then reply another way.' And then Nigel and I would have this great interaction going with each other. It set me off balance at first. I wasn't sure why he was telling me how to act. And then, I believe it was my dad who said to me, 'In England, he's a great actor. If he gives you any help, take it!' At one point, I just wanted to obtain any knowledge Nigel could offer me. Off the set, we sat in chairs next to each other once in a while, but he seemed to be extremely introspective. I believe he was drinking, too. I think he was hiding it, and quite well at that. I know I smelled alcohol on him once, but not often. I didn't think it was a problem. I just figured, 'Oh, he must've been drinking last night.'"

"In regard to Mary Badham, I did not know her prior to *Let's Kill Uncle*. I was well aware of the fact that she starred in *To Kill a Mockingbird*, and I knew she was nominated for an Oscar for that. I had seen *To Kill a Mockingbird* several times because I used to sneak into the theaters on Colorado Boulevard in Pasadena. I watched it over and over again because the film was about kids. And I loved it. It was a great film. When I met Mary initially, she didn't look like the girl in the film. We met in the casting office. We recited lines together, and she was very personable and extremely friendly. I just attributed her personality to the fact that she was from the South and people in the South seemed friendly, at least according to the television shows I watched. We arrived on the set, and Mary worked on the first scene. On the first day of production, I didn't work. Mary did, and I felt a little jealous. I was also intimidated by her Academy Award nomination, thinking, 'How good can she be? If she's that good, this is going to be a problem. This is going to be trouble.' I think part of my overacting in the film was me trying to shine above what she was doing. And I pretty much thought I had that under control until I went into the screening room and saw that I was very much over the top. The first day on the set, Mary did her scene, and then she came off the set. She looks at me, grabs my head, and says, 'They cut your hair! They cut your hair! I can't believe they cut your hair!' I was in shock and wanted to be as far from the studio as possible. But through the course of the film, Mary was just so friendly and lovely and such a lady that she was different from any girl I had ever met. I was fourteen years old and dating Diane Sherry at the time *Let's Kill Uncle* was produced. But I needed some stability in a relationship. Although Mary lived in Alabama, we visited each other back and forth a couple of times following the film's production. She stayed with us at our house. I was convinced I wanted to marry her. By the time we were seventeen years old, I proposed. Mary looked at me and said, 'You just don't think, do you? Are you crazy? Do you know how old we are?' And I replied, 'Yeah, but I know this is right. This is what it has to be.' And she says, 'You're out of your mind.' Mary then told her brother, John, all about it. She was staying with him at the time. John later approached me and said, 'Oh, Patrick, Patrick, Patrick, you've got a lot of life to live.' They both were trying to steer me in the right direction. Mary and I eventually lost touch, but around 2005, I did a search and found her. I then sent her a message with my phone number and she called me. When Mary and I both realized we were finally in contact with each other

Pat Cardi and Nigel Green.

after so many years, we laughed for five minutes straight before beginning our conversation. It's a great memory."

"One day on the set of *Let's Kill Uncle*, Bill let me come in and view the rushes, also known as the dailies. Prior to seeing myself on the screen, he made me promise that I wouldn't change my performance, that I wouldn't change my character because of what I was about to see. And when I looked at what was going on, I was really shocked and thought, 'Oh no! That's what I'm doing?' And I wanted to change my performance. Then, we had a discussion about the fact that I thought the character of Barnaby should be different. Castle replied, 'You know what? We're already a quarter of the way into the film and you can't change. You have to be that kid. And that's the kid I want.' And after a couple of days, I got back into it. But I had these thoughts going on in my head the whole time, thinking, 'My performance is really bad!' It really bothered me. I think that was the first time I really realized that I wasn't that great of an actor. I was just a kid acting out, and I didn't really have a philosophy or good point of view as an actor. After all, I was only fourteen at the time of production."

"There were times when Bill would take me aside just to be with me. When he was working with boys, like Charles Herbert of *13 Ghosts*, Castle always offered words of encouragement. He became an uncle with whom I wanted to have fun. He gave me things. Aside from a model of a Beechcraft Bonanza, Castle gave me a script book with my name in gold engraved onto it. The book had a spring in it, so a script could be inserted and the whole thing would just snap shut. Castle also gave me a bag of magic tricks because I had earlier told him that I enjoyed going to the Burt Wheeler Hollywood Magic Shop during the weekends. Either he or somebody went down there and bought a bunch of stuff and put it in a bag for me. And then Castle wanted me to show him the magic stuff. I was amazed, thinking, 'Why is he so interested in what I'm doing?' He was the best, and I will never forget the times I spent with him."

Let's Kill Uncle was Castle's final film for Universal. To reiterate, it is not as gruesome as the title suggests. The only death of the film, befalling upon the character Castle portrays, transpires seconds after the picture begins. Uncle, proud author of *Killing the Enemy*, harbors a malicious nature, but we never see him commit murder. The audience is simply exposed to one attempt after another. A particular scene depicts Uncle using arson as a means for murder. But a sudden thunderstorm, complete with a torrential downpour of rain, rapidly extinguishes the fire (similar to what is seen with the liberation of the entrapped Israelites in *Slaves of Babylon*).

In regard to the film's setting, the addition of a haunted hotel to Castle's island environment is reminiscent of old dark houses of previous pictures. Rohan O'Grady, when asked her opinion of the novel's adaptation, replied, "I'd set the book on one of the Gulf Islands [of British Columbia] and there was a cougar in the story. They'd switched the whole thing to some tropical island off Mexico or Texas. The cougar became a shark. Sometimes, I think all they really bought from me was the title."

CHAPTER FIFTY-THREE
THE BUSY BODY (1967)

"I surrounded [Sid Caesar] with a cast filled with comedy stars," William Castle said of *The Busy Body*, based on the Donald E. Westlake novel of the same name. Castle, under contract with Paramount Pictures, was at a point in his career where he was determined to make his audiences laugh. However, comedy is difficult. But Castle was up for the challenge. It had been almost five years since the release of *Zotz!*, and he wanted another chance to prove himself to the general public. Ben Starr was brought in to adapt the screenplay, which does not stray too far from the original plot of the novel. In order to attempt another foray into the realm of comedy, Castle relied on what he knew best and was sure to include particular elements of the macabre at just the right moments.

George Norton (Caesar), recently promoted within the ranks of organized crime, is ordered by his boss, Charley Barker (Robert Ryan), to unearth a corpse in search of $1 million. The fortune is hidden within the lining of the deceased's suit. When the coffin is discovered to be empty, Norton visits the mortuary in search of answers. But things become more complicated when the mortician turns up dead. Margo Foster Kane (Anne Baxter), a mysterious widow, accuses Norton of the murder. The police soon dismiss him, but Margo does not, leading to a mutual attraction between the two. Norton tries to stay focused on finding the money. But the downward spiral continues when Kurt Brock (Dom DeLuise), the assistant mortician, is murdered, and Barker, suspecting insubordination, orders Norton's death. On the run, and through his own investigation, Norton uncovers an insurance scam concocted by Margo and her husband, Murray Foster (Jan Murray), who is not only alive, but is also responsible for stealing the corpse and murdering those of the mortuary. The Fosters, completely unaware of the hidden fortune, are soon apprehended. Later, Norton finds the suit and immediately summons Barker in an attempt to win back the latter's approval. Instead, he is almost killed upon learning the harsh truth that Barker, out to embezzle the million, set him

Sid Caesar and Robert Ryan.

up as a patsy to take the fall. In the end, it is Barker who meets his demise, thus enabling Norton to begin a new life.

Prior to its theatrical release in January of 1967, *The Busy Body* received a lot of publicity. A headline from the Paramount press book claimed that "all this picture has is SEX, GANGSTERS, STRIPPERS, A MILLION STOLEN BUCKS, 3 STIFFS IN ONE COFFIN, and some of the other little Happenings in life." Not only did Castle want to direct a successful comedy, he wanted to produce a blockbuster hit that people would remember for years to come. Today, although not as popular as other Castle films, *The Busy Body* still manages to entertain the average audience. Much of this is due to its ironic undertones, the idea that less is more, and Castle's signature repertoire.

As the film begins, Vic Mizzy's score commences with organ music, as if we might be in church to attend a funeral. But it is not long before the notes quickly fade, blending into a quirky tune reminiscent of a 1960s sitcom. The organ music foreshadows what is to come with Officer Muldoon's funeral. Like the film's opening track, what is originally perceived as somber soon becomes comical. And the irony, which is sometimes humorous, enables Castle to be a few steps ahead of his audience. It begins with the opening credits, but also evolves around the missing fortune (the one factor to keep the characters on their toes).

The ironic undertones of *The Busy Body*, evident from the get-go, are more apparent after one has completed an initial viewing of the film. Many names are displayed during the opening credits, and almost all of them are filled with holes, shot up by a pistol we can hear, but cannot see. As the titles conclude, we are immediately brought into Barker's boardroom, where he and his associates analyze a crime short filled with nothing but shooting guns. Within the sequence of events, Castle alludes to a classic, shoot-'em-up narrative that could potentially follow, and this is what select members of an audience may come to expect. Yet, not a single person is shot throughout the entirety of The Busy Body. People are murdered, and quite creatively at that, but nobody meets their demise via gunshot. Of all the performers whose names are displayed, only one name is not shot up, and it is that of Paul Wexler, who stars as Merriwether, the murdered mortician. Coincidentally, Merriwether is stabbed instead of shot. But the irony extends beyond the scope of the opening credits.

"We're sure gonna miss Muldoon."

It is not long before Norton's million-dollar objective lures the audience into his world, and the fortune and its existence are arguably the most ironic elements of the film. Barker sets the stage for what is to follow as he orders Norton to recover the missing money. Along the way, people are killed, and a murderer with purple suede shoes is on the loose. But the $1 million remains to be the primary concern of the audience, because its disappearance is what got Norton into trouble in the first place. He will not rest until it is found. Eventually, all conflicts are resolved, and the film concludes with Norton relaxing at home with his over-possessive mother (Kay Medford) and Bobbi Brody (Arlene Golonka). Archie Brody (Bill Dana), aka the missing corpse, is Bobbi's late husband.

Not only is it ironic that Norton ends up with Brody's widow, but it is also ironic that the million dollars, the very catalyst for the film's premise, is never seen by the audience. Yet, the mere existence of the money creates conflict, and without conflict, Castle would be unable to produce his film. Sometimes, the less the audience sees of a particular character or object, the better.

In 1855, Robert Browning, the famous English poet, published *The Faultless Painter*, in which the phrase "less is more" was first coined. The idea is that overexposure could lead to disaster. Although some critics and film historians have referred to *The Busy Body* as a wacky comedy, it is also an intriguing murder mystery. But in order for the narrative to be engrossing, the audience must be kept guessing up until the murderer is finally unmasked. Browning's concept keeps the audience in suspense in regard to the killer's identity. A colorful pair of purple suede shoes, in addition to several talented comics, is afforded a limited amount of screen time because of Browning's age-old philosophy.

Brief flashes of purple suede shoes, which accompany the deaths of Merriwether and Brock, inadvertently build suspense. Castle's depiction of Bobbi's musical act keeps us on the lookout during the entire scene. By the time Norton seeks refuge in her apartment, the audience is very much privy to the murderer's shoes. Purple, by nature, is more of a feminine color and is less likely to be associated with males. Bobbi, an attractive female, is a suspect. The scene during which she sings for Norton is approximately eight minutes in length. It is an enticing period of time, and Castle avoids the exposure of Bobbi's feet until the scene's final seconds. A sudden appearance of her golden sandals reduces suspicion, but not before the audience is subjected to minutes of uncertainty. In regard to the mysterious purple suede shoes, as well as Bobbi's golden sandals, Castle puts a strict limitation on what we are allowed to see, and his strategy extends beyond the exposure of flashy footwear.

Although a select group of comedians, aside from Sid Caesar, comprise a portion of the film's cast, the audience does not have the opportunity to see that much of them, and this simply makes them more mysterious. Shortly after Brock is murdered in his own apartment, Mike (Godfrey Cambridge), an associate of Barker's who has rarely been seen at this point of the film, suddenly appears at the rear window. His presence is one for concern, especially since he does not react to Brock's motionless corpse. Later, Felix Rose (Ben Blue), a strange character, accuses Norton of slander for no apparent reason, again arousing suspicion. Some murder mysteries make the mistake of giving a character who is secretly the murderer too much screen time, and it is a tactic that can sometimes make a film more predictable. But Castle does not make this mistake with *The Busy Body*. Mike and Rose arouse suspicion partly due to their limited screen time, but a better example of less being more is found elsewhere in the narrative.

Godfrey Cambridge, Sid Caesar, and Marty Ingels.

Approximately twenty minutes into the film, comedian Jan Murray makes a brief appearance, and because the audience will not see him again until the picture's conclusion draws closer, he is the last person people would suspect as the murderer. His appearance as a cemetery night watchman is sudden, but in 1967, it was a pleasant surprise for some. Prior to starring in *The Busy Body*, Murray spent a significant amount of time hosting various game shows. His face was easily recognizable across America. Hence, when Foster, Murray's character, caught Norton in the cemetery, the scene was rather surprising, yet comical, to theatergoers. Seconds before the events transpire, Norton finds himself questioning the disappearance of Brody's body:

> NORTON (to himself): Why steal an entire Archie when all they had to do was grab the million and run? So, where am I? (snapping his fingers) Nowhere!

Suddenly, a light shines in Norton's face as Foster, pretending to be the cemetery night watchman, approaches.

FOSTER: What are you doing here?

Norton's initial reaction is one of shock, but it quickly dissipates as he plans his response.

NORTON: You know what I'm doin' here!

FOSTER: No, I don't.

NORTON: Good!

Norton immediately dashes out of the cemetery. Instead of going after Norton, Foster turns his attention to the freshly dug grave. His reaction to the new addition, which is intensified with Mizzy's score, simply adds to the laughs. Murray's humorous, yet brief, appearance takes the suspicion off of him, leading some to think his character will only emerge once (especially since the audience is unaware he is pretending to be somebody he is not). There are several comedians in the film whose screen time is minimal, but with Murray, his exposure is handled differently. Following the cemetery scene, he does not appear for an entire hour, and it is during his second appearance that he is revealed to be the killer, thus catching many in the audience off guard. Much of Castle's repertoire evolves around several elements, including that of surprise.

When Castle purchased the rights to Westlake's novel, he and screenwriter Ben Starr took the story and made it their own. But they were careful not to stray too far from its original plot. After all, Westlake had a knack for humor, and Castle wanted a narrative that would fill the theaters with laughs. But some have criticized Castle for placing too much of an emphasis on humor instead of assembling an entertaining film devoid of plot holes. Nevertheless, the integration of cigars, movie premieres, and references to several of his earlier films reminded audiences of the signature Castle touch.

A reflection of the director's persona is seen just seconds prior to Brody's death. Barker, in typical William Castle fashion, pops a cigar into his mouth before the fatal flame is lit. Westlake's novel is completely devoid of the barbeque explosion. Castle's addition of the event provided him with the perfect opportunity to implement his persona, similar to the way an artist would sign a painting. In fact, the circumstances of Brody's death are somewhat different in the novel. The cause of death, which is a heart attack, transpires before the story begins. Page one commences with Brody's funeral, and funerals occur just as much in Westlake's novel as they do in the film. But Castle's approach is unique.

Officer Muldoon's funeral is filled with chaos and suspense, just as it is in the original story, but Castle makes a special modification to the eulogy. In the film, a priest speaks highly of Muldoon's character and accomplishments, sadly noting that "he met his death by getting trampled in the rush of a crowd at a premiere at a famous movie." Castle was a director who thrived on movie premieres, often traveling from city to city, attending multiple premieres for the same film. It was merely his way of reaching out to the public. It is no wonder he would insert a brief reference to the festive tribute, despite its aura of death. But without the concept of death, many of Castle's films would lack the solidity that made them successful in the first place, and although he intended for *The Busy Body* to be a comedy, he was able to leave some room for the macabre at just the right moments.

Castle pays homage to many of his previous films by making slight alterations to Westlake's characters, settings, and props. In

Dom DeLuise as the cleaver-wielding Kurt Brock.

some cases, no alterations are made, but the references remain. For example, the digging of a fresh grave, present in both the novel and film, is a direct reference to *Macabre*. One could make the same argument with *Mr. Sardonicus* because, like *The Busy*

Body, its plot involves the burial of money, or, at least, some form of it.

However, there are significant themes of the picture, added by Castle, that cannot be found anywhere in the novel. First, the main character of *The Busy Body* is named George Norton, but in the novel, his name is Aloysius Engel. In *House on Haunted Hill*, a previous owner of the house is named Mr. Norton. And in *Johnny Stool Pigeon*, the main character's name, George Morton, differs only by a single letter. Second, shortly after Merriwether is killed, we see a pair of purple suede shoes from behind the curtains. In *The Old Dark House*, Cecily Femm is yet another killer who uses a curtain as concealment. Third, every time Rose faints, Norton pours Coca-Cola onto his head in order to revive him. In *Strait-Jacket*, the advertisement of another major cola is present, as the kitchen of the Cutler Ranch contains a six-pack of Pepsi. Fourth, during the climax of *The Busy Body*, Barker chases Norton across a rooftop. In *Zotz!*, Professor Jones flees Russian agents during a climactic rooftop chase. Fifth, when Norton is first introduced as a board member, there is mention of Brody's trip to New Orleans, which is the setting of Castle's *New Orleans Uncensored*. Sixth, and again, during Norton's initial board meeting, Barker speaks of LSD after we, the audience, watch a movie within the movie, both references to *The Tingler*. Seventh, Westlake's novel is set in New York, whereas Castle's film is set in Chicago, the same setting for *Undertow*. Eighth, Norton's mother has aspirations of her son opening a haberdashery. In *Cave of Outlaws*, Pete Carver frequents the local haberdasher shortly after arriving in Copper Bend. Ninth, when Norton and Brock first meet in the hallway of the latter's apartment building, Brock reaches for a concealed key to unlock his front door, similar to the way Miriam Webster opens her shop in *Homicidal*. Last, and perhaps the most significant theme of all, is evident during Norton's aforementioned encounter with Brock. In the novel, the meeting is somewhat uneventful. The exchange of information occurs, and Brock is left unharmed. In the film, however, the events are quite different. Tempers flare, a knife is thrown, and Brock grabs a meat cleaver. One is easily reminded of Emilio, the cleaver-wielding apparition of *13 Ghosts*.

In regard to *The Busy Body*, what began as a simple inquiry becomes tragic, as Brock meets his demise. Murder and mayhem, two concepts that have enabled many of Castle's films to thrive, ensue. Castle essentially took Westlake's comical premise and added his own spin of the macabre, resulting in a unique, but memorable, combination of both elements.

The Busy Body premiered in New Orleans prior to its nationwide release. The reviews were mediocre at best, referring to the film as a pleasant comedy, but advising potential theatergoers to not go out of their way to see it. Today, its primary claim to fame is that it is the screen debut of the late, great Richard Pryor.

It is also the longest film directed by Castle, with a running time of 101 minutes. Some critics panned the picture, claiming Castle tried too hard to make it funny. For example, the character of Felix Rose faints only one time in the novel, but Castle arranged for him to faint multiple times as a means of adding more humor to the story. Apparently, this was interpreted by some as more annoying than funny. In 1967, Castle believed his "small empire was beginning to collapse." The future was not looking good. Nevertheless, he had another project in the works and, again, wanted Sid Caesar to star as the film's protagonist. Castle, in essence, prepared himself for one final experiment with the intricacies of comedy.

CHAPTER FIFTY-FOUR
THE SPIRIT IS WILLING (1967)

In 1965, Chas Addams, the famous cartoonist who had earlier provided his artistic talents to the opening credits of *The Old Dark House*, designed the cover art for *The Visitors*, a novel about a family's misfortune of moving into a seaside, ghost-infested mansion. Its author was Nathaniel Benchley, son of the noted American humorist, Robert Benchley. William Castle read the novel, and upon finishing it, acquired the rights to adapt Benchley's work into a major motion picture.

Originally crafted as a suspenseful ghost story, *The Visitors* does, at times, contain its share of subtle humor. Ben Starr, screenwriter of *The Busy Body*, was hired to adapt a script that focused more on comedy and less on suspense. Castle wanted a different premise, specifically one that evolved around the sex lives of ghosts. Furthermore, Benchley's title was eventually changed to *The Spirit Is Willing*.

Nestor Paiva and Robert Donner. Sadly, Paiva succumbed to stomach cancer shortly after completing his scenes and did not live to see the film.

In 1898, Felicity Twitchell (Cass Daley), wife of New England sea captain Ebenezer Twitchell (Robert Donner), murders her husband along with his lover, Jenny Pruitt (Jill Townsend). However, seconds before dying, Ebenezer manages to kill Felicity. The three are immediately transformed into ghosts, inhabiting the coastal house in which they met their demise. Many years later, Ben Powell (Sid Caesar), a magazine editor on extended leave, rents the house with his wife, Kate (Vera Miles), and teenage son, Steve (Barry Gordon). Shortly after their arrival, Steve encounters the ghosts, but his parents refuse to believe what he has seen. Kate's millionaire uncle, George (John McGiver), visits the home. Felicity attempts to kill him, but the blame is placed on Steve. In an attempt to placate the situation, George invites the troubled teen aboard his yacht, which is anchored in a nearby cove. But when the vessel, courtesy of the ghosts, plunges to the bottom of the sea, the blame is again placed on Steve. He eventually meets Priscilla Weems (Townsend), who not only confirms the presence of the ghosts, but is also a relative of the deceased Jenny. Steve desperately wants his parents to understand the danger of their situation. He concocts a plan to summon the ghosts out of hiding. A masquerade party in honor of Steve's sixteenth birthday is thrown. At Priscilla's urging, "men of the sea" are invited. George, the ideal guest, attracts the attention of Felicity. She successfully converts him into a ghost by pushing him off of a cliff. A mutual attraction is instantaneous, and they are married.

The Spirit Is Willing marks the second and final collaboration between Castle and Sid Caesar. Again, humor was a priority. Caesar, in his portrayal of Powell, remained true to Benchley's original creation, but also took the character to the next level. Back problems, for example, are not only more common in the film than in the novel, they are also more comical. However, despite Caesar's status as a popular comedian, as well as being the highest-billed performer of the film, his character's so-called summer vacation merely serves as the subplot to a more important story. *The Spirit Is Willing* is a romantic comedy of the most unusual kind, with the narrative's focus centered primarily on the character of Felicity. And Castle's portrayal of the ominous events deftly enables her to stand out from the fellow apparitions of Ebenezer and Jenny. The use of color, Felicity's interaction with the audience, and her courtship of George are clear indicators of her importance to the story.

Jill Townsend and Barry Gordon. In addition to The Spirit Is Willing, *Felicity's headstone appears in* The Busy Body, *as it is briefly visible during the film's funeral sequence.*

Castle's use of color reveals that Felicity, sporting bright red attire, is the most significant of the three ghosts. Her revelations are unlike those of Ebenezer and Jenny. For example, a stream of red smoke usually precedes Felicity's untimely appearances. Her multiple unveilings contrast faultlessly with whatever background is present, because red is a color composed primarily of the longest wavelengths of light perceptible by the naked eye. Ebenezer and Jenny not only lack the smoky entrance, but the colors of their clothes are devoid of the vibrancy that is associated with Felicity's red attire. And it is clear from the beginning where the focus of Castle's film lies.

When Felicity's character is first introduced in the film, she engages not only Ebenezer's attention, but that of her audience. Castle affords theatergoers a precise point-of-view shot through the captain's spyglass. As Ebenezer catches the first glimpse of his future bride, Felicity jubilantly raises her teacup at him (and us) in acknowledgement. Clearly audible are the squawks of a seagull. It is a bird considered by some cultures to be symbolic of versatility, freedom, and a carefree attitude. Coincidentally, these are the very qualities Felicity will exhibit as a ghost, specifically during her initial encounter with George. She blithely pushes her unsuspecting victim down the cellar stairs, and again, interacts with the audience by looking directly into the camera. A smirking Felicity then rubs her hands together and walks towards us,

Vera Miles.

getting as close to the screen as possible before disappearing into thin air. It is clear she is on the prowl for a soulmate.

Felicity's courtship of George is central to the plot of the film. The destiny of George's character differs greatly between the narratives of Benchley and Castle, as the latter creatively depicts an eternal union between husband and wife. In the novel, George has a spouse named Estelle, who later leaves him to start a new life of her own. Within the latter part of the story, he eventually retires to South America, never to appear again. But in Castle's film, George's continued presence is necessary, as only he can set Felicity free. The concluding shot of the picture reveals the Powell family, having finally attained happiness, to be driving out of town. However, the emphasis is on the ghostly newlyweds, because the narrative's conflict has finally been resolved. In short, upon George's demise, three is no longer a crowd. He and Felicity, in addition to Ebenezer and Jenny, are free to thrive in eternal happiness.

The Spirit Is Willing was released in July of 1967. A portion of the filming was completed on location in the quaint, seaside town of Fort Bragg, California. It served as the ideal double for the tides of the New England coastline. Castle, who rarely appeared in the films he directed, has a brief cameo as a mentally unstable plumber who works for George's prosperous toilet bowl company. In regard to the film's reception, it did not do well at the box office and has received little attention through the years.

Nevertheless, *The Spirit Is Willing* is remarkable because Vera Miles, an A-list performer who worked with some of the greatest directors of all time, starred in the role of Kate Powell. As usual, her performance was nothing short of amazing. Castle, however, was disappointed with the film's reception. He figured that television movies were gradually becoming a "formidable enemy" of theatrical films. But Castle, at fifty-three years of age, had no intention of quitting.

CHAPTER FIFTY-FIVE
PROJECT X (1968)

Following the lackluster reception of *The Spirit Is Willing*, William Castle's comedic endeavors had formally come to an end. But he was not ready to abandon the director's chair. The genre of science fiction was becoming increasingly popular amongst mainstream audiences, and Castle wanted to be a part of it. He took an avid interest in the works of L. P. Davies, an author whose stories explored many themes, particularly human cognizance and memory. Two of the writer's novels, *The Artificial Man* and *Psychogeist*, piqued Castle's interest, and a new idea eventually began to take shape.

Edmund Morris, a screenwriter best known for his work on Edward Dmytryk's *Walk on the Wild Side*, composed a script based on concepts from both novels. Similar to the stories of L. P. Davies, Castle's penultimate film, *Project X*, sought to establish an underlying tone of mystery and ambiguity.

The year is 2118. Hagan Arnold (Christopher George), a geneticist, has returned from a mission of espionage in Sino-Asia. For security purposes, the government erases his memory. But a discovered recording of Arnold's final words prior to erasure claims the "West will be destroyed in fourteen days." Desperate to understand the meaning behind his message, a team of scientists places him in a controlled state of apprehension with the hopes of salvaging his subconscious memories. Because Arnold is well-versed in the culture of the 1960s, he is transferred to an artificial, rural setting that resembles the time period. The environment, or matrix, is established within close proximity to a processing plant. Arnold has a chance encounter with Karen Summers (Greta Baldwin), a plant employee. Unaware of the circumstances behind the matrix's construction, she questions its design, claiming "such houses are no longer built." Gregory Gallea (Monte Markham), Arnold's accomplice in Sino-Asia, is presumed dead by the government. But he emerges from seclusion and speaks of a planned alliance between Dr. Crowther (Henry Jones), the lead scientist, and Sen Chiu (Keye Luke), head of the Sino-Asian Empire. The scientists push their experiment to the limit, spawning an ominous apparition of Arnold. The wraith, apparently vengeful, murders Gallea. An analysis of the victim's brain is conducted. Gallea's memories unveil the existence of a deadly Sinoese weapon. A bacterial culture, composed of multiple plagues, will destroy the West. Crowther and his team learn that Gallea, the ultimate traitor, infected Arnold with the virus. The threat is quickly eradicated, and Arnold is given a different identity so that he can begin a new life with Karen.

Henry Jones as Dr. Crowther.

Deep into the narrative of *Project X*, a noteworthy event transpires. Colonel Holt (Harold Gould), head of government security, demands to see Crowther's experiment in action. He looks on in amazement as a hologram reveals Arnold's subconscious memories. Within the image, Arnold and Gallea are seen to be meeting for the first time. Shortly thereafter, the two are ambushed by Sino-Asian forces. A struggle ensues, and Arnold is subsequently imprisoned. He eventually comes face-to-face with Sen Chiu. There is talk of feudalism, nuclear energy, and a plan to conquer the West. Meanwhile, in the laboratory, Crowther wishes to temporarily suspend the experiment, believing its continuation will result in permanent brain damage to Arnold. But Holt is eager to obtain additional information from the hologram and learn more of Sen Chiu's plan. Following a brief argument, the colonel orders Crowther to continue with the experiment. Holt's abuse of power, albeit foolish and irresponsible, is the most important aspect of the narrative because it sheds light on an otherwise ambiguous perspective of Crowther. Furthermore, the extension of the experiment facilitates the conclusion of a popular Castle motif, and it also serves as the catalyst for a one-of-a-kind sequence.

Holt's eagerness to delve deeper into Arnold's subconscious casts Crowther, a man suspected of treason, in a different light. The doctor's intentions are initially unclear to theatergoers, and Gallea's accusatory remarks further heighten our suspicions until the experiment is pushed to the limit. Gallea's discreet conversation with Karen marks a turning point in the narrative:

> GALLEA: Hagan Arnold was in Sino-Asia. While there, he learned something which will cost him his life . . . if we don't get him away from Dr. Crowther.
>
> KAREN: Who?
>
> GALLEA: You haven't met the esteemed Dr. Crowther?
>
> Karen shakes her head.
>
> GALLEA: He's one of the leading scientists in the West. Now, Hagan learned that Crowther and Sen Chiu planned an alliance which will deliver the West to Sen Chiu without a shot being fired. That's why Crowther brought Hagan here...to keep him from revealing the truth. He'll destroy Hagan's mind.

Minutes later, as Holt and Crowther view the hologram, the latter behaves in a manner that is not at all reflective of Gallea's rhetoric:

> HOLT: What is this plan Sen Chiu spoke about?
>
> Dr. Lee Craig (Phillip E. Pine), a colleague of Crowther's, immediately expresses a desire to learn more.
>
> CRAIG: We'll soon see.
>
> CROWTHER: I'm afraid not. Time's up.
>
> HOLT: No, let it continue. Sen Chiu never boasts.
>
> CRAIG: Let the hologram continue a little longer, doctor.

CROWTHER: Can't risk brain damage.

HOLT: I insist!

CROWTHER: I'm sorry! George?

Crowther gestures to Dr. George Tarvin (Robert Cleaves), another colleague, to deactivate the hologram.

HOLT: Let it continue! That's an order!

CROWTHER: You'll destroy him!

HOLT: Did you hear me? That's an order!

Crowther reluctantly allows the experiment to continue, and theatergoers cannot help but question his demeanor. He does not appear as one who wishes to destroy the mind of his subject. Hence, Gallea's credibility begins to wane. We reach a point of the narrative where its ambiguity is deliberate. Select characters of *Project X* cannot be trusted, and perhaps, the audience feels as lost and alone as Arnold. But Crowther does not exhibit the characteristics of a traitor. Instead, he appears to be deeply concerned for Arnold's safety and well-being, especially as the experiment is pushed to the point of no return.

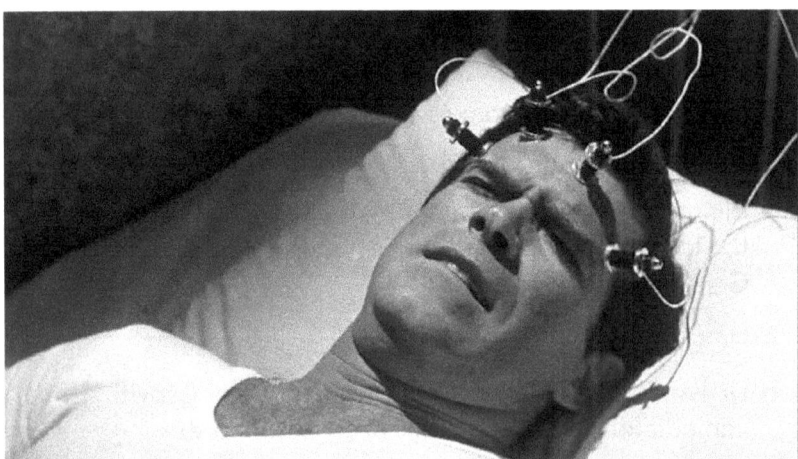

Christopher George as Hagan Arnold.

Holt's blatant disregard for Crowther's scientific principles not only facilitates the summoning of Arnold's apparition, it also affords Castle the opportunity to conclude his recurring motif of ghosts.

As the wraith-like entity's objective is revealed to the audience, Castle's general use of his motif becomes clear. Arnold's ghost locates and dispatches Gallea, the true antagonist of *Project X*.

Furthermore, a closer examination of Castle's previous "ghost" films reveals a slew of character qualities that are more desirable than detrimental. Throughout the history of motion pictures, ghosts have traditionally been portrayed with negative connotations. Yet, Castle's approach is different. For example, in *House on Haunted Hill*, we never see the ghosts, and their contact with the film's characters is minimal. In *13 Ghosts*, a majority of the apparitions are not only harmless, but they strive to help the Zorbas through their predicament. *The Spirit Is Willing* features a trio of ghosts who are more concerned with quarreling amongst themselves than haunting those of the natural world.

Finally, in regard to *Project X*, Arnold's apparition and its termination of Gallea is a representation of what Castle has conveyed to audiences for years. Ghosts are not to be perceived as evil apparitions, but instead, as righteous spirits that are vital to the success of a film's narrative. In fact, an image of Arnold dominates the theatrical poster of *Project X*, as it vividly depicts a form of energy that will eventually become his ghost. Castle's special effects contribute to the film's entertainment value, but the contributions of a celebrated animation studio are also noteworthy.

Holt's order to continue the experiment reveals a one-of-a-kind sequence within the hologram, courtesy of Hanna-Barbera. The studio's primary objective was to establish an ultra-futuristic design within Arnold's memories. William Hanna and Joseph Barbera, founders of Hanna-Barbera, were more than qualified to handle an endeavor of this sort. A few years earlier, the two successfully produced *The Jetsons*, a futuristic cartoon entailing a flashy, utopian setting. The television program takes place one hundred years in the future.

In comparison, the setting of *Project X* takes place 150 years in the future (at the time of the picture's release). There are many aspects of the film's animated sequence that deserve recognition, but Arnold's journey to the underwater prison colony is especially memorable. The audience is afforded a glimpse of the facility's tube transport system. We gradually submerge beneath the sea, only to discover the heart of the prison. It is a spectacular sequence of events. Arnold is not imprisoned for long, as Gallea eventually arrives on the scene. At this point, the audience learns that the colony is underwater because the land is "too valuable to waste on convicts." The statement is ironic, as any film producer knows that underwater photography is traditionally more costly than that which transpires on dry land. Nevertheless, Castle was willing to pull out all of the stops in order to ensure a futuristic look for his film. Throughout his storied career, he had the opportunity to experiment with several genres. But Castle's collaboration with Hanna-Barbera enabled him to tread through the intricacies of animation, a magical aspect of film production that many of Hollywood's greatest directors did not have the opportunity to experience.

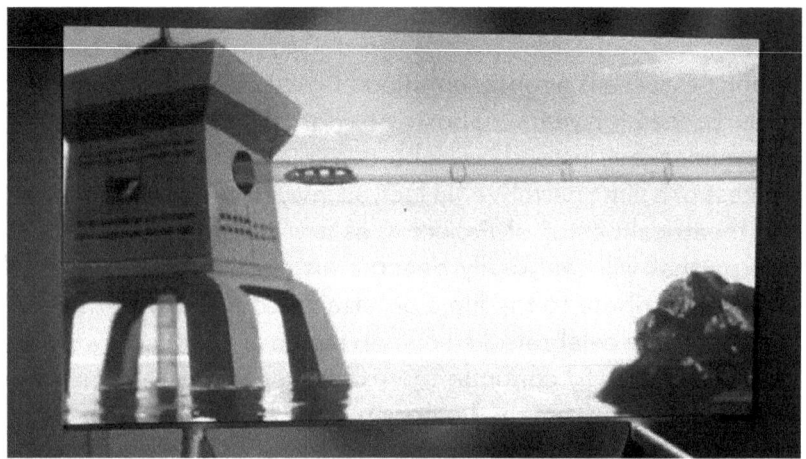

Arnold's journey to the underwater prison colony is depicted through an animated sequence of images, courtesy of Hanna-Barbera.

Project X was released in May of 1968. It was given a UR (Unrated) rating according to the Hays Code, which had the power to approve or disapprove the distribution of a film on the basis of moral content. Months later, the Motion Picture Association of America (MPAA) adopted a new ratings system. No longer would the industry hinder the distribution of so-called immoral films. Instead, theatergoers, especially parents, became empowered to make decisions according to the new set of ratings. The entertainment industry was clearly changing, and Castle himself was reaching a turning point in his illustrious career. Six years would pass before his direction of another film. And Castle was adamant about returning to the director's chair altogether. Yet, through the art of persuasion, one of the greatest entertainers of all time made it happen.

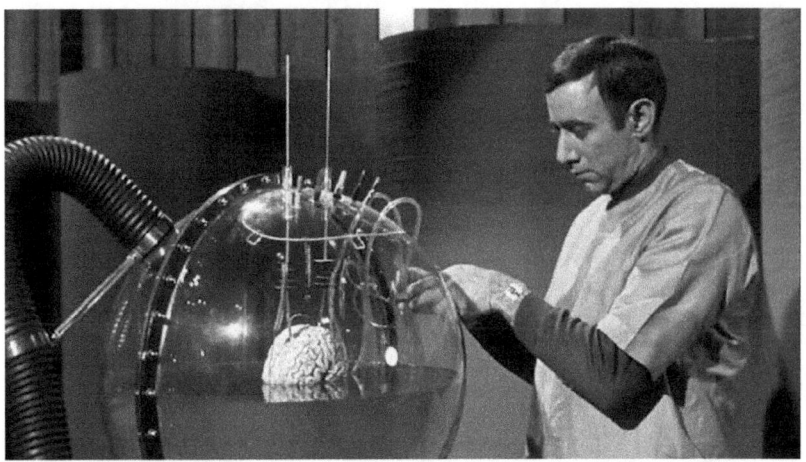

Dr. Tony Verity (Lee Delano) prepares to analyze Gallea's brain.

CHAPTER FIFTY-SIX
SHANKS (1974)

Shortly after being introduced to the great Marcel Marceau, William Castle pitched what he believed to be an idea for "a grim fairy tale." The world-renowned mime took an immediate interest in the project, but many of its details needed to be finalized before production commenced. Marceau had concerns about what kind of film his fans might expect to see. He did not necessarily want *Shanks*, the title assigned to the project, to be a horror film. But Castle did not want to stray from the genre he knew best. Furthermore, Marceau insisted that Castle direct the film. Six years had passed since the release of *Project X*, and Castle believed his directing days to be well behind him. Nevertheless, Marceau was demanding. It was ultimately decided that *Shanks* would be a film of fantasy, not horror. In addition, Castle agreed to direct with the clear understanding that the production would be done his way. Marceau acquiesced, believing "that's the way it should be."

Malcolm Shanks (Marcel Marceau), a mute puppeteer, lives in despair with his stepsister (Tsilla Chelton) and her drunk, abusive husband (Philippe Clay). His greatest admirer is Celia (Cindy Eilbacher), a teenage girl who yearns for a special puppet show in honor of her upcoming birthday. Shanks becomes employed by Old Walker (Marceau), a wealthy man in the village. At the latter's estate, a bizarre experiment involving a dead frog is conducted. The lifeless amphibian, hooked to several wires, exhibits movement with the flip of a switch. Walker makes modifications, implementing wireless capability through the use of metal pins. Days later, the old man dies. But Shanks resurrects Walker by replicating the details of the frog experiment. He spends all of his time at the estate and studies the intricacies of reanimation. Barton, his alcoholic brother-in-law, eventually storms the mansion in demand of money. Shanks kills him with the beak of a reanimated chicken. Later, his stepsister meets her demise while running into the path of a speeding car. Shanks then converts the deceased into human puppets and uses them for Celia's birthday show, which transpires at Walker's estate. She initially struggles to cope with the reality of the situation, but eventually accepts it. The festivities are cut short when an evil motorcycle gang arrives on the premises. Shanks fights back with his puppets, including that of Walker. Celia is killed during the fracas. After a lengthy battle, good prevails over evil. Shanks consequently finds himself performing a puppet show for a group of children. Some of the miniature puppets include Barton and Old Walker. Celia, alive and well, is there to enjoy a retelling of the recent events.

Following the production of *Shanks*, Castle invited Marcel Marceau to his beachfront home in Malibu for an afternoon of relaxation. During the visit, there was much discussion about the film and its impending release to the American public. Marceau

Marcel Marceau as Malcolm Shanks and Old Walker (below).

sought reassurance that he and Castle had accomplished their objective in making a classic film that "will play forever." But Castle was uncertain. Nevertheless, combining his world of horror with Marceau's art of mime was a challenge he was willing to confront.

With *Shanks*, Marceau was given his first opportunity to star in a leading role in a motion picture, and he wanted his performance to be nothing short of captivating, especially for his devoted fans. Castle knew that Marceau would rely more on visual expression than anything else. And due to a special cinematic effect, series of intertitles, and restricted level of dialogue, Castle's direction of *Shanks* was in sync with Marceau's ambiguous realm of pantomime.

A special cinematic effect, used as a means to transition between scenes, bears a striking similarity to a style of lighting previously used in Marceau's popular stage show. Castle implements the effect shortly after the passing of Old Walker. Shanks returns home to console Walker's puppet, but Barton strips it away and crushes it to pieces. Despite the sorrow, an idea is born. Shanks faces the camera. A slight smile forms on his lips as an Iris-In effect, moving inward from all directions until the screen is enveloped in complete blackness, concludes the scene. The following Iris-Out effect, beginning as a pinpoint of light and then expanding to reveal the motionless corpse of Old Walker, marks the onset of a human puppet show, which is the film's main attraction. Castle had earlier observed the same effect while attending Marceau's stage show in Paris. As in *Shanks*, the effect served as a prelude to a momentous event (detailed in Castle's

Tsilla Chelton and Philippe Clay.

autobiography). But aside from cinematic elements, Castle relied on a traditional method of narration when transitioning from one scene to the next.

Numerous intertitles, frequently seen throughout the duration of *Shanks*, provide the look of a silent film, a medium in which pantomime is paramount. The titles, thirteen to be exact, set a decorous manner for the narrative, but also expose the underlying issue of alcohol dependence. The opening intertitle introduces the audience to "the town drunk with a shrew for a wife and a deaf mute for a brother-in-law." The wording places more of an emphasis on Barton and his abuse of alcohol than it does on the film's title character. Intoxicants appear to be commonplace.

As the film begins, the first image we see is that of a sign. It reads, "WE BUY BEER BOTTLES." The opening credits follow, thus leading to a bizarre puppet show. During the performance, a miniature version of Old Walker continuously spins next to an empty beer bottle. As the dazed, supposedly inebriated puppet proceeds to walk off of the stage, a single pebble blocks its path. The minuscule Walker successfully navigates around the impediment, thereby evoking applause from the many children in attendance.

A few scenes later, the film's fourth intertitle boldly announces "the first experiment," but not before Shanks and Old Walker toast each other with a festive libation. The consumption of alcohol is a recurring custom in the films of William Castle (i.e., Jack Gaines

Old Walker's strange mansion.

of *The Gun That Won the West*, Watson Pritchard of *House on Haunted Hill*). In *Shanks*, a severe dependency is evident within the character of Barton, and the film's intertitles confirm it.

To reiterate, Castle strived for his world of horror to be compatible with Marceau's art of mime, and the intertitles essentially provide *Shanks* with the appearance of a silent film. But the lack of a customary cinematic element also contributes to the picture's unique presentation.

Audible dialogue, powerful enough to control the narrative of any post-silent era film, is not often spoken in Castle's picture. On his way home following the success of "the second experiment," Shanks encounters a group of children playing in a grassy field. He stops to entertain them, using his hands as a means of mimicking a butterfly. Indistinct chatter emanates from the children, and no dialogue is clearly audible. Instead, the focus is on Shanks as he swiftly transforms into Bip the Clown (sans makeup), his real-life alter ego and arguably his most famous persona. For a brief moment, Castle allows Marcel Marceau to be himself instead of Malcolm Shanks. Due to the film's restricted level of dialogue, the presentation closely resembles the appearance of a silent feature. Of the fifty-six motion pictures directed by Castle, *Shanks* is the one to contain the least amount of dialogue. Throughout his storied career, Castle never had the opportunity to direct, or be affiliated with, a silent. But his collaboration with Marceau allowed him to fulfill a missed opportunity of sorts.

Prior to its theatrical release, *Shanks* was promoted as "a new concept in the macabre in which the Good come out of the grave and the Evil are sent to fill the vacancy." Approximately one hour into the film, Castle uses an intertitle to expose his audience to "the outside world of evil." A battle ensues during which "the dead fight the living." The final third of the film, dismissed by some critics as unnecessary, fulfills the tagline's promise as the Evil are, in fact, sent to their graves.

Shanks did not live up to its expectations with the general public. A. H. Weiler, a critic of *The New York Times*, wrote that the characters of *Shanks* "leave a viewer uncommitted, if not confused, by their largely far-out, somber fiction." Upon the film's conclusion, Castle borrows a quote from William Makepeace Thackeray, the English novelist of the nineteenth century. It states,

"Come . . . let us shut up the box and the puppets – for our play is played out." Not only was this true for Castle's fifty-sixth film, but for his directorial career as well. Although he would continue to work in the industry as a producer and actor, he did not live to direct another film. *Shanks*, in essence, is Castle's swan song. Coincidentally, his trademark silhouette is nowhere to be found on the film's theatrical poster. But a particular scene of the picture reveals Shanks to be puffing on a cigar in typical William Castle fashion. Perhaps, this was Marceau's way of paying homage to the master showman with the most popular Castle motif of them all.

Old Walker, now a puppet, rises from the grave to wreak havoc on uninvited guests.

AUTHOR'S NOTE

Following *Shanks*, William Castle produced *Bug*, based on Thomas Page's novel, *The Hephaestus Plague*. The film's primary claim to fame was its featured gimmick, a million-dollar life insurance policy taken out on "Hercules" the cockroach. *Bug* was the final motion picture to be produced by Castle. That same year, in 1975, he appeared in two films. The first was Hal Ashby's *Shampoo*, in which Castle portrays Sid Roth, a producer. The second was John Schlesinger's *The Day of the Locust*. This time, Castle was cast as a director. It is evident that his passion for show business never wavered, especially during the latter part of his career.

Castle wrote his autobiography in 1976. Shortly thereafter, he began pre-production on *2000 Lakeview Drive*, an MGM thriller that was to take place in an elegant, high-rise apartment building. The film's tagline referred to the featured street address as "An Address of Extinction," as the story was supposed to evolve around a killer lurking within the confines of the building.

The picture was never produced. Sadly, on May 31, 1977, Castle suffered a fatal heart attack at his Beverly Hills home. He was sixty-three years old. Through the years, his legacy has continued to thrive. In 1993, Joe Dante's *Matinee*, starring John Goodman as schlock producer Lawrence Woolsey, was released in theaters across the country. The film served as an homage to Castle and also raised awareness of his contributions to American cinema. Whenever I have had the opportunity to attend retrospectives of Castle's work, it has been a pleasure to encounter people from all walks of life in attendance. I especially find it refreshing to see many younger individuals within the theater. These are the people who had yet to be born as Castle's films were initially released to the American public. As I bear witness to a new generation of theatergoers who continue to develop a passion for the cinema of William Castle, I am reminded of the marker that adorns his grave in Glendale, California. Aside from his name and the designated years of his life, it consists of a single word, and it not only defines Castle's very existence, it promotes his enduring legacy. The word is *FOREVER*.

BIBLIOGRAPHY
BOOKS

Benchley, Nathaniel. *The Visitors*. McGraw-Hill, 1965.
Benefield, Barry. *Eddie and the Archangel Mike*. Reynal & Hitchcock, 1943.
Castle, William. *Step Right Up! I'm Gonna Scare the Pants off America*. G.P. Putnam and Sons, 1976.
Davies, L.P. *The Artificial Man*. Doubleday, 1965.
Davies, L.P. *Psychogeist*. Doubleday, 1967.
Durrant, Theo. *The Marble Forest*. Knopf, 1951.
Karig, Walter. *Zotz!* H. Wolff, 1947.
O'Grady, Rohan. *Let's Kill Uncle*. Macmillan, 1963.
Priestley, J.B. *Benighted*. W. Heinemann Ltd., 1927.
Russell, Ray. *Sardonicus and Other Stories*. Ballantine, 1961.
Westlake, Donald E. *The Busy Body*. Random House, 1966.
Yerby, Frank. *The Saracen Blade*. Dial Press, 1952.

ARTICLES

Barber, Lester E. "This Rough Magic: Shakespeare on Film." *Literature/Film Quarterly*, Vol. 1, No. 4, 1973.
Buhle, Paul. "The Last of the Hollywood Ten." *The Progressive*, Vol. 65, No. 1, January, 2001.
Cooledge, Dean R. "Dames in the Driver's Seat: Rereading Film Noir." *Literature/Film Quarterly*, Vol. 35, No. 1, 2007.
Cripps, Thomas. "Camera, Star, Studio and Politics: Four Approaches to the Film Image." *Literature/Film Quarterly*, Vol. 3, No. 2, 1975.
Fischel, Jack. "Reds and Radicals in Hollywood." *The Virginia Quarterly Review*, Vol. 79, No. 1, 2003.
Kempley, Rita. "Movies; 'Matinee': In the Glow of the Atomic Age." *The Washington Post*, January 29, 1993.
Lovenheim, Robert. "The Creative Producer in the Hollywood Market." *American Cinematographer*. Vol. 58, No. 7, August, 1977.
Sobchack, Thomas. "Genre Film: A Classical Experience." *Literature/Film Quarterly*, Vol. 3, No. 3, 1975.
Telotte, J.P. "Faith and Idolatry in the Horror Film." *Literature/Film Quarterly*, Vol. 8, No. 3, 1980.
Wong, Herman. "George Montgomery Visits His Fans: A Folksy Matinee For Old-time Actor." *Los Angeles Times*, April 2, 1985.

ONLINE RESOURCES

INTERNET MOVIE DATABASE. WWW.IMDB.COM

OLD TIME RADIO NETWORK. WWW.OTR.NET

TURNER CLASSIC MOVIES. WWW.TCM.COM

WWW.WILLIAMCASTLE.COM

Index

13 Frightened Girls! (1963) 6, 19, 291-292, 292p, 293, 293p, 294-295, 295p, 296, 296p, 306
13 Ghosts (1960) 19, 74, 216, 245-246, 246p, 247-248, 248p, 249, 249p, 250, 250p, 251, 251p, 252, 252p, 253, 253p, 254, 254p, 255, 255p, 257, 295p, 335, 352, 360, 373
2000 Lakeview Drive 383
20th Century Fox (studio) 159
Abbott, John 38
Ace the Wonder Dog 56
Adam's Rib (1949) 99
Adams, Cedric 254
Adams, Gerald Drayson 191
Adams, Julie XV, 101
Addams, Charles 305-306, 363
Adventures of Rusty, The (1945) 55-56
Advice to a Raven in Russia (poem) 139
Agee, James 32
Alaniz, Rico 124
Alcaide, Chris 195-196, 199, 199p
Alexander, Van 317
Alfred Hitchcock Hour, The (tv series) 333, 335
Allen, Lester 11
Allied Artists Productions (studio) 220-221, 231, 235
American Broadcasting Company (ABC) 102
Americano, The (1955) 173-174, 174p, 175-176, 176p, 177, 298
And Now Miguel (1966) 341, 347
Anderson, Dusty 37
Anderson, Leona 225p
Anna Lucasta (1949) 41
Ansara, Michael 129, 159, 179, 182p, 194
Archainbaud, George 65
Arless, Jean (see Marshall, Joan)
Arnaz, Desi 62
Arnold, Edward 195
Arnt, Charles 48
Artificial Man, The (novel) 369
Ashby, Hal 383
Astar, Ben 117, 138

Atwater, Edith 308
Aumont, Jean-Pierre 137, 138p
Backus, Jim 105, 210, 211p, 216p, 283, 286, 286p
Bacon, Irving 118, 121
Badham, John XV, 347, 350
Badham, Mary 337, 340p, 347, 349-351
Baker, Diane 307, 311p, 312p, 321p
Baker, Fay 75
Baldwin, Greta 369
Ball, Lucille 62
Barbera, Joseph 373
Barker, Jess 21
Barker, Lex 191
Barlow, Joel 139-140
Barnum, P. T. XIII
Barrier, Edgar 159
Barry, Gene 171, 195-196, 196p, 199p
Bat Masterson (tv series) 171
Bates, Florence 72
Bates, Jeanne 4
Battle of Rogue River (1954) 121, 143-144, 144p, 145-146, 146p, 147
Baxter, Anne 353
Baxter, Warner 37, 47, 59, 65, 67p, 74-75, 78
Bells of St. Margaret's, The (nursery rhyme) 306
Benchley, Nathaniel 363-364, 366
Benchley, Robert 363
Benefield, Barry 72
Benighted (novel) 299, 305
Bennett, Bruce 88
Benton, Garth 293
Bergman, Ingrid 27
Best, Willie 34
Betrayed (1944). (see *When Strangers Marry*)
Bice, Robert 185, 187p
Black Marketing (short) 179
Blake, Pamela 51
Blind Alibi (1938) 56
Bloch, Robert 307, 323
Blue, Ben 357
Bluhdorn, Charles X-XI

Blythe, Betty 101
Bochner, Lloyd 324, 325p
Boetticher, Budd 173, 177
Bondi, Beulah 21-22
Booth, Karin 138
Boston Blackie (film series) 3, 7, 20
Boston Blackie (radio) 7
Boyle, Jack 3, 7
Brackett, Leigh 60
Bradley, Leslie 129, 153
Brady, Scott 85, 163, 166
Branch, Houston 10
Brandt, Frances 133
Breslin, Patricia 257p, 258, 265p, 268p, 330
Bricker, George 33
Bridges, Lloyd XV, 21
Briggs, Charlie 292, 292p
Briskin, Irving 3-4, 7
Brocco, Peter 101
Brown, James 267-268
Browne, Cicely 133
Browning, Robert 356
Bruce, David 167
Buchanan, Edgar 107
Bug (1975) IX, XI, 344, 383
Bull, Peter 297, 298p, 304p
Bunce, Alan 258, 259p, 268p
Burns, Paul E. 51, 54
Burr, Raymond XV, 111, 115-116
Bushman, Francis X. 101
Busy Body, The (1967) XV, 31, 157, 240, 353-354, 354p, 355, 355p, 356-357, 357p, 358-359, 359p, 360-361, 363, 365p
Busy Body, The (novel) 353, 358-361
Bwana Devil (1952) 117
Caesar, Sid 353, 354p, 355p, 356, 357p, 361, 364
Calvert, John 33
Cambridge, Godfrey 356, 357p
Cameron, James 20
Cameron, Kate 20
Cardi, Pat XV, 337, 338p, 341-348, 348p, 349-351, 351p, 352
Cardwell, James 41
Carey, Macdonald 107
Carleton, Claire 59
Carter, Janis 33

Carver, Tina 202
Castle (Falck), Ellen 74-75, 78-79, 162, 210
Castle, Georgiana 162
Castle, Terry XV, 231
Cat Ballou (1965) 109
Cavanagh, Paul 102, 163, 166
Cave of Outlaws (1951) 105, 107-109, 126, 360
Chambers, Wheaton 68
Chance of a Lifetime, The (1943) 3-7, 9, 12-13, 179
Chaney, Lon 95, 240
Chaplin, Charlie 101, 241
Charge of the Lancers (1954) 137-138, 138p, 139, 139p, 140-141, 141p, 142-143
Cheirel, Micheline 65
Chekhov, Michael 71
Chelton, Tsilla 377, 379p
Christian, Linda 129
Ciannelli, Eduardo 38
Clark, Fred 101, 287
Clark, Jim 341
Clay, Philippe 377, 379p
Cleaves, Robert 372
Clemens, William 51
Clementina (novel) 154
Cleveland, George 9
Cliff, John 149
Clouzot, Henri-Georges 209
Clover Productions (studio) 201, 206
Cobb, Lee J. 195-196
Cohn, Harry IX, 3, 13, 24-25, 33, 36-37, 39, 55, 65, 68-69, 74-75, 78-79, 105-106, 111, 116, 160, 209, 220, 233, 320, 323
Colbert, Robert 212
Colmans, Edward 125
Columbia Broadcasting System (CBS) 37, 102, 348
Columbia Pictures Corporation (studio) 3, 14, 20, 24-25, 33, 37-38, 55, 60, 65, 69, 71, 74-75, 78-79, 89, 105-106, 111, 116-117, 137, 149, 159-160, 163, 167, 177, 179, 194, 201, 206, 209, 233, 235, 240, 281, 284, 307, 320
Connor, Whitfield 159
Conquest of Cochise (1953) 123, 123p, 124-127, 127p, 128, 147
Conte, Richard 101, 129
Cook, Elisha 221, 224p

Coolidge, Philip 233-234, 234p, 242p
Cooper, Jeanne 197, 198p
Corbett, Glenn 258, 259p, 264p
Corby, Ellen 212p, 215
Corrigan, Lloyd 4
Corsaro, Franco 37
Cos, Vicki 307
Costa-Gavras X
Costello, Don 15
Cowling, Bruce 167, 170p
Cox, Mitchell 308, 316p
Craig, Carolyn 221, 224p, 225p
Crawford, Joan 307-309, 310p, 312p, 316p, 318p, 320, 321p, 329, 334-336, 336p
Crest, Patricia 310
Crime Doctor (1943) 37
Crime Doctor (film series) 20, 37, 39, 47, 49, 59, 65
Crime Doctor (radio) 37, 66, 278p
Crime Doctor's Courage, The (1945) 37
Crime Doctor's Gamble, The (1947) 7, 65-69
Crime Doctor's Man Hunt (1946) 59-63
Crime Doctor's Secret, The 69
Crime Doctor's Strangest Case (1943) 37
Crime Doctor's Warning, The (1945) 37-39, 47, 59
Cugat, Xavier 177
Curfew (poem) 139
Curtis, Tony XV, 83
Curtiss, Ursula 329
Cutts, Patricia 234, 237p
Dale, Paul 89, 92p, 93p
Daley, Cass 363
Dalton, Audrey 269, 276p
Dana, Bill 355
Dann, Roger 65
Dante, Joe 166, 383
Darrell, Steve 163
Davies, L. P. 369
Davis, Bette 58, 308
Day of the Locust, The (1975) 383
DeCamp, Rosemary 245, 251p, 252p, 253p
Dehner, John 191
Delano, Lee 375p
DeLuise, Dom 353, 359p
DeMille, Cecil B. 129

Denning, Richard 143, 185, 187p
Dennis, Mark 55, 57-58
Dexter, Von 228, 242, 249, 281
Dey, Howard L. 179
Dhiegh, Khigh 291
Dietrich, Marlene 335
Dillinger (1945) 41
Dillon, Robert 306
Dinehart, Alan 18
Disney, Walt 284
Dix, Richard 13p, 14-15, 16p, 33, 41, 42p, 51
Dmytryk, Edward 369
Don, Carl 288
Donaldson, Ted 55, 57
Donner, Richard 347
Donner, Robert 363, 363p
Dormant Account (short story) 33
Douglas, Mike 267
Dow, Peggy 85
Dracula (play) VII, 73
"Dracula" (fictional character) VII
Drew, Ellen 59
Drums of Tahiti (1954) 43, 133-136
Duel on the Mississippi (1955) 191-194, 243, 251
Duff, Howard 79
Dumas, Alexandre 159
Duncan, Pamela 160
Dunn, Kathy 291, 292p, 296p
Dunn, James 71
Dupas, Ralph 181, 181p
Durrant, Theo 211
Duryea, Dan 79
Eagle-Lion Films (studio) 89, 93
Eddie and the Archangel Mike (novel) 72
Egg and I, The (1947) 24
Eilbacher, Cindy 377
El Cid (1961) 41
Eliscu, Fernanda 140
Ellender, Allen J. 179
Elliott, Dick 25
Engel, Roy 198
Erickson, Leif 307, 316p, 331
Evans, Charles 145
Evans, Douglas 331
Evans, Robert X-XI
Evelyn, Judith 234, 234p, 239p, 242
Fairbanks, Douglas 154, 241
Farnum, William 101

Farrell, Glenda 10
Fat Man, The (1951) XV, 95-100
Fat Man, The (radio) 95-98, 100
Faultless Painter, The (poem) 356
Ferniel, Daniel 86
Field, Margaret 90p
Fielding, Fenella 298, 304p
Fiske, Robert 30
Fitzgerald, F. Scott 33
Fleming, Rhonda XV, 111, 115, 115p, 116
Flynn, Errol 63
Foch, Nina 21-22
For Love or Money (play) 202
Ford, Glenn 173, 174p, 177
Ford, John X
Forde, Eugene 49, 59
Foreign Correspondent (1940) 101
Fort Ti (1953) 117-121, 133, 149, 277
Foulger, Byron 19, 30, 49
Fowler, Phyllis 118
Fowley, Douglas 4
Fox, Michael 112
Foxes of Harrow, The (novel) 159
Frankel, Benjamin 304
Franz, Arthur 179, 181p, 183p
Frawley, William 60-62
Frees, Paul 323p
Friedhofer, Hugo 262
Garland, Beverly 179, 183p
Garralaga, Martin 165
Garrett, Andi 329, 330p
Garth, Otis 163
Gates, Nancy 168
Geer, Will 89, 92p
Gentleman from Nowhere, The (1948) 75-78
George, Christopher 369, 372p
Geray, Steven 66
Gibson, Helen 101
Gilda (1946) 199
Gilligan's Island (tv series) 105, 157
Goddard, Paulette 138, 138p
Goetz, William 79, 100
Golonka, Arlene 355
Gone with the Wind (1939) 3
Goodman, John 383
Gordon, Barry 364, 365p
Gordon, Bernard 163-164
Gordon, James B. (see Kent, Robert E.)

Gordon, Roy 185
Gould, Harold 370
Graff, Wilton 48, 75
Granger, Michael 143, 146p
Grant, Cary 27, 336p
Green, Gilbert 268p
Green, Nigel 337, 339, 339p, 343p, 346p, 348p, 349, 351p
Gremlins (1984) 166
Grenfell, Joyce 297, 301p
Griffin, Robert 124, 127p, 129
Griffith, James 149, 163, 167, 170p
Guderman, Linda 210
Guilfoyle, Paul 33
Gulliver's Travels (novel) 90p, 91
Gun That Won the West, The (1955) 141p, 185-187, 187p, 188-189, 189p, 381
Hale Jr., Alan 155, 157, 163, 166
Hale, Barbara 195, 198p, 199
Halliday, Andrew 202
Hamilton, Margaret 74, 245, 253p, 254p
Hamilton, Murray 291, 292p
Hamilton, Neil 25
Hamlet (play) 47-49
Hamlin, Walter B. (Judge) 180
Hammer Films (studio) 297, 302
Hammer, Will 302
Hammett, Dashiell 96-97
Hanna, William 373
Hanna-Barbera (studio) 373-374, 374p
Hanson, Lorna 276
Harmon, John 4
Harris, Stacy 180, 181p, 183p
Hart, Dorothy 85
Hawks, Howard X, 58
Hayes, John Anthony 307
Hayworth, Rita 199
Healey, Myron 59
Henry, Thomas Browne 89
Henry, William 167, 179
Hepburn, Katharine 99
Hephaestus Plague, The (novel) IX, 383
Herbert, Charles 245, 249p, 251p, 352
Herman, Pete 181, 181p
Heyes, Douglas 133
Hickman, Darryl 235, 236p, 243
Hickman, Dwayne 57
High Noon (1952) X
Hinds, Anthony 302

Hitchcock, Alfred X-XI, 26-27, 101, 257, 267-268
Hodiak, John 123p, 124, 128
Hoffman, Howard 215
Holliday, Judy 99
Holloway, Dona 323
Hollywood Reporter (magazine) 7
Hollywood Story (1951) XV, 101-106, 240, 286p
Homicidal (1961) XIV, 22, 31, 36, 83, 217, 240, 257, 257p, 258-259, 259p, 260, 260p, 261, 261p, 262-264, 264p, 265, 265p, 266-268, 268p, 269, 289, 325, 327, 360
Homolka, Oskar 270, 272p
House on Haunted Hill (1958) XIV, 31, 35, 103, 109, 127, 156, 214, 221-222, 222p, 223, 223p, 224, 224p, 225, 225p, 226, 226p, 227, 227p, 228-229, 229p, 230-231, 232p, 233, 245-247, 275p, 325-326, 360, 373, 381
House on Haunted Hill (1999) XV
Houston Story, The (1956) 31, 137, 171, 195-196, 196p, 197-198, 198p, 199, 199p, 201, 306
How to Plan a Movie Murder (featurette) 307
Howland, Olin 60
Hoyos Jr., Rodolfo 173
Hudson, Rochelle 307
Hudson, Rock XV, 88, 95, 100
Hull, Henry 101
Humpty Dumpty (nursery rhyme) 306
Hunter, Kim 25, 28p, 31p
Hyer, Martha 143, 144p
I Love Lucy (tv series) 62
I Saw What You Did (1965) 320, 329-330, 330p, 331-336, 336p
If I Die Before I Wake (novel) 36
Ingels, Marty 357p
Invisible Agent (1942) 34
Invisible Man Returns, The (1940) 34
Invisible Man, The (novel) 34
"Invisible Man, The" (fictional character) 34
Ireland, John 329, 335, 336p
Iron Glove, The (1954) 153-157
Irwin, Charles 139, 155
Irwin, Coulter 37

It's a Small World (1950) 7, 31, 54, 89-90, 90p, 91-92, 92p, 93, 93p, 94, 94p, 95, 142
It's About Time (tv series) 347-349
Jaffe, Leo 307
Jagger, Dean 25
Janti, David 277
Jason, Rick 159
Jenks, Frank 198
Jesse James vs. the Daltons (1954) 127, 136, 149-152, 282p
Jetsons, The (tv series) 373
Johnny Stool Pigeon (1949) XV, 79-83, 85, 360
Johns, Mervyn 297, 304p
Jones, Carolyn 159
Jones, Henry 369, 370p
Jory, Victor 107
Journet, Marcel 65
Just Before Dawn (1946) 30, 47-50, 272
Kaplan, Marvin XV, 99-100
Karig, Walter 283-285
Karloff, Boris 300
Karns, Todd 93p
Katzman, Sam 111, 114-116, 129, 133, 137-138, 141-142, 149, 160, 162, 195, 201, 206, 235
Kazan, Elia 58, 195
Keaton, Buster 241
Keith, Ian 191
Kellaway, Cecil 283
Kelley, Barry 79
Kellogg, Ray 150
Kelly, Emmett 95, 97, 100
Kennedy, George 308, 315p
Kent, Robert E. 118, 120-121, 133, 137, 141
Kenton, Erle C. 9
Kidd, Jonathan 210, 211p
Kilbride, Percy 21, 24
Kilburn, Terry 129
Kine Weekly, The (newspaper) 297
King Brothers Productions 25
King Solomon's Mines (1950) 107
King, Brett 149
King, Frank 25-26, 30, 41
King, Hymie 25-26, 30, 41
King, Maurice 25-26, 30, 41
Klondike Kate (1943) 9-13
Koshetz, Nina 89

Kosleck, Martin 47
Kramer, Stanley X
Kuhn, Mickey XV, 55-58
Lady from Shanghai, The (1947) 63, 71
Laemmle, Carl 298, 300
Lafitte the Pirate (novel) 182
Landers, Lew 36, 51, 54
Lane, Abbe 175, 177
Lane, Charles 49, 51, 76
Lane, Richard 4
Lane, Sarah 329, 330p
"Lassie" (fictional character) 55
Law vs. Billy the Kid, The (1954) 126, 163-167
Lawrence, Barbara 149
Lawson, Linda 337, 342p
Lederman, D. Ross 51
Lee, Jack 62
Left Handed Gun, The (1958) 166
Leigh, Janet 334
Leigh, Nelson 151, 159
Leonard, Sheldon 9
Leontovich, Eugenie 257, 257p
Les Diaboliques (1955) X, 209-211
Let's Kill Uncle (1966) 337-338, 338p, 339, 339p, 340, 340p, 341-342, 342p, 343, 343p, 344-345, 345p, 346, 346p, 347-348, 348p, 349-351, 351p, 352
Let's Kill Uncle (novel) 337-341, 352
Leven, Boris 313
Lewis, Ronald 269, 271p, 276p
Lifeboat (1944) 27
Lincoln, Pamela 234-235, 236p
Livingston, Stan 347
Locke, Sharyl 329
London, Jack 9
London, Julie 95
"Lone Ranger, The" (fictional character) 128
Long, Richard 223, 224p
Longfellow, Henry Wadsworth 139
Louis, Jean 116
Lovejoy, Frank 173-174
Lovelace, Richard 139-140
Lubin, Lou 25
Lugosi, Bela VII, 73
Lugosi, Bela G. VII, XV
Luke, Keye 369
Lundigan, William 111, 116

Lynn, Diana 71
Ma and Pa Kettle (film series) 24
Macabre (1958) 19, 31, 93, 209, 209p, 210-211, 211p, 212, 212p, 213, 213p, 214, 214p, 215-216, 216p, 217, 217p, 218, 218p, 219, 219p, 220, 220p, 221, 233, 235, 238, 286, 286p, 306, 325, 359
MacLane, Barton 51
Madison, Guy 71
Madison, Noel 75
Main, Marjorie 24
Majors, Lee XV, 310
Mallinson, Rory 149
Mander, Miles 38
Marble Forest, The (novel) 210-211, 218
Marceau, Marcel 377-378, 378p, 379, 381-382, 382p
Mark of the Whistler, The (1944) 33-36
Markham, Monte 369
Marlowe, Hugh 292p
Marsac, Maurice 65
Marshal, Alan 221, 224p
Marshall, Joan 257, 257p, 261p, 268
Martell, Alphonse 120
Marvin, Lee 109
Mason, Alfred E.W. 154
Mason, James 347
Masterson of Kansas (1955) 128, 157, 167-168, 168p, 169-170, 170p, 171
Matinee (1993) 383
Matthews, Lester 117
Max, Edwin 99-100
Maxwell, John 167
Mazurki, Mike 51, 54, 182p, 288-289, 289p
McCrea, Joel 101
McGiver, John 364
McIntire, John 79
McKennon, Dal 244p
Meade, Julia 283
Meadows, Jayne XV, 95
Meadows, Joyce XV, 329, 333-335
Medford, Kay 355
Medina, Patricia 133, 191, 201, 202p
Meeker, George 47
Meet a Body (play) 32, 36, 41
Men of Annapolis (tv series) 206, 210, 234
Menefee, Dave XV
Meredith, Judi 324

Merrick, Lynn 41
Merrill, Louis 117, 154, 191
Meskill, Katherine 103
Metro-Goldwyn-Mayer (MGM) (studio) 107, 383
Michel, Lora Lee 89
Mike Douglas Show, The (tv series) 267
Miles, Vera 364, 366p, 367
Miller, Lorraine 89, 94p
Miller, Marvin 47
Millerson Case, The (1947) 65
Millhollin, James 287
Milner, Martin 245, 250p, 251p
mise-en-scène XIV, 222, 225, 229p, 265
Mitchum, Julie 223, 224p
Mitchum, Robert XV, 25, 31p, 224p
Mizzy, Vic 323p, 354, 358
Monsour, Nira 160
Montalban, Georgiana 162
Montalban, Ricardo 159-160
Montgomery, George 117, 121, 143, 144p, 146p, 167, 170p, 171
Moon, Lynne Sue 291, 295p, 296p
Moore, Ida 21
Morgan, Dennis 185, 201
Morgan, Michael 186
Morgan, Russ 310
Morley, Robert 297, 300p, 302p, 304p
Morris, Chester 2p, 3
Morris, Dorothy 210
Morris, Edmund 369
Morrow, Jo 245, 250p, 251p, 253p
Morrow, Susan 210
Motion Picture Association of America (MPAA) 374
Motion Pictures, Inc. (studio) 89, 93
Mowery, Helen 51
Mr. Sardonicus (1961) 269, 269p, 270-271, 271p, 272, 272p, 273-274, 274p, 275, 275p, 276, 276p, 277-278, 278p, 279-281, 282p, 283, 359
Murphy, Audie XV, 72
Murphy, Donald 169
Murray, Jan 353, 357-358
Mysterious Intruder (1946) 51-54, 289
Naish, J. Carrol 15, 18p, 19p
National Broadcasting Company (NBC) 102, 171, 348
Navarro, George 173

Neal, Tom 9
New Orleans Uncensored (1955) 54, 137, 179-181, 181p, 182, 182p, 183, 183p, 191, 289-290, 360
New York Times, The (newspaper) 159-160, 381
Newmar, Julie XV
Night Walker, The (1964) XIV, 306, 323, 323p, 324-325, 325p, 326-327, 328p
Niles, Ken 95
North to the Klondike (1942) 9
North, Zeme 284, 289p
Notorious (1946) 27
O'Houlihan's Jest (novel) 337
Oboler, Arch 117
O'Brian, Hugh 107
O'Grady, Rohan 337-341, 352
Ohmart, Ben XV
Ohmart, Carol 221, 222p
O'Keefe, Dennis 133
Old Dark House, The (1932) 298-301, 305
Old Dark House, The (1963) 157, 251-252, 290, 295, 297-298, 298p, 299, 299p, 300, 300p, 301, 301p, 302, 302p, 303-304, 304p, 305, 305p, 306, 360, 363
Olsen, Larry 4
On the Beach (1959) X
On the Waterfront (1954) 195
Othello (play) 272
Out of the Dark (novel) 329
Owen, Rica 154
Page, Joy 124
Page, Thomas IX-XI, XV, 383
Paiva, Nestor 363p
Palmer, Mavis Neal 281
Pantages, Alexander 10
Paramount (studio) X, 345, 353-354
Parnell, Emory 68, 143
Parsons, Louella 231
Penn, Leonard 161
Perry Mason (tv series) 199, 269
Peters, Erika 275p, 277
Petrie, Howard 117
Pettitt, Wilfrid H. 41
Phantom of the Opera, The (1925) 240
Pickering, Robert 337, 342p
Pierlot, Francis 59
Pine, Phillip E. 371

Playboy (magazine) 269
Polanski, Roman XI, XIII
Poston, Tom 283, 284p, 289p, 290, 297, 298p, 299-300, 300p, 301p, 304p
Power of the Whistler, The (1945) 36, 51, 54
Price, Vincent XIII, 221, 222p, 232p, 233, 233p, 234p, 235-237, 237p, 238p, 242p, 243, 245
Priestley, J. B. 299, 305
Prince, William 210, 213p, 218p, 219p
Project X (1968) 369-370, 370p, 371-372, 372p, 373-374, 374p, 375, 375p, 377
Pryor, Richard XV, 355p, 361
Psycho (1960) 257, 268, 334
Psycho (novel) 307
Psychogeist (novel) 369
Public Defender, The (tv series) 173
Radar, Allan 41
Radilak, Charles H. 275
Ray, Frankie 182p
Raymond, Paula 185
Return of Rusty, The (1946) 55-58
Return of the Whistler, The (1948) 51, 54
Rhodes, Grandon 76
Richards, Paul 195
"Rin Tin Tin" (fictional character) 55
Ritch, Steven 124, 128, 147
RKO Radio Pictures (studio) 56, 173, 177
Roberts, Adelle 47
Rode, Walter 291
Rodgers, Mark 337
Rolf, Erik 4, 21
Rolfe, Guy 270, 274p
Romero, Cesar 173, 174p, 177
Rorke, Hayden 324
Rosemary's Baby (1968) X-XI, XIII, 83
Roux, Tony 140
Russell, John 85, 95
Russell, Ray 269-271, 271p, 272-275, 279-280, 283
Rust, Richard 257, 264p
Rusty (film series) 55, 58
Rusty's Birthday (1949) 58
Ryan, Robert 353, 354p
Sande, Walter 6
Sanders, Hugh 108
Saracen Blade, The (1954) 159-162, 166, 194, 286
Saracen Blade, The (novel) 159-162

Sardonicus (novella) 269-271, 271p, 272-275, 279-280
Saturday Evening Post, The (magazine) 244
Savage, Ann 9
Saxon, Lyle 182
Scavino, Leonardo 61
Scheuering, Joseph L. 182-183
Schlesinger, John 383
Schreiber, Otto 89
Schwartz, Maurice 129-130, 132
Schwartz, Sherwood 347-348
Schwarz, Jeffrey XIV-XV
Scott, DeVallon 160
Scott, Jacqueline 210, 212p, 213p
Scott, Janette 297, 304p
Sears, Fred F. 55
Seay, James 117
Secret of the Whistler, The (1946) 51, 54
Serpent of the Nile (1953) XV, 111-115, 115p, 116
Shadows in the Night (1944) 37
Shakespeare, William X, 48, 272
Shampoo (1975) 383
Shanks (1974) 377-378, 378p, 379, 379p, 380, 380p, 381-382, 382p, 383
Shaw, George Bernard 128
She Was a Phantom of Delight (poem) 140
Sherlock, Charles 86
Sherman, George 51, 54
Sherry, Diane 350
She's a Soldier Too (1944) XV, 21-24
Sholter, Anne 90
Silverheels, Jay 128
Skal, David J. XV, 241
Skinner, June (see O'Grady, Rohan)
Slaves of Babylon (1953) XV, 129-132, 194, 352
Smart, J. Scott 95-96, 98-100
Smith, Alexis 107
Snyder, Jacqui 89
Sokoloff, Vladimir 270
Sousa, John Philip 304
Spine Tingler! The William Castle Story (2007) XIV
Spirit Is Willing, The (1967) 363, 363p, 364-365, 365p, 366, 366p, 367, 369, 373
St. John, Betta 159, 163, 166
St. John, Howard 308
Stack, Robert 124, 127p, 153, 157

Stanton, Helene 183, 183p
Stanwyck, Barbara 324, 325p, 327, 328p
Stapley, Richard 137
Starr, Ben 353, 358, 363
Stein, Herman 338, 341
Step Right Up! I'm Gonna Scare the Pants Off America (Castle's autobiography) VII, XI, XIII-XIV, 63, 73,78, 107, 130, 281, 320, 380, 383
Stevens, Robert 55
Stevens, Warren 191
Stevenson, Janet 164
Stevenson, Philip 164
Stewart, James 58
Stone, George E. 2p, 3
Strait-Jacket (1964) XV, 306-309, 309p, 310, 310p, 311, 311p, 312, 312p, 313-315, 315p, 316, 316p, 317-318, 318p, 319, 319p, 320, 321p, 323, 325, 360
Stuart, Gloria 16p, 17, 20
Sullivan, Francis L. 133
Sundberg, Clinton 99-100
"Superman" (fictional character) 14p, 20
Swift, Jonathan 90p, 91
Talman, William 201
Tamblyn, Russ 108
Taylor, Eric 49
Taylor, Joyce XV, 291, 293p, 295-296
Taylor, Robert 324, 327, 328p
Taylor, William Desmond 101
Ten Commandments, The (1923) 129
Ten Commandments, The (1956) 129
Texas, Brooklyn, and Heaven (1948) XV, 22, 71-74, 283
Thackeray, William Makepeace 381
Thiess, Ursula 153, 173-174, 176p, 177, 327
Thir13en Ghosts (2001) XV
Thirteenth Hour, The (1947) 51
Three Stooges (shorts) 285
Thurston, Carol 124
Time (magazine) 32
Tingler, The (1959) 156, 233, 233p, 234, 234p, 235-236, 236p, 237, 237p, 238, 238p, 239, 239p, 240, 240p, 241-242, 242p, 243, 243p, 244, 244p, 245, 247, 262, 275p, 289, 323, 360
Titanic (1997) 20
To Althea, from Prison (poem) 140
To Kill a Mockingbird (1962) 349

Tol'able David (1921) 241, 243p
Tonge, Philip 210, 214p
"Tonto" (fictional character) 128
Toomey, Regis 52
Townsend, Jill 363-364, 365p
Tracy, Spencer 99
Trikonis, Gina 295p
Truffaut, François 12
Twain, Mark 344
Undertow (1949) XV, 85-89, 360
United Artists (studio) 71-72, 74
Universal (studio) VII, 9, 34, 298, 323, 333, 343, 345, 347-348, 352
Universal-International (studio) 79, 83, 85, 89, 93, 95, 100-101, 106, 108, 111, 117
Uranium Boom (1956) 201-202, 202p, 203-204, 204p, 205, 205p, 206
Van Dreelen, John 247
Van Rooten, Luis 75
Van Zandt, Philip 205p
Variety (magazine) 7
Visitors, The (novel) 363-364, 366
Vohs, Joan 117
Voice of the Whistler (1945) 39, 41-42, 42p, 43-45, 47, 240
Waldis, Otto 153
Walk on the Wild Side (1962) 369
Waring, Joseph 124
Wasserman, Lew 345-346
Wayne, John 58
Weaver, Tom XV
Webster, M. Coates 10
Weiler, A. H. 381
Welles, Orson 7, 38, 73, 204p
Wells, H. G. 34
Westerfield, James 257
Westlake, Donald E. 353, 358-361
Wexler, Paul 355
Whale, James 298, 301, 305
What Ever Happened to Baby Jane? (1962) 308
When Strangers Marry (1944) XV, 25-26, 26p, 27-28, 28p, 29, 29p, 30-31, 31p, 32, 41-42, 260p
Whistler, The (1944) 13, 13p, 14, 14p, 15-16, 16p, 17-18, 18p, 19, 19p, 20, 25-26, 30, 35, 45, 75, 239
Whistler, The (film series) 14, 20, 33, 36, 45, 50-51, 53-54

Whistler, The (radio) 14, 20, 53
Whistler, The (tv series) 54
White, Christine 210, 216p, 217p, 218p
White, Lester H. 152
White, Robb 210-211, 215, 219, 220p, 221, 235, 243, 257-259, 269
Wiesenthal, Sam 176p
Wilcox, Frank 201
Williams, John T. (see Gordon, Bernard)
Williams, Lucy Chase XV
Williams, Rhys 41, 42p
Wilson, J. Donald 14, 54
Winters, Shelley XV, 79
Wiseman, Donald 132
Wizard of Oz, The (1939) 74
Wood, Douglas 43
Woodbury, Joan 15
Woods, Donald 245, 251p, 252p
Woolrich, Cornell 33
Wordsworth, William 139-141
Worth, Constance 9
Wyler, Richard 153
Yates, George Worthing 160
Yerby, Frank 159-162
Yordan, Philip 41
Young Guns (1988) 166
Your Show Time (tv series) 85
Z (1969) X
Zaremba, John 195
Ziv Television Programs, Inc. (studio) 206
Zotz! (1962) 30-31, 54, 240, 272, 283-284, 284p, 285, 285p, 286, 286p, 287-289, 289p, 290, 353, 360
Zotz! (novel) 283-285

www.ingramcontent.com/pod-product-compliance
Lightning Source LLC
Chambersburg PA
CBHW050417170426
43201CB00008B/446